MARIA MALIBRAN

*The faculty to move hearts
is the supreme goal of art.*
François Talma

*Many singers of my time were great artists . . .
but there were only three true geniuses:
Lablache, Rubini, and that child so spoiled
by nature, Maria Felicita Malibran.*
Gioacchino Rossini

MARIA MALIBRAN

A Biography of the Singer

Howard Bushnell

Foreword by Elaine Brody

The Pennsylvania State University Press

University Park and London

Library of Congress Cataloging in Publication Data

Bushnell, Howard.
Maria Malibran: a biography of the singer.
Includes bibliography and index.
1. Malibran, Maria Felicità, 1808–1836.
2. Singers—Biography.
ML420.M2B87   782.1′092′4 [B]   79-14880
ISBN 0-271-00222-0

for

Joan Sutherland and Richard Bonynge

CONTENTS

ACKNOWLEDGMENTS

I am happy to acknowledge the assistance given me in preparing this book. I want to express my gratitude to the staff members of the Princeton University Library, the New York Public Library, the University of Chicago Library, the Library of Congress, and the Yale University Library. I am particularly indebted to Herbert Cahoon, Curator of Autograph Manuscripts, the Pierpont Morgan Library, New York; Margaret Webster and Margaret De Motte, Sub-Librarians, Central Library, Manchester; Louise Goldberg, Reference Librarian, University of Rochester; Charles E. Greene, Keeper of the Rare Book Reading Room, Princeton University Library; Mary E. Janzen, MSS Research Specialist, Special Collections, University of Chicago Library; Mary Ann Jensen, Curator of the Theatre Collection, Princeton University Library; Ernesto Milano, Direttore, Biblioteca Estense, Modena; James E. Mooney, Director, Historical Society of Pennsylvania, Philadelphia; Maurice O'Leary, Research Assistant, Special Collections, University of Chicago Library; P. J. Porter, Assistant Keeper, Department of Manuscripts, British Library, London; C. A. Ryskamp, Director of the Pierpont Morgan Library, New York; Susan T. Sommer, Head, Rare Books and Manuscripts, Library & Museum of The Performing Arts, New York. Thanks are also due to my brother, Francis M. Bushnell, Jr., Agnes Constance, Allen Dutcher, Herbert O. Hagens, Anne and François Hoffmann, David Loerke, and Scotia MacRae.

FOREWORD

Maria Malibran, an artist whose meteoric career ended abruptly with her death at the age of twenty-eight, belongs among the legendary singers of all time. A performer at the age of five in the 1813 Naples production of Paër's *Agnese*, Malibran tenaciously held the stage until a few days prior to her death in 1836. The freneticism, daring, and audacity that characterized her highly unorthodox lifestyle all anticipate today's liberated woman. To comprehend the extraordinary phenomenon that was Malibran, we must know something of her background, her remarkable musical family, and the musical and social spheres where she made her conquests.

Although Italians dominated the world of opera, particularly serious opera, in the eighteenth century, it was in Paris that comic opera became an international success. A performance of Pergolesi's *La Serva padrona* in 1752, twenty years after it was written, reactivated the traditional rivalry between proponents of French and Italian opera and suddenly these *intermezzi*, comic interludes with characters based on stock figures in the commedia dell'arte, assumed importance. First performed between the acts of serious operas, these pieces later became organic units of their own. Comic operas were about common people, and the audience could readily empathize with the business of the plot. A simple servant like Figaro outwitted his master, to the audience's delight, thus guaranteeing a successful engagement. Comic operas under various names—ballad opera in England, vaudeville in France, *Singspiel* in Germany, *zarzuela* in Spain—appeared throughout Europe. Except for the Italian opera buffa, all comic operas included spoken dialogue instead of recitative. Sung in the vernacular, using fewer characters, no chorus, and reasonably believable plots, these operas appealed to the middle classes.

In the 1780s, Mozart made remarkable strides in the technique of musical characterization, combining elements of both serious and comic opera. *The Marriage of Figaro,* in which the nobility is outwitted by their shrewd and clever servants, made a statement sufficiently powerful to worry the Austrian censors, who felt that it might encourage rebellious behavior in the Emperor's realm. In this opera the Countess's music, in her aria "Porgi amor," expresses a woman's heartbreak more eloquently than words.

In *Don Giovanni* the composer writes distinctly different music for each of his principal female roles: the aristocratic Donna Anna, the bourgeois Donna Elvira, and the peasant maid Zerlina. With equal ingenuity, Don Giovanni's music is made to blend with each one of them! In *Die Zauberflöte*, rather than offering us genuine human beings, Mozart focused on concepts and imbued his drama with the symbolism of Freemasonry.

Beethoven's *Fidelio*, based on a true story, typifies the plots of the popular rescue opera: it depicts the rescue of a brave man unjustly imprisoned by a tyrant who is himself eventually captured through the fidelity and efforts of the prisoner's wife. *Fidelio*, first performed in 1805 in Vienna, met with a hostile reaction from an audience of soldiers in Napoleon's army of occupation.

Paris emerged in the nineteenth century as the operatic center of Europe, a distinction it retained for fifty years. As a result of the political situation in France, spectacle operas (featuring mob scenes and processionals) and rescue operas became very popular. Spontini, Napoleon's favorite and a composer whom Wagner esteemed highly, achieved considerable success early in the century with *Fernand Cortez* and with *La Vestale*, a work whose extensive ensembles and choruses anticipated the grand operas of the 1830s. Also successful were Méhul, Grétry, Gossec, and Catel, native Frenchmen. Cherubini, an Italian, reigned supreme not only at the Opéra but also at the Conservatoire, the French national music school established in 1795 and still in operation today.

Paris was the mecca for musicians intent on financial and professional success. Foreign composers writing for the French capital had to consider seriously the conventions for productions at the Opéra or the Théâtre-Italien: the corps de ballet, the number of acts (always five at the Opéra), the order of dances (a divertissement in the second act and a full-fledged ballet in the fourth act), the language (which had to be French), and the conductor (somebody other than the composer). Operas in this era were divided into numbers. First came an overture, whose music was not necessarily related to the music of the rest of the opera, but would simply allow the public to find their seats. Arias and duets accounted for most of the musical content in the opera. These pieces alternated with recitatives by which the plot moved forward. Operatic conventions also called for the addition of trios, marches, processionals, occasional quartets, choruses, and ensemble finales, popular since Mozart wrote the remarkable second-act finale in *Figaro*. Gothic tales and the chivalry of the Middle Ages attracted the attention of young romantic composers; knights in shining armor, magic scenes, outdoor scenes, and nature in all its grandeur became standard operatic fare. Conventional arias—those of vengeance, jealousy, greed, anger, despair, and love—were so much a part of the operatic clichés that composers could reuse them with almost no changes. Each item in an opera was a self-contained unit capable of being transplanted from one work to another.

Composers customarily wrote with specific singers in mind. Singers remained singers, not actors. Although resident theatrical companies participated on occasion at the opera, professional singers busied themselves with the music and not with their gestures. Singers, however, still embellished their arias, sometimes so excessively that it was rumored that Rossini once sarcastically asked an overeager soprano, "Tell me, who is the composer of that piece?" referring, of course, to his own music.

Opera orchestras, composed of professional and amateur players, were unbelievably poor. As late as the 1840s, Wagner and Liszt commiserated with one another over the poor quality of performers at the court in Weimar, where the level of culture exceeded that of almost any center in Europe. Rehearsals were minimal. Beethoven's Ninth Symphony, performed for the first time in May 1824, had only three rehearsals—and only one of them with chorus!

The virtuoso, one of the typical features of nineteenth-century musical romanticism, appeared ever more in evidence as audiences responded to their technical expertise. Violinists like Paganini, de Bériot, and Sarasate, pianists like Liszt, Chopin, Clara Schumann, and the lesser known Thalberg, Kalkbrenner, and Czerny, found their operatic counterparts in Malibran, Viardot, Pasta, Grisi, Rubini, Mario, and Lablache.

Wilhelmine Schröder-Devrient, among the earliest German artists to break the hold of Italian singers, was the daughter of baritone Friedrich Schröder (the first to sing the role of Don Giovanni in German) and Antoinette Sophie Burger, one of the greatest dramatic actresses of her day. She was eighteen when she astonished Viennese opera audiences in 1822. Inspiring numbers of composers, she made a particularly strong impression on Richard Wagner, who says in his biography that seeing Schröder-Devrient's 1829 Leipzig performance in *Fidelio* convinced him to become a musician. The era of the actress-singer—an era presaged by Maria Garcia Malibran—had begun.

Of all the great musical dynasties of nineteenth-century Europe, the Garcia family stands supreme. Manuel Garcia, the first to bear the name, was born on January 22, 1775, in Seville, a city remembered as the locale of some of the most popular operas in the repertoire. His obscure parentage—he was raised for a time in an orphanage and later by foster parents whose name he adopted—has given rise to speculation that he was either of gypsy or of Jewish, probably Marrano, origin. Restless, talented, adventurous, shrewd, and highly motivated, young Garcia at six became a chorister at the Seville Cathedral and by seventeen had achieved a reputation as a conductor, actor, singer, and composer who had already written numerous *tonadillas,* Spanish comic operas shorter than the French operetta or the German *Singspiel.*

A popular tenor, Garcia sang to enthusiastic audiences in Cadiz,

Malaga, and Madrid. He married a fellow artist, singer Joaquina Sitches, and their son, Manuel Patricio Rodriguez, was born in 1805. For some time, Garcia had desperately wanted to live in Paris, to perform in Napoleon's capital for those he assumed to be among the most cultivated audiences of Europe. After sending Pablo Sitches, Joaquina's brother, to make the necessary arrangements, the family moved to Paris where, within a year, Manuel Sr. was acclaimed at the famous Théâtre-Italien. In 1808 a second child, daughter Maria Felicita, arrived. By the time she was old enough to walk in 1811 they moved again, this time to Italy.

In Naples, Manuel became friendly with Rossini, then living with the Spanish soprano Isabella Colbran. Garcia may have met Colbran earlier, and he certainly would have known her by reputation, for she had already sung at some of the leading opera houses of Europe, but he was not her teacher, as some authorities have indicated. When Rossini wrote *Elisabetta, regina d'Inghilterra* for Colbran, he sketched the role of Norfolk for his friend Garcia. Evidently pleased with Garcia's singing, Rossini proceeded to ask his assistance in the composition of music for *Il Barbiere di Siviglia.* Some Spanish elements in the score probably derived their inspiration from Garcia. Also, because of the speed with which Rossini completed this work, the count's cavatina, "Ecco ridente il cielo," in the first act, was not yet ready on the occasion of the premiere. In its place Garcia sang an aria of his own composition. Singers at this time generally were paid more than composers, and the Rome premiere in 1816 was no exception. Garcia received three times the sum of money Rossini obtained for his opera!

Garcia was restless. He could not remain long in one place and decided he must return to Paris. There he found that the singer Angelica Catalani had become the new manager of the Théâtre-Italien. Unable to work with her, he broke his contract and left for London, where salaries were reputedly higher than in Paris. In the British capital, he presented the first English performance of *The Barber of Seville* at the King's Theater. Thereafter, he and his family continued to crisscross the Channel, alternating between London and Paris, where in 1819, Garcia offered the first French-language production of *The Barber of Seville.* In 1821 a second daughter, Pauline, was born in the French capital.

In England, Maria, now seventeen, made her debut as Rosina on June 11, 1825. Her sensational success in the Rossini opera brought invitations to sing at festivals in Manchester, York, and Liverpool. A few months later Garcia left for New York with a troupe comprised principally of family and friends. From November 29, 1825, to September 30, 1826, he gave seventy-nine performances at the Park and Bowery theaters. He staged five first performances of Rossini operas, including a splendid *Otello* with Maria as Desdemona, and he presented the first *Don Giovanni* on American shores with the seventy-six-year-old DaPonte, who was then a teacher of Italian at Columbia University, in the audience.

Looking for new worlds to conquer, Garcia set out for Mexico, but this time Maria refused to go along. She had dutifully studied singing in France, piano and theory in Italy and from the age of fourteen endured her father's notoriously severe tutelage. While the family worked in New York, she had sung in *Otello, Tancredi, La Cenerentola,* and *Il Barbiere di Siviglia* of Rossini; in *Don Giovanni* she sang Zerlina, which, at the time, was considered the prima donna role; and she sang in two of her father's own operas, *L'Amante astuto* and *La Figlia dell'Aria.* In America, she had met and married a French businessman, François Eugène Malibran, whose name she would immortalize, although his ineptitude in matters of both business and romance cost him his wife. Their short-lived marriage ended unofficially in 1827, when she left for Paris, where her success was such that she could demand ever more exorbitant fees for each engagement.

After her successful Paris performance in *Semiramide,* Malibran continued her promotion of Rossini operas, competed enthusiastically with reigning singer Giuditta Pasta, and eventually won violinist Charles de Bériot, rejected suitor of another rival, Henriette Sontag, as her husband. Malibran and de Bériot had two children. One died in infancy; the other, born in 1833, became the respected pianist and composer Charles de Bériot, teacher of Granados, Ravel, and Ricardo Viñès at the famed Conservatoire in Paris. Younger sister Pauline always remembered the humiliation the family had suffered when Maria gave birth to two children out of wedlock. (Despite General Lafayette's intervention, Malibran could not obtain a divorce and settled instead for an annulment so that she could marry de Bériot.)

In 1829, after a disastrous tour in Mexico where their music was lost and Manuel was forced to copy from memory the scores of the two operas that they intended to perform, *Don Giovanni* and *Il Barbiere di Siviglia,* Garcia and family returned to Paris, where he devoted himself exclusively to teaching. To his credit, he had already sung in a considerable number of operas, sometimes sharing the bill with his daughter Maria and, for one season, singing with Sontag, too. Besides his son and daughters, Adolphe Nourrit was Garcia's best known pupil. At his death, Garcia left seventy-one Spanish operas, nine Italian and seven French ones. Manuel Jr. also became a pedagogue, first in Paris and later in London, where he taught until 1895. He was the inventor of a kind of laryngoscope that allowed singers, with the aid of a mirror, to look into their own throats. For his effort, he received an honorary doctorate from the University of Königsberg. Drawing as well on his father's training, he created a method for singers which remained in extensive use throughout the century. Manuel Patricio Rodriguez Garcia died in London on July 1, 1906, at the ripe age of 101. Among his pupils were his wife, Eugenie Mayer, Jenny Lind, and Julius Stockhausen.

Pauline Garcia, thirteen years younger than her sister, studied piano with Liszt, voice with her parents, and harmony with Beethoven's friend Anton Reicha, the Czech composer living in Paris. Like Maria, Pauline made her debut in London; she sang Desdemona in Rossini's *Otello* on May

9, 1839. The same year she was invited to sing at the Théâtre-Italien by its director Louis Viardot, whom she married in 1841, although he was many years her senior. Pauline Viardot created Fidès in Meyerbeer's *Le Prophète,* Sapho in Gounod's opera by that name, and Orphée in Berlioz's revival of the Gluck opera. In 1859 she sang this role 150 nights to overflowing crowds at each performance! A mezzo of extraordinary ability, she was also a consummate musician, pianist, composer, and friend of Chopin, Heine, Sand, and above all of the Russian writer Turgenev, who lived in a *ménage à trois* with the Viardot family until his death in 1883.

In later years, Viardot exerted considerable influence on the musical scene through her expertise as a teacher. She taught several young Americans including Annie Louise Cary and Antoinette Sterling as well as the Belgian singer Desirée Artôt, who was for a short time engaged to Tchaikovsky, and Johanna Wagner-Jachmann, Richard Wagner's niece. Viardot's celebrated Sunday matinees at Baden-Baden, where she attracted a following that included Bismarck, Dostoevski, Brahms, Clara Schumann, and the German poet Storm, were followed by her Thursday evenings in Paris, where de Musset, Gounod, Flaubert, Renan, de Maupassant, Doré, and Michelet enjoyed the music and the company. After 1875 she was associated with the Conservatoire in Paris.

Viardot spoke six languages fluently and she was known as a delightful hostess. She was a close friend of Chopin and her own piano compositions, understandably, show traces of his style. Apparently Germans, too, thought highly of her talents. Robert Schumann in 1840 dedicated his *Liederkreis,* op. 24, a setting of Heine poems to Pauline Garcia. This generous woman in 1892 bequeathed the holograph of Mozart's *Don Giovanni* to the Bibliothèque Nationale. Like her brother Manuel, Pauline Viardot, too, was blessed with a longevity usually reserved for conductors. She died in Paris in 1910 at the age of eighty-nine.

Maria Malibran's arrival on the operatic scene coincided with the appearance of other singers whose names have since made history: Giuditta Pasta (1797–1865), Henriette Sontag (1806–1854) and Giulia Grisi (1811–1869). Heralding a new style in vocal music, these women replaced the castrati, male sopranos whose extraordinary vocal prowess covered a multitude of aesthetic and moral sins. For centuries, while the presence of women on stage was severely restricted, these gentlemen, with perfect equanimity, sang the most elaborate female roles. Italian audiences accepted this archaic tradition, occasionally even articulating their approval of the brutal process responsible for such white voices with the cry "Viva il coltello! [Long live the knife!]." Eventually the public awoke to the knowledge that real women, trained to handle the fioriture and embellishments previously tossed off so effectively by these bizarre eunuchs, could sound even more tantalizing.

With the disappearance of the castrati, the way cleared as well for the advancement of male singers, among them Giovanni Battista Rubini (1795–1854), Antonio Tamburini (1800–1876), Adolphe Nourrit (1802–1839), and the tenor who called himself simply Mario (1810–1883), although his real name was Mario Cavaliere di Candia. The bass Luigi Lablache (1777–1856) had entered the lists earlier, and together with Tamburini, Rubini, and Grisi, they became a well-known ensemble, a celebrated quartet after their first appearance together in 1835 in Bellini's *I Puritani*. (Admittedly not a quartet in the traditional sense, this group comprised of a bass, baritone, tenor, and soprano figured as one of the eyes and ears of audiences who heard them.) In 1839 Mario replaced Rubini in the ensemble; he married Grisi five years later and together in 1854 they toured the United States.

Rubini acquired an international following and competed both for salary and popularity with the women. Whereas earlier tenors had concerned themselves primarily with Rossini operas, Rubini became associated with the operas of Donizetti and Bellini, with Giuditta Pasta usually singing opposite him in the principal soprano role. Giulia Grisi, reputed to have had a more beautiful voice than either Malibran or Pasta, did not provoke the same frenzied response from her audience, conceivably because there was always less risk involved when she performed. Audiences tend to identify with those on stage. Singers who cultivate their voices, who first train and then continue to fight to sustain their achievement, elicit the support of their public. A performance then tends to resemble a highwire act at the circus, the successful completion of which evokes hysterical applause.

Maria Malibran, undoubtedly a product of her times, proved herself a remarkable artist. With a range of three octaves, she sang contralto as well as soprano roles—coloratura parts as well as those for dramatic soprano—in thirty-five operas, and in a few works, she would perform two or more of the leading roles. She was equally at home in tragedy and comedy. With fearless originality and with a relentlessness belied by her diminutive figure, she brought the new style of singing to audiences in Europe and the new world. She created only a few roles, but once having sung a particular character, she made her portrayal uniquely her own. An extrovert, she attracted the public even before she impressed the critics. Her sister Pauline, more studied and less instinctive, possessed superior musicianship and would eventually capture critical and popular acclaim, but in that order.

Malibran acted on impulse. She did what she wanted to do when the fancy struck her. She cared not one whit for what people thought. She lived and breathed and fought and battled for her special kind of performance—total identification with her role. The electricity that coursed through her body could not help but charge any audience before whom she appeared. Her competitive spirit left little time for repose; the gnawing need to best her opponents ultimately cost her life. Dashing here and there, never leaving for the morrow what could be done today, she quickly reduced whatever physical resources had been hers. She was strong, but also brittle. Determined to keep pace with her female partner, Madame Caradori, in their last duet no matter what the cost—and she did tell Sir George Smart, who was directing the Manchester orchestra in this performance, that it would mean her life if she continued—she gathered her energy for a final repeat and collapsed immediately afterward backstage.

From Arne to Zingarelli, Malibran's roles encompassed the literature. Not only did she sing the bel canto heroines, but on occasion, both she and Giuditta Pasta undertook the male leads in some of these operas. (Within the short space of time, approximately fifteen years, that separated Malibran's career from that of her sister Pauline Viardot, the tradition had changed so drastically that women in male roles were totally unacceptable.) Besides singing at the King's Theater, at Covent Garden and at the Drury Lane in London, at the Théâtre-Italien in Paris, Malibran sang at the Teatro Valle in Rome, at both impressive opera houses in Naples, in Bologna, in Milan, and in Venice, where a theater was named after her.

In 1833, singing in English, Malibran introduced Bellini's *La Sonnambula* to London audiences. She also sang in French, Italian, Spanish, and German. With an energy and vitality unmatched until the likes of Maria Callas in our own day, Malibran seized life and all it had to offer. In the haste with which she tackled every role, she may have sensed that time was short. Although known primarily for her interpretation of operatic roles in works of Rossini, Donizetti, and Bellini, Malibran also performed in operas written for her by Halévy, Balfe, Giovanni Pacini, Lauro Rossi, and Giuseppe Persiani. A kind of savage overreach, a desire to make the world her oyster, an exhilaration that dazzled all who heard her brought this artist international recognition. Toward the middle of the century, Schumann, Wagner, and even Verdi turned their backs on the style of singing introduced and fostered by Malibran. But style changes and so does taste. In recent years, audiences have demonstrated renewed appreciation of florid song, thus bringing into favor singers like Callas, Caballé, Sutherland, and Horne—and reminding us that Malibran was there first.

After her death, de Bériot was inconsolable. Some even said that he was so caught in the magic of her music that the sound of her voice, her soul, now emanated from his fiddle. Malibran today rests in the de Bériot family mausoleum in Brussels. The French poet Lamartine composed her epitaph; in her honor Alfred de Musset wrote his famous *Stances à la Malibran*. In 1837, a year after her death, Vaccai, Coppola, Donizetti, Mercadante, and Pacini joined forces to write a memorial cantata which was performed at La Scala. Otto Nicolai composed an allegorical cantata commissioned by the Bologna theater. Moscheles and Cramer both created piano fantasies in her honor. Liszt, Clara and Robert Schumann, and even Wagner mentioned her name with respect.

Malibran, the archetypal prima donna, has not yet received her due. We are therefore indebted to Howard Bushnell for this definitive study, this genuine labor of love prompted by a desire to know more about a remarkable artist lost to the world at a far too early age. Music lovers, opera buffs, feminists, and readers in search of a good story—for her life was indeed stranger than fiction—will rejoice in his achievement.

In a recent television documentary devoted to the life and times of Maria Callas, Gian Carlo Menotti recalled that "she was the Paganini of opera. She could create a tension on the stage . . . the sense of fight with herself created an enormous excitement in the theater . . . her presence was hypnotic. . . . She had a kind of histrionic power just by walking on a stage." He might well have been speaking of Malibran.

ELAINE BRODY

CHAPTER 1

Beginnings

Maria Malibran's father was no ordinary man. The illegitimate offspring of gypsies and an orphan at age six, Manuel del Popolo Vicente grew up a ward of the Catholic Church at the Seville Cathedral. There he received a thorough musical education. From the age of seventeen, as Manuel Garcia, he achieved great renown throughout Spain as a composer and tenor, developing an impassioned performing style that expressed an excitable Andalusian temperament both charming and violent in turns. It was said that had he not been a musician he would have made a good toreador, and he would have looked the part well with his dark curls and flashing black eyes. Certainly religion made no impression on his character during his years at the Cathedral. According to his second daughter, "He believed neither in God nor the Devil—his personal religion was *life* with all its most ardent passions."[1] But his intense nature revealed itself in a permanent and debilitating frustration that often thwarted his own ambitions and brought misery to those closest to him. "If your father had had as much 'savoir faire' as he had 'savoir musical,' " declared Rossini to one of the Garcia children, "he would have been the foremost musician of his time."[2] But neither tact nor diplomacy would ever be among Garcia's many accomplishments.

By the time he was thirty years old, the young tenor had become dissatisfied with musical life in Spain. In the spring of 1807 he and his wife Joaquina, a performer whose flexible nature and cheerful disposition made her a perfect foil to her demanding husband, began the journey to Paris and Napoleon's glittering court. Their two year old son, Manuel Jr., remained in Madrid with his maternal grandparents, thereby placing less of a financial burden on his parents, for despite his successes Garcia had little money and intended to finance his trip by giving concerts along the way. Crossing the French border in late May, he found the musical situation discouraging. In both Bayonne and Bordeaux the wealthier people had departed for their summer homes in the country and at the beach, and when he did perform the French agents handling the ticket sales contrived to cheat him of his earnings. Reaching Paris in the last days of June, he somehow managed to survive the summer and fall. By November he began to give concerts, but because of his expenses he made no profits, and his attempts to join the Feydeau Theatre and the Théâtre-Italien were thwarted by jealous performers. Adding to his difficulties was Joaquina's second pregnancy, now almost six months along.

He appealed to the Duchess of Osuna, a Spanish aristocrat and patron of the arts who had offered him "limited financial help just once" in the event of "extreme necessity."[3] But Garcia did not use the money to return to Spain, as he had indicated to her, for his luck soon improved. An invitation to sing before the French Court at the Palais Saint-Cloud brought him to the attention of Ferdinando Paër, an Italian composer popular in Paris, who offered the newcomer a role in his *Griselda,* to be presented at the Théâtre-Italien. And so, on February 11, 1808, almost nine months after his arrival in France, Manuel Garcia made his operatic debut before the Parisians. He succeeded immediately; critics praised him for his natural acting, great feeling, and a voice that was "sweet, pleasing, of great range, and extreme flexibility."[4] "I love the Andalusian passion of that man," remarked a critic. "It animates everything." Within one month Garcia had become "the leader of the troupe" of the Italien.[5] This long sought success made the birth of a daughter on March 24, 1808, a happy occasion, which the two Spaniards demonstrated by choosing the name Maria Felicita.

Garcia's French success was soon equaled in Italy and England. In 1811 he accepted an engagement as leading tenor of the Royal Theaters of Naples, where he remained for five and a half years, and where he enjoyed the distinction of having major composers, including Gioacchino Rossini, write several operas specifically for his talents. In addition, he studied with Giovanni Ansani, one of the last disciples of the old vocal school of Naples. In an October 1816 return engagement in Paris his voice was found to be "much more flexible, of greater range, and more powerful."[6] Unfortunately, he was less highly regarded as a composer there than in Spain and Italy, but he continued to write operas for Paris, making their production a condition of his contracts so that the theater receiving his talents as a performer also participated in his failures as a composer. With the passage of time critics would become more and more intolerant of this "musical rent," as one called it.[7] Ideas came to him so quickly that he did not take time to select the good from the bad, and his librettos were considered deplorable.

England first discovered Garcia on March 10, 1818, when he made his debut at the King's Theatre in a role Rossini had written especially for him, that of Almaviva in *Il Barbiere di Siviglia.* Both tenor and composer were new to the English, who, despite their cultural ambitions, were in no way as musically sophisticated as their Parisian and Italian neighbors. Both Garcia and Rossini achieved the greatest success. It would soon be "soup for breakfast, soup for dinner, soup for supper, and soup for breakfast again," as a critic wrote of Rossini's operatic invasion,[8] and Garcia led the conquest, not only in London, but in Paris. He spent his next seven years commuting between the two cities, securely establishing himself as the greatest tenor in the world, and his arrogance increased in proportion to his salary, which was soon the highest of any tenor in Europe. But despite his fame, his highly embellished style and unparalleled vocal virtuosity did not appeal to everyone. An English critic made much fun of him, saying he "went running about in vain with his gratuitous notes like a dog that scampers about ten miles to his master's one."[9] In reviewing a performance of *L'Italiana* in 1819 the same journalist observed that "every crotchet was literally suffocated with quavers, like the flutterings of so many mosquitos." A joke much bandied about wondered what the tenor would think of Shakespeare's *Twelfth Night* delivered by a dramatic actor in the following manner:

If music be the food of—*fally ral de riddle iddle, tum te iddle*—love, play—*tum, tum, riddle iddle fal de rally*—on.

Give me excess of—*tot lot de fiddle fol, liddle toddle*—it; that surfeiting

The appetite may sicken, and so—*ti tum de tiddle liddle, tiddle toddle ro—ri tol fal de riddle tum te iddle*—die.[10]

By 1823 extreme embellishments were necessary to disguise the ravages of time. Garcia's prime years seem to have lasted well into his forties, but as he approached fifty a beat, even a tremolo, marred his sustained notes, and the immense volume of sound that had previously characterized his singing diminished. This decline did not mellow his excitable temperament: in earlier years he had been content with flagrant exhibitionism, for example, singing straight through an aria exactly one key higher than the one in which the orchestra was rehearsing, or, in the case of a displeasing opera, stepping onstage at its premier to sing a vocal line of his own improvisation. But now he arrogantly demanded to sing only what and when he wished to sing. This impertinence created more feuds than ever before, many of them violent, and he became even more difficult with his family, in particular with Maria, whose voice he had begun to train.

As the daughter of a premier tenor, Maria Garcia had long been exposed to music and musicians of the highest order. She learned to read notes before she could read the alphabet, and, by the time she was five years old, she had already made her stage debut at the Teatro Fiorentini in Naples as the child in Paër's *Agnese*. Although she did not sing in this role, she immediately gave her father evidence of her prodigious musical instincts; after several performances she knew the music of the opera, and one evening when the prima donna suffered a momentary lapse, Maria, without hesitation, took up her music until the startled soprano regained her voice. Manuel Jr., who had been sent from Madrid to join his family, remembered the feat as the first of those inimitable effects upon the public that no other singer in his memory ever equaled—and he lived to be 101. Maria had her own ideas about her premature success. "I sounded like a dog and I'm not going to sing anymore!" she declared flatly.[11] Her father thought otherwise, however, and selected Auguste Panseron and Louis Hérold, both recent winners of the coveted Prix de Rome, to teach his children solfeggio and piano. On the family's return to Paris, he tutored them himself.

Maria Garcia acquired and maintained her vocal abilities through infinite perseverance. Despite her obvious musical interests and sensitivities—sensitivities so acute that when she first heard Beethoven's Fifth Symphony, she was carried out of the hall in a faint[12]—nothing indicated that she would become a prima donna, certainly not "the most wonderful singer of her age."[13] Her natural voice, unrefined by training, was small, uneven, and lacking in flexibility. The lower notes were rough, the middle ones unfocused, and the upper register limited in range and shrill in tone. Nor did it quickly respond to exercise. "Hard and wayward" was Joaquina's own evaluation of her daughter's voice.[14] Furthermore, she sang so off key that it seemed she might be tone deaf.

The development of Maria's voice was the result of her father's untiring efforts. He subjected his daughter to a training as arduous as his own had been, if not more so. Maria was allowed to sing only exercises, exercises that were the product of Garcia's studies with Ansani and which were derived from those of the old Neapolitan school of singing. She repeated these again and again as her father sought to extend her range, to equalize her scale from top to bottom, to join her three registers, and to increase the flexibility of her voice until she could easily manage every conceivable embellishment. But he added another requirement: the ability to sing all except the notes at the extremes of her vocal range in any of the three registers, an uncommon skill that lent itself to unusual powers of expression and interpretation.

Since Garcia was famous for his skill at improvisation, he stressed development of that ability in all his students. Chastising a pupil who had only three cadenzas for a given aria, he declared: "A true singer ought to be able to improvise ten, twenty, as many as he likes, for the real singer must be a real musician as well."[15] To insure that his daughter would never lack this faculty, he turned to the concerti of the master violinist Giovanni Viotti, and had Maria write out numerous embellishments with which to enhance Viotti's melodies.

Garcia would not admit human limitations and would accept neither excuses nor apologies for failure. One day Maria and a friend were singing a duet into which Garcia had introduced some embellishments. Maria attempted the interpolation, failed, tried again, failed, and after exhausting all her efforts, finally said, "I can't, Papa." Her teacher turned his blazing eyes on her and asked, "Did I hear you correctly?" In an instant she succeeded in singing the passage. Later questioned on this unexpected achievement, she clasped her hands together and cried, "Oh! One angry look from my father and I am sure I could jump off the roof of the house without getting hurt!"[16]

These victories were not prompted only by fear or the desire for praise from one who gave little; they were also the manifestations of a perfectionist. Maria had an uncompromising will to succeed regardless of the effort. Sometimes she fainted when she fought to overcome a difficulty, and yet she could resist her father when necessary. During one class, Garcia tried to teach a difficult run to a student. "You must force it," he said, with a sweep of his arm. But when he was called out of the room for a moment, Maria, who had watched the pupil's agonies, ran over and said, "Don't, it will kill you," and was back in her seat at her father's return.[17] However, when she exercised caution, lessons were interrupted as Spanish tempers clashed. One day, after an hour's work, Garcia groaned in disgust, "You'll never be anything but a chorister!" "A chorister with more talent than you!" shot back his daughter.[18] Once Paër was walking with a friend near the Garcia apartment. Screams were heard through the open windows, and the friend exclaimed in alarm, "Someone is being murdered!" "No, no," replied Paër calmly, "it's only Garcia teaching his daughter to sing."[19]

Vocal perfection came slowly to Maria. Because of the constant exercises to extend her natural mezzo-soprano range downward to the lowest contralto notes and upward to the highest soprano tones, the middle register of her voice was weak. A critic who heard her at the time of her early successes noted that "the voice of Mme Malibran wasn't exactly beautiful; one could even find rather large faults in it, particularly in the tones of the middle register, which were indistinct and unequal."[20] Although clever at disguising this fault, she never ceased working to eliminate it, priding herself on whatever advances she made from year to year. A friend once heard her preparing a performance of *Il Barbiere,* practicing trills over and over with an occasional angry comment to her voice: "I will *make* you obey me!"[21] At the peak of her fame, when her every note could guarantee an ovation, she sang a brilliant concert in Liège for which her sister Pauline complimented her. "No," she replied. "It wasn't good. Didn't you hear my crescendo on the last A? It was forced. If our Papa were here he would be very unhappy with me, and for your own benefit I am telling you that one must always work, always make progress."[22]

Garcia's contract with the King's Theatre kept his family in London from March 1818 until September 1819. During that year and a half Maria attended the convent school of Hammersmith, proving herself too much for the nuns to control. Even at age ten she exhibited the qualities and contradictions that would later make her seem strange, even eccentric, to those who knew her. She made friends easily but, being absolutely unable to hide her feelings, she was frank to the point of bruskness. Her natural vivacity and warmth contrasted with violent outbursts of temper, although she was sensitive and quick to apologize for her behavior and could be charming when the occasion demanded. The incongruities of temperament that would prove both her doing and her undoing were evident. Her moods swung in cycles from depression to gaiety, and she vacillated between maturity and childishness, masculine strength and feminine weakness. Her obstinate will was too strong for her physical resources; when her body could not follow her passionate enthusiasms, she would have nervous attacks or fainting spells, which afflicted her throughout her life.

But despite her reputation as a "terrible little vixen,"[23] the coldest observer pitied this emotional and wayward young girl, because her worst faults were attributed to her renowned father, from whom she must have inherited them. The treatment suffered by the Garcia children at their father's hands rapidly became a conversation topic in London. One day a visitor to the Garcia home was asked if he would like to hear the patriarch's latest composition. An affirmative reply produced a full-throated roar that thundered throughout the house: "LA FAMILIA!!!" Joaquina, Manuel, and Maria obediently appeared to perform the piece and were summarily dismissed at its conclusion. Garcia must have approved of this recital. He did not approve of a public performance at the Catholic Chapel, where he exploded in a storm of fury that brought the concert to a finish. At yet another performance, which involved singing some quartets, the audience watched in embarrassment and pity as Maria, who, unfortunately, stood in front of her father, received a quick slap in the face every time he was displeased.

Her bold spirit testifies to her strength of character, but the treatment she received from her father marked her for life, and she always remembered her childhood as "stormy."[24] She envied other children: they played and had friends; she worked and suffered. Her one real pleasure seems to have been dolls. She never outgrew this passionate love, and no child could have shown more pleasure at a puppet theater than did Maria Malibran as an adult. Never having had a normal childhood, she would spend her life enjoying the delights she had missed in youth. When rebuked for his behavior, Garcia replied, "I am aware that the world blames me, but I am right. Maria can never become great but at this price: her proud and stubborn spirit requires a hand of iron to control it."[25]

Maria's stay in London was not without accomplishment, despite a poor education. Yet here she learned English, her fourth language; she already spoke Spanish, French, and Italian. The poet Alphonse de Lamartine once complimented her on her linguistic aptitude, and she replied, "Yes, it's very convenient. I can thus clothe my ideas in my own way. When a word I want in one language doesn't come to me, I take it from another. I borrow a sleeve from English, a collar from German, a bodice from Spanish. . . ." "That gives you a charming harlequin suit" observed the poet. "So be it!" she told him. "But there is never a mask."[26]

Both poet and singer were correct. Maria always said exactly what she thought, and her letters drift through several languages, sometimes changing within a single word, which might have a French root and an Italian conjugation. She was at home in all and in none.

While in England she also learned to play the piano, her performances of Bach being particularly admired. But her vocal prowess interested her father, and the ordeal of studying with so demanding a teacher continued without respite, both in London and in France, where the family returned in 1819. As she grew older she longed to escape her father's tyranny and the violent fights that increasingly punctuated her music lessons. Not even Joaquina's concerned intervention could prevent the friction between father and daughter, nor alleviate its effects. When Garcia raged at her she would turn her head or move behind his chair where he could not see her tears, meanwhile singing in a voice unaltered by weeping. When asked, throughout her career, about this seemingly impossible ability, Maria always said she learned it from these confrontations with her father.[27]

CHAPTER 2

The Debutante

From 1821 to 1825, Garcia's principal musical partner, both in Paris and in London, was the soprano Giuditta Pasta. Pasta had made her first operatic appearances in minor roles in minor Italian theaters, and, although she received no particular encouragement, she ventured with her husband Giuseppe as far as London, where she performed in 1817 without success. Pasta had neither the attributes of a singer nor great beauty; her figure was short and clumsy, and she walked heavily, even awkwardly. But as an impresario noted, "Other singers find themselves with a voice, and leave everything else to chance. This woman leaves nothing to chance and her success is therefore certain."[1] Returning to Italy for further study, she worked ceaselessly to improve a second-rate mezzo-soprano voice that would never overcome its many faults.

Pasta's return to the stage in 1819 proved far more successful than her appearances in London had been. For her debut as a major artist in Paris on June 5, 1821, Rossini adapted and revised his *Otello* for the famous performances in which Garcia* played the Moor to her Desdemona. The greatest music connoisseurs in Paris praised the pair for their extraordinary musical and dramatic interpretations, many being of the opinion that the work had, in effect, received a second premier. Stendhal observed that "Garcia, as Otello, shows unusual powers, not only as a remarkable singer, but as a considerable tragic actor; no one could show a finer grasp of every thread in that infinitely subtle web of thought and feeling which goes to make up the violent and impassioned character of Desdemona's lover . . . his acting is full of fire and fury; he is most truly the *Moor*."[2]

The date marked the beginning of an important international career for Pasta. But even now her voice was far from perfect. Its unexceptional range extended from A to as high as D, sometimes D sharp, and it was not particularly powerful. The tones, although described as "rich and sweet,"[3] lacked the clarity and vibration of a true soprano and became harsh when forced. Some notes were always more or less off pitch, especially at the start

---

*The role of Otello was one that Garcia made so completely his own that it became common, if erroneous, knowledge that Rossini had written the part for him. Garcia appears to have been in no way connected with the original production of the work, which was first presented at the Teatro del Fondo, Naples on December 4, 1816, long after his return to Paris, and in which Andrea Nozzari played the role of Otello to the Desdemona of Isabella Colbran.

of a performance, and her scale was uneven, a portion of it retaining a veiled quality. But Pasta had learned to use her voice to express whatever emotion she wished, and she had mastered the precise skill that Garcia was developing in his daughter: the ability to sing various notes in various registers. Thus she could carry the force of her chest tones as high as G above the staff and the "sweetness, softness and ductility" of her head tones into her middle range.[4] "Madame Pasta may indeed sing the same *note* in two different scenes," commented Stendhal, "but if the spiritual context is different, it will not be the same *sound*."[5] Although Pasta was unwilling or, more probably, unable to sing with the extreme coloratura embellishments essential to Garcia's art, her comparatively plain style manner focused attention on her great dramatic abilities, which surpassed those of any operatic performer before her. Her features were now described as "noble," and her ability to portray grand emotions more than compensated for her vocal deficiencies. Even her stature had changed: the lumbering walk was now one of "terrible grandeur."[6]

On April 24, 1824, she returned to the English stage for the first time in seven years, again in the role of Desdemona, again opposite Garcia's Otello. But although the audience was overcome by her performance, the critics were less so. The reviewer for the *Times,* while admitting her improvement, observed that "some of her notes are . . . sharp almost to harshness. We do not think her improvement warrants the excessive praises which have been showered on her by our Gallic neighbors."[7] He and others noticed the coarseness of her tone compared with other singers,[8] the upper notes that were sometimes sour and off-key in rapid passages, and the "forced and harsh" quality of her chest register.[9]

But some critics praised her while admitting her faults. One observed, "There are few singers who have made more successful or more touching appeals to the feelings than Madame Pasta . . . she is unquestionably very great, even considered relatively to singers of the first class."[10] Yet another concluded, "In so far as respects the triumph of art, she exceeds them all,"[11] and soon his opinion was voiced by European critics who began to see her as the example by which to judge other singers.

Inspired by his partner's example, Garcia sang with a brilliance that did not come easily anymore. His final performances of Niccolo Zingarelli's *Romeo e Giulietta* demonstrated the excellence of which he was still capable. "His soul is in every note," wrote a reviewer.

He seems let loose from earth, and the more boundless his flight, the more full of ecstasy is his song, for herein lies the grand difference between Garcia and every other florid singer it has fallen to our lot to hear. He makes every passage expressive by the ardour and the ease and the feeling with which he "wantons in the wiles of sound." His last aria, "misero che faro," gave proofs never to be forgotten of the deep sensibility with which he entered into passages of pathos. The words *misero* and *mia figlia* were uttered with a tone and emphasis that touched the very soul.[12]

Pasta's inspiration fired more imaginations than Manuel Garcia's: his daughter, ten years younger than the great singer, was infatuated with her, not only for her art, but for herself, and she would remain so for many years. Subjected to a grueling training, she could not have failed to appreciate Pasta's determination to overcome her own insuperable hurdles, and this common bond, combined with Pasta's ultimate success, made her Maria's idol. When Garcia was performing with the soprano, Maria became friendly with her, and when Pasta left London in the fall of 1824, she promised to write to her young admirer. The letter did not arrive quickly enough, however, and Maria soon wrote one of her own.

"Carissima Judith," she began. "I am very sorry not to have received a letter from you, which my mother had announced. I don't believe that you will have had enough time, and so that's why I am writing you, with the intention of stimulating you to write me, even though it be only two lines." She signed it "Your good friend who loves you from the heart, Marietta Garcia."[13]

Eventually a letter did arrive from Pasta, who may have regretted writing it when she received Maria's response. She never again wrote to Maria, despite Maria's many letters, pleas, and even anger. The letter, and others that would follow, is bold, confused, and immature: it shows the overly excited imagination of one who had been isolated all her life from society at large. At age sixteen her unbounded fantasies as expressed on paper conveyed more than she may have intended.

Mia cara judith,

Imagine my joy when I actually saw the two little words that you wrote me. It made me see that you have not forgotten me the way that I had imagined you did. Do me a favor and ask sister Carolina* if she received any of the crazy things I sent, and please let me know if she approved of my taking such liberty. We have heard that brother Curioni† was ill. Let us know, my dear bride. You already know that if I were near you, you would have neither face nor body, because I would eat all of you. Love me, love me the way I love you, and if you should have the chance, *for the love of God!* write to me even though it be only two lines. Tell sister Carolina and your mother to do me *the favor* of writing me.

Pardon the errors that you find in my letter, but I never learned [Italian] and I don't know how not to make mistakes. Give my regards to sister Rachele‡ and your husband.

I kiss you with all my heart.

                                                            Marietta Garcia

Tell me if you are coming to London this year.[14]

Maria had made significant advances in her musical studies. Late in 1822 she had appeared before the members of her father's exclusive musical circle in Paris, and one year later she created the contralto role in Rossini's

---

*Possibly refers to Carolina Naldi, with whom Pasta had sung in Paris.
†Alberico Curioni, the well known tenor with whom Garcia frequently sang.
‡Rachele Negri, Giuditta Pasta's mother.

Penalver Cantata. The conflict between art and nature still showed in her voice, which lacked size and evenness in certain passages, but its potential was becoming more obvious. Physically she was of medium height, of beautiful stature, and had inherited her father's dark complexion and flashing black eyes. Her eyes entranced her audiences, for with her sensitive and mobile features they mirrored and reflected her vivacious and ever-changing moods. Furthermore, she began to develop a stage presence, as well as the ability to influence the emotions of an audience as she wished.

During the London season of 1824, she had been singing in the chorus of the King's Theatre, and on June 9 she joined her father for Rossini's second subscription concert, in which the composer himself sang. No public notice was taken of this inconspicuous debut beyond its announcement, but the event led to appearances in numerous private concerts during the following winter and spring when she sang with famous singers such as Giuditta Pasta, who returned to London at the beginning of May 1825, and the castrato Giovanni Velluti.

Velluti had just arrived from Milan where he was enormously popular. A curiosity in London, he was disgusting to many and pitiable to others. Any appreciation of his art was colored by these two emotional reactions; few sincerely admired his singing. During the spring of 1825, however, he appeared only in private concerts and so did not provoke the outspoken diatribes that newspapers would later publish. But although the public did not yet know Velluti, the singers who performed with him did, and they disliked him for consistently displaying a disagreeable temperament, no doubt exacerbated by his status as a near freak.

One concert at which the castrato was to appear included a duet from Zingarelli's *Romeo.* Neither Pasta nor Giuseppina Ronzi-de Begnis would join him in the piece and Garcia suggested that Maria learn the duet. On the morning of the concert, she rehearsed it with Velluti, who, as was his custom, practiced without embellishments, both to avoid unnecessary strain to his voice and to ensure that his partner would not benefit from his example.

The concert that evening was attended by an audience capable of appreciating Maria Garcia's daring and accomplishment. But, in addition to being clever, her performance indicated the career and even the life that lay before her. Velluti sang his solo, embellished it, and finished with a brilliant cadenza. The audience applauded excitedly. As Maria moved to the footlights, he turned aside, barely noticing her. She sang her solo, and then, to his consternation and to the amazement of her listeners, exactly duplicated the embellishments she had heard for the first time only minutes before, giving them a finish and charm no castrato could hope to achieve. A dazzling cadenza concluded her piece and won her an ovation from the astonished audience.[15]

Her talents soon earned her greater notice from the dilettanti and she took a more prominent figure in the private concerts. On June 2 she sang with Pasta at Prince Leopold's soirée; the two joined talents in a quartet from Giacomo Meyerbeer's *Il Crociato* and finished the evening with the difficult duet "Ebben a te ferisci" from Rossini's *Semiramide*. Maria's expertise in her art can be assumed. Four days later she participated in a Philharmonic concert that produced the first public review of her singing. The critic from the respected *London Literary Gazette* wrote, "Rossini's 'alma invitta' was sung in a very superior manner by Signora [sic] Garcia, who appeared here for the first time. With a voice naturally so beautiful, and under so excellent a tuition as that of Garcia, her father, she cannot fail to become a first rate vocalist."[16]

She had already been brought to the attention of John Ebers, manager of the King's Theatre, who was having a difficult season. In addition to the problems presented by Pasta's imminent departure for Paris, where she was due by June 8, he faced Ronzi's chronic illnesses and Elisabeth Vestris' increasing preference for the dramatic stage. Pasta's final appearance took place on June 4, and she hurriedly left for Paris. Mozart's *Così fan tutte* had already been announced for Saturday, June 11, with Garcia, Maria Caradori-Allan, and Vestris, when the two ladies canceled. In desperation Ebers proposed that Garcia perform in *Barbiere* with his daughter as Rosina. Garcia accepted the proposal, making monetary demands that took full advantage of the impresario's plight, and on Thursday Maria rushed into rehearsal to learn her role. She had known the arias by heart from childhood, and now, in two days, she mastered the recitatives and stage action.

The preparations were so rushed that in all London only one newspaper advertised Maria Garcia's operatic debut, or anything at all for the King's Theatre on the evening of June 11.* On the day of the performance the *Morning Chronicle* gave her a cordial greeting.

We remark with pleasure, that Mademoiselle GARCIA is announced at the King's Theatre for this evening's performances; we have heard much of this young lady's talent, and great credit is due to Mr. Ebers, for having added her to his establishment, already considerably thinned by illness and other unexpected circumstances.

Immediately below this announcement appeared the theater's own bill.

King's Theatre—This evening will be performed Rossini's Comic Opera, in two acts, entitled IL BARBIERE DI SIVIGLIA; in which Mademoiselle Garcia will make her first appearance. The other Characters by Miss Willis, Signor Garcia, Signor Remorini, Signor Porto, Signor Crivelli, and Signor de Begnis.

Maria's appearance won her immediate favor from the public: her dark Spanish eyes, her beautiful figure, her youth and vivacity, all combined in a perfect Rosina. Nor did her vocal abilities disappoint. Ebers

*Due to an error in the *Harmonicon*, virtually every biography and biographical sketch of Malibran gives the date of her debut as June 7, 1825. The correct date is June 11.

was pleased with the outcome of his gamble, finding her performance "filled with a degree of talent and of stage tact rarely witnessed in so young a debutante" and her voice, "a contralto, and managed with great taste."[17] The *New Monthly Magazine* published a complete review in which a critic considered Maria Garcia's debut "the most important novelty of our month."

Mademoiselle Garcia trod the boards with a confidence and ease seldom witnessed on a first debut, and evinced the germ of comic powers which bid fair to expand into first-rate perfection. . . .

With regard to Mademoiselle Garcia's vocal qualifications, she appears to us to be quite as much indebted to art and cultivation as to physical organisation. Her voice is a mezzo-soprano, mastering a scale of two octaves without effort (a to a″) and capable of a note or two beyond these extremes. The lower half of this compass is of sufficient power and roundness, but the upper notes, ascending from e″, want, at present, at least, strength and vibration. This was particularly observed in the concerted pieces, in which her soprano part proved often quite inefficient; and on such occasions we recommend greater effort. Within their natural range Mademoiselle Garcia's notes are extremely pleasing, partaking of the full-bodied, fresh and healthful timbre of her speaking voice and of its distinct and perfect general articulation. . . . But it is to art and culture, and, we must add, to great innate taste, that this young lady owes the distinguished success which she has met with. Art has done, we might almost say, wonders in her case—has done—shall we dare to add?—perhaps too much.

As for her embellishments, the reviewer professed to be astonished and delighted by their "taste and delicacy," their "gracefulness," and "the plenitude of musical feeling displayed in their execution." "Such perfection in this respect was probably never witnessed in a performer of her years. It is scarcely conceivable, and well merited the rapturous approbation which it called from every part of the house. All our experience does not furnish an instance of a first debut at such an age attended with equal, and equally deserved, success."[18]

Maria was under contract to Ebers for the remainder of the season at the exorbitant salary of £500, which, considering the number of performances she sang, equaled her father's fee and probably even Pasta's. She continued to perform in *Il Barbiere* before large, enthusiastic audiences, and began learning a second part, Felicia* in Meyerbeer's *Il Crociato,* an opera new to London which was being produced under the direction of Velluti, for whom the role of Armando had been written. Working with him proved valuable to Maria, for he directed all the musical preparations, giving her a complete course of training in the study of her role. Velluti also worked with her, and with the other performers as well, on the interpolated embellish-

---

*Originally assigned to Vestris, who so detested Velluti that she was said to have offered the management of the theater "any sum" to find another singer for the part. *London Magazine,* cited by Pearce, *Madame Vestris,* pp. 115–16.

ments, thus ensuring stylistic uniformity among cast members. He always prepared three sets of ornaments for any given passage, choosing the one he wanted while on stage. Maria learned much from him, and later in her career critics claimed to find his influence in her style of embellishment.

Il Crociato had an extended rehearsal period; its initial performance was to have taken place on June 3, but there were several postponements before it finally appeared on June 30. Anticipation was great, not only because this was the first of Meyerbeer's operas to be presented in England, but because no castrato had been heard publicly in London for over twenty-five years. This fact alone excited curiosity over Velluti's debut, not all of it favorable. "Our opinion was that the manly British public and the pure British fair would have been spared the disgust of such an appearance," fumed a *Times* journalist. "His shameless patrons have dared to insult not only the British nation, but even humanity itself by thrusting forward this non-creature upon the stage" (30 June 1825).

The performance provoked unkind comments from critics and music lovers alike. Velluti made so strong an impression that the music and his own abilities as a singer were all but ignored as the audience became so many voyeurs. Tall and thin with high shoulders and a round back, he did not look the part of a chevalier, and his lank face half hidden in a helmet tied at the chin with a bow of white satin did not help. His shrill first notes sent a cold shiver down the spines of the men in the audience, and people were heard to suck in their breath as if in pain. "In the upper tones [his voice] often emulated the nocturnal serenades of the feline race," observed the *Examiner*'s critic, who found the performance "very revolting." "It is quite clear that had it not been for the furious support of a large assembly of dirty foreigners in the pit, he would never have been heard to the end of the opera" (3 July 1825, p. 417).

Maria, however, succeeded both as singer and actress, and she was the only performer encored. Several critics compared her to Pasta, and one predicted that she would "certainly gain an eminence in her profession which few have passed."[19] However, the substitution of one of her father's songs for the aria "pace ci reca," which Garcia considered too demanding for her at this early age, met with unanimous and outspoken disapproval. Forcing the issue at the dress rehearsal on June 29, he won a violent argument with the theater management by pointing out that Maria's contract allowed her to make any changes in the music that she wished.[20] The critics grumbled. "Nothing could be more ill-judged," wrote one. "We pitied Mademoiselle Garcia. How can the managers suffer such preposterous interpolations?"[21]

With the conclusion of the opera season in mid-August, the critics remembered Maria's contribution as significant and promising. "From the first hour when Maria Garcia appeared on stage," wrote Henry Chorley, "it was evident that a new artist, as original as extraordinary was come—one by nature fairly endowed not merely with physical powers but also with that inventive, energetic, rapid genius before which obstacles become as nothing, and by aid of which the sharpest contradictions can be reconciled."[22] Another critic warned her that the acclaim she had received did not mean she had already reached the summit of her art. "That lady's Rosina . . . warrants great expectation of signal success as a Donna Buffa," he wrote, "while her Felicia . . . holds out less decisive anticipation in regard to a serious line of characters. In this respect, however, time may greatly operate in Mademoiselle Garcia's favour, provided she entertains that modest opinion of her talents which will enable her to profit by good advice and example."[23]

As Manuel Garcia's daughter, Maria had little chance to be carried away by success, but a typically strange and cryptic letter to Pasta written shortly after the close of the season indicates that she was enjoying the applause. "Your dear, beloved husband* will already have told you, I imagine, the news of my debut and of my Orestian furors, thus it will be pointless for me to say anything on this particular. Signor Crociato is done with, which displeases me, and which wasn't done with you, but almost!† Were some opera to be done with you, either as your lover or your mistress, the two empty holes would become big enough to become my tomb. For love of all the devils in Paradise, write me two lines, even though you say nothing other than M . . . ."

After wishing all of Pasta's relatives well, Maria concluded, "For you I say nothing, because I am not able to fill my intentions. In effect, it would be to melt you with kisses and this I can't do because you are a hundred thousand leagues away, rascal, witch, gossip, infamous one, go, you are missing a tooth." She signed this unnerving epistle "Addio, heart of my hearts, don't forget your always mad girl, Maria Garcia."[24]

Because of England's continuing shortage of prima donnas, Maria was invited to participate in the York Festival, which began on September 13. There public praise abruptly ended. Many felt that her youth and sprightly stage action had gained her too much praise as a prima donna when in reality she was merely a very promising debutante. If the directors of the festival were willing to pay her "the extravagant, the ridiculous sum"[25] that her father demanded, they no doubt hoped that Maria Garcia would at least equal the effect she had produced in London. They were sorely disappointed.

The first day of the festival she sang "Una voce poco fa," and more than one critic agreed that "Madlle. Garcia, in attempting to do much, failed."[26] Another song came too late in the afternoon to be appreciated, and Maria was forced to watch the audience departing while she sang. In

---

*Giuseppe Pasta was still in London.
†Pasta sang Armando, Velluti's role, when *Il Crociato* was presented in Paris on September 22, 1825.

the second concert she attempted Handel's "Rejoice Greatly" from the *Messiah,* and failed so completely that the English singers were heard to grumble about her salary.[27] Other pieces were well received, but in general she made a negative impression.

Maria's reviews must have ignited Garcia's ire. He had little to be pleased about at this time, for his own critical notices over the past few months had emphasized his declining vocal powers, and Ebers admitted that his voice had reached the point where it could not be relied on from one day to the next.[28] Soon the tenor and impresario became embroiled in a widely publicized feud involving a performance of Mozart's *Così fan tutte,* in which Garcia was assigned the baritone role of Guglielmo rather than his accustomed tenor part of Ferrando. His vanity rankled, for he could see in this decision the management's belief that he was no longer a great singer. To appease the furious tenor, Mr. Ayrton, acting director of the King's Theatre, pointed out that with alterations the role assigned to him had always been sung in London by a tenor, and that Garcia had many times performed Don Giovanni, a bass-baritone part.* To Ebers Ayrton observed that since 1823 Garcia's salary had risen from £260 to £1,250, and considering the tenor's reasonable working schedule, he should have been willing to sacrifice if necessary for a theater which "grants him such generous terms."[29]

Ebers now attempted to negotiate with Garcia, who offered to take the unwanted role if he could be dropped from a later performance of *Semiramide* in which the management wanted him to sing the very high, florid part of Idreno. To this proposal came the following reply from Mrs. Ebers for her husband, a delegation of duty which, with its implication that a woman was adequate to handle him, infuriated Garcia still further.

Mr. Ebers is delighted to learn that Signor Garcia has no further objections to accepting the role of Guglielmo in Cosi fan tutte, which has always been filled in England by a tenor . . . although composed in the same clef as that of Don Giovanni, a role Signor Garcia has often sung. Mr. Ayrton will set up a rehearsal of this opera . . . at which Signor Garcia will be expected to appear.

Mr. Ebers is not able to give a positive response to Signor Garcia relative to Semiramide; Mr. Ayrton is the Director of the Theatre, and Mr. Ebers has delegated his powers to him. If it is possible to mount Semiramide without Signor Garcia, Mr. Ebers is certain that Mr. Ayrton will be pleased to do without him in this role, but Mr. Ayrton must be guided in this decision by what is owed to the subscribers and the public.

27 Old Bond Street, Thursday April 7, 1825

Garcia's furious reply was by return courier.

---

*But Garcia sang the Don (another part he made his own) as a tenor, common practice for the times. Indeed, tenor Dons achieved greater success than the baritones during that period, raising the arias by as many tones as were necessary (Nourrit raised "Fin ch'han dal vino" by a fourth) and either transposing low notes up in the concerted passages or rewriting the vocal line to fit the music being played.

Signor Garcia sees clearly by the response of Mr. Ebers that he has not clearly understood, or doesn't want to understand, the proposition he has made to him *to play the role of Guglielmo in Così fan tutte, provided that he does not play in Semiramide. Signor Garcia will not consider playing Guglielmo at all* until he has received *in writing* the order that he will not have to play in Semiramide. If M. Garcia has performed the role of Don Giovanni, despite the fact that it is written for a bass, it was done as an obliging act for the good of the establishment; since he is engaged to sing as *"premier tenor"* he is not obliged to sing bass roles.

Ebers, having received his tenor's "very impolite letter," refused to promise anything and pointed out that

Signor Garcia has already, in singing imprudently in certain concerts, deprived the Theatre of his talents three nights out of the eight which have been given, and he has otherwise intentionally neglected his duty; he should thus be one of the last people to inconvenience the management.

Signor Garcia has accepted conditionally the role of Guglielmo; it is evident now that he *is able* to sing it, but that he does not wish to do so without making a demand which could, if one grants it, bring harm to the theatre. But M. Ebers will put the subscribers and the public immediately in a position to judge the conduct of Signor Garcia.

Old Bond Street, Wed, April 8, 1825

Whatever result Ebers may have expected from the publication of these letters, their appearance in the June *Quarterly Musical Magazine* could only have embarrassed him, for by then Garcia had won the battle, appearing as Ferrando in *Così* as well as playing Idreno in *Semiramide.* But the fifty-year-old singer was faced with the realization that eventually even the greatest voice must succumb to the inexorable demands of time and that the future promised only further deterioration of his once magnificent vocal powers.

At this time Dominick Lynch—amateur singer, wine merchant, and Chairman of the Board of the Park Theatre, New York City—appeared in Garcia's life. As agent for Stephen Price, co-manager of the theater, Lynch traveled to Europe to engage accomplished performers to appear in his theater, and, more specifically, to bring an Italian opera troupe to a country that had not yet experienced the cultural pleasures enjoyed by Europeans. Exactly when he arrived in England is not certain, but he seems to have begun recruiting singers in August 1825. Despite a glib tongue, he was not immediately successful.

Garcia appears to have been the first to accept Lynch's promise of fame and fortune, and with little resistance. His eagerness can be understood easily, for the United States would be a less demanding audience for his declining powers and would also provide an ideal training ground for his daughter, who could gain valuable experience under less exacting conditions than Europe could offer. The inclusion of Joaquina and Manuel would provide the basis for an entire troupe.

Having signed up the Garcias, Lynch used the tenor's contacts in the music world to engage Domenico Crivelli, son of the famous Gaetano Crivelli, as well as Paolo Rosich and Carlo Angrisani, undistinguished basso-buffo and baritone, respectively. Maria Caradori-Allan declined a large offer to join the troupe, but Lynch's biggest disappointment was in failing to hire Giuditta Pasta, who saw no sane reason to endure a five-week sea voyage to sing in the provinces of America when she was already reaping tremendous artistic and financial benefits in Europe. Acting through her husband Giuseppe, who was still in London, Lynch attempted to change Pasta's mind.* His promises may be seen in Giuseppe Pasta's comments to his wife: "All agree that in New-York they are crazy for music, especially Italian music," he wrote, without offering any explanation of how they could be crazy for something they had never heard. "That country will be a promised land. No one else from Europe has tried to establish an Italian Theatre under more favorable circumstances. . . . If my Giuditta decides to go, she will leave a fortune in Europe, and will go and make a better one in America; and in a short time. We are young and why don't we see new and big countries of the world?"[30]

Pasta was not impressed, and now Garcia attempted to persuade her.

London, Sept. 21, 1825

Mia cara amica,

I am not losing hope of seeing you again in the United States soon—my happiness would overflow. While you are deciding, you may be sure that all that is needed I will take care of for your husband, and that nothing will be lacking while I am here. You know that you can count on me as a true friend.

We will leave from here for Liverpool the 26th, and from there for Philadelphia† the first of October. What a coup if you were with us! Embrace your mother's good pasta for me, and regards to my god-father Paër, and tell Rossini that I admire him for whatever he's worth. The director general [Lynch] sends you his best regards. I am and always will be yours.

Emanuele Garcia[31]

But Pasta had already decided she would not go.

The venture was not planned without snide remarks from the London journalists, who considered the troupe poor and the Americans thoroughly uncultured. The *Harmonicon* expressed the view of many.

Mr. Price has obtained the Spanish family of the Garcias, consisting of husband, wife, son, and daughter. How an opera is to be got up by such slender means we cannot guess, for although Madlle Garcia is clever, she possesses a contralto voice, not a soprano, though the latter, of course, must be wanted; and the father is liable to such frequent indispositions that he cannot always be counted on; besides which he is no longer young. Madame Garcia some years ago in

*In the New York Public Library at Lincoln Center are three letters, dated 21 August 1825, 23 August 1825, and 27 August 1825, from Giuseppe ("Peppino") Pasta to his wife, attempting to persuade her to join the Garcia troupe.
†The ship sailed not to Philadelphia, but to New York.

Paris took the inferior parts, and once made an unsuccessful attempt in the same in London. The son has never appeared. But our transatlantic brethren have no experience in this kind of musical representation, and, therefore, will not perhaps be very discerning. The sums said to be secured to these persons are past belief, all circumstances considered. We have hitherto been the laughingstock of Europe for the preposterous manner in which we pay foreigners, but the ridicule will now be transferred to the Western continent if the statements put forth—which we cannot credit—should actually prove true.[32]

The engagement of a young singer named Mme. Barbieri solved the problem of a soprano for the troupe, and on October 1, aboard a ship appropriately christened *New-York,* the Garcias and their opera company sailed from Liverpool for America.

CHAPTER 3

New York

The voyage from Liverpool to New York could have been tedious, taking as it did five and one-half weeks, but the Garcia troupe provided the passengers with entertainment that few transatlantic passages could boast. Weather permitting, the singers rehearsed on deck to appreciative and friendly audiences. The favorites were Maria and her four-year-old sister Pauline, whose precocity made her the pet of both passengers and crew. She spoke four languages almost equally well and alternated rapidly between French, English, Spanish, and Italian, depending on which was needed at the moment. This feat astounded those who heard the little girl conducting one of her frequent polylingual conversations. Quiet but gregarious, she lacked the emotional fervor of her father and sister, and consequently she fared better with Garcia than did Maria, who was increasingly at odds with him.

The young men on board considered Maria "a most interesting girl, simple, bright as could be, charming in conversation, a general favorite,"[1] and very attractive. She also seemed to be in poor health, which was blamed partly on "that terrible Spaniard, her father." When Maria's and twenty-year-old Manuel's performances did not please Garcia, he treated them brutally. He was so violent at one rehearsal that his daughter seemed mortally afraid of him. When it was over she and a young man sat down on a deck sofa to play chess, and at first she appeared to be almost as lively and bright as usual, but before the game ended she turned pale, her head sank to her partner's shoulder, and had he not caught her, she would have fallen to the deck. He carried her down to the cabin where she remained in a faint for some time.

Manuel suffered too. One afternoon the passengers summoned the captain when Garcia, having accused his son of rehearsing carelessly, struck Manuel suddenly and with such force that he fell to the deck "as if shot." The captain informed Garcia that he would protect his passengers, even if that meant throwing the Spaniard below deck in irons. "In irons!," he thundered. "Do you understand that?"

Garcia understood and muttered some unintelligible excuse as the captain walked away. But he took the captain's warning to heart. Although he continued to scold and grumble, no one on board ever again heard him use insulting language or witnessed any more physical attacks on his children. As long as everything accorded with his wishes, Garcia was polite, even obliging to the passengers; he wrote the music for a poem composed by one of them which was later published with great success in New York under the title "Ebor Nova."

On the morning of November 7 the travelers sailed into New York harbor, its deep blue waters stirred by a light breeze and marked with myriad white sails. Beyond, the spires of New York shone bright in the clear sunlight of a fresh autumn day.

In 1825 New York was primarily a mercantile city. Business was pursued almost to the exclusion of art forms which Europeans, both the aristocracy and populace, enjoyed. But the rising monied class looked across the Atlantic for more intellectual and cultural refinements. They were interested in Paris fashions, English books, and, soon, Italian music. English operettas, as well as English translations of French operas-comique, had been played in the city for some time. In 1823 Weber's *Der Freischütz* had been performed at the Park Theatre (also known as "The New-York Theatre") in an English translation and was repeated in subsequent seasons. In recognition of America's rising cultural awareness, acting companies from Covent Garden had ventured to the new world, and famous individual performers had amassed fortunes by playing to a curious American public. But although the drama was known to some, Italian opera had never appeared on an American stage; its imminent arrival at the Park Theatre was both exciting and confusing.

Ten days after the Garcia troupe landed in New York, articles describing Italian opera began appearing in the newspapers, with detailed structural analyses that, if not entirely accurate, were sincere attempts to describe this new musical form. Proper etiquette and attire for the opera were also explained. At the same time the following announcement appeared:

Italian Opera—Signor Garcia respectfully announces to the American public, that he has lately arrived in this country with an Italian *troupe* (among whom are some of the first artists of Europe) and has made arrangements with the Managers of the NEW-YORK THEATRE to have the house on Tuesdays and Saturdays; on which nights the choicest Italian Operas will be performed, in a style which he flatters himself will give general satisfaction.[2]

Prices were announced at two dollars for the boxes, one dollar for the pit, and twenty-five cents for places in the gallery, a large increase over the Park Theatre's usual rates. A full house of 2,500 customers would gross over $3,200: every seat had a full view of the stage, and the theater was considered exceptionally good even by European standards.

The bills promised that "The opera of 'Il Barbiere di Seviglia' [sic] is

now in rehearsals, and will be given as soon as possible." Indeed, rehearsals
began the moment the troupe unpacked and lasted as long as twelve hours
a day. To Dr. Francis, a New York physician who soon knew the singers well,
it seemed that a President of the United States or a Lord Chancellor could
be more easily reared than a Maria Garcia.[3] While other members of the
troupe helped build and paint the scenery, Garcia organized a twenty-five-
piece orchestra, considered large at that time, which was culled from the
Philharmonic Society and other musical organizations; and Domenico
Crivelli took on the unenviable task of turning the rawest musical recruits
into a chorus. In three weeks all had been prepared, and on November 29,
1825, *Il Barbiere* was presented for the first time in America, with the
following cast:

Rosina	Maria Garcia
Berta	Mme Garcia
Almaviva	Sr. Garcia
Don Basilio	Paolo Rosich
Figaro	Manuel Garcia, Jr.
Fiorello	Domenico Crivelli

The orchestra was conducted by Mr. De Luce, and the performance
prompted from the pit by Mr. Etienne at the piano, who also gave the pitch
when needed.

The theater opened its doors at 7:30 in the evening, and by 8:00,
curtain time, it had quietly filled with one of the most fashionable
audiences ever seen in New York, one that included Joseph Bonaparte,
former King of Spain, James Fenimore Cooper, Fitz-Green Halleck, the
poet, and very probably a prominent merchant named François Eugène
Malibran. The anticipation preceding the performance was fully justified
by *Il Barbiere*. When the curtain fell at 11:30, a critic noted that the remarks
of the departing audience were more enthusiastic than any he had
previously heard on similar occasions, and the reviews of the following
morning echoed the audience response to Italian opera.[4]

"Until it is seen, it will never be believed that a play can be conducted
in *recitative* or singing and yet appear as natural as the ordinary drama"
began the *Evening Post*. "We were last night surprised, delighted, enchanted;
and such were the feelings of all who witnessed the performance." The
question of whether the American public could accept Italian opera
seemed settled. "We predict," continued the critic, "that it will never
hereafter dispense with it. . . . We may boast that we begin with as good a
troupe as London, Paris, or Naples can furnish."

All the performers met with the highest praise, both as singers and
actors, but Maria was "the magnet who attracted all eyes and won all
hearts."[5] Her dark expressive eyes, her playful smile and perfect teeth, a
figure described as "ravishing,"[6] led one reviewer to wonder "but how, or in
what language shall we speak of Maria Garcia? How can our feeble pen

portray the loveliness of this admirable creature's face and figure?" Despite the fascination of her personal appearance, the "witching wonders of her almost unequalled voice" were not overlooked. "Compass, sweetness, taste, truth, tenderness, flexibility, rapidity, and force do not make up even half the sum of her vocal powers, and her voice is only one of the rare qualities with which Nature has endowed her" marveled an infatuated journalist, who considered her acting equal to that of any actress yet seen in New York, and who, in addition, found her embellishments to be "a rich stream of overflowing and almost overpowering melody. . . . Her shake is good, her appoggiaturas beautiful, and her roulades, whenever introduced, are thrown off with wonderful rapidity and ease."[7]

Such praise must have redeemed her in her father's eyes and led him to forgive her for the disastrous notices she had received at the English festivals four months before. His daughter was now America's first prima donna, and she was quickly to prove herself the major force behind the troupe's success.

Assured of public patronage, the company began to add further productions to its repertoire. On December 17 Garcia raised the curtain on a work he had written especially for New York to a libretto by Rosich entitled *L'Amante Astuto*. The plot of *L'Amante* closely resembled that of *Il Barbiere,* but it gave Maria, as its heroine, opportunity for appearing in situations not only of comedy but of pathos. In one scene she cried real tears as she clung despairingly to her father's cloak and made "a deep and indelible impression" on the whole audience. But in the score lay the undoing of the work, for Garcia had written such taxing music for Rosalia that by the time Maria reached the finale, carefully designed to show off her voice in its full glory, she was too exhausted to provoke more than "painful sympathy" by her resolute determination to get through it.[8] After two performances* the work was, of necessity, withdrawn.

The popular *Barbiere* continued to delight and on December 31 met with a worthier companion in Rossini's *Tancredi.* Critics were uneasy at the prospect of tragic opera, wondering aloud if it would prove as appealing as the comic *Barbiere.* Because of "the Signorina" it did. Although the critic for the *Evening Post* (11 January 1826) lamented her conversion into "a warrior maiden" whose costume concealed "those surpassing charms with which nature has so liberally adorned her," he admitted that "few tragedians could play it better" and noted how much her successful impersonation owed to her father's direction.

But despite Garcia's domineering influence, Maria already demonstrated what would become a major characteristic of her performing style. This was not the result of training but an expression of her own genius which distinguished her from all other actresses and singers. "She has a perfect and animating conception of her parts, and after having seen her

*A third was presented February 21, 1826.

often in the same piece, one perceives that she plays variously at various times and under the excitement of the moment." With what would prove surprising prescience the critic continued: "This is the inspiration of genius, and it is this which makes us so confidently hope and believe that our youthful favorite, who is but beginning, and, as it were, training in her profession on our favored soil where no competitor is to be found, may at no distant period, when she shall enter the lists before more experienced and severe judges, divide the prize with the Pastas and Catalanis of Europe" (*Evening Post,* 11 January 1826).

Maria's personal success continued to grow. In late January, when the opera company appeared in concert with the Philharmonic Society, she sang the aria "Bel Raggio" from *Semiramide* with such effect on the small audience that "one would have thought that the spell of enchantment in which they had been bound was never to be broken. It finally terminated in the most rapturous applause and encore that we ever witnessed. She repeated it with an effect, if possible, increased by her cheerful compliance and untiring efforts to please, discovering a taste and science in her extemporaneous variations that both astonished and delighted those who could justly appreciate such a display of talent."[9]

But despite the enthusiasm of the audience at this and other performances, the halls were not always filled to capacity, and were, in fact, sometimes almost empty. These disappointments could not be attributed to the weather, which was unusually mild during the winter of 1825–26, nor to the minor outbreak of influenza. Garcia now saw the glowing picture painted by Dominick Lynch of New Yorkers crazy for Italian music as a fabrication. But by American standards the opera was successful enough to arouse the jealousy of other performers trying to support themselves in New York. After a performance of *Julius Caesar,* the Shakespearean actor Mr. Cooper lambasted the audience for its partiality toward the troupe, which he termed a "foreign influenza."[10]

Although Garcia was not making the promised fortune, receipts justified staying in America, and he added to the company's repertoire, this time another Rossini work, *Otello.* Mme. Barbieri had originally been intended for the role of Desdemona, but Maria's artistic development, not to mention her drawing power, led Garcia to use her for the part and to put Barbieri in the male role of Roderigo, perhaps Maria's original assignment. She was given six days to learn the part, and her protests were in vain, for her father set about teaching her the role. The dress rehearsal was fearful: Garcia's dissatisfaction with her acting in the last scene invited a barrage of abuse. He outlined the scene as he wanted it: "You will do it, my daughter, and if you fail in any way I will really strike you with my dagger!" Convinced that he meant what he said, she played the part as he directed.

On opening night, as Otello advanced to murder her, she was terrified to see her father holding a real knife, not the stage prop she had expected.

Forgetting the audience she screamed: "Papa, papa, por dios no me mates!" (". . . for God's sake don't kill me!") She fought furiously with him, biting his hand so hard that he screamed. Garcia later explained that he had been unable to find the stage knife and at the last moment had substituted one of his own.[11] Perhaps he deliberately anticipated the effect of a real dagger on his daughter's acting. The audience, knowing neither Spanish nor Italian, thought this improvisation part of the action and noticed nothing except the wonderful realism of Maria Garcia's performance, for which she was highly praised.

Rarely have such elegance, dignity, grace, beauty, passion and pathos been united in any female who ever trod the stage. . . . The most fastidious criticism would say that she was faultless, and a generous admirer might be permitted to pronounce that she was almost perfection. . . . Perhaps action and sound never united to produce grander effect than when Desdemona, in the first act, sinks shrieking to the earth beneath the malediction of the father, and amidst the piercing expression of horror to all present. . . . In the chamber scene where Otello kills his wife, their impassioned acting, the accompaniment of the orchestra, and the concert of the elements abroad, apparently conscious of the event, combined to produce in the audience sensations of sublimity and terror beyond which no imagination can reach.[12]

At this time Maria wrote about being a prima donna in New York to Giuditta Pasta.

[February 18, 1826]

Carissima Judith mia,

How cruel you are; you haven't sent me even one tender little note since you left, not even once. As you see I am the only one who remembers you, tyrannical and sweet friend; perhaps I have written you too often, because, (you know) whenever I had a friend who was leaving, to you and for you alone have I written, and you have never deigned to return those attentions to your poor Arsace;* go, I forgive you because this is one of the beautiful qualities (of which I boast) which are of heroes, which is that of generosity. You probably know that in the three months we have been here in N.Y. we have played four operas, the *Barber, Amante Astuto,* papa's opera, *Tancredi,* and *Otello,* in which I am Desdemona, and this evening it is being played for the third time. Here they are already half crazy for Italian opera, and I, as you can imagine, am the heroine!!! How wonderful to be in a country where they don't understand!! In spite of this it is known that they have a taste for music, and even when they are sixty years old they can still bray like donkeys.

Your husband is well, and has recovered so well from an illness he had that he is even better than before. Why haven't you written to me, even to tell me if you are pleased that I write you? I am afraid of boring you, and so I finish this crowning work and requiem eternam. I swear to you that I adore you, that I go into spasms for you, and that I melt just in thinking of my diva, and that if you

*Refers to the duets from *Semiramide* that Maria had sung with Pasta at private concerts in England.

had only a slight inkling for me, I would die this evening content, for to tell the truth papa scares me when he kills me. God bye [sic] dear, cara, querida, chère Judith, love me as your mad girl loves you.

Marietta Garcia[13]

This letter gave no hint of the turn Maria's life had taken in recent weeks. Long resentful of her father's harsh treatment, she chose the only means of escape that seemed possible: marriage, and it was far from being a new idea. In England, perhaps as early as 1824, she had become friendly with a young musician in the orchestra of the King's Theatre. How far their relationship developed is uncertain, and nothing of the musician is known other than his lack of means. Perhaps Garcia put an end to their romance. An obscure sentence from a letter Maria wrote to Pasta late in the summer of 1825 may refer to this unknown man: "You can tell that I don't want to speak clearly, so as not to make your Good Modesty blush, by telling you that I am *not* planning to get married anymore, because of certain discoveries which I *fortunately* made."[14]

Since her departure from England she had been tenuously linked with other men. On the *New-York* she made a great impression on an English officer named Captain M'Donald, who was described by a passenger as "young and handsome."[15] And in New York she became friendly with the American poet Fitz-Green Halleck, another relationship supposedly terminated by Garcia, but not before Halleck had written his youthful poem to the troupe:

> No! if a garland for my brow
> Is growing, let me have it now,
>   While I'm alive to wear it;
> And if, in whispering my name,
> There's music in the voice of fame
>   Like Garcia's, let me hear it![16]

A letter from Maria to W. Rogers, a man somehow associated with the troupe's performances, shows a sensitive, perhaps lonely girl of few defenses and great naiveté. Although Maria's response to Rogers' rebuff indicates that he had accused her of being too forward, it is ambiguous without more knowledge of prior events. The letter is scribbled in pencil on a tiny piece of paper, her handwriting becoming increasingly agitated as it progresses.

Mon chère ami [sic],
    Your little letter is delightful, for although it humbles me, it also makes me see clearly that if I were a little (a lot) more informed, I would in no way have dared to take the first step in letting you know *by too much* how very dear you are to me. I would not expose myself to what I call *friendly, but hardly indifferent* manner. I did say it, *I would always be miserable,* and instead of being flattered by any of the flirtations and compliments of any man, I would only be annoyed (as I have always been when flattered) and the thought of you would only be heavier on my mind and in my *heart.* Don't try to take me as a joke, or laugh to

yourself about my *too strong* feelings, for I think you would make me very sad, since I see that your letter, although friendly, is rather *dry*. I think I might be annoying you, by too much tenderness, and I finish here, so as not to talk any longer with someone who could be mocking me while reading of my feelings, which a girl should not have been the first to declare. Adieu, have pity on the too miserable,

F.[17]

But none of the men Maria had known could offer her the advantages she saw in Eugène Malibran. Forty-four years old, perfectly mannered, elegantly dressed, this wealthy merchant offered liberation, security, and a respectable position in society. According to legend, Eugène, who had long admired Maria from the audience of the Park Theatre, was introduced to her after a performance by none other than Lorenzo DaPonte, then living in New York.

The son of a French father and a Spanish mother, François Eugène Malibran had been born in Paris on November 15, 1781, the youngest of seven children and the only one not born in Spain. Eugène's brother Pierre owned a large plantation in Cuba, and in 1817 Eugène had established an import-export company in New York to ship his brother's produce to America and Europe. On the docks at 38 South Street, near the tip of Manhattan, the business succeeded, and he became an American citizen.

Malibran's business ethics were questioned on at least one occasion: in 1821 he was found in violation of the strict laws against slave trading. There is no indication that he was jailed, but he did change his business address to 34 South Street. That he could be conniving is an irrefutable fact, but apparently he was not a shrewd businessman, nor particularly intelligent. The major force behind his business—its prosperity and its illegalities—was probably Pierre.

Whatever faults Eugène's polished manner concealed were not evident to the Garcia family. He was not handsome, having a pocked complexion, but his opulent style of living and flattering attentions appealed to Maria. Even that fearsome obstacle to romance, Manuel Garcia, was lulled into complacency, for Eugène spoke fluent Spanish, and Garcia, who spoke little English and was never entirely at home in French, delighted in meeting someone in New York with whom he could converse in his own tongue. The merchant frequently visited the Garcia household, and before the patriarch knew what was happening, a full-blown love affair was being conducted behind his back.

Her boldness untempered by the experience with Rogers, seventeen-year-old Maria seduced Eugène Malibran. As she imagined herself into her roles, so she imagined herself in love with this middle-aged man. Although she would later deny ever having loved him, her letters show the initial conviction of her feelings. Too inexperienced to analyze her emotions, she did not realize she had fallen in love with the idea of becoming Madame Malibran, with the security, independence, and, above all, peace of mind that title represented. But so strong was her desire to escape her father's domination and his theatrical life that had she been more mature her actions would probably have been no different. Eugène, on the other hand, fell in love with Maria Garcia. He saved every one of Maria's letters to him—proof of his sincerity. Not even when they became insulting, not even when he was ultimately scorned and thrown aside did he part with any of her correspondence, and at his death it was found intact.

Maria's earliest notes to Eugène were later found wrapped in a piece of paper on which Eugène Malibran had written: "Little notes from Maria before our marriage—1826." They reflect the haste and secrecy of her arrangements to meet him.[18] The first was scribbled so fast that the last word of the closing "Soyez moi fidèle" was omitted.

Cher bon ami, I would like to be able to see you today at 4:00, and despite the fact that they are home, I hope to tell you *two words*. Adieu, amiable friend, Be true to me.

The second is similar:

Cher Eugène, I have to go with mamam this morning and I can only see you tonight at the theater. Adieu, love me well.

At times the intrigue caught up with her; the beginning of the next note contradicts the end.

Cher Eugène, Since I have permission to stay to see you and talk to you, I ask you to come to our place at exactly 12:15. No one will be here as there is a rehearsal.

The response will be to see you and if you *do not want to,* let me know. No one has any idea that I am writing to you and that I am entrusting myself to your discretion.

Adieu, dear friend, I *am waiting for you.*

Not much time could have elapsed between these letters. The romance quickly ripened, and Maria soon expressed her feelings in stronger terms.

Mon bien aimé Eugène, I want to write to you so as to leave you in no doubt whatsoever, for since papa told me tonight not to talk too much about you in front of everyone, I think that I feel more and more affectionate toward you, and don't know how to express it; I ask you, as a favor, to come tomorrow at the same time as today and tell me exactly what has happened between you and my parents.

Good Eugène, I think that the more I see you, and the more I am near you, the more I am enchanted by you.

Oh! Cherish me, love me, think about me, and dream ceaselessly of your faithful friend.

And then, in an imaginative interweaving of truth and fantasy, she revealed her confused state of mind. This remarkable page was not a letter to Eugène but was apparently an attempt to analyze her thoughts, or at least to express them. It sums up seventeen-year-old Maria Garcia's immaturity, inexperience, and most of all her inability to separate reality from vivid illusion. Indeed, the paper reads like an operatic monologue of the sort she sang at the Park Theatre.

What, you say that you love me, Oh! happiness, you are marrying me; I can't believe in so much happiness, a poor girl without talent, without education, without sense, without spirit, without any attributes except a passable voice, and a cold could get rid of that, who—— but she has a kind heart, a tender heart, devoted for life to the one whom she adores, whom she idolizes. I would like to prove to him that I love him, that were he poor, and were his existence to depend on my work, I could make him happy and fulfill my duties. But I must believe that it is not only for interest that I feign to love him—no I do not want to stop at that wretched idea, it distresses me. I want to think only of the happiness of pleasing him, of being his for life, oh you! paper to whom I confide myself, you will not betray me, you will never show yourself to him whom I love, you will not tell him that my heart pours itself out on you, no I do not even want, if a good God grants that I could one day be his by legitimate ties, you will be hidden from all eyes and hearts more than any other. Oh my Eugène, why should paper be the recipient of the feelings that I would want to see you share with rapture and delight. I am crazy. I am straying, for I am stupid to delude myself with thoughts that are too precious, but has he not told me that he adored me—would it be in derision—no, his mind is too well born to deceive a girl who he can tell loves him.

Oh Eugène, sweet friend, should I call you by that name which repudiates love, and should I crave that sentiment, without knowing if your heart is at all predisposed? I cannot believe your heart indifferent to my advances, for every moment of the day I look for ways to make you understand my tender feelings which no other has been able to inspire in me. What sweetness, what friendliness, what good manners and what grace, and as all these qualities spread before other ladies, and that marked preference for some other women has made me think that your heart was not at all in those cold attentions. How jealous I am of a pretty demoiselle whom I do not know but with whom you danced yesterday evening, and who seems to me to have carried off the apple you gave. But one thing (which has completely deprived me of peaceful sleep, which I used to enjoy before knowing you)—while entering the carriage! First you squeezed my hand, my heart became as big as the entire world, you told me at the same time "Je vous adore!" Oh! happiness! Oh! It was so unexpected, the pleasure, the doubt, have deprived me of sleep, and in my dreams I felt my hand in yours, I awakened—it was a dream. Oh that I would always dream thus—but my waking is only a frightful nightmare, and to believe, or doubt to be loved, is the heavy daydream that suffocates my heart.

This fantastic overflow of imagination was written by a young girl about to embark on an affair with a man almost three times her age. Her waking would indeed prove to be a frightful nightmare; and her professed desire to make Eugène happy, even if he were poor, was a romantic delusion that would soon be put to the test.

With her next letter, one involving a lover's quarrel, Maria used the *tu* form for the first time. That she also used the term "husband" may indicate that she and Eugène were now lovers, for throughout her life a lover was a husband, regardless of how society defined the situation.

Oh! mon Dieu! Pardon me and I will be more than happy. I love you, why do these silly things have to be . . . why do I say that I am not guilty at all? Have I not let it happen myself, and caused the one whom I *adore* to leave without even saying adieu? I complain only about my wretched character, which has put an end to the divine patience of my angelic husband: if these tears that I am shedding this very minute could obtain my pardon . . . ! but no . . . I am not worthy of it . . . and I give up.

The pardon was granted, and Maria's relief led to another letter. Her parents did not know of her amorous escapade. The couple was being aided in their trysts by a Mme. Pelletier, and that lady, the wife of a wine merchant, lived a good ten blocks north of the Park Theatre in an outlying neighborhood far from prying eyes.[19]

Mon bon petit ami, I am very appreciative of your goodness and your little letter gave me the greatest pleasure, *as much as I could have now.* I will do everything possible to amuse myself; I have seen Caseau, I have an appointment to dine with him at two o'clock; and at three we will part. I do not know at what time I will be able to return, but I think I can go to the home of good little Mme Pelletier. Adieu, my good friend, all yours, Mariquita.

The final letter in the series increases in depth of feeling. Playfulness and confidence in her relationship with Eugène supersede the fears and doubts of earlier weeks. It is clearly a letter to a lover.

Darling, you're a kitten; you're an angel, I love you! M. Tessier has had the goodness to make me a present of the most beautiful pears he could find, and it is really nice of him. Tell me, little pussy-cat, don't you love me? Oh! It's yes, I can tell; I would like to have a little golden *lacrymatoire* to catch your sweet tears, and I would like to perfume myself with the sweet smell of your breath. What momentary foolishness! No matter, it doesn't stop the lively and ardent feelings of my boiling heart.
Adieu, bm, bm, bm, there, you have three kisses that I'm sending you, and a half page blank so that you can imagine as much as you want.

Ultimately Eugène loved more, but he was also far more realistic than the dream-ridden girl he met so secretly. As Maria confided her thoughts to paper, so did her lover, but with the benefit of more experience. He could be a man of scruples and foresight, one who clearly saw what the future might hold for such a mismatched couple. Unfortunately all his worst apprehensions were to come true. He noted the disproportion of their ages, the exaggerated accounts of both his reputation and his fortune, the uncertainty of his business affairs in Cuba, whose political state was always a question, and the obstacles Maria's parents could create for them. He underlined that he was *"all hers for life,"* but he questioned whether Maria's talents did not put her in a position to be independent of anyone, if her parents would want her to leave them, and if she really had a desire to abandon the stage, as she had told him. He showed a strong jealous streak, and was particularly tortured by Maria's friendship with the young musician in London. She mentioned that she had been on the verge of marrying him, and now Eugène wanted to know the name of this anonymous lover, his nationality, his status in life. Was he rich or poor? How long had he courted her?

Although she kept her love affair a secret until the situation was well beyond her father's undoing, Maria knew that eventually he would find out. The first Garcia knew of it was when his daughter announced that she intended to marry Eugène Malibran. Exploding with all his Andalusian fury, he ordered Eugène out of the house forever; Maria was never to speak to him again. It was a question of honor: his daughter was too young to marry, especially a man old enough to be her father. Furthermore, the troupe was returning to Europe soon, and Maria could not be left behind in this provincial land—nor could the company withstand such a loss. The house echoed with screams, and war was waged as never before in the Garcia family. Father and daughter were adamant; never had Maria defied him with such determination. She threatened to kill herself unless Garcia permitted the marriage, Garcia promised to murder her if she persisted in her madness, and Joaquina vainly tried to reconcile them.

Money finally appeased Garcia. Eugène offered to pay him $50,000 for the loss of his daughter's talents.[20] Since his total New York earnings would come to $56,685,[21] Eugène's generosity was no doubt appreciated. The marriage contract lists a dowry of $25,000, but as it is unlikely that Garcia could have afforded such a sum, or would have been willing to pay it, Eugène Malibran may have been coerced by the unhappy Garcia and his unbending daughter into absorbing this in addition to promising the $50,000 compensation fee.

They also agreed that Maria would not leave the troupe during its New York engagement, and attempts were made to extend its stay indefinitely by forming a corporation to be known as "The New-York Opera Company." On March 21, 1826, a meeting was held at the fashionable City Hotel for the purpose of raising $200,000 in capital by the sale of shares at $250 each. Though Eugène was a member of the committee, these plans came to nothing.

The promise of marriage was legally recorded as having taken place on March 14, and three days later the news was printed in the papers. Under the title "Gossip of the Day," the *Evening Post* lamented the coming nuptials. "The admirers of the Italian Opera have within a few days been reduced *au desespoir,* as the French say, at learning that their dear little favorite, who has every night of her appearance been making more and more advances into their hearts, is about to devote the remainder of her days to the sole solace and delight of a single individual, whom report says is an opulent French merchant. *Sic transit gloria mundi.*"

The marriage contract was drawn up and signed on March 22 before the French Consul in New York, Count Charles-Louis d'Espinville, acting in his capacity as a French official upholding the civil laws of France. And on Thursday, March 23, at St. Peter's Church, Father Peter Malou performed the wedding ceremony in the presence of the Garcia family. One day before her eighteenth birthday, Maria Garcia became Madame Malibran. She would regret it for the rest of her life.

CHAPTER 4

Madame Malibran

By marrying Eugène, Maria sought to escape her father's tyranny, but she was also anxious to give up the life of a performer, a wish with which her husband concurred. She succeeded in marrying, but as the most important factor in the opera's success, she could not be dispensed with for long. Thus the honeymoon, if it could be called that, was a short one. Having played last on March 21, she again appeared at the theater on March 28. New roles included Zaida in Rossini's *Il Turco in Italia,* Semiramide in Garcia's second new work for New York, *La Figlia dell'Aria,* and Zerlina in *Don Giovanni.* In June and July she would perform Angelina in Rossini's *Cenerentola* and Romeo in Zingarelli's *Romeo e Giulietta.*

The engagement of the Garcia troupe was to terminate in mid-August, and by that month appraisals of its success began to appear in the public press. The out-of-town newspapers vociferously proclaimed failure. "This dramatic speculation has proved a failure as was anticipated," trumpeted a Charleston paper. "There is no city in the Union yet ripe for this species of entertainment." The journalist continued by observing, no doubt in a spirit of jealousy, that New York, despite its large population and relative wealth, was "more like Liverpool than London—more like Bordeaux than Paris. The pursuits of her wealthy citizens are in closer connection with the counting houses than the coteries of fashion, where clashing claims in literature, the elegant arts, and of course music, are discussed and decided on in the spirit of cognoscenti."[1]

A New York newspaper quickly noticed this unflattering evaluation and, still smarting from the *Harmonicon*'s snide remarks of the previous fall, furiously replied. "This 'dramatic speculation' has *not* proved a failure; nor was such a result anticipated by any but the Cockney Magazines of London. The writers in those periodicals seem to know as little about Italian opera in general as they do of the city of New-York, its wants, its resources, and even its *locality.* . . . It may also be worthy of remark, that of the educated part of the audience, as great a number in proportion probably understand the language to the sweet sound of which they listen, as are usually found at the English operatic 'speculations' whereof these cockney scribblers *twaddle.*"[2]

But whatever Americans thought of this operatic venture, all considered themselves worthy of Garcia's troupe. The leader of the enterprise, however, had his own ideas about America, which he bluntly stated in a letter to Giuditta Pasta.

Querida Giuditta,

How it displeases me not to be able to foresake this country to go to Italy, as your husband will inform you. . . . Since he is aware of everything that has happened, I don't want to bore you with a long letter, and I conclude by telling you that I have been deceived in everything by everyone, and that this country cannot be compared with the worst of Italy. I have learned about your triumphs and you know how interested I am in everything you do. You already know that Maria is married, and that she will retire from the stage because her husband doesn't want her to follow this career; and to tell the truth, it's a shame because she could have become an excellent little prima donna. On the other hand, his being rich will get her away from such a labyrinth. We will leave for Florence after finishing this engagement, and I will get settled there. Addio my beautiful Giuditta, I will see you in Italy. Your Garcia[3]

In spite of this letter Garcia's troupe played on at the Park Theatre through September, presenting a series of benefits, one for each member of the family. On September 30 the last of these, *Il Barbiere,* was greeted with "an overflowing audience."[4] Garcia was considered to be in his best voice, and Maria exerted all her powers to please, singing in the lesson scene English, French, and Spanish songs, some of her own composition. Although the audience requested a continued engagement, the theater had already booked other performers for the weeks ahead, and thus the Italian opera came to an end. On Monday, October 16, the troupe, less Paolo Rosich, Carlo Angrisani, and Maria Malibran, sailed for Vera Cruz on the brig *Brown.*[5]

As her family departed for Mexico, Maria's brief singing career seemed ended, and as Madame Malibran she took her position in New York society as the wife of a successful merchant. Her new role was congenial. Unlike Europeans, Americans tended to judge individuals on their own merits rather than on those of their ancestors; the young and pretty Maria Malibran was unusually interesting, not only because of her musical accomplishments, but for her international background and vivacious affability. In no time she was a prominent matron in New York, and the beautiful white stucco house at 86 Liberty Street that Eugène rented shortly before their marriage became what was probably the city's leading salon. For three months she made no public appearances, enjoying her independence and peace. But this respite was perhaps the only one she would ever know, for the seeds of new disasters had already been sown.

In June 1826 a general economic instability began to be felt and in

July several banks closed. Exactly how these failures affected Eugène Malibran's business is not certain, but he was obliged to borrow large sums of money. This would not necessarily have been alarming, but by December the situation was such that he could not repay them.

"I would like to prove to him that I love him, that were he poor, and were his existence to depend on my work I could make him happy and fulfill my duties," Maria had once written, and now the sincerity of that innocent declaration was tested. Volunteering her services for a benefit concert at the Grace Church on December 22, she quickly became an unparalleled attraction, and within days a contract was arranged for her reappearance at the theater. She was to sing in English opera (a form of theater consisting of dialog and the occasional introduction of songs), under "the most munificent terms" prompted by "her misfortunes" and an "unexpected failure," as the *Evening Post* delicately expressed the situation (5 January 1827). Indeed, her salary of $600 per night was the highest ever paid a performer in America. She first appeared on January 15 as Count Belino—a male role—in Charles Edward Horn's *The Devil's Bridge*. "Her accent is not too foreign to add to the interest with which she is ever received," wrote a critic. "For a lady apparently not 20 years of age [Maria was eighteen yeas old], educated amidst a Spanish, Italian, and French community, with all her habits, languages, and even foreign dialect, to perform in *English* opera may indeed be considered a phenomenon."[6]

Despite Maria's high fee, Stephen Price received more than he had contracted for. Maria's theatrical experience enabled her to teach and prompt the other performers, rehearse the orchestra, and direct the whole production. And each night of this brief engagement, the agreed upon sum was delivered to Eugène Malibran, thus alleviating, however temporarily, his most pressing debts.

Perhaps Maria was not really upset by returning to the stage. She knew no other life; her training and talents were too much a part of her to be so easily denied. Still, she must have felt uneasy at being left by her family in a strange country with a husband who no longer could support her and who had become instead the beneficiary of her own labor. Doubts about Eugène entered her mind. Surely he knew the condition of his business affairs when he married her, but he had kept it secret from her and her family. Perhaps he had married her thinking of her earning power. But for now she gave her husband the benefit of the doubt and made every effort to forestall the direst results of his debts. She did not yet realize that his business was beyond repairing with the earnings of a singer, even a very highly paid one.

But whatever her feelings about resuming her career, this was clearly not a temporary situation. Her engagement with the English opera was renewed, earning her in total the handsome sum of $6,000, and she presented occasional concerts which, despite the high prices charged for tickets, were attended by large, fashionable audiences. From time to time she lent her talents to the needs of others: at a benefit for the Greeks given at St. Paul's Church, she sang Handel's "Angels ever Bright and Fair."

During the performance of the song so silent was the audience that not even a whisper was to be heard. She performed it beautifully, as a matter of course, although the admirers of the simplicity of Handel had to regret the introduction of so much ornament. She was clad in robes of virgin white and at the words "Take, oh take me to your care," she raised her hands and eyes in an imploring attitude to heaven in so dramatic and touching a manner as to electrify the audience, and to call down a universal outburst of approbation, a very unusual occurrence in a church of this country.[7]

White was a striking color on Maria, and her preference cannot have been an accident, for she was well known for her effective use of clothing. When she was young it set off her dark coloring and flashing black eyes; when she was older, and the glow of youth had been replaced by the pallor of fatigue and ill health, she used white for its ethereal effect. Madame Merlin remembered her in white muslin the day Maria came to seek her help; Princess Victoria wrote of her "dressed in white satin, so merry and lively"[8] when she sang at the Princess's sixteenth birthday party; as she leaned from her coach to wave to the actor William Macready he was struck by her "bridal attire."[9] Whatever the reason, every contemporary reference to Maria Malibran's dress speaks of white.

Her church singing was such an attraction that to enlarge his congregation a minister or priest had only to enlist her talents. She cheerfully complied with as many requests as she could. However, Father Malou, the Catholic priest who had performed her marriage ceremony, was upset at the care with which she was training the Protestant Grace Church choir. Even worse, he feared that her friendship with Reverend Wainwright might lead her to convert to protestantism. In trying to persuade her to relegate her singing and worship to the "religion of her fathers," Father Malou resorted to flattery, religious threats, pleas to filial obedience, and, worst of all, attempts to instill fear and guilt in her mind. "Free me, I beg you, of the cruel pain I experience," he wrote.

You are gifted with extraordinary talents, you are the idol of a certain group, but will it last? A malady could destroy your face, fade your talents, and no longer having that to beguile the public. fantasies and enjoyment, it will be for you, my child, as for so many others who have preceded you and will follow you. The world will leave you and will entomb you in forgetfulness if death, whose moment is so uncertain, does not terminate your career. Reconsider then, I implore you, for the love of He who will never abandon you, when the world will abandon you, and will never let you perish. . . . Once again! don't take lightly a course that will cause you a day of bitter regrets and unhappiness.[10]

Maria's fury at receiving this letter must have equaled any of her father's tantrums. Rather than "consulting the pros and cons with educated people" as the old priest had suggested, she fired off a letter not to

Father Malou, nor to her "guiding minister" as he referred to the Reverend Jonathan Wainwright, but to the Bishop of New York, who weakly explained,

So many simple lay people have spoken to me of the supposed change that has taken place in your feelings. I had rejected these tales as unworthy of you—but when a respectable ecclesiastic whom Mr. Malou knows, as well as I do, came to tell me that next Sunday was named as the one on which you deviate, one would say, to be received into the Anglican Church and that someone has been preparing you for a long time for the denial of faith, I fear a longer silence would have the air of indifference. You are very young, surrounded by all the marvels that can mislead a mind less strong than yours. Even friendship has its snares.

But the Bishop retreated before her fury. "I have concluded nothing against the purity of your faith, of your diligence to the choir of the Protestant Church," he told her. "I have seen in that only the goodness of your heart, which cannot refuse on any occasion to oblige, especially some friends who have shown the greatest interest in you. As for your friendship with Mme. Wainwright, it proves nothing more than what I myself have for her husband. Christian charity unites all men, and is the best proof of our love for God."[11] And so the matter was dropped. Maria sang where she wished, gave her friendship as she pleased, and no more was said.

Since the arrival of the Garcia troupe in New York, there had been talk in Philadelphia of bringing the company to the Chestnut Street Theatre. The papers debated this hotly, as though the coming of the opera were of the greatest civic importance. "Our Theatre is doing very well as it is," asserted the editor of the *Gazette*, who admitted to being unmusical.[12] Still, lest New York gain a cultural advantage on its smaller and even less cosmopolitan neighbor, the editor quickly declared the troupe's failure after its first two months at the Park Theatre. "The fact is that excepting as a matter of curiosity, a nine-days wonder, an opera company cannot be supported in America."[13]

Although Garcia never bothered with Philadelphia, there were recurrent rumors that his daughter might visit the city. Undoubtedly the Malibrans read about the success of William Macready and Miss Kelly in Philadelphia. The actor and actress had earned between them in a short period of time nearly $17,000, a fortune in 1827. Thus plans were made for Maria to sing in Philadelphia. When she arrived on June 13 she was the only important singer ever to have been there, and the first to introduce Italian opera. Her initial concert took place on June 16 at the Music Fund Hall, and afterward she wandered through the auditorium, extemporizing to her accompanist's piano playing and admiring the acoustics.[14] She was in a good mood, for it seemed that all had gone well on this first foray far from

husband and family. Too excited to sleep, she was up at dawn the next day
to write Eugène about her success.

> Sunday
> Philadelphia, June 17, 1827
> 5:30 AM
>
> Mon cher petit chou,
>   As you can see, I am up early to chat with you! My concert has succeeded
> *non plus ultra.* There were a great many people *from what one tells me,* but I can
> affirm to you that I had all the *crème de la ville; fashionable to the last degree.* The
> pieces gave pleasure by degrees. First they liked *chè farò* very much, and
> applauded well, then *more* for *batti*—enthusiasm for *sweet home,* the *variations* and
> *di tanti*: they applauded for a long time when I finished; I see from this that they
> were delighted by the concert. The piece that I performed with Mr. Gibbs gave
> extreme pleasure. I do not know how much the receipts were, in any case I am
> going to prepare for another. Make Rosich come, have him bring his *duo de la
> leçon,* the *capellini* air, and *the other one* that he sang at my benefit, and send me
> the corsage of white Rosina from Naples and tell la Forgis to arrange the
> ornaments of white satin, which you will find in the chest where the old
> woman's costume is. They are with some black velvet and spangles, Tancredi's
> costume. Now ask Mme Brugière if she thinks I could play that scene from the
> Barber like I did at my benefit, and *di Tanti in costume* and tell her it is my
> particular desire. You could make Mr. Boyle come, and he would sing the duet
> from Tancredi in *costume,* having sung before in evening dress a duet in the scene
> from the Barber, or even in costume as if he were my father. If this could be,
> everything would be fine, eh? What do you think? It seems like a good idea to
> discuss this with Mme Brugière, and send me the response *with the costume.* You
> see what an early riser I am. Don't forget to send me the white plumes that are
> in a white box. This must be done soon, as soon as said. Adieu good friend, I
> leave you to go to mass. Adieu, adieu, with good heart I embrace you.
>
>   M. G. Malibran[15]

"I see Mr. Bayland and his wife," she added later. "I have asked him to write
you and tell you that *I am charming.* As you see, it is without pretension."[16]

    Although she was so wound up in her plans that she treated Eugène
like a valet or manager, Maria was still affectionate at this stage of their
marriage, as is indicated in other letters from Philadelphia. "Do me the
favor of not writing me in half pages, but in 4 pages," she told him; and
again, in a more seductive mood, "Tell me forever that you really love me
and try to raise your . . . head . . . and we won't lack for any furniture . . .
except a cradle (you know what I mean.)" She signed this letter "Adieu,
adieu, chou chou, your wife who loves you, Marie Félicie."[17]

    The first flush of victory quickly faded. Although the concert grossed
$2,000, Maria perhaps expected more. Something was not going well, for
only three days later she was as depressed as she had been gay.

> June 20, 1827
>
> Mon pauvre petit chou,
>   I didn't write you at all yesterday, but let you wish that I had. I am tired,
> humiliated, annoyed, grieved, saddened by the success of my first concert.

Messieurs les Philadelphiens are . . . don't make me say what for I could only curse. I'm not eating very well, for instead of getting sleep, I get worried. I am not going horseback riding, that isn't done here at all. I went to the *Scoolkill mountains,* and I saw the *prison* and the *Waterworks,* and the *museum*; that's all. Tell me if Rosich is coming, for I am unhappy in waiting. I don't see the time when I will come to rejoin you. I absolutely want to get some rest, for here I have to be dressed all day long, *as early as morning,* to receive the visitors that come. I need *good air* and *solitude.* Embrace *Mme Wainwright and her husband.* I have the *blue devils* horribly today. I have raw nerves frightfully. I would have really liked to hang myself . . . from *your neck* . . . mais bernique. Tell me about good old Mr. *Fauterfink.* Now don't scold me because you haven't gotten any news from me, but the blue devil, it's his fault. I must finish for I feel like crying. Tell me if there aren't any letters at all from *Papa and Mamam,* they say he has arrived in New York, tell me about it for *the love of God!* If you knew how I have grieved to have to reappear at the Theater, and to have the certainty that all will go badly! Let's not speak of it anymore, for my head is spinning. Adieu chou, your wife who embraces her man.

M. F. Malibran[18]

By June 22 the orchestra Maria expected from Baltimore had arrived, and all was prepared for her second concert the following night.

June 22, midnight
Old papa Teisseire grumbles because he says it is too late, and doesn't want me to write you, but as I couldn't write you and besides Sunday I could have been buried, for Saturday I could have *died from fatigue.* I am passably well satisfied with my orchestra, all goes well except that I am *exceedingly tired.* We will leave Tuesday at six AM. I wanted to leave Monday, bernique, Mr. Tesseire could only leave Tuesday. I'm not going to be long, for time passes and I have to get up at 8:00 tomorrow. I have to rehearse with the orchestra at 11:00 tomorrow, I have to *tranquilize* myself.——

Have you ever known me to be at peace? Neither have I. Adieu. I embrace you with all my little *sleeping heart,* and eyes filled with sleep. I kiss you while yawning. Adieu.

Everyone says nice things to you, embrace Venus and her retinue. *Love sings.* . . .

Maria[19]

The second concert, which sold out at the Chestnut Street Theatre, presented scenes in costume from various operas and was more successful. After this performance Maria and a group of musicians and friends moved into the Philadelphia suburbs, presumably for further concerts. "I am marvelously well," she wrote Eugène. "I eat like an Ogress, I drink like a drunkard, I run like a *deer,* I swim like a fish, I sing like a siren, I ride horseback like Napoleon (the late) and I sleep like a woodchuck."[20] She also indulged in pranks.

You can't imagine what a good time we are having with this good Gibbs. We tease him delightfully. I must tell you that Mr. Etienne wanted to play a trick on Mr G. That is to write him an anonymous letter in Italian. I then had a very funny idea. I wrote to him in English, as if it were from an old woman—she tells him that having heard it said that he was traveling for pleasure, she would offer him a chance for some fun. That she had a daughter thirteen years old, pretty as the sun shining on a mountain, who vanished with the Shaker's cult. She appeared disposed to run here and there, and that if he wanted to prevent the loss of a girl, he would do well to take her in friendship. The address of the hotel is: Pigs Hotel No. 1. There is not one place like that in Hudson, but that's allright. Eh bien. Would you believe that G.—swallowed all that? that he spoke of it to Mr and Mme E, and that he wants to keep it a secret from me because he believes the honor of a young girl has been compromised? This could make an evening comedy, for the letter is just since this afternoon.[21]

Sometimes she seemed to forget why she was on tour. Eugène undoubtedly shuddered at her wish to give $50 to a Philadelphia doctor who had helped her when she hurt herself swimming in the river, "not as payment of my debt to him, but as a small sign of my thankfulness."[22] This sum, immense for the times, was being offered as a token of appreciation by the wife of a man attempting to avoid bankruptcy. If Eugène had not realized it before, he now knew that his wife had little sense of pecuniary values.

Maria was happy to be back in New York by mid-July. But soon she faced the fact that her husband's business affairs continued to deteriorate. On August 10 seven judgments totaling $25,000 were pronounced against him.[23] There is evidence that he offered to pay them off at eighty cents on the dollar,[24] and since New York had no bankruptcy law, this proposal may have been accepted by his creditors. However, the problem was not the legal judgment, but how to pay the debts, and the Malibrans assessed the situation: in Europe Maria could earn more money and more fully realize her talents than she could anywhere else. America had served her as a valuable training ground; she could return to France as a seasoned professional, no longer a mere debutante. She and Eugène agreed that she should go back to Paris, where he would join her when his business affairs were settled. The details of this plan will probably never be known. In Paris it was widely believed that Maria was sending back money to pay off her husband's debts, but there is little evidence for this. Whatever the arrangement, they parted amicably, hoping for a prompt reunion in France.

To finance her trip Maria accepted one last engagement to begin on October 9 at the Bowery Theatre. Her return to the stage prompted cogent remarks and prophecies from the press.

Signorina Garcia—Our readers before now will have generally learnt that this young lady has made an engagement with the managers of the Bowery. That engagement is extremely brief, being confined to four nights, and we regret to say that it will be the last time of her singing before an American audience. She has resolved, we hear, to return to her profession: a profession of which she was one of the most brilliant ornaments, which was to her a scene of fascination and triumph. Singers of loftier and wider fame undoubtedly exist. Catalani, Pasta, and Sontag, possess in Europe a recognized supremacy. But the two former marched by gradual steps to pre-eminence and reached it after years of trial and practice. They were nearly twice the age of Signorina Garcia before they came into the fullness of their reputation. Mlle Sontag is still young, and report says, very lovely. It is said too that much of her popularity is due to her personal charms. At any rate, she is as well known by the anecdotes of her projected marriages with Peers and Princes as for her musical talents. There is no instance of so high a celebrity being gained at so early an age as that of the Signorina. Nor can there be any doubt that had she remained in Europe she would have now been in the very first rank of her profession.

It is gratifying to our pride to know that her fame has not diminished among us, though it is painful to our musical likings to know that it is that unlessened fame which calls her back to Europe. We are told that for a time she will pursue her studies under Paer, and then appear as prima donna at the Italian Theatre of that city. At the Bowery Theatre she will sing four nights only. . . . Those who have not heard her will seize the opportunity; those who have will not miss it.[25]

The four evenings of her contract became six, and then the Bowery announced Maria's reengagement "due to popular request" for a last performance on October 29, when she assumed a role new to her, that of the Princess of Navarre in an English translation of François Boieldieu's *Jean de Paris*. The occasion was emotional on both sides of the footlamps, and her performance throughout reflected her unsettled mood. At the program's conclusion she came forward for an encore and sat down at her harp but she seemed so overcome that she could not sing, and rose again. Mr. Etienne, the pianist, began playing the introduction to a farewell song she had composed for the occasion, which, once she regained her composure, she sang "in a most touching and effective manner."[26]

New York regretted the departure of its first prima donna, fearing that "this amiable girl" would never return. "She has been winning the regard of all who knew her, either in public or private. Perhaps there never was an instance of a public actor making so deep an impression on private affection," lamented a correspondent, adding, "there is something peculiarly interesting in the history and destinies of this lady, and we cannot think of them without a feeling of sympathy."[27]

On November 1, 1827, Maria Malibran sailed from New York on the *Henri IV* to seek her fortune in Paris.

CHAPTER 5

Return to Paris

As she sailed bravely away, Maria once again traded one uncertainty for another. Alone, her family in Mexico, her husband in New York, she was returning to Paris, where she had few real friends and no public recognition. And yet, as she so confidently told the New York journalists, she intended to make a career at the Théâtre-Italien, the most artistically demanding opera house in Paris, if not Europe. Such ambition called for more than courage: it required talent, audacity, and luck.

Because of bad weather, she and the other passengers were seasick for days on end. And she was less than enchanted with her chaperone, Eugène's nephew Jules Chastelain. On November 12, halfway across the Atlantic, she wrote Eugène, "We have had all the time up until now a good wind, 10 miles an hour, up to 12. Today I am fine; I have been constantly sick more than I can tell you. Chastelain has been, and still is, sick. So sick that as soon as he eats a little he throws it up right away, and he is very annoying. All he does is spit, and he does it in a way that would make you vomit."[1] Only her young maid Victoire pleased her; she even avoided seasickness.

Maria's feelings toward her husband were confused, reflecting not only the affection she felt she owed him—a sentiment heightened by homesickness—but her as yet unexpressed disappointment in one who had failed her. "Mon bon petit ami, mon cher petit chou," she wrote him,

I must make a thousand and a thousand apologies to you. The cruel day of our separation my heart did not have the strength to say anything. I left without telling you so many things that I had wished to tell you, but the restraint in which I held myself so as not to cause you any pain prevented me from letting anything show which could hurt you. . . . Tell me, cher ami, how are you keeping yourself busy? What are you doing? At first you thought of me, next you dreamed of me, and then you spoke of me with your friends. That's all very well, but I want to know where you are living, and I want and demand that you enjoy yourself.[2]

Sickness and the rolling ship prevented her from continuing her letter until eight days later, when she took it up again in a sentimental mood. "Mon cher bijou . . . I think of you morning and night. Once in the day, that is to say from morning until night . . . I need to see you now, that's natural, but it is not one of those every-day needs, but for you yourself, your good little heart, which, I don't doubt, thinks of me, and perhaps through some tears! . . . . . . Oh! Mon bon Dieu! I wish you could read my mind, petit ami, you would like to take advantage of me for it."[3]

But in the last addendum to this much-continued letter, Maria expressed her confused feelings about Eugène; their marriage was already showing signs of its fragile foundations.

Thirteen days ago I told you "I finish for the present." I have been sick, or even the rolling prevents me from continuing. It is now November 25. Perhaps we will arrive tomorrow or the day after. I need to see you and to tell you a thousand things. Write me a packet of six pages. Say hello to everyone. (my friends) hem! Mme Brugière and the gentlemen who are our friends. Mr. and Mme Etienne. Please let me know how you are coming with your creditors.

Remember me to your brother, let him know what it costs me to have left you. Tell him how hard it is to be separated from persons whom *one loves,* from you. Pauvre ami. I assure you that I have never had a passion for you as I have already told you, but since I am no longer near you, your good qualities come to mind so vividly that I see I was mistaken in thinking that I loved you only *faithfully.* My stomach is turning over, bon ami. I leave you for awhile.[4]

On November 28 at 5:00 in the afternoon the ship docked at Le Havre, and with Jules Chastelain Maria traveled to the heart of Paris to live with Eugène's widowed sister at 23 Rue Neuve-Saint Eustache. Her greeting at the Chastelain home was more than cordial. "I am charmed with my family," she told Eugène happily of the large household, which included nieces, nephews, sisters-in-law and other relatives. *"I am like a coq en pâte. Everyone* addresses me as "tu." What pleasure that gives me! I lack absolutely nothing except you for it to be the *ne plus ultra.*"[5]

Her joy increased when Manuel arrived on the evening of December 10. His sister's plans to return to Europe had given him the courage to leave his family and the troupe in Mexico: life with his father had become unbearable. The elder Garcia had decided that on the all too frequent evenings when he was vocally indisposed his son would take his place, and transposed the tenor music to fit Manuel's baritone voice. Manuel suffered nervous agonies on these occasions and, as Maria had before him, he now felt the need to live his own life on his own terms. Maria was delighted to see him again. "What joy! What happiness!" she rejoiced to Eugène. "All I need is you! With that, the prospect of having papa, mamam!, my little sister!!"[6]

Maria Malibran the woman received a warm welcome in Paris, but Maria Malibran the prospective prima donna received an inauspicious, even ignominious acknowledgment. One newspaper observed her arrival: "Mlle Garcia (Mme Millibran) has just arrived from N.Y. at Havre, aboard the packet-boat *Henri-Quatre.* One speaks of her coming debut at the Théâtre-Italien."[7]

At the time of this announcement only Maria spoke of her imminent engagement at the Théâtre-Italien. And she wasted no time. Within days of her arrival in Paris, she sought the help of her old friend Countess Merlin, who could bring her to the attention of influential people in the city's music circles.

Maria de la Merced Santa Cruz y Montalva was born in Havana, but while a child she moved to Paris, where she received her schooling. As a girl she studied voice with Garcia, becoming an accomplished singer. Despite the nineteen years difference in their ages, the two Maria's came to know each other well and frequently sang duets together for Garcia during their music lessons. Now married to Count de Merlin, a lieutenant general in the French military and a member of the Legion of Honor, the Countess presided over one of the most brilliant salons in the French capital. But this beautiful, charming woman was not selfish with the power granted by her position, and she was among the first of her class to consider artists as equals.

The Countess vividly recorded her meeting with Maria in the first week of December.

A recollection of the regard I had cherished for her in girlhood induced her to come to me. This interesting young creature, a wanderer from a distant land, presented herself to me. Her dark silken hair hung in long ringlets on her neck, and she was simply attired in a dress of white muslin. Her youth, her beauty, her intelligence, her friendless and destitute condition, all combined to excite my deepest interest. I gazed on her with mingled feelings of sympathy and admiration. She seated herself at the piano, and I was charmed with her performance.

She expressed a wish to sing a duet with me, but she had not sung many bars when suddenly stopping, and throwing her arms around my neck, she exclaimed, "Oh! how this reminds me of the times when we used to practice together in papa's school! How perfectly we understood each other!" Then she resumed her singing, to which I listened with wonder and admiration.[8]

During her two years in New York Maria's voice developed remarkably, and now it ranged an astonishing three octaves from low D to high D, sometimes more, pure and even throughout the scale. The quality, that of a rich contralto with a soprano register superadded, was distinguished by a strange and exciting timbre that combined at the same time both a rough and sweet tone. The sound throughout was clear and brilliant, resembling, if it resembled anything, "the richer tone of the flute."[9] The upper notes possessed a liquid sweetness;[10] her contralto notes were richer and had a singular power and smoothness. "There is no sound in nature which can convey any idea of her lower notes," observed Mme. Merlin.[11]

Maria's voice was not outstandingly beautiful; but its remarkable range and her powers of expression raised her above her rivals. She, like Pasta before her, had learned to take the same notes in different registers to vary the color for purposes of expression: her middle voice could be sung in either the brilliance of her soprano register or the rich power of her chest tones, which she used frequently and with more force than any singer before her.[12]

Manuel Garcia, Senior

Joaquina Sitches Garcia

Manuel Garcia, Junior
(drawing by Pauline)

Pauline Viardot

The Park Theatre, New York, where the Garcia troupe
presented the first Italian opera in America.

Announcement of the New York arrival
of the Garcia troupe.

Malibran's Paris debut as Semiramide.

Maria Malibran

Charles de Bériot

Malibran at 46 rue de Provençe.

Charles de Bériot

Gioacchino Rossini

Henry Phillips

Mr. Mutlow, organist and conductor at the Gloucester summer festivals. According to Henry Phillips he was "a gentleman of eccentric habits and appearance, very short and fat, an epicure of no ordinary stamp, the length of whose arm was as near as possible the measure of his baton."

Caricatures by Maria Malibran

Maria as Romeo   Maria as Desdemona

Caricature of Maria Garcia, 1825.

Letter from Rossini to Maria Malibran, dated January 14, 1832.
"To Madame Malibran, celebrated composer, singer, player, painter, florist, costume designer, declaimer, dancer, etc. etc. etc. etc."

The phrase, as Bellini wrote it, is as follows.

- - vi-amo, ci for - mi-amo un ciel d'a-

mor, Ah nel-la ter . . . . . . ra in cui vi

via . . . . . mo, ci for - mia

mo un ciel d'a - mor.   etc.

Madame Malibran sang it thus:—

- - vij-amo,   ci for-mia-mo   un ciel d'a-

mor, Ah nel-la   ter . . . . . . ra in cui vi-

via . . . . mo, ci for-mia - - mo un

ciel   d'a - - mor   etc.

Malibran's embellishments
on a passage in *La Sonnambula*.

Allegro brillante

Nell' ebrez - za dell' a - mor   quanti

pianti cho ver - sai   quanti pal - pi - ti   pro-

vai   tutto spar - ve dal pen - sier   dal pen-

sier   u. s. w., zuletzt:

- m'è - - piu   ca - ro un tal   mo-

men - to che una vi - ta di pia - cer si di piacer si

A passage from one of Maria's arias
in Persiani's *Ines de Castro*.

☞ Extraordinary Attraction!!

THEATRE ROYAL, COVENT GARDEN.

It is respectfully announced, that in consequence of the attraction of

Madame MALIBRAN,

in her TWO POPULAR CHARACTERS
of La Sonnambula, & The Students of Jena.

she has been prevailed upon to perform them TO-NIGHT, at
this Theatre; in consequence of which arrangment

The heavy Scenery and Machinery,

connected with those Dramas, will (by permission of Captain Polhill) be
removed on that occasion from Drury Lane Theatre, in addition to
which attraction

MADAME VESTRIS

will perform her celebrated Character of KATE O'BRIEN.

This Evening, FRIDAY, June 14, 1833,

Their Majesties Servants will perform (*for the 16th Time*) a New Grand Opera, entitled

LA SONNAMBULA

(*With the whole of the Music by the celebrated composer BELLINI, for the 15th time on the English Stage*)
Arranged and Adapted to the English Stage by Mr. H. R. BISHOP.

Count Rhodolpho, - Mr. SEGUIN,
Elvino, Mr. TEMPLETON, Alessio, Mr. MARTYN.
Notary, Mr. F. COOKE. Joanno, Mr. YARNOLD. Pedro, Mr. AYLIFFE.
Amina, - - - Madame MALIBRAN,
Térèsa, Mrs. C. JONES, Liza, Miss BETTS.

Villagers, Peasants, &c. &c.

Messrs. TAYLEURE, BADLAND, WALSH, BRACE, ALLCROFT, TOLKIEN, S. JONES, G. SMITH,
BRADBERRY, WHITE, CARTER, S. JONES, FRY, T. JONES, HONNER, WIELAND,
J. BAKER, BECKETT, RUSSELL.
Mesdames CROUCH, MAPLESON, EAST, PENLEY, SOMERVILLE, NEVILLE, HUGHES, BROWNE,
FENWICK, LIDIA, HUNT, GILBERT, SHAW, VALLANCY, GEAR, WEBSTER, CLAIRE,
FROUD, WEST, GILMAN, RICKEY, THERESE, JEFFERSON, &c. &c. &c

After which, the popular Farce of

PERFECTION

Sir Lawrence Paragon. Mr. BARTLEY. Charles Paragon, Mr. BALLS, Sam, Mr. HONNER.
Kate O'Brien, ... Madame VESTRIS

In which she will introduce the favorite Song of

"TO THE GAY TOURNAMENT."

To conclude with, (*for the 4th Time*) a New Operetta, called The

STUDENTS of JENA

Or, THE FAMILY CONCERT.

(THE MUSIC ENTIRELY NEW, BY MONSIEUR CHELARD.)

Monsieur Roulade, (*an old French Professor of Music, residing at Weimar*) Mr. SEGUIN,
Ernest. (*a Student of Jena*) Mr. TEMPLETON,
Students—Karl, Mr. BALLS, Eberhard, Mr. YARNOLD. Rudolph, Mr. S. JONES,
Signor Solfeggio, (*Maitre de Chapelle to the Grand Duke*) Mr. STANLEY,
Adele, { *Daughter of Monsieur and Madame Roulade,* } Madame MALIBRAN,
{ *intended for the Stage.* }
Gertrude, (*Servant to Roulade*) Mrs. CROUCH Madame Roulade. Mrs. C. JONES.

☞ As the greater part of the Boxes are already secured, it is necessary
to state, that NOT AN ORDER WILL BE ISSUED; and every privilege
(excepting those of the Public Press) will be suspended.
⁎ *AN EXTRA PIT DOOR WILL ALSO BE OPENED.*

The doors will be opened at Half-past Six o'clock, and the Performances commence at Seven.

☞ For the better accommodation of Parties residing at the West End of the Town, Mr. EBERS, has been
appointed Sole Agent for the disposal of Private Boxes and Stalls, the prices of which are as follow:—

Private Boxes, £4. 4s.—£3 3s. and £2. 2. .... Stalls, 10s. 6d. each.

N. B.—The STALLS are fitted up in the same commodious and elegant style as those erected at Drury Lane Theatre.

S. G. Fairbrother, Printer, Theatre Royal, Drury Lane.

Malibran as Norma.

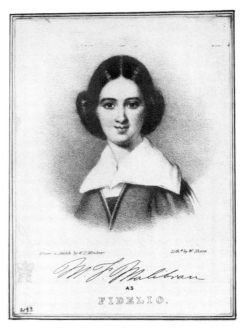

Pasta as Norma.

Malibran in *Fidelio*.

I. R. TEATRO ALLA SCALA.

Dal giorno 15 al 17 del corr. Maggio avranno luogo
due Recite, nelle quali agirà Madama **MALIBRAN**
rappresentando il Melodramma

NORMA

La Compagnia sarà composta inoltre dalle

Signore Garcia Ruez	. . .	ADALGISA
„ Ruggeri Teresa	. . .	CLOTILDE
e dai Signori Reina Domenico	. . .	POLLIONE
„ Marini Ignazio	. . .	OROVESO
„ Vaschetti Giuseppe	. . .	FLAVIO

Nell'intermezzo dei due atti vi sarà un PASSO A
SETTE, espressamente composto dal sig. *Egidio Priora*,
eseguito dallo stesso, e dalle signore *Rabel, Ancement
Bonalumi, Braschi Amalia, Frassi Adelaide e Romagnoli.*

Con altro avviso sarà indicato precisamente il giorno
della prima recita, restando fissato quello della seconda
nel succennciato giorno 17, e saranno pure indicati i
prezzi d'ingresso e delle Sedie chiuse.

Dal Camerino dell'I. R. Teatro alla Scala il 3 Maggio 1834.

I. R. TEATRO ALLA SCALA.

In questa sera di Sabbato 24 Maggio 1834 si darà L'ULTIMA RECITA
DI MAD. MALIBRAN coll'Opera

OTELLO
OSSIA
IL MORO DI VENEZIA

Musica del Maestro Cavaliere sig. Gioacchino Rossini

PERSONAGGI

DESDEMONA	. . . Signore	MALIBRAN MARIA.
EMILIA	. . . . „	BAVILLOU FELICITA.
RODRIGO	. . . . „	GARCIA RUEZ.
OTELLO	. . . . Signori	REINA DOMENICO.
ELMIRO	. . . . „	MARINI IGNAZIO.
JAGO	. . . . . „	BALFE GUGLIELMO.
DOGE	. . . . . „	MARCONI NAPOLEONE.

Dopo il primo atto, essendo indisposto tuttora il sig. *Priora*, avrà luogo un
PASSO A QUATTRO fra le allieve dell'I. R. Accademia, signore *Ancement
Ciocca, Romagnoli e Zambelli.*

Prezzo del Biglietto	Al Teatro . . . lir.	6	austriache.
	Al Loggione . . „	2	
Per una Sedia chiusa „	1.5		

Daranno accesso alle File chiuse due ingressi a dritta e sinistra nell'atrio
del sudetto Teatro. — Ciascun concorrente conserva il Biglietto a ga-
ranzia del posto.

Al Camerino si affittano Palchi di quinta Fila.

Lo Spettacolo incomincierà alle ore otto e mezzo.

IN BOLOGNA
NEL GRAN TEATRO DELLA COMUNE

Nella Primavera 1834.

SI RAPPRESENTERANNO DUE OPERE

LA PRIMA SARÀ IL DRAMMA INTITOLATO

OTELLO

Musica del Celebre Maestro Cavaliere ROSSINI

LA SECONDA SARÀ IL MELODRAMMA INTITOLATO

LA SONNAMBULA

Musica del Celebre Maestro Cavaliere VINCENZO BELLINI.

Interlocutori della prima Opera   *Attori*

OTELLO Moro al soldo de Veneti	LORENZO BONFIGLI
DESDEMONA Amante, e Sposa secreta di Otello	MARIETTA F. MALIBRAN.
EMILIA Amica di Desdemona	ASSUNTA ROCELLI.
ELMIRO Patrizio Veneto, amante di Otello	LUCIANO MARIANI.
RODRIGO Amante, e pretendente di Desdemona, figlio del Doge	PIETRO FONZOLINI.
JAGO Nemico secreto di Otello, amico finto di Rodrigo	PAOLO GARZONI.
DOGE	N. N.
LUCIO Confidente di Otello	N. N.

Coro di Senatori, di Seguaci armati di Otello, di Damigelle del seguito di Desdemona, di Popolo
Maestro Istruttore dei Cori Sig. FILIPPO VANDUZZI Avv. Id.

CORISTE

Portrait of Bellini by Malibran.

Portrait of Bellini by Malibran.

My Dear Mr Bunn

I cannot promise to play the part of cont Belino — The music is exceedingly week, and after the sunnambula I am not capable of singing baby's music — however I dont say positively no untill I have seen, both the music and the pice again — for it is about 8 years that I have not even herd of the part — therefore be so good as to send the whole to me & I shall give you a conscientious answer quite

à la Malibran.

Maria and her impresario Bunn — a struggle of wills
concerning future roles. *(See page 156.)*

Malibran at the Opera, by Chalon.

Drawing from the portrait medallion struck in Milan
and presented by Malibran to Dr. Belluomini.

SOUTH TRANSEPT of the CHOIR of the COLLEGIATE CHURCH MANCHESTER,

EXHIBITING the INTERMENT of the REMAINS of the UNIVERSALLY LAMENTED

MADAME MALIBRAN DE BERIOT.

during the reading of the Funeral service at the Grave, drawn on stone, from a faithful sketch
taken at the time, by the public's most obed' Serv'

Henry Harris

London. Published by C. Tilt 86 Fleet S'. Rittner & Goupil, Paris & Grundy & Goadsby Manchester.
Printed by T. Papuck Manchester.

De Bériot and the memorial portrait
bust that he sculpted.

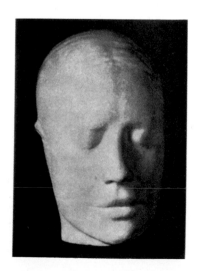

Death mask.

MALIBRAN!

From an Italian journal.

Garcia's training had made her a complete musician as well as an outstanding singer. Her enunciation and intonation were perfect, and her sight-reading was so remarkable that she could walk into a composer's studio, pick up any piece of music, and sing it to her own piano accompaniment, all without an error.[13] She executed the greatest coloratura difficulties with as much brilliance and accuracy as could be heard from any singer then before the public.[14] Her arpeggios and trills were astonishing both for agility and extreme duration, and her ability in improvisation and embellishment seemed to be without limits. She used this great facility to conceal a slight weakness in the notes between her mezzo-soprano and soprano registers, frequently alternating between high and low notes in great leaps of startling rapidity and accuracy for distances of up to three octaves and more. Her use of ornamentation for dramatic effect made her art unique.

That evening at the Théâtre-Italien Mme. Merlin described her impressive experience of the morning. Her friends, suspicious of such extravagant praise, doubted her word and even suggested that this Maria Malibran's Spanish background was unduly influencing her judgment. "Surely if she were so wonderful we would have heard of her," they commented.[15] But the Countess held to her convictions and arranged a concert at her home to which she invited the doubters. Never, perhaps, has a musical reputation been made so quickly. From the moment of Mme. Merlin's soirée, Maria became the engrossing topic of conversation in music circles all over Paris. Invited to sing in all the fashionable salons, she was heard by the major critics and impresarios alike. Just one month after arriving in France she wrote Eugène ecstatically:

You should know that I sang this past Sunday at the home of Mme la Duchesse de Berry. Mme Pizaroni, Mr Galli, Mr Lavasseur, Mlle Blasis and Mr Donzelli [were there]. *I made a furore.* Mme Pizaroni has great talent, but she is ugly, very ugly, and grimaces while singing. As I'm quite passable, and as I do not grimace, that alone should assure my success, but put your mind at ease, it's not like that. I have sung in succession at Mme Merlin's, who had a beautiful reception, and where I had all the success to which I could aspire. One speaks only of my technique, my voice, my manner of singing. They call me the worthy successor of Mme *Pasta,* and they grant me many superiorities over her. You are going to tell me: "that's what flattery gets you, and you let yourself be seduced by praise." Be reassured, my friend. These are only the *ladies,* I do not say what the men say. But when Rossini, when Mme Rossini [Isabella Colbran], who in her whole life never gave a compliment to anyone, approached, arms open, before a numerous group, to embrace me, to pay me a thousand compliments, then I can see that everyone is enchanted. Everyone is talking about the concerts afterwards and telling me that I have had so much success. That's a reason for me to believe something. Moreover, have no fear that I will gain a swelled head, and that I will consider myself too grand in my little specialty. What can give you even more of an idea of my success is that Mr Laurent, director of the Théâtre-Italien, was at Mme Merlin's, and as soon as he heard me he spoke to me to try and engage me for the Bouffe [Théâtre-Italien]. He is, at the same time, director of the Theatre of London. I warn you that if he engages me, he will probably want to engage me for his theater over there. Put your mind at ease, I see you already upset. It is absolutely necessary that I know when I will have the happiness of being with you, because I could say in the contract that I will only go to London when you come, at such and such a time.[16]

Maria was conscious of Eugène's apprehensions. From the moment she set foot on French soil, he voiced his worries to her and questioned her behavior. His fears were further fanned by a letter from a family friend in Paris. Greatly annoyed at his lack of trust she angrily told him that

the letter Eveline wrote to you has gone to your head. What fright all of a sudden! You, who knows me, do you really believe that if I were to contract myself to the Theater, and if you were not there, that I would have to fear seduction, and all the things which E. has crammed into your head?! You are not thinking, my friend. If I were disposed to being bad or letting myself be seduced, *whether it was you who were here or the Eternal Father,* it would make *no* difference at all. Also my good little friend, set your mind at ease, and prepare to know that my first and last names will be on the placards one of these mornings. You know very well that if I were made advantageous offers for the theater, whether it be in London or Paris, I would not lose good engagements because of the frightful panics that so suddenly grip you. . . . One more time, my dear little husband, get it into your head that I desire only *what is good.* Never, even when the angels of heaven come to tempt me. I will resist like St. Anthony.[17]

"I am enjoying a great deal of respect in Paris, which pleases me because I deserve it in the way that you desire," she assured him.[18]

Maria did not like Paris as much as New York. To her Paris meant pretty hats, beautiful gowns, dazzling jewels, and shallow women concerned with little more than their appearance. "I can't seem to find a Mme Brugière or a Mme Wainwright!"[19] she wailed, never failing to supply Eugène with lists of New York women to whom he should pass on her greetings. But the rapid progress of her career precluded much nostalgia for New York or much preoccupation with anything other than music.

One of her first paying concerts was a benefit at the Paris Conservatory on January 12, for which she received 250 francs. The crowd was immense and anticipation high, for the public had read about Maria Malibran but had not yet heard her. The audience studied her with curiosity as she sat on the platform with the other performers. There was nothing particularly striking about her appearance. Her small bonnet hid half of her face but did not disguise her youth. She seemed no more commanding than a schoolgirl. When it was her turn to sing, she removed her hat and walked to the piano to play her own accompaniment. The writer Ernest Legouvé, who was hearing her for the first time, described the effect she made:

First, her coiffure astonished by its simplicity; no curls, no cleverly piled up tresses; flat and smooth bands of hair outlining the shape of her head. A somewhat large mouth, a rather short nose, but such a pretty oval face, such a shapely neck and shoulders that beauty of features was replaced by beauty of outline. And finally, eyes the likes of which have not been seen since [actor François] Talma, eyes that had "an atmosphere of their own." . . . Well, Maria Malibran had, like Talma, eyes floating in some indescribable electric fluid from which her glance, at the same time both luminous and veiled, shot out like a ray of sunshine through a cloud. Her every look seemed completely charged with melancholy, with reverie, with passion. She sang the "Willow Song" from *Otello*. After a few bars the audience was conquered, at the end of the first stanza it was inebriated, at the end of the piece it was insane.[20]

Greater opportunities were already imminent. In two days Maria would make her operatic debut in the title role of *Semiramide* for the benefit of Fillipo Galli, an old family friend with whom she had sung in the salons. In addition to the performance of *Semiramide*, the gala evening included the fourth and fifth acts of Shakespeare's *Romeo and Juliet*, in French, with Miss Smithson and Mr. Abbott, and the first act of *Il Barbiere* with the enormously popular soprano Henriette Sontag.

Sontag, the leading singer of the Théâtre-Italien, lacked great dramatic ability, but she had an extremely beautiful, flexible, voice. Since her French debut in June of 1826, this young and beautiful woman had aroused a fanatical enthusiasm termed "Sontag fever." A German actress described her first impressions of la Sontag on stage:

And then she opened her little rose-bud mouth, just as a little wood-bird opens its beak; so naturally, so unaffectedly, and the sweetest, clear, bird-warble filled the house with joyous tones. Her voice was neither full nor strong, but pure as a bell, transparent as a pearl, with a ring of silver, sonorous, especially in the middle tones, very flexible, every note distinctly articulated, and of seductive sweetness. And how beautifully she trilled—like the jubilation of a soaring lark! Then again there was the brilliance of her singularly high head tones in the most difficult passages and roulades—as precise as a delicate musical clock. Incomparably, enchantingly, she sang mezzo and sotto voce. And all this came forth with such playful ease, so effortlessly from the charming little mouth, that the listener had but to relax and enjoy it, confident that nothing could go wrong.[21]

"Mon dieu! How can she sing so beautifully?" cried Maria on first hearing Sontag.[22] Maria would have preferred the role of Rosina for Galli's benefit rather than that of Semiramide, which was new to her repertoire and, in addition, one of the most difficult and fatiguing parts written for the soprano voice. As a newcomer, however, she could not yet claim a role that virtually belonged to "the northern nightingale," and with Manuel's help she set about learning her assignment.

On January 14, 1828, the night of Galli's benefit, Maria felt stage fright for the first time in her life, not only because of her role, but because the auditorium of the Académie Royale de Musique was the largest in which she had yet sung, and the audience, as glittering as Paris could muster, expected much of Garcia's daughter. "Mme Malibran, Mlle Smithson, Mlle Sontag at the same time!," exulted a critic. "What a debut was that of the new Semiramide! What chandeliers, what torches, what brilliant stars! What danger, but also what victory!"[23]

At her entrance Maria was greeted with warm applause by a public at once captivated by her bearing and youthful appearance. As she began to sing this reception seemed justified, but almost immediately the phrase "Trema il tempio," a hideously difficult tongue-twister sung on a flurry of fiorature, proved her undoing. Frightened by this stumble she let her voice drop and did not attempt the final passage, leaving the audience disappointed and skeptical. The prodigious talents displayed by Rosamunda Pisaroni in the subsequent scene provided an unflattering comparison, and when Maria returned to the stage she was coldly received. Undaunted, she courageously essayed the aria "Bel raggio lusinghier," exhibiting a voice of such range and sonority that the audience forgot her earlier failure and applauded with enthusiasm. Inspired by this success she dared to interpolate the most difficult embellishments. "Applause such as I do not remember ever having heard paid her back for her efforts, and indemnified her usuriously," wrote a critic.[24]

From that point on the evening was hers. Admiring reviewers excused her initial accident. François Fétis declared the troublesome passage "an ungrateful phrase which is not fit for the voice."[25] And in *Le Figaro,* which devoted its entire front page on January 15 to the brilliant evening, a critic commented that "Mme Garcia dares to place on her head the diadem whose weight has bruised Mme Pasta herself. . . . When one realizes the extreme youth of this charming singer, who already can compete with the first talents of the times, one can foresee what a brilliant future is destined for her."

Fétis, the most critical of the reviewers, admired her singing. "I will say that nature has gifted her with the most precious qualities, with a rare voice that unites the powerful sounds of the most beautiful contralto to those of the highest soprano . . . that her facility in singing the most difficult passages is prodigious, that her rich imagination provides her with new and elegant embellishments, finally, that she has soul and verve."[26] He then modified his praise by stating that her vocalism was "absolutely devoid of taste," and that her embellishments, good by themselves, were "incoherent" and inconsistent with the music they were intended to complement. He also criticized her breathing, which was affected by nervousness, noting that she often altered the music's flow in order to breathe. Maria did not argue with this observation, but she knew exactly what ornamentation pleased the audience. "My dear grumbler," she addressed him, "there may perhaps be two or three connoisseurs in the theater, but it is not they who give success. When I sing for you alone I will sing very differently."[27] But she took his advice to heart and her style became more restrained.

Her success, achieved in a mere six weeks and against formidable odds, changed her outlook on life. In one evening she acquired a new self-confidence, a faith in her destiny, and a different attitude toward Eugène. She suddenly saw herself not as the hardworking wife of a bankrupt husband but as an individual in her own right, independent of anyone. The day after her first triumph, she wrote a brusque, almost rude letter to Eugène that indicated a new phase in their relationship. Anticipation of his arrival in Paris became more worrisome to her with every passing day. Eugène Malibran was not only a nuisance but a cause for alarm.

> Paris, Jan. 15, 1828
>
> Mon cher Eugène,
>
> I am writing you just two words to tell you that I made my debut last night. As for knowing if I had any success, I will leave it to you to learn from others rather than from me. It doesn't matter to me. I am not under contract, I performed on the occasion of the benefit of Mr. Galli, an old friend of my father's.
>
> Remember Eugène, that you should write me to let me know when you are arriving. You have no idea how I am beseiged with offers for contracts both at the Théâtre-Italien and at the Opéra.
>
> I don't under any pretext want to be engaged to the latter. Not for millions. The other one is different. I warn you that if I am made brilliant offers, I will engage myself *at once*.
>
> My brother is leaving for Italy.
>
> Remember Eugène, when you arrive in this country, *to behave yourself. Remember that your imprudence has made me sick.*
>
> I don't trust yours too much, and although you have much experience, you make *mistakes,* and *very big mistakes.*
>
> I am behaving a lot better than *when I was in New York.* Adieu, my friend, I embrace you.[28]

For the first time she signed a letter to her husband "Maria Malibran" rather than including her middle name or preceding her signature with "your wife."

In the first days of December, after Maria had made her appearance in Mme. Merlin's salon, Rossini approached her about an engagement with the Opéra, the company that performed French opera and of which he was now musical director. Maria's interest, however, lay with Italian opera and consequently with the Théâtre-Italien, which was superior and more highly regarded by the music lovers of Paris. "The Opéra," commented Stendhal, "is populated with superlative talent, trained and cherished with boundless patience—and is without an iota of genuine musicality."[29] Audiences also differed. At the Italien silence was mandatory; to lose a note was a public calamity. At the Opéra it was said the audience slept through the performance and was silent during the dance.[30]

Initially Rossini was so persistent in trying to engage Maria that she had difficulty getting him out of her home. To dissuade him she demanded 30,000 francs per year and a three-month vacation. No more was heard from the music director until the morning after her performance at Galli's benefit, when a note arrived inviting her and Manuel to his apartments. They accepted his invitation and, as they had suspected, were presented with renewed offers, this time a four-year contract at 25,000 francs per year. Rossini explained that he had not offered such a sum previously because, although he thought Maria was brilliant at the private concerts, he wondered whether her voice was large enough to fill a hall as big as the Académie Royale and whether she could hold the interest of an audience as large and blasé as that of the Opéra. Such doubts, of course, had been dispelled by the preceding night's performance. But Maria was not interested in singing French opera and once again refused him: she had made up her mind to wait for the Italien to meet her terms.

The Opéra did not give up easily; the management increased its offer to 35,000 francs per year and a three-month vacation. Soon the issue was debated publicly and in the newspapers. Most, including Fétis, hoped that she would join the Opéra, for the Italien already had Sontag as a drawing card and its rival company needed a popular singer following the departure of its soprano Laure Cinti. "I would suggest granting Mlle Garcia anything she wants, in order to finally have someone who can assure the future of the institution and who can pull in the receipts," wrote Fétis in *La Revue Musicale.* "I know this kind of example is dangerous, for after the indispensable talents come serviceable talents, which also have their own pretensions. This progressive augmentation in payment of performers is a very bad thing; it is this which wrecks theatrical enterprises, but this evil, which is a consequence of the rarity of its cause, will cease only when useful measures have been taken to develop a large number of singers."[31]

No amount of public pressure could change Maria's mind, and the Opéra resorted to Machiavellian intrigue. Emile-Timothée Lubbert, director of the Opéra, visited Mme. Naldi, an old friend of the Garcia family, and adroitly informed her that the person who could persuade Maria Malibran to join his theater would receive 2,000 francs. Meanwhile the Vicomte Sosthènes de la Rochefoucauld, director of the government Beaux-Arts Council, instructed Laurent that he was not to engage her for the Italien. Unaware that Maria knew of this, the Vicomte made every attempt at civility whenever he saw her, never failing to inquire when she was going to join the Opéra, and Maria, in her forthright manner, would tell him, "Never will I join, under any pretext, no matter what."[32]

In the meantime she confirmed her rising reputation with two more performances of *Semiramide,* at enormous fees, and the private salons fought over her, offering her up to 300 francs for a single concert, a sum made even more significant by her willingness to perform more than once in an evening. Unfortunately she appeared at so many soirées that she gained a not altogether flattering reputation as a "singer of the boudoir" and was severely criticized for wasting her time.[33]

All these problems were resolved by the conclusion of Henriette Sontag's contract with the Italien. The Opéra, seeing that Maria would never accept their offers and that their intrigue was useless, gave up the fight. Laurent offered her 800 francs per performance for the remainder of the season and a four-month vacation. Her debut was arranged for April 8, again as Semiramide.

Although Maria Malibran managed her public life with perfect aplomb, dealing with the Chastelains was a problem. By the third week in February her relations with Eugène's family were so unbearable that she left 23 Rue Neuve-Saint Eustache and went to live with her mother's old friend Mme. Naldi. Each party to these domestic squabbles blamed the other, and Eugène, 3,000 miles away, was left to judge for himself.

Problems arose after Maria's operatic debut, toward the end of January. "It is extremely disagreeable for me to let you know how disagreeably I am lodged with my sister-in-law," she wrote Eugène on February 6, in the first of many letters that he must have found most annoying.[34] She declared that when she first arrived in Paris she had been determined to love the Chastelain family as if it were her own. She shared every thought with her new relatives. Not a letter came or went that they did not see, and her money was placed in the hands of Mme. Chastelain, whom she called mamam. Her new mother and Victor Chastelain chaperoned her everywhere she went. She gave them all presents for New Year's and reiterated her love and pleasure at living with them. True, she had noticed a lack of education, a dearth of social polish which was not shared by the more sophisticated and traveled Eugène, but she was willing to overlook these faults because *"I believed them to be good."*[35]

Waiting for the Théâtre-Italien to engage her led Maria to bouts of depression, spells of weeping, and loss of appetite. Irritable, she took greater offense at the commonness of her in-laws, whom she began to resent. It now seemed that Jules spoke condescendingly to her, as though she were lodging for free, which was not the case, and as though she were a mere child in the custody of Mme. Chastelain. A doctor, correctly diagnosing her mental state, advised her to find more distractions and amusements. At the same time her mother sent her the address of Mme. Naldi and wrote her old friend asking her to help Maria as though she were her own daughter.

Marie Naldi, who lived with her daughter Carolina and son-in-law the Count de Sparre, immediately took the miserable girl under her wing. Unfortunately Maria's reliance on her new guardian made matters worse in the Chastelain home as she spent more and more time with Mme. Naldi and her daughter. Her relatives questioned her about these absences; they told her that she no longer seemed to love them as she had in the beginning and asked if she would tell them why. Maria's brutal frankness could hardly have helped ease the situation: she replied that the Chastelains annoyed her and that she was quite capable of passing the day where she wanted. "Besides," she snapped, "you know very well where I'm going."[36]

After this retort her relatives felt they owed her no favors, and in her immaturity Maria was baffled by their unwillingness to oblige her. Their first sign of disapproval involved chaperoning. Victor Chastelain did not consider the social and paid parties equally important and commented, to Maria's mind very insolently, "I am willing to accompany you when you have paying concerts, but not to your dinners or balls."[37] Furious, Maria made it plain to Eugène that in her opinion Victor was obligated to accompany her wherever she wanted to go, be it for money or her own pleasure. But when she saw that his decision was final, she began attending the dinners and soirées alone, regardless of social opinion.

"You will ask me, 'Why haven't you asked my sister?,' " she wrote Eugène in anticipation of his reaction. "I answer you that I *have* asked her to accompany me, but she said she does not have the proper attire, and that she can't make that expense. It would be me, then, who should make it? Oh! for that, no. I have enough expenses as it is, and besides, since my reputation is now made, and since I am liked and respected, I do not need to spend capriciously. Not for your nephew, nor for your sister, who does not strike me as being anything but a blockhead when she is with me, for she knows nothing to say."[38]

A more serious problem than chaperoning was Maria's financial situation, and here Mme. Naldi played a professorial role. She immediately saw that her charge knew nothing of business and provided her with a practical education in money management. Maria learned quickly, and the more Mme. Naldi taught her about economizing, the more horrified she was at how the Chastelains had handled the money she had so willingly entrusted to them. "How many times they told me, 'you should buy this, that,' " she complained to Eugène. "I asked 'is it expensive?' 'No, that doesn't cost so much' and so I bought. What do I know?! I would have thought that people who were accustomed to economizing down to the last cent would surely urge me to be economical—Eh bien! It was completely the opposite."[39]

The Chastelain's accusation that she was suddenly becoming economical annoyed her still more. "There is a beginning to everything," she retorted sharply.[40] With her tutor's help she calculated the expenses she had incurred in the Chastelain home and discovered that her stay from December 3 through the end of January had cost her the outrageous sum of 5,776 francs.

The rent was 2200 francs per year. She wanted me to pay half of it. I didn't want to, having only a bedroom and the enjoyment of a parlor. The wages of my maid come to 300 francs, and 600 for food, which makes 900 francs for the good woman. Then my food, my lighting (not counting the wood) comes to 116 francs per month. The upholsterer, for renting the furnishings, 120 francs per month, without counting the wash. Thus we have calculated, according to the accounting that Victor made me this morning, that my food, lighting, rent, maid and upholsterer, all come to (without counting the wood and washing) 4645 francs. Now let's put in what it should be for my clothes, being obliged to have something decent, always, let's put it at 2000 francs. Do you know that when one does not earn in proportion to what one spends, it is frightful to see how it all disappears?

No doubt Eugène knew only too well how it all disappears. Then Maria almost dared to consider the unthinkable. "If I were alone. . . . that's all very well, but we must consider our future, and this way of life doesn't suit me at all."[41]

Victor Chastelain's meddling in her negotiations with the Opéra also bothered her. When Lubbert visited Maria, Victor assured the director that it was not fitting for her to join his theater. But behind her back he had told Lubbert to speak to her again, that she would join the Opéra if offered enough money. Although Maria did not mind causing intrigue, she did mind being personally involved in it, and Victor's remark, which soon reached her ears, gave the world the impression that she was matching the Opéra's own wiles.

The Chastelains sought to defend themselves by implying to Eugène that his wife's behavior was not as virtuous as he might like to think, and Maria was once again forced to calm his fears. "I am annoyed that in your letters you always speak to me of certain things that displease and disgust me," she told him angrily.

You tell me to love you: I love you as in the beginning, not at all Amour, for I have known only friendship. That is all I can promise you if you deserve it, and if your conduct towards me is like the words in your letters. I can tell you, to put your mind at ease, that all the men I see, beautiful or ugly, are like statues or bushes for me, no more effect than that. I never experience the least desire, and even if one speaks of something that pertains to what you seem to like so much, I feel disgust—ah!—I don't even like to think about it . . . I am your wife, solely *your wife.*[42]

On February 19, at midnight, she sat down and wrote Mme. Chastelain a long letter in which she aired all her complaints: Mme. Chastelain's mistreatment of Maria's maid while she was spending her days with Mme. Naldi, the unpleasantness over her measures of economy, the slurs against her character. As for her new habit of traveling about unchaperoned she wrote,

Don't bother to be disturbed over what my husband could think of it; for were he here, he could shut me up in a tower, but that would not prevent me from being the worst of all women (if I were disposed to be). . . . So leave me alone to earn money *for my husband* and for me, without troubling his heart or mine. Remember that *he has only me.* Remember also that *I will do everything* so that he

can spend his life agreeably, as long as he can behave himself with me, as I
believe merits him . . . and instead of sullying the motives of my actions, bear in
mind that I will only do what is perfectly appropriate.[43]

She finished her long and passionate epistle by hoping that the misunderstanding might be resolved and that they would be reconciled. *"As for me,"*
she concluded, *"I feel no ill-will."*

Madame Chastelain's reaction to this letter cannot have been favorable, for two days later Maria moved out of her in-laws' house and went to
live with Mme. Naldi. In her explanation to Eugène she stated that the
family had thrown her out and that she had then decided to move in with
Mme. Naldi.[44] Mme. Merlin's impression was that "one day, in a moment
of irritation, she sent for a coach and taking with her her trunks, she
drove off, unknown to her relatives, and took up her abode with Madame
Naldi."[45] The separation was inevitable. In her heart Maria sincerely
believed the Chastelains were in the wrong, and she waited before telling
Eugène because "I wanted to give them free rein to say whatever came into
their heads. However, I hope that they will have told you the truth. . . . You
know me, you know them—You know that I *never lie,* thus you will judge us,
and if you do not give me justice, I am angry about it, but that will change
nothing in my point of view, or actions, which like everything else, only
honors you."[46]

Maria may have sought a father substitute in Eugène Malibran; she
now found a surrogate mother in Marie Naldi, "my good and true friend
. . . whom I can never repay for the really maternal kindness she has shown
me." Her life became more peaceful under this lady's care. Although Mme.
Naldi did not have a large apartment in the Count de Sparre's residence
and couldn't give Maria more than half her own bed, her foster child could
tell Eugène, "I am treated like a daughter of the house. *I am getting fat here,*
(and I am happy)."[47]

The Chastelain affair put another wedge between husband and wife,
and the following weeks brought Eugène letters of increasing anger. His
attempts to soften Maria's interpretation of his sister's financial demands
provoked a stream of sarcasm that clearly indicated how much his wife had
learned from Mme. Naldi.

Don't be surprised if I laughed in reading the accounting you made me. One
could really say it was a laughing matter. I have never been a businessman; I
only count with my fingers on my nose. That's enough for me to see that five
thousand francs in two months doesn't seem to you to be too much (result of
your generosity). You grant me three thousand more for six months (result of
your avarice). Neither one sum nor the other is correct. Five thousand for two
months is too much, eight thousand per year is too little. From this you can see I
know more than you. You fear that I will become avaricious (a fault I would not
like to have) but I certainly will want to take care of my affairs, knowing how
much I will need for my old age. I will always be just as I am with your family.
I paid (despite the fact that I had nothing in writing) a month's and a half rent

for an apartment—I do not owe one sou more. I am told that you have offered *generously* to pay everything entirely. If that is so it proves two things to me, that you find me wrong, and that you have money. I would like to settle in my mind two contradictory things which have been told to me. They are: that you are coming back soon, and that you have settled nothing with your creditors. How can that be? In the first case, it is certain this can only be when you will have permission from your creditors, *for I don't suppose that you would bring me a dishonored name,* which in my situation could no longer serve me as Mentor and from which I would have to blush. In the second case, why, if you have money, do you not give it to your creditors? That would at least diminish your debts by a little. One must be generous according to his means. If you don't have any, why play the big man with your family and give them false hopes?[48]

While she was on the subject of money, Maria brought up their wedding contract. The Garcias had not forgotten Eugène's debt to them. "I received a letter from my mother," she told him, "and she always puts as a condition of their coming to rejoin us the payment of the debt you owe my parents. . . . If you don't think you can fulfill your obligation to them, I ask you not to give them any false hopes. Don't make them believe *that I will pay what I in no way owe,* understand?"[49]

But worse was yet to come. "You know that in marrying, each party has his motives in view. Mine was to be happy and peaceful. You know that I have a loving nature, and it has been only for you. Thus it continues, but remember . . . . . one can pardon but never forget. There is my motive. Yours I would not want to know." When her husband expressed his indebtedness to her, she added, more charitably, "I will tell you that when I married you and when I believed that I would not have to work anymore, I did not think of myself as being indebted to you. Now that things are reversed, I think of nothing other than my duty. Whether the burden be light or heavy makes no difference to me, and I don't think of you as being indebted to me."[50]

Maria's debut at the Théâtre-Italien was arranged to coincide with the departure of Henriette Sontag in early April. Probably because of her father's fame she wished to be billed as Garcia and had in fact sung under the name of Mme. Garcia for her initial performances. This name, however, presented problems; only a year before a young soprano named Marietta Garcia had appeared in Paris, and some critics had already confused Maria Malibran with this singer.[51] Her name had to clearly distinguish her from other singers, so on March 3 she wrote Eugène, "I warn you that I am announced as Madame Malibran née Garcia—as it is a name *that I honor* I want to bear it."[52]

In early April the posters appeared announcing the debut of Mme. Malibran-Garcia with the Théâtre-Italien, again as Semiramide. The night before the performance, Maria wrote to Giuditta Pasta about the pressure created by her growing reputation.

Paris, April 7, 1828

Cara la mia Giuditta,

I wrote you four times from New-York without having ever received any news about you other than your fame . . . and this is it! I believed for a time that you had forgotton about poor Marietta, but then I thought that perhaps your not having time to write me, you would be thinking of me, and so I live in hope. Cara Judith! I have a *passion malheureuse* for I am afraid of not being answered; enough, if you wish only to tell me three words, "I love you!," I am happy. Tomorrow I make my debut! How frightening! in the small part of Semiramide (nothing fatiguing as you know). I haven't slept for eight days, my heart is beating like an anvil, in short, I'm overwhelmed with fright. Pray to God for me! . . . Love me, and know that I adore you.

your most affectionate
Marietta Malibran

Rue de Choiseul No. 7
I am staying with Marietta Naldi and Carolina[53]

Despite Maria's fears, her triumph exceeded her earlier successes. As the evening began her voice was tremulous, but she rallied her powers and attacked the phrase "trema il tempio" with a force that seemed too strong for her physical resources.[54] In the subsequent "Bel Raggio" the beauty of her voice, her vocal colors, her grace and expressive features won her the greatest applause, and as the performance progressed the artistic gains she had made in the past three months became apparent. Although Fétis again accused her of overembellishment, he did admit that her style was now "most pure, and at the same time most brilliant," and he found the way she sang the coloratura difficulties "charming." He also noted an innovation: her embellishments were not meaningless ornaments but served the dramatic situation. Although he still considered her acting inferior to Pasta's, he observed that she had a "remarkable superiority" in singing and predicted for her "the most brilliant reputation if her health holds up, for nature has given her everything in the way of talent; experience will supply the rest."[55] Some still unconquered faults were also recognized. Because of her great exertions, fatigue was occasionally obvious throughout the evening, and she was advised to pace herself carefully for the sake of her future.

For the remainder of the season Maria drew on her New York repertoire, unveiling those roles one by one in order to display her versatility as brilliantly as possible. She wanted the Parisians to see that not only could she sing soprano and contralto, but she also could perform comedy as well as tragedy, "trouser roles" as well as female characters. At the same time she challenged Giuditta Pasta on her own ground by singing parts that, in the eyes of the public, literally belonged to the beloved Italian soprano. Assuming the role of Desdemona on April 15 was even more dangerous than singing Semiramide, despite the fact that it suited her better, for to the Parisians Desdemona *was* Pasta. To everyone's astonishment, Maria succeeded completely. "The memory of Mme Pasta is a terrible barrier that, as far as we are concerned, Mme Malibran has succeeded in crossing," wrote the critic for *Le Figaro* (7 May 1828).

Maria did not attempt to duplicate Pasta's interpretation of Shakespeare's heroine. Pasta had played her as a grown woman, noble and resigned, in the classic tradition. Maria made her a young girl of no more than sixteen. She gave her an innocence, a touching weakness and vulnerability, a childish naïveté marked with outbursts of terror and anger that sent shivers through an audience that had never before seen so realistic a conception of the part. She wept in the Willow Song, reduced her voice to an excruciatingly emotional pianissimo in the prayer—a pianissimo of such finesse that it was almost silence—and burst out "like a thunderbolt" in the last duet with the murderous Otello. When the Moor approached with his dagger raised, Pasta had anticipated death, heroic in her virtue and courage; Maria ran from it, she leaped for the doors and windows. As Otello tried to grab her by the hair she attempted to climb the walls in her desperation and fright.[56]

That Maria's vaunted superiority in singing was matched by an unprecedented histrionic talent stunned the Parisians. Fétis declared that the public was "vanquished without return"[57] by *Otello,* and Maria received the first of those hysterical ovations that would follow her to her final moment on the stage. But he also noticed a trait that had been commented on in England after her first performance of *Il Barbiere* and which perhaps resulted from an effort to pace herself and to avoid strain in her upper register. "In ensemble pieces that are rather loud, Mme Malibran can't be heard," he complained. "Is she saving herself to avoid fatigue, or is she incapable of forcing her voice as one must do in concerted passages? Mlle Sontag, despite the light quality of her voice, could still produce an effect in the loudest passages. I fear that Mme Malibran's voice lacks bite for these things, which would be very unfortunate."[58]

But in spite of the care she took, weakness was still apparent, as in the second performance of *Otello* two days later; yet her expressiveness in the last act was much admired. How much restraint she could exercise at this stage of her career is questionable, for once under the drama's spell she rarely thought of preserving her powers. A friend suggested that she not make Otello pursue her for so long in the final scene of the opera, and she replied that when she played a character she never thought of effects but imagined herself the person she was portraying. In the case of Desdemona, she often felt as though she were about to be murdered and would frequently admonish her tenor to catch her as best he could.[59]

From the purely vocal display of *Semiramide* and the intense drama of *Otello,* Maria turned to comedy, and seven days after playing her first Desdemona she appeared, with great success, as Rosina in *Il Barbiere.* But not until her impersonation of Angelina in *La Cenerentola* on May 1 were her comic gifts fully appreciated. The critics compared her performance to Sontag's high soprano version, but they admitted that the newcomer "proved herself to be as skillful a singer as [she was] an intelligent comedienne." She gave the character "a new color and temperament" and sang the finale, the rondo "non piu mesta" and its exceedingly difficult variations more slowly than had Sontag, but with such an outpouring of sound that the full house gave her an ovation. Her versatility was not overlooked: "It really takes an astonishing flexibility of talent to appear with such success and variety in the parts of Semiramide, Desdemona, Rosina and Cenerentola," observed *Le Figaro*'s critic (3 May 1828).

Maria had barely enough time to keep Eugène informed of her activities. "I am engaged at the Théâtre-Italien," she wrote him on May 8, exactly one month after the fact. "I played *Semiramide,* which made a furore, and then *Otello,* which was a crescendo with a vengeance, the *Barbiere,* which is the same, and this very night I played *Cinderella* for the second time. There is much enthusiasm. I will not tell you whether it is just or not, but I can tell you that I have a hold on my public, and that everything I do pleases them."[60]

On the same day she found time to pen a final letter to her unresponsive rival, Giuditta Pasta.

I am writing to you for the last time if I don't receive a line from you. Tell me now; do you think of me? I don't think so, but you love me a little, I am sure, and I love you so much that it seems impossible to me that it is not reciprocated. I had the courage to sing *Otello, Semiramide,* and now in a little while, *Romeo*; this takes great effrontery! Addio, my Giuditta; I am afraid to bother you and therefore I finish with wishing you the success that you deserve and of which I have no doubt.

Your M. Malibran Garcia[61]

As Romeo, another role in which Pasta excelled, Maria first fully displayed her rich, smooth contralto register. The last act in particular received the greatest praise; when Romeo prepared to die with Juliet Maria's voice sounded hollow and stifled; the audience shivered and continually interrupted the scene with applause that seemed never to end. At the final moment the theater was filled with shrieks as ladies jumped to their feet at the frighteningly real sight of Romeo dropping in a free fall flat upon the stage. "The vigor of this young virtuoso surpasses anything we could say," remarked Fétis.[62]

Romeo was the last new role Maria presented to the French. For the final month of her engagement she paraded her repertoire of five characters before the public to ever growing appreciation of her talent. A later performance of Desdemona moved a critic to write: "I have already vaunted several times her superiority as a singer, but here this superiority is equal to her acting . . . with her all is instinct, nature; she divines the art that she has not yet had time to learn. May such a fortunate constitution not tire before its time, and preserve its health!"[63] And with each performance Giuditta Pasta faded further from the minds of the dilettanti.

Many parallels have already been drawn between the new singer and she of whom the remembrance is still strong. Without wishing to pronounce between them, without especially wanting to appear forgetful or ungrateful, it seems to us that despite the depth of her acting and the power of her effects, despite the majesty of her poses and the sublime expression of her features, Mme Pasta could envy her young rival for her abandon, her artlessness, her freedom, which always makes something inspired of what she does, something unexpected, improvised. Possessing in addition a decidedly superior voice, Mme Malibran is capable of embellishing her singing with all the charm of the ornaments. But what is especially striking is the flexibility, the variety, the immense resources of this young talent.[64]

Maria's final performance was announced for June 24, and a critic sadly anticipated the end of the opera season: "Just one day more and we are going to lose one of the most beautiful talents that we have possessed, one of those gifted individuals that a stingy nature rarely grants us. . . . Until now a richer, a more brilliant union of all the qualities demanded by the art of song has never been encountered."[65]

The following evening Maria was granted a farewell reception such as Paris had never before witnessed. In her own estimation she played the role of Desdemona "better than I usually do,"[66] and she made a travesty of the law forbidding an artist to take curtain calls. At the conclusion of the second act someone threw a crown of flowers at her as she sang her aria "s'il padre m'abbandona" ["If my father abandons me"], dramatic music in which Desdemona's voice rises despairingly against Rossini's thunderous orchestral backdrop. When the curtain fell the choristers, stage crew, and other artists crowded about her and tried to put the crown on her head, but she refused, thinking only of how she could thank the audience without breaking the law. As the curtain rose for the third act, she stood on the stage, head bowed, with the crown in her hands. The theater exploded with an ovation that lasted for four minutes, and at the conclusion of the performance the audience remained, applauding and calling for la Malibran. The curtain was again raised so that the manager could explain the law regarding curtain calls, but no sooner had he opened his mouth than the audience booed and hissed him off the stage. The students in the theater began smashing the benches together while the ladies stood in the boxes calling and waving their handkerchiefs. When the commissioner of police appeared and attempted to mount the stage, he was grabbed by the neck and dragged back before he could forbid Maria to reappear.

By this time Laurent had called the commissioner into the wings and demanded that he either address the uncontrolled crowd or accept liability for the havoc being done to the theater. Frightened at the noise, and fearful of being attacked by the excited crowd, the official retreated, and in disgust Laurent told Maria to greet the audience. The hysteria that met her was such that she took the time to write Eugène about it at 2:00 that morning. "I can't let this moment pass without giving you the comfort of learning about the most beautiful triumph that has ever been seen in years," she told him. "The curtain was raised, I appeared. Everyone was standing on the benches, screaming, howling, bellowing, the noise reaching all the way to the dressing rooms. Someone threw me another crown with some verses that you will read in the paper, and each lady from the first, second, and third tiers and from everywhere threw me their bouquets of flowers, while the screaming continued, undiminished, for ten minutes, and the uproar redoubled at each falling bouquet. Really, it was like a rain of flowers."[67] It was, according to Mme. Merlin, the first time that flowers had been thrown on the stage of the Théâtre-Italien.[68] The evening finally ended as Maria threw a gracious kiss to her admirers.

No benefit was specified in Maria's contract, but her popularity made the unwilling Laurent listen to requests that she be given one. Having been offered engagements in Naples, Vienna, Venice, Parma, Milan, and St. Petersburg—at an enormous sum—she let the press know that she would probably not accept a return engagement at the Italien for the following season. Laurent gave in and offered her the desired benefit for July 1, to consist of a reduced version of *Il Barbiere* and the last two acts of *Otello*. The public was overwhelmed by her versatility in moving from the comic Rosina to the tragic Desdemona. Rather than stabbing her in the final act, Maria's tenor, Domenico Donzelli, killed her in his arms, dropped her body to the stage, and threw his cloak over her. "Don't crush my flowers!,"[69] she murmured to him, for they were already littering the stage. At the final curtain he brought her forward to a twenty-minute ovation during which the poems and flowers—seventy-two bouquets according to one member of the audience—fell as they had the week before.[70] Only a token effort was made to invoke the law, and the public cheered Maria without provocation.

Maria had been in Paris exactly seven months, since *Le Moniteur* had announced the arrival of "Madame Millibran." She had found friends, contended with disagreeable relatives, kept a bankrupt husband at bay, and wrangled with theater managers and government intrigue. She had established herself as the most remarkable and popular singer in Paris, while at the same time vastly improving her powers. "I can tell you without fear of exaggeration that the French public adores me", she told Eugène happily.[71] Observed an eminent critic: "To be placed at the head of all the singers of her age, she needs only two or three years travel in the principal cities of Europe."[72]

Maria Malibran was twenty years old.

CHAPTER 6

The Actress

At the end of June 1828 Maria considered herself "ravishingly well and noticeably fat." But some felt she had overtaxed both her physical and mental resources during the past seven months, and they were happy to see her depart with Mme. Naldi and Carolina for an extended vacation at the Chateau de Brizay, the de Sparre ancestral home in the Touraine. She left Paris with her "guardian angel" in the first days of July, happily anticipating the joys of becoming "a complete peasant" for four months.

Still conscious of her obligations to Eugène, she did not make even this small move without advising her husband of her plans. Nor was she any less concerned with the rumors being spread by the Chastelains. "Your charming nephew Mr. Victor amuses himself by slandering my conduct," she wrote him lightheartedly. "Even people who do not know me stand up for me, and there is a close friend of Victor's who is falling out with him because he wants so badly to persuade his friend that I have a lover. I can hear you (I am sure of it) laughing like crazy over these petty vengeances, which are born of a bad heart and a very inferior mind." But she knew that Eugène was not laughing, and had Mme. Naldi add a comforting postscript to her letter, an addendum that bears signs of having been carefully thought out and dictated to the good woman. "You may put your mind at ease on the fate of your wife for as long as she relies on me," Mme. Naldi assured him.[1]

At Brizay Maria forgot the cares of the theater. "I'm putting my whole heart into my fun here, and I am never tired," she wrote Eugène. "I run, I jump rope, I am embroidering a collar for Madame Naldi's birthday. I have composed three tyrolian duets and three barcarolle duets. I don't sing much, but enough to exercise my voice. I am respected by the men and loved by the women, but trust in neither.[2] An enthusiastic equestrienne, she rose at daybreak to go hunting or exploring, and choosing the most spirited mount she could find, she would disappear at a gallop. She dressed in male attire, which, in addition to being comfortable, disguised her sex and identity.

Maria's public and private personalities coincided. According to Ernest Legouvé, who knew her well, "The singer and the woman were one, at least in the face of danger. The same audacity in life as in art. . . . She had not only disdain, but a passion for danger." One day in Paris she went riding with a friend. The party came to a large ditch and one of the riders leaped it.

"I want to jump it too", she said right away.

"But you don't know how to jump, Madame."

"Show me."

"But your horse might not want to do it."

"Yours jumped it well enough."

"But . . ."

"There aren't any buts. Since you did it, I can do it!" And she did, laughing uproariously upon her success.[3]

Legouvé, who apparently rode with her often, recounted another excursion.

She descended the banks of dangerous ravines at a triple gallop. I set out one day with her on a black horse and returned on a white one, the course she had led us on for the duration of the day being so difficult that the horse was completely lathered up. Back at six o'clock, we retired to the soirée given by the Count Moreni, where she had promised to sing. She sang as she had ridden the horse, or as if she had not ridden it. We parted at one o'clock in the morning. My first concern on returning home was to forbid my valet to wake me before eleven o'clock. At seven o'clock my door opened.

"What is it?"

"A note from Mme Malibran."

"Bon dieu! What's the matter?" I opened it and read: "Nine o'clock on horseback, rendez-vous with our friends at the Place de la Concord."![4]

When accused of seeming masculine in her attire and vigorous sports, she pleaded guilty and cut her activities not at all.[5] Such was the woman who refused to acknowledge any physical limitations and spent her life trying to sing as high as Sontag and as low as Pisaroni.

Although she sang little at Brizay, Maria's theatrical abilities were occasionally called upon. One visitor at the Chateau was a doctor, a good, generous, and kindhearted man, but overconfident of his romantic appeal. Having experienced one of his inept passes Maria played a trick on him. Disguising herself as a peasant girl, complete with costume and sunburned complexion, she stuffed wads of cotton into her mouth to fatten her cheeks and called on him. Unrecognizable and speaking the dialect of the region perfectly, she explained that her mother had broken her arm, and she offered in addition such a heartrending tale of poverty and woe that the doctor, completely convinced, gave her money and sent her on her way. Maria repeated the visits several times, the peasant girl growing bolder until she at least revealed her strong affection for the physician. The duped old man, relating these incidents to Maria and the guests, never suspected the hoax, and Maria always pretended disappointment at not having seen this remarkable girl.

Finally the doctor's beneficiary declared, within earshot of the others, that she loved him. Everyone was amused, and the doctor, sharing their mirth, murmured sarcastically, "I have made quite a flattering conquest!" The peasant girl came forth with a quick slap. "Whenever have you done better, ungrateful man?," she cried in her own voice, and tore off the disguise.[6]

The doctor would soon experience another side of Maria's nature. His old sister, who lived in the south of France, suddenly lost her house and all her possessions in a bad fire. The doctor sent her money, which he could ill afford to do, and planned a trip to his sister's town. When Maria heard of this, she had a friend in Paris contact the mayor of the town, in great haste and secrecy, and arranged to rebuild the house at a cost of several thousand francs. By the time the doctor had arranged for the trip, he received a letter from the mayor acknowledging the receipt of the doctor's money, assuring him that it would be spent as directed. So well was the secret kept that neither the old man nor his sister learned their benefactor's identity until after Maria's death, when her personal papers revealed the story. At that time a plaque was set into the front of the house:

Cette Maison a Eté Rebatie
Par Les Soins Bienfaisants
De Madame Malibran[7]

The summer brought bitter recriminations against Eugène Malibran. Maria wrote a note to Mme. Wainwright, which she enclosed in a letter to Eugène with instructions to forward it to her friend. The note was not sealed, and Eugène read it. "God bless him and keep him over there," she confided to her friend. "I have no need of him here."[8] Eugène's response is known only by its reflection in Maria's next letter to him, for she would later destroy all his correspondence. It bears no greeting at all:

I don't know what you mean when you speak to me of an unsealed letter that I sent, and that you have not forwarded to the one for whom it was intended. If the letter contains something that regards you and that displeases you, I can assure you that what I say can only be true. Furthermore you know that I have never liked to deceive anyone, and because of my excessive frankness you should be the first one to perceive that fact. In addition, I declare to you that whatever might be the contents of it, I repent nothing of what I might have said, and if there is something that you do not understand I will explain it to you, even though it be to your disadvantage.—I consider you *very wrong* not to have sealed and sent it.

Having vented her ire about the Wainwright letter, she moved on to everything else that had been bothering her recently, and even from the beginning of their relationship. The fact that Eugène saved this letter along with the others indicates that he still loved the girl who was irretrievably lost to him. Maria left no question about her own feelings.

Furthermore, that is not the only thing I could reproach you for, and here you
are: My brother-in-law, Mr. Colladon, let me see a letter that you wrote him—in
which you were telling him to stop by the columnists for the papers that had
said nice things about me to thank them for it! Are you crazy? You should know
how much I detest everything that pertains to intrigue. How many times have I
asked you emphatically not to involve yourself with what the papers might say
about me, good or bad - especially in Paris—where these people are only under
obligation to say good or bad (in general) by the powerful motive of money. In
effect, what makes my triumph complete in this city is that without newspapers,
without free tickets, without paid friends, I have obtained the support of the
journalists, who at first said bad things about me just so that I would subscribe,
and those who said good things about me did so in the hope that I would
subscribe, or even because they thought so. I will tell you that I know of two or
three whom I often told that I didn't like to court anyone and that I did not
want to subscribe from fear of influencing their opinions. You must have learned
of my last successes, which I do not want to attribute completely to my talent,
but rather to the benevolence of the public, which really is fanatical and
enthusiastic about me.

As a final blow, she brought up his business failure, assuring him that she
had reached her own conclusions. "Unfortunately I understand your
business affairs only too well my myself," she declared flatly.

I have never doubted that your bankruptcy was dishonorable and
premeditated—*I told you that by myself.* So I do not believe that you can ever
satisfy me in this regard, and, as the Spanish proverb says [about excuses], "he
who makes one basket makes a hundred." You shouldn't be surprised that I
have been able to develop some suspicions, which come from what I told you
one certain day, because you have lost your rights to my respect. In a word, I
must try and forget the past—For I am *ashamed* to speak of your affairs to
anyone.

As if to confirm what she had said in the note to Mme. Wainwright,
she now told Eugène, "You should be happy to know that I'm getting along
like a charm, and that I am perfectly happy. . . . For my happiness to last I
need only to spend all my time in the theater, as I am now. For it is enough
for me to know that you are in good health."[9]

By late September Maria was back in Paris. Her new contract with
Laurent again specified 800 francs per performance, 35,000 francs for the
six-month engagement at the Italien, and was to be followed by three
months at the King's Theatre in London at 40,000 francs and a free benefit.
"I see you calculating how much I will earn with my benefit," she told
Eugène somewhat caustically, "but stay calm and don't build castles in
Spain."[10] Independently wealthy, Maria no longer needed to share a bed
with Mme. Naldi, but carefully considering her reputation, a reputation
questionable by her very profession, she persuaded her mentor to live with
her in a rented house at 10 Rue d'Artois. Manuel, back from Italy, joined

them in these accommodations, which were luxurious by Chastelain standards. The house consisted of an antechamber, dining room, drawing room, three bedrooms, two servants' rooms, two wine cellars, and a kitchen; it was furnished agreeably with curtains, bed linens, and carpets for the winter, all at the reasonable cost of 400 francs a month. Even Mme. Naldi could approve.

Maria told Eugène not to expect another letter for some time, at least not until she reappeared at the Théâtre-Italien and had something interesting to tell him. "I will be devilishly busy this winter, and will hardly have time to sneeze!!," she warned him.[11] But his constant chiding for news provoked her enough to write him a letter on September 28. "You are really unique, my dear Eugène! You complain that I don't write you and yet I remember having told you everything that I know. Do you think that I like to write you when I have only two words to tell you, and do you think that it gives me pleasure to send you a little piece of paper like you sent me?"[12]

Nevertheless, in late July there was very interesting news in Paris about Henriette Sontag. La Sontag had suffered an accident: she had slipped on a cherry-stone in her boudoir, twisted her knee badly, and consequently was unable to appear on the stage or in society.[13] This was the story presented to the public, but in fact the northern nightingale was pregnant by her lover, Count Rossi, the Sardinian ambassador at the Hague. Her situation was particularly difficult because polite society considered her better than others of her artistic caste; she was accepted not only as a singer, but as a beautiful and charming lady.

This choice tidbit of gossip found Maria at her most ungracious, although she attempted to hide her glee behind a show of righteous indignation. That her rival, who moved in the company of princes, should have met with such disgrace! "Behold this Mlle Sontag, who had been pronounced virtue personified," she wrote with relish to her ever-suspicious husband.

Not that I would want to believe all the bad things that are said about her, but she went to London, she did not make a furore, and then she came to Paris. She made her debut in *La Donna del Lago,* and then *Cenerentola,* which I did, and in which I made a furore. But in that role they say her voice is greatly diminished, *that she doesn't have such a pretty figure* . . . . . . and she has dropped in public favor like a fallen soufflé . . . I swear to you that I am very angry about this, but very angry! for she was very nice and one overlooked many things about her because of her respectability. See then how goes the world; all Paris knows it. Eh bien! I fell from the seventh floor in learning of the series of unpleasant things she was experiencing. However, as I told you, I do not want to believe anything until I find out for myself. Meanwhile I enjoy flourishing health and *respect.* That helps to fatten also—but that is enough to get fat from without need of a second stimulant.[14]

Maria's turn would come, and she would suffer as much as her rival, perhaps even more. But at the moment she was too busy with the theater to empathize, for she was to assume Sontag's roles for the immediate future in addition to performing her own. She told Eugène saucily that "I am going to learn *La Gazza Ladra,* in which Mlle Sontag *made a fiasco,* and during the whole period of her pregnancy I will play *The Barber of Cinderella.* You see how I must tweak the news I give you."[15]

On October 2, 1828, Maria Malibran reappeared at the Théâtre-Italien as Desdemona. To the crowd it was obvious that Maria's summer in the Touraine had restored her to perfect health; still, in the first scenes she was a little weak vocally, a condition ascribed to the emotional effect of returning to an audience eager to applaud her,* but in the course of the evening her singing and acting improved. "I made my reappearance—furore!,"[16] she told Eugène, and the reviewers seconded her opinion. One critic wrote, "The role of Desdemona, so congenial to the expressive sensitivity of this great singer, was a new occasion of triumph for her. Never has her art been greater, never has she so moved an audience. It was said that the emotion she herself experienced was so strong that she had suffered a violent attack of nerves after the performance."[17] The report was true. In the last act her emotional identification with her role had become so complete that the tears ran down to her shoulders. Barely had the final curtain fallen than she fainted.

The new opera season so drained Maria's emotional and physical energy that barely a week after her first performance she dared put in writing a thought that had been on her mind for some time. In a letter to Eugène she explained her feelings about her career, which had become her reason for existing.

I just had an idea which occurs to me often and which I postponed communicating to you, but as you know how frank I am, you will take it in good faith and you will do what I am going to tell you. I think that a career in the theater demands great tranquility and a celibate life, which suits me perfectly. I find myself *very happy* as *I am now*.

I am telling you this so that you will not hurry to return—for, my friend, listen. You are well, you are getting fat—Me too, and I earn peacefully. Thus it is better that we not see each other until my *fortune is made*. This way I will have only one duty to fulfill. Some things are worth nothing to me. It would be better then for your happiness and mine if it happened like this. Don't show my letter to anyone. This idea ought not to be known by anyone except we two. So take my advice—stay—and let me follow my career honorably as I have done so far, and when all will be concluded, we will see each other again in peace. Mme Naldi, from here on, (I do not doubt) will serve me as guide and guardian—and as for me, I will be at peace all the time. I will know you to be in good health

---

*The critic was perhaps influenced by a characteristic of her performance that was often attributed, wrongly, to her emotional or physical state. A friend once accused her of being too tame in the opening scenes of her roles and she replied, "I look on the heads in the audience as so many wax candles. If I were to light them all at once they would soon burn out, but by lighting them gradually I produce a brilliant illumination. My system is to light up the public by degrees" (Merlin, *Memoirs,* vol. 1, pp. 209-10).

by correspondence, and everything will be the best in the world . . . Adieux, cher Eugène.[18]

In the eleven months since she had left her husband in New York, Maria's feelings changed from anticipation of seeing him again, to anger and annoyance, and finally to an almost complete severing of relations. From this time her letters were pleasantly vacuous, as though to a distant relative not really in her thoughts or concerns, but whose existence nevertheless deserved an occasional acknowledgment.

The early months of the 1828–1829 season brought a failure for the Garcia family, the first that the patriarch had experienced if one excludes Joaquina's limited accomplishments. On October 7 Manuel made his Parisian debut as Figaro in *Il Barbiere* with his sister as Rosina. The reviews were unfavorable. "Manuel Garcia does not justify all that one hoped from the name he bears," commented the disappointed critic for *Le Figaro* (9 October 1828). "His voice is not yet formed, his tones are not well placed; he lacks study and experience." This dismissal was no doubt painful for one struggling to establish himself in a field in which his name was so well known and in which his father firmly expected him to succeed. His sister's reviews for the same performance gave rise to humiliating comparisons. "Mme Malibran possesses in the highest degree every necessary talent," wrote Fétis, who again stated that "just two more years of work and reflection on her art, and Mme Malibran will have arrived at the highest point of perfection possible in the art of song and dramatic expression."[19]

Four days later Maria declared, "He won't perform anymore since he doesn't like the theater, and since he didn't please very much." Manuel wrote to his father in Mexico with the bad news, including several newspaper clippings with a note that read, "You see that I can never hope to become an operatic artist. From now on I am going to devote myself to the occupation which I love, and for which I believe I was born."[20] The occupation he was referring to is not clear, for he would try being a teacher, doctor, soldier, mathematician, and finally a voice teacher. By the end of October 1828, however, he announced that he would become a sailor.

After *Il Barbiere*, Maria played *La Cenerentola* and learned the role of Ninetta in Rossini's *La Gazza Ladra*, all parts to have been sung by Sontag. Her Angelina in *La Cenerentola* received the highest praise. *Le Figaro*'s critic spoke of "unexpected upward passages from low to high, brilliant arpeggios, roulades of great length performed in full voice, which attest to the range and power of her voice" (16 October 1828). And Ninetta became one of her greatest roles. The part of the village girl falsely accused of, and nearly executed for, the magpie's theft of some silver spoons challenged Maria vocally and gave her the opportunity to act in the style for which she was rapidly becoming known, a style more natural and impassioned than anything previously seen on the operatic stage. "The role of Ninetta provides her with a new occasion to display all that she has of intelligence, variety, [and] dramatic power," wrote a critic, declaring her a "consummate actress."[21]

There was, however, some criticism. Apparently Maria was never at her best the first time she played a role. She needed time to reflect on it and to learn from her stage experience what suited the character best. Between the first and second performances roles would be rethought and reinterpreted. In retrospect it was seen that her first performance in *La Gazza Ladra* lacked the polish that Sontag had demonstrated in the work. "Strongly felt emotions sometimes became exaggerated," wrote a critic, but he observed that "the most useful lessons Mme Malibran can learn are those she takes upon herself." Her Ninetta rapidly became "a beautiful conception well rendered".[22]

A special honor awaited Maria this winter; the young French composer Jacques Halévy had been commissioned by the Théâtre-Italien to write an opera especially for her. *Clary* went into rehearsal late in October. Maria later developed a passionate interest in having a great opera written for her talents, one that would seal her artistic immortality. Although she met with regrettable failure in this ambition, *Clary* was one of the better attempts. Rossini cried "bravo!" at a final rehearsal,[23] and the work was enormously successful at its premier on December 9.

The critics praised Maria ecstatically for her singing and acting as Clary. For the first time she was not struggling against previous impressions left by another singer; the reviewers judged her on her own terms. Most could not determine whether the work itself was of merit or whether Malibran deserved the credit for its success. Fétis, the "dear grumbler," wrote what was probably the least emotional review. "As great an actress as a singer, this virtuoso was perfect from one end of her role to the other, but in the third act especially, she was beyond all praise."[24] In this final act Maria made an "ineffaceable impression" as Clary; resuming her peasant garb, Clary prepares to leave the wealthy Lothario who has deceived her. She opens the window to escape into the street when a ray of moonlight falls on her lover's portrait, and she pauses to gaze at it. According to Mme. Merlin, "It would be vain to attempt to describe the admirable tones of her voice while she bid a last goodby to the picture."[25]

Even Maria, rarely satisfied with her own performances, was content. "You have been pleased with me, and me with me too," she told a friend.[26] In Mme. Merlin's opinion the opera contained much beautiful music and was a credit to its composer; yet once Maria ceased to sing it, the work was dropped from the repertoire. Halévy had tailored it too perfectly to Malibran's unique talents.

Maria received the attention accorded a first-rank performer returning from the theater after every performance or rehearsal with bundles of letters stuffed into her pockets. "I don't read any of them," she told a friend. "They are all alike, offensive offers of 'protection' and propositions."[27] One contained a promissory note in the amount of 30,000 francs, which she returned to its sender with a note: "If I were vile enough to sell myself, you offer me 30,000 francs more than I am worth. If ever I give myself, all your gold could not pay me."[28] But some letters were worth saving.

Madame, I have a stong desire to speak with you before your departure and I beg you to please let me know just where I can find you. Perhaps you say that it is quite indiscreet for a wicked rogue to want so much to annoy the personage of Semiramide and Desdemona, but I hope you have the goodness to excuse me because of the admiration I have for your. . . . . I lack the word, I don't know what to call it for you have more than genius and I mean it when I confess to you sincerely that you have made such an impression on me that I need to see you.

Please accept, Madame, the offer of my respectful homage.

F. Liszt

Rue Montholon No. 7 Bis.[29]

A certain Baron supposedly was in love with her, and her friends teased her about it. "Yes," she said, "I think he loves me, but what of it? I don't love him. Probably I will fall in love some day—I am young, financially independent, married to a man three thousand miles away who is old enough to be my grandfather—but you can be sure that when I do meet a man I can love I will tell him I love him, and my feelings will never change."[30] What would Eugène Malibran have thought of such a statement, coming from the wife who had so long protested her virtue and who had just told him that the life of a celibate suited her perfectly?

During her year in Paris Maria made many friends from all classes of society. However, social strictures discouraged the mixing of artists and the *haute monde,* for Europeans, unlike New Yorkers, generally honored aristocracy of birth before aristocracy of talent. At the conclusion of a concert given by a particular baron, many society ladies left, refusing to remain for the ball because the performers, whom they had applauded moments before, had been invited. Although some aristocrats honored artists such as Henriette Sontag with their friendship,* only a performer of exceptional charm could hope to cross the "silken cord" that divided entertainers from polite society at most social events. In the more modest salons, where music was loved for its own sake, the social rules did not prevent Maria from remaining after the concert to delight the guests with her lively conversation. She gradually, and proudly, gained acceptance into the society of barons and princes because of her attractive personality.† But this accep-

---

*Sontag's mother had given birth to twelve children, only three of whom were sired by Herr Sontag, who was a severe alcoholic. Both her parents were traveling performers.

†And she would go to extraordinary lengths to maintain an important friendship. Realizing she had missed a dinner in which she had been invited by a distinguished Marquise, Maria went to the lady's mansion despite the post-midnight hour, and rushing past the protesting doorman, she burst into the chambers of the Marquise. Falling on her knees, she kissed the sleeping woman awake and implored her pardon with such sincerity that all was forgiven (Maynard, pp. 304–7).

tance was precarious, and occasionally an insult cut her to the core. She responded to one invitation: "I would be very happy to go to this ball, and I would even confess that I have an enormous desire to do so, but not having ever liked to go where everyone is not equally glad to receive me, I prefer to do without the pleasure."[31]

Particularly galling was the condescending praise she sometimes received. Occasionally she would return home from a soirée to which she had been invited—and paid—to sing, crying, "I'm only the opera singer, nothing more, the slave whom they pay to give them pleasure!"[32] And yet if a lady did invite her to a party for herself, with no request to sing, she would leave annoyed because no one had asked her to display her talents. But the day would come when she could demand a pair of scissors, and before a breathless crowd quite literally cut her way across the silken cord.[33]

Maria's new apartment on the Rue d'Artois enabled her to give small soirées for her friends, regardless of their situation in society, and she made herself the central attraction of these evenings, which included not only musical performances but short plays and charades as well. One of her first parties was described briefly in a letter to Eugène.

I have learned some roles—I am going to explain to you how. I had some people for a soirée—I gave two proverbs. —I had in my home the highest society of Paris, both men and women. So there have been jealousies on all sides. But as one cannot say bad about it, it's all the same to me. I gave "the fad of proverbs"* and "the cobbler and the financier." It was charming. I invited Mr. Canet, who I received with my best, per your recommendation. He was enchanted with my soirée. I had my house like a little lighted jewel, and in short, all my arrangements were perfect.[34]

She liked nothing better than to amuse her guests by appearing in grotesque and comical parts in which she could masquerade as old hags, child prodigies, or other humorous types. There was little that she could not imitate on the spur of the moment. A brilliant improvisation occurred during an evening concert when the festivities were interrupted by the unmusical sound of a man playing a hurdy-gurdy in the street outside. He refused to leave. Turning to some singer friends she said, "We'll drive him away by a hurdy-gurdy of our own," and then had the men hold bass notes on a common chord while pinching their noses. She squeaked an imitation of the organ-grinder. Everyone found this enormously amusing, and the poor man departed.[35]

She did not stop at proverbs, songs, or imitations of organ-grinders. She loved doing impersonations, usually unflattering, of people she knew whose eccentricities she emulated to hilarious perfection. How she escaped more notoriety is a mystery; when the humor of the moment struck her and an audience was at hand to enjoy her inspiration, she never thought of consequences. One of her legendary specialties was an imitation of society

*See Appendix; *Additional Letters,* letter to Monsieur Cavalier, January 1829.

ladies attempting to sing with perfect sincerity—and with cracked tones and wavering pitch—a sentimental song such as "Home Sweet Home."

Unfortunately, one parody achieved such acclaim that it reached an indignant public press. As she had indicated to Eugène, the rooms of her house were too small to permit large crowds, and some were always disappointed, or worse, at not having been invited to these popular gatherings. One disgruntled individual, connected with the British embassy,[36] learned that Maria had concluded one of her inspired evenings with her impersonation of an Englishwoman and he attempted to discredit her before the English in order to endanger her imminent engagement in London. On February 4, 1829 an article appeared in *Galignani's Messenger*, a newspaper circulated in both London and Paris, in which the writer cleverly insulted the British while accusing Maria of the same impropriety. He proclaimed her "singular folly . . . a base impertinence resulting from an abject education, and especially not becoming a person who, if we have a good memory, is personally indebted to the hospitality of that nation which she holds up to ridicule; a nation which, despite its small pretensions of taste for music (a lack which has been particularly the object of the signora's satire) is nevertheless the nation of the world which most munificently patronizes musical talent."

This priggish attack was not overlooked by Malibran's admirers, among them the Baron de Trémont, who, although he had never met her, took it upon himself to defend her. With the greatest difficulty he persuaded *Galignani's Messenger* to publish his lengthy rebuttal, in which he informed the journal and its readers that "whether or not artists are liable to the censure, or especially the criticism of the paying public when they appear before it, this criticism has no right to follow them into their homes nor into their private relations."[37]

Whatever the truth behind this ridiculous frolic, Maria had no bias against the English, or for that matter against any nationality, although she was always willing to poke fun at any of them and would comically roll her eyes heavenward at the mention of America. On at least one occasion she argued against the condescending attitude the French directed toward the English, contending that each country had its own musical forms and folk melodies and that none could be singled out as inferior. Pointing out the beauty of Scottish, Irish, Welsh, and old English airs, she declared that if compositions of such contemporary composers as Horn or Bishop were published as the works of Signor Vescovo or Señor Cuerno, Europe would accept them as equal to any of Italy or Spain. As proof she sang a new Spanish song by Don Chocarreria:

> Maria trayga un caldero
> De aqua, llama levante
> Maria pon tu caldero
> Ayamos nuestro té.

With her embellishments and variations, this merely proved to her audience the superiority of European to English songs. Without arguing, Maria stated that the piece, which she had sung adagio, would be even better when sung presto. To her own great amusement, the guests suddenly recognized the melody as "Molly put the kettle on."[38]

During Henriette Sontag's pregnancy Maria was the salvation of the Italien, a fact that did not go unnoticed or unappreciated by the public and press, but by January 1829 Sontag resumed her career. Maria both respected the singer and feared her return. Despite her catty gossip to Eugène, she took her rival's talents seriously. When a friend tried to please her by stating that Sontag had a pretty voice but no soul, Maria cried: "No soul? No sorrow! She has been too happy, that's her misfortune. I have a superiority over her, and that is to have suffered. Let something happen to make her weep and you will see what tones come forth from that voice you treat so disdainfully as pretty!"[39]

Parisian music lovers looked forward to seeing the two singers perform together, an opportunity Laurent quickly seized. As early as January 15, 1829, he announced that his prima donnas would soon perform in Rossini's *Tancredi*. For several weeks the event was postponed, partly to build up as much anticipation as possible. Meanwhile the salons fought for the chance to present the women together in concert. Many hostesses and musicians claimed to have instigated the first Sontag-Malibran duet, and all agreed that the undertaking involved intrigue.

Rossini may have been responsible for their first vocal collaboration. On friendly terms with both, he had them invited to a soirée, each to sing her own program of songs and arias. Their performances were saved until the other musicians had finished their own recitals, and at last they appeared. At the conclusion of their solo arias, in which each singer outdid herself trying not to be effaced by her rival, Rossini proposed that they sing a duet from *Semiramide,* "Ebben a te ferisci," and was flatly and emphatically refused. But the guests pleaded and coaxed until further protest would have meant embarrassment, and thus coerced, they warily approached the piano together. Rossini began the introduction, and the little audience was rapt as the two singers, inspired by the challenge, sought to surpass each other. Encouraged by the opportunities for embellishment, they filled the music with every ornament they could conjure up, and the piece became a full-throated duel. In the andante "T'Arresta O Dio," their voices "united, or rather melted into one another with incomparable smoothness." The guests were thrilled, and quite overcome, Rossini cried, "Oh! That was too beautiful!" Embracing them both, he pushed them toward one another that they might shake hands or kiss. Maria stepped back and Sontag turned away.[40]

A few weeks later, Countess Merlin, who also claimed her soirée as the scene of the first duet, reconciled the two singers. On this occasion they seemed delighted in the combination of their voices, and on concluding the piece they joined hands and kissed.[41]

On February 16 Maria Malibran and Henriette Sontag made their first public appearance together, as promised, in *Tancredi*. Those present agreed that such singing had never before been heard. "As for the flexibility of her vocalization," wrote a critic of Sontag, "[she] left nothing to be desired; her throat is a veritable compendium of vocal fioratura. Her facility is prodigious, and one could say that it cost her less effort to execute difficulties than to sing with simplicity." Malibran's flexibility was equally praised, but instead of Sontag's exquisite birdlike sounds, Maria brought spontaneity, nervous energy, original embellishments, and "emotions that she could impart to the coldest spectators."[42] Once again a critic compared her to the great Pasta.[43] The duets, "like the performances of one singer with two voices," were the evening's high points.[44] Their execution "left nothing to be desired,"[45] wrote one critic, echoing the sentiments of everyone who had ever heard the singers perform together. This perfection established a dangerous precedent: all singers were expected to accomplish the same miracles, and for decades afterward the comparison remained.

Parisian opera lovers had fallen into two groups, the "Malibranistes" and the "Sontagistes," creating a feud enjoyed by both audience and impresario alike. And yet the voices and styles of the two singers were so dissimilar, and each was so perfect in her own way, that direct comparisons were difficult, if not impossible. An exultant habitué of the Théâtre-Italien admitted that "Mme Malibran and Mlle Sontag had been for me divine graces, and for nearly two years I had no other religion, no other hope, no other happiness, no other joy than music."[46]

The two prima donnas sang together as frequently as Laurent could arrange it in *Tancredi, Don Giovanni,* in which Maria played Zerlina to Sontag's Donna Anna, and *Semiramide,* in which Maria played Arsace for the first time. *Le Figaro* considered the *Semiramide* "an extraordinary performance in every sense of the word," declaring that memories of other singers in the roles had been obliterated. The duets were sung "in an inimitable manner. Never has one heard more perfect execution, an ensemble more ravishing: the voices of the two singers lent to them a completely new charm; nothing could equal the enthusiasm of those who heard them" (25 March 1829).

For nearly four months Maria found herself too preoccupied to write to Eugène. Finally she wrote: "Can you believe that I wrote you a letter that I didn't send you, because after having written it I didn't have time to send it, but I am sending it to you all the same so that you will not believe me negligent in writing you. Only I have been, very much, in sending it to you." The tiny three-month-old note was dated October 30. One wonders what her husband could have thought of her happiness without him in reading: "In a word—I am always on the *Pinacle,* as they say—and will remain there, I hope, until the *extinction* of my voice."[47]

Almost two months passed before another letter crossed the Atlantic. "It certainly has been a long time since I have written you!," she confessed.

It's true—but when one is far away, when one has rehearsals, concerts, visits, dinners in town every day, it is impossible, when, with all that, one goes to bed at 2:00 in the morning. I assure you that for me, the complete end of the world is getting up at 1:00 in the afternoon, dressing, and going out to begin again the same course of life. When once one is glorified in the world it is impossible to get out of it. I played *la Gazza ladra* and had the greatest success. The last time, even, that I played it, I was called back after the opera and cries, yelling and hurrahs, hats and handkerchiefs accompanied my exit. To thank the public I played the role of Arsace in *Semiramide,* and I had the greatest success.

With no apologies or excuses she continued, "I am going to London and I leave Paris around the 5th or 6th of April. I can't absolutely promise to write you often, for good friend, you have to put yourself in the place of an unfortunate who leads the life of a horse." She expressed her pleasure at his having paid her parents some of the money he owed them, "for you can't have too much in funds," and she added gratefully, "If you need money, tell me. I will send you what I can, provided the sum isn't more than a million."[48]

Maria's final performance of the season took place April 2, and she prepared to leave for London. The strenuous winter had taken a toll on her abilities. "Our apprehensions have been for some time converted into serious fears," wrote *Le Figaro*'s critic. "It seems to us that Mme Malibran has never abused her beautiful combination of talents more" (5 April 1829). It was true. Emotional involvement with her roles allowed Maria no limits to her exertions; her physical resources were at the mercy of her inspirations.

"In sum, all goes for the best," she told Eugène. "Money, esteem, honor, and almost health."[49]

CHAPTER 7

England

Shortly before March 25, 1829, the Garcias landed at Bordeaux and set foot on French soil for the first time in more than four years. The Mexican expedition had been a great financial and artistic success. "I would have been able to show my Mexican troupe without fear to the Parisian public, which would not have found it unworthy," declared Garcia proudly.[1] But the performers were now bereft. When he set out from Mexico City for Vera Cruz, Garcia joined a caravan of about thirty people that was escorted by an armed guard of soldiers. His earnings, about a thousand ounces of gold, were carefully hidden in the bottom of the wagon that held the troupe's possessions.[2] Such precautions proved in vain. Near Tepeyagualo, in the valley of the Rio Frio, about sixty outlaws attacked the convoy. Joaquina recognized one of them as the leader of the soldiers paid to defend the travelers.[3] Garcia appealed to Eugène Malibran, who seems to have paid part of his debt to Garcia, thereby enabling the family to continue their journey.

Arriving in Bordeaux, the family sent word to Maria that they would soon be in Paris. Their letter shocked her. Her father's announcement that he was destitute made her financially responsible for her family, and the specter of a permanent reunion enforced by economic necessity presented itself. "I don't know if you remember," she wrote to Eugène, who remembered only too well, "that I often tell you that the principal goal in my marrying had been to separate myself from my family so that I wouldn't have to live with them. You can thus imagine that I have had great fear that their arrival not put me again in the necessity of living with them."[4] Although she had previously turned down the chance for a benefit on April 2, she quickly changed her mind and with the help of her friend Adolphe Nourrit presented the scenes from *La Gazza Ladra* and *Otello* that netted her the enormous sum of 40,000 francs at doubled prices.[5] At the same time she wrote her father a letter, both fearful and frank, explaining that she did not want to lose her independence and that she would not be responsible for paying Eugène's debt to him. So that he would not have to take engagements, which, at his age, would only tarnish his reputation, she offered him an income of 4,000 francs a year and the support of her sister Pauline, including her education.

These proposals infuriated Garcia. "One finds that I have not used measured words," she complained to Eugène. "Unfortunately I use those that my frankness dictates. . . . They are offended, saying that the sum of 4 thousand francs is a 'cochonnerie.' If I had offered 20 thousand francs instead, nothing would have been said." Already her father was proving that her fears were well grounded by attempting to meddle in her affairs, but she refused to answer any questions about the size of her fortune or where it was invested because "I would have been tormented even more if they knew. Thus I am determined never to live in the same house with them—and not to permit them to mix in my financial affairs. Unfortunately I know from experience that they don't agree on that, since for the many years that my father has worked he has not been able to put money aside and invest it well. . . . I will be delighted to do what I can for them, but *never* live together." In passing she uttered a prediction that would prove only too true: "I work as much for them as for me, for the more I have when I die, the more will be left to them."[6]

Maria's earnings raised the problem of their proper investment, which interested her less than it did Eugène. She answered his questions about her money casually: "You alone will know that it is placed with Mme Naldi's, and that even she does not know where it is—it is invested by the Count de Sparre."[7] This nonchalance brought an immediate reply from New York that amused Maria greatly. "I received your letter in which you sent me a piece of private paper,"* she told Eugène. "I confess that I laughed over your panic-stricken terrors. . . . I believed—when I wrote you that I know nothing of my affairs—that you would have understood that I did not want to tell anyone about them and that that would stop all questions. Now one last time, I am telling you that you needn't worry. So when friends come to ask you out of national spirit, and, what dominates New York so much, *curiosity,* how much do I have? where is it kept? how is it invested? etc., tell them 'Her affairs are in good hands; she runs *no risk for the future.*' That's all. I don't like to satisfy the curiosity of people who, just for chit-chat, ask a lot of questions."[8]

But her cryptic comments were not the whole truth; she contributed much of her money to charity. When Maria admonished Eugène to be generous according to his means, she in no way preached a virtue she did not practice. Never was she too preoccupied to give to the unfortunate, nor was her charity ever performed for acknowledgment or applause. Often her beneficiaries did not know the source of their unexpected good fortune. One morning an artist in debtor's prison woke up to find a large sum of money stuffed under his pillow and no indication of its origin.[9] "Pray for me and don't tell anyone," she would frequently tell a grateful beggar. Her motivation for this compulsive benevolence seems to have been the joy she

---

*Refers to Maria's habit of showing all her mail to Mme. Naldi.

felt in helping the needy. "My heart, like yours, feels all the happiness of others, and shares their feelings," she once told Lafayette.[10]

The recipient of the following two letters is unknown.

November 29, 1829

Can you come Monday at 5:00? I will give you the five thousand francs I offered you, but in secret, without even my own mother suspecting anything, for I haven't said anything to her. I am already rather annoyed that you were aware of the use that I wish to make of it. It is so sweet to hide it even from the most intimate friend! I fear that you might be a little talkative, and then, goodbye pleasure! I hope this monsieur, whose name I don't even want to know, does not suspect that I have anything to do with his affairs. This should be done with *complete honor.* So long as I know that this good so-called porter is out of a predicament that could have perhaps compromised the setting-up of his daughter, *that is all* that my heart desires. The blessings which have been directed to you by that family are due you; for without your compassion for them I would never have known the unhappy state in which they were living.

Thus, I do not necessarily see what you do . . . Take care!

January 16, 1830

It's me again, who comes to *beg you on bended knee* to hear this excellent little woman whom I am sending you, satisfied that you will do all you can to give a job, even as maître d'hôtel, to her husband, M. G. . . . *They don't have a sou. Find something!* Oh! I beg you! If you knew how heavy my heart is! I would like to do something to enable them to get out of the complete misery in which they find themselves. Don't make it seem as though you know too much about their miserable state. . . . With their theater salaries they have indeed seen bad times, even before paying their debts, which are not completely paid off. They have a baby. . . . When they have sold their meager furnishings they will be *absolutely destitute.* You are a good person, you will do everything in the world to pull them from the abyss that is only a step away, and in which they will fall if you don't come promptly to their aid!

Pardon, a thousand times pardon, for my imposing on you like this, but I am very concerned about this *childhood friend,* as much by her misfortune as by old acquaintance, and I can't recommend her to you enough, as well as her husband.

Please accept this expression of my strong gratitude.

M.-F. Malibran[11]

She gave more than money. During her years in Paris she regularly worked several mornings a week in the Catholic hospital for children. A beggar was just as likely to be taken in, washed, clothed, and fed, as given money. Once she ran down the street after the police, who had just arrested a young boy for stealing. She went to the magistrate, had the boy freed in her custody, and put him into a music conservatory, her favorite choice of schooling regardless of her beneficiary's talents or interests.[12]

But while one hand gave, the other demanded. In March 1829 she wrote Eugène, "Everyone is torturing me for new engagements." Although a rumor spread that she demanded 100,000 francs per year, she denied it vigorously. "I ask 40,000 for five months and a free benefit. That's reasonable enough."[13] A little calculation would have shown her that her reasonable request, figured on a yearly basis, came to 100,000 francs and more with the free benefit. But her oversight did not matter; scandalized impresarios, ever mindful of her effect on the receipts, rarely failed to find the sums she demanded.

Maria's imminent trip to London left her little time to see her parents, and she was probably grateful. On April 6 she and Mme. Naldi took the coach from Paris to Calais, and three days later, at 3:00 A.M., they boarded the ferry for Dover. Maria did not consider Eugène's opinion about her trip, thinking it sufficient to explain that she was traveling with Mme. Naldi, "who is respected in society . . . and who understands all its proprieties. So you ought not to complain about anything, and I would find it very out of line on your part if you seemed to be afraid . . . to dread . . . to doubt."[14]

Although a singer in Paris led "the life of a horse" as Maria had once described it, in retrospect that life was idyllic compared to the performer's life in London, which a contemporary described: "One knows what the life of a singer is like in the capital of England, the life of a dramatic singer of talent. Three or four afternoon concerts awaiting him after rehearsal, and when the curtain falls, and he is able to escape from the theater, the soirées begin, lasting until dawn. The virtuoso climbs into his coach to go from one to the other."[15] Faced with the same situation years later, Pauline Garcia commented, "Good gracious, how can one call that *faire de l'art*! I call it *faire de l'ar . . . gent!*"[16] But money attracted artists to England; London theaters paid more for talent than theaters in any other country in the world.

Maria threw herself into the English musical circuit with a fury. In answer to Eugène's complaints that she never wrote him or her friends in New York, she countered, "I have written to those ladies as long as I had time to eat a little and to sleep, but since I don't even have the consolation of remaining peacefully in my bed to rest my weary bones, nor to eat slowly, and since regardless of everything I eat and sleep on the run, I confess to you that it is completely the end of the world when I can write you once a month."[17]

The London summer season of 1829 was particularly brilliant: Pasta, Sontag, and Pisaroni divided the honors with their new rival. Pasta's presence was of special interest, for in late September 1828 a friend had advised her to be there, explaining, "If la Sontag goes to London in April, she will not be more than a secondary subject. All the curiosity, thus all the interest will be for Malibran."[18] But Pasta was very much aware of her new rival's progress and of the constant comparisons with herself. Her vocal style, always exceptionally plain, had, in the last year, become more florid, and although she was not capable of extreme ornamentation, she did her best to provide some of the touches that delighted Malibran's audiences.[19]

All the excitement and curiosity did fall to the newcomer, for the English had heard of her triumphs in Paris and had not forgotten that she first appeared professionally on their own soil only four years before. Since then Maria's voice and art had matured greatly. Because of her extraordinary volume, especially in the lower register—considered the most admirable part of her range—she no longer held back in the ensembles. Along with the power had come more discipline; she now saved her spontaneity for dramatic climaxes, and though few realized it, she gave her acting careful study.[20] No longer could she be criticized for the exhaustion that once marred her performances; no matter how great her efforts, no matter how violent the passions she projected on stage, her voice never weakened. The most demanding works began and concluded with the same vocal brilliance.[21]

Now, more than ever, she was less an imitator of Pasta than her superior. But the English—"a public as apt to be scared as allured by original genius," according to Henry Chorley—did not quickly perceive her as the finest singing actress in Europe.[22] For one thing, Maria pitted herself against Pasta in roles that the English, like the French before them, accepted as Pasta's own, with an impassioned style of performance that, despite its originality, was too easily compared to her predecessor's, and a method of singing that employed the same technique of using different registers for the same notes. For another, the English, ever the cultural underdogs, were eager to prove their sophistication by denigrating a singer who had so thoroughly conquered the cultural capital of the world. And yet, despite these disadvantages, some judged her on her own merit, without prejudice.

On April 21, 1829, she appeared as Desdemona at the King's Theatre before an exceptionally large audience. The comments on her personal appearance were generally favorable although the passage of time and her exhausting schedule had somewhat altered the youthful prettiness so evident in 1825. One critic described her as "rather below the middle stature, but well made. She is not handsome, but her countenance is capable of much expression, and her personal appearance is rather in her favor."[23] Chorley found her intriguing. "She may not have been beautiful, but she was better than beautiful, insomuch as a speaking Spanish human countenance by Murillo is ten times more fascinating than many a faultless angel-face such as Guido could paint. There was a health of tint, with but a slight touch of the yellow rose in her complexion; great mobility of expression in her features; an honest, direct brightness of eye; a refinement in the form of her head and in the set of it on her shoulders." He noticed the gold coin held at her forehead by a fine Venetian chain entwined in her braided hair—a style utterly in defiance of convention yet perfectly suited to her features—and wondered if it did not indicate the character of a woman "thoroughly, fearlessly, original."[24]

Chorley considered her voice "not naturally . . . of first rate quality," although he recognized that arduous training had accomplished much. Less severe, the *Times'* critic admitted "the impossibility for any but very highly gifted singers to undertake the part with the least prospect of doing it justice," and he considered her vocal talents as "belonging to the highest order" (27 April 1829), an opinion with which most other reviewers agreed. Her impersonation of Desdemona met with more criticism. Many critics concurred that her performance was "an imitation of Madame Pasta's, but with additional exaggerations of passions and so super-abundant a vehemence of action . . . as to be sometimes outrageously at variance with theatrical decorum." One found her to have "less grandeur, less simplicity" than Pasta, and to lack "that richness of intonation which made her predecessor's voice a treasury of passionate expression," but he admitted that "she commands a stronger body of auxiliaries; she has a softer and more feminine sweetness; a thousand changes of attitude and gesture which are graceful beyond any thing we have seen on the stage."[25]

The *Examiner* published perhaps the most flattering review, finding her "almost . . . perfect, both as an actress and a singer," and her performance "one of the most splendid exhibitions of talent ever witnessed." While admitting Pasta's influence on her artistic style, the writer observed that Malibran was no "mere servile imitator."

In youth and beauty she certainly has advantages over her predecessor: no female could look more truly feminine and intellectually beautiful than she does in the more quiescent scenes, nor no one could rise into more energy and passion than subsequent events in the drama elicited. Her voice much resembles that of Pasta, and is of a most sweet and liquid quality throughout, combined with all the firmness and decision of the finest wind instrument. It is extremely flexible, and capable of every modulation that the most ardent admirer of the Rossini school could desire . . . .

Her face is of a most exquisite expression, combining great feminine softness with its rare accompaniment, a power of expression at times terrific. It will not be easy for any one to forget that situation of agitation in which she remains while waiting the result of the combat between Otello and Rodrigo, the excess of joy portrayed when she hears that Otello lives, and the sudden check when, on turning round, she discovers herself in the presence of her father. The last scene, when she mourns over and sings in broken accents to her harp, was a perfect portrayal of complete and heart-broken sorrow. We do not point out these passages as being the most remarkable, for the performance throughout abounded with instances of the finest perception of character of a finely-regulated mind, and of grace and picturesque action not to be surpassed. We could dilate on this subject to, we fear, a tedious length, and will therefore conclude with intreating everyone who has a spark of feeling or taste not to miss the opportunity of gratifying them to the utmost by as perfect an exhibition as ever did honor to the drama. As critics, we suppose we ought to have discerned some fault among such beauties, but we confess our incapacity to find one, and any severity we may possess has been fairly beaten out of us. [26 April 1829, p. 262]

Critical reservations wilted further with each character she presented. A reviewer compared her performance of Rosina to that of her debut in 1825, noting that "her progress, both as an actress and singer since that period, presented a striking contrast between last night's and the original personation," although another questioned the wisdom of her singing the part as a soprano, warning her that "she who sings *highest* sings not the best."[26] Her Ninetta in *La Gazza* was found by the *Athenaeum*'s critic to be "by far the most vivid representation of the character itself which we have seen, or hope to see, or fancy that we can see," and the reviewer praised it for being "as impassioned a piece of acting as any that an English audience of this generation can remember . . . to enumerate the beauties of this particular performance is beyond our wish—beyond our power."[27]

Another critic described the scene in which Ninetta, having been proved innocent, barely escapes her death sentence.

Madame Malibran is brought upon the stage in a swoon. She shows gradual symptoms of restoration to life—her recollection wavers—but on her absolute return to sense the remembrance of her father rushes upon her—she seeks him with a preternatural vehemence and eagerness through the crowds, she meets him at his entrance, and throwing herself into his arms, abandons herself to the feelings of the moment, so tumultuous, so overpowering, and again sinks into a temporary insensibility. As she recovers from the hallucination partially and by degrees, she endeavors to convince herself of the reality by running her hands along the shoulders and arms of her father while locked in his arms, and she does this with such terrific verisimilitude that we have seen the actor engaged in the scene with her visibly and strongly affected . . . .

Her constitution, strength, and her self-command must be astonishing, and those are the qualities that lead to greatness, even more surely than technical attainments in art.[28]

Some appreciated Malibran's new style, but others, whose conceptions of stage decorum were rooted in the past, found the realism of her portrayals shocking. "In love scenes she often outsteps the modesty of her sex, and seems to forget that 'woman should be wooed, and was not made to woo,' " observed a scandalized journalist. "With her, however, it is quite the reverse; and the manner in which she sometimes *paws* about the person of her lover is really indelicate."[29] Still, five weeks after her initial appearance, she wrote Eugène, "I am making a furore in London more and more each time."[30] One compliment, however, never reached her ears: Felix Mendelssohn, on hearing her for the first time, wrote to a friend that "Malibran is above all praise. There are voices whose very sound moves one to tears; she has one like that, and in addition sings earnestly, passionately, and tenderly, and acts well too. You should see her!"[31]

Despite the attention lavished on Malibran, Malibran and Sontag together were the sensation of the summer. On May 4 Sontag returned to the London stage in *La Cenerentola*. Her frail appearance was attributed to her pregnancy, but the public received her enthusiastically. "Her vocal powers of execution have made no progress since the period of her last exhibition of them at this theatre," wrote the *Times*'s critic, "because they had already attained a degree of perfection which it is not, perhaps, allowed to the faculties of the human voice to surpass" (6 May 1829).

Opera patrons in London wanted to hear Malibran and Sontag sing the Rossini duets that had displayed their joint perfection in Paris, and the Philharmonic Society quickly seized the spectacular attraction, presenting them for the first time at the Argyll Rooms on May 30 in a concert that included Giovanni Velluti and the brilliant young violinist Charles de Bériot, several of whose difficult variations were sung by Maria to his accompaniment. The evening concluded with the duet from *Tancredi*, which so affected the overflowing audience that the critic for the *Times* did not even try to describe it. "Words can convey no idea of this extraordinary performance and it may be safely affirmed that only those who have heard Sontag and Malibran singing Rossini's music can form any idea of the perfection to which vocal execution in this particular style may be carried" (1 June 1829). Of particular interest, although the English seem not to have been aware of it, was that the embellishments for these duets were composed by Malibran. (In the fall of 1829 Ignaz Moscheles published "Gems à la Malibran," his piano transcriptions in two volumes of Malibran's ornaments and cadenzas.)

The concert of the following week brought forth similar praise for the duet, and special commendation for Maria. "Malibran sang exquisitely! Her extraordinary compass of voice is astonishing, and probably unparalleled: on the present occasion she sang down to F sharp on the fourth tone in the bass clef, and she has sometimes been heard to skip with the most extraordinary exactitude from the E flat of the bass to the E natural upon the third ledger tone above the treble stave,—the surprising, difficult, and uncertain distance of three octaves and a semitone!" On this occasion the two singers closed the concert with a duet from *Semiramide*. "This was the grand attraction of the evening; and we hesitate not to say, after witnessing every species of vocal performance in this country from the days of Mara in the year 1800 to the present period, that nothing has been heard so finished, so beautiful, or so interesting: in the immediate duet parts every breath, every aspiration, was given so simultaneously and so perfectly, that the two voices seemed to be actuated by one person only."[32]

A journalist wondered "whether any two voices ever went so well together, and whether any two singers ever sung with such a generous rivalry, not to distinguish each herself, but to make the most of the composition."[33] But problems arose in the generous rivalry. When, at the conclusion of one concert, the audience threw bouquets at the singers,

Maria leaned over to pick up one at her feet when a voice from the pit cried out sternly: "Leave it there, it's not for you!" "I wouldn't deprive Mlle Sontag of the flowers," she replied evenly. "I would rather give them to her myself!"[34] And she did. A few weeks later Sontag returned the favor at her own concert and offered Malibran a garland from those that had been thrown on the stage.

The private concerts brought Maria into another, more difficult, competition with Sontag. The aristrocrats accepted Sontag not only as a singer, but for herself, her beauty, and her engagement to Count Rossi. Although she lacked Maria's charming vivacity, her sweet reticence passed for refinement and she was able to brush aside the silken cord that still barred her more interesting colleague. In London as in Paris, rebuffs cut Maria to the quick and left her depressed for days. Mendelssohn saw her at a private concert, sitting in a remote corner, looking shut out and miserable.[35]

Meanwhile the management of the King's Theatre, hardly deaf to the opportunity at hand, presented the two singers together in staged performances of *Tancredi, Don Giovanni,* and *Le Nozze di Figaro,* sometimes providing a contrast unflattering to Sontag. In reviewing *Le Nozze* a critic spoke of Sontag's "unimpassioned" acting as the Countess. "This impassible languor—not to call it frigidity—was rendered the more perceptible by the contrast with the Susanna of Madame Malibran, in whose organization Nature really seems to have concentrated a quintessence of life and spirits, ever in motion and action. What an inexhaustible exuberance of by-play! What significance of looks! What endless variety of expression in the features, to suit every word this lady has to utter!"[36]

In *Don Giovanni,* Sontag's Donna Anna faded into the shadow of Malibran's Zerlina, which became the opera's main attraction. Maria's Zerlina at first mystified audiences accustomed to "lady-like and drawing room Zerlinas," for she made her a "coarse, vulgar country lass, agog for enjoyment, and running to or from her *caro Masetto* just as the inclination of the moment prompts her." Her dancing at the ball, where she "jumped and jigged about, out of time and out of place," conformed to her idea of the role, but this original combination of "vulgarest nature and highest art," as it was described, did not meet the expectations of those who demanded refinement before truth.[37] "Mad. Malibran's Zerlina has the fault of her Ninetta," harped the *Harmonicon*'s music editor, who had long nurtured the belief that writers for other publications were being paid to print favorable reviews of Maria's performances and who was incensed not to have been approached with a similar proposition. "She makes her sing like an educated lady and act like a vulgar peasant. . . . If Zerlina can sing skillfully and in time she as certainly can, and as assuredly will, dance in the same manner. It is next to impossible to imagine a Spanish girl well informed in one act and abominably ignorant in the other—so instructed and so barbarous as Mad. Malibran hypocritically represents her. But this young lady, it is too evident, has a most exalted opinion of her own judgement" (1829, p. 178).

Others, including the *New Monthly Magazine,* found her Zerlina a revelation.

Her performance is not likely to be soon forgotten. She perhaps over-acted the part in a slight degree: an objection—if objection it be—which attaches to some other characters undertaken by this lady. But in the case of Madame Malibran Garcia, the term "over-acting" scarcely expresses our meaning. When she goes, a mere shade perhaps, beyond the expected line of demarcation, the transgression, instead of being the result of affectation, as is frequently the case with others, obviously proceeds from an exuberance of vivid feeling, an ardent fancy, an overflowing fund of humour, a buoyancy of animal spirits, of which we can scarcely find a parallel in our theatrical recollection. It is delightful to witness the youthful freshness, the fun and frolic she throws into every word, action, and gesture; and if there should be a trifling excess of these now and then—supposing the possibility of that being the case, it, after all, is but real nature in a higher state of action and excitation than what we are ordinarily accustomed to, on, as well as off, the stage. Instead of finding fault with it, we perhaps ought to welcome this uncontrolled display of genuine nature as a source of enhanced enjoyment. With these qualifications, united as they were to rare advantages of voice and scientific cultivation, Madame Malibran's Zerlina constituted the main attraction of the opera. [27 (1829): 298]

On June 27 the bill at the King's Theatre consisted of *La Cenerentola,* with Sontag, followed by the tomb scene from Zingarelli's *Romeo e Giulietta,* in which Sontag played second place to Maria's spectacular Romeo. Even the usually hesitant critic of the *London Literary Gazette* capitulated. Had she not embellished her aria "Ombra adorata" in a manner quite unlike Pasta's performance of it, the reviewer declared that her Romeo would have been "faultless." Her startling final fall, accomplished "quite a la Kean," provoked screams from the ladies in the boxes, who had never seen such a feat on the operatic stage, and the lurid effect was heightened by the dropping of the curtain behind the dead lovers so that the audience witnessed the stagehands removing their prostrate bodies.[38]

But in falling, Maria cut her arm, either on a piece of glass or a section of the scenery. The next day, feeling unwell, she fainted in church and canceled all her operatic performances for the following week. The unsympathetic Laporte, aware of how her absence would affect him financially, demanded a doctor's written statement that she could not sing. Retaliating in kind Maria not only produced the certificate, but had it published in the newspapers, a deed that did not ingratiate Laporte with the Malibranistes.

After a semiconvalescence of nearly three weeks, during which the press, annoyed at her slow recovery, dropped increasingly disparaging remarks about her unreliability, she introduced a character new to her repertoire, the old hag Fidalma in Domenico Cimarosa's *Il Matrimonio Segreto*. This small role was of the type her mother had played, and indeed Joaquina had once appeared as Fidalma. Maria also loved to play these character parts at her private soirées where they were so successful that she now attempted to bring her fun to the public stage. Not at all averse to undertaking a minor role, she once remarked that she would like to play Berta in *Il Barbiere* just so she could wear the comic costume.³⁹

Never before had a major singer appeared in a small part, one flattering neither to her appearance nor to her voice, and as Fidalma, Malibran raised an uproar among both audiences and critics alike. "We feel rather at a loss what to say upon the choice of Madame Malibran as regards the part of Fidalma," began a reviewer. "To see a lady of twenty-two or so, the Tancredi, the Romeo, the Ninetta of the season disfigure her spirited, intellectual, youthful countenance by artificial wrinkles, a powdered wig, &c.; to behold the gay Zerlina, the arch Susanna, totter about the stage in buckram of the fashion of Queen Anne's time, with shaking head, trembling hands, and tremulous voice; to hear her squeak in childish treble pipes from beginning to end—to witness such a transformation was a feature in the cast of characters which few of the audience were prepared for. The preposterous travesty can only be regarded as a wayward freak of caprice."⁴⁰

The *Times* considered the part "far beneath this lady's talents and high station on the theatrical boards, but [one] which she undertook probably with the view of showing what she can make of every character in which she chooses to appear." The critic nevertheless admitted that the role "was rendered important and highly amusing by the comic humour which Madame Malibran threw into it with a skill which evinces a versatility of power rarely, if ever, to be met with to an equal extent" (17 July 1829).

Maria had spent all her energies during her stay in London, not only in public but in the private salons, and she continued to cancel performances for the remainder of her engagement. And yet contracts lay ahead in Belgium and in the English provinces for the fall festivals. Beyond that loomed her new engagement with the Italien. Exhausted, she let the London season end as an anticlimax. She wrote to Eugène,

Now I am fine, my life is peaceful, as is necessary for the type of life that I must lead. I hope that nothing will change it in the slightest. Do you understand me? Think about what *I once told you*. I don't want this to make you unhappy, but I assure you that I must continue to live like this as long as I follow this profession. Thus, since you have your occupation, you will do well, my friend, to continue to keep busy, and to try to reconquer by your *good conduct* and your work, the respect that you have lost. You know how I think on the subject of all the matters that have, unfortunately, taken place on the subject of the bankruptcy—So think it over, and since you seem to desire the continuation of my happiness, we must stay like this. I will write you more often and I will give you as many details as I can, so as to keep you current with what I am doing.[41]

In this, her last letter to the husband she had not seen for nearly three years, Maria reiterated all that she had told him before. But in a few weeks her life would change irrevocably, and her belief in a celibate, peaceful life would vanish, forgotten forever, in the course of one evening.

CHAPTER 8

Charles de Bériot

In 1827, at about the same time Maria Malibran first appeared in Paris, the young violinist Charles de Bériot also made his name known in the French capital, with notable success. Six years older than Maria, he and his sister Constance were the sole survivors of an aristocratic Belgian family. Orphaned at the age of nine, he had been raised by Monsieur Tiby, a professor of music in Louvain who quickly recognized his musical talents and became not only a father to the boy but his music teacher as well. By the time he was nineteen years old Charles had progressed sufficiently on the violin to be accepted at the Paris Conservatory, where he studied under such masters as Giovanni Viotti, Pierre Baillot, and Charles Lafont. But life at the Conservatory did not appeal to him, and fearing that his individuality would be lost, he left after only a few months to study privately and to begin his career as a performer.

De Bériot appears to have had no difficulty establishing himself as a first-rank violinist. In 1826 he was well received in London and on his return to Belgium was appointed First Violinist to His Majesty King Wilhelm. One of his biographers described his playing as having "a peculiar charm . . . that was perhaps never possessed by any violinist of this century; and thus early in his career his playing was characterized by a most refined taste, a rich and charming tone, and wonderful execution."[1] Another noted his "unfailing accuracy of intonation, great neatness and facility of bowing, grace, elegance, and piquancy."[2] Not even the advent of Paganini diminished his standing as a great violinist, and many considered him superior to his grandstanding rival. The Baron de Trémont, who preferred to be moved rather than astonished, remarked that no matter how many times he heard de Bériot he always found new delights to enjoy, whereas Paganini's acrobatics became predictable and tiresome. "Paganini dazzled me, but rarely touched me,"[3] he declared, an opinion shared by many music authorities.

In Paris Charles had fallen in love with the beautiful Henriette Sontag, and her pregnancy by Count Rossi left him heartbroken and bitter. Soon the entire city knew of his anguish. Maria Malibran sympathized with him; she had known him since her return from America and had performed with him many times in the salons. She had even been moved to tears by his playing.[4] But there was no real attraction between them, for Charles was preoccupied with Henriette, and Maria, as she declared to Eugène, considered men "no more than statues or bushes," so busy was she with her own career. "Never, even when the angels of heaven come to tempt me," she told her fearful husband. "I will resist like St. Anthony."[5]

After her engagement with the King's Theatre, Maria traveled briefly to Belgium for several concerts,* including one at the Chateau of the Princess de Chimay where she sang several Spanish songs to her own guitar accompaniment. Charles de Bériot, also present by invitation of the Princess, played one of his own compositions with unexpected inspiration. His handsome face bore the marks of his emotional trauma; pale and thin, with a nervous tic in one eyelid, he maintained an attitude of constant bitterness and melancholy that, whether he knew it or not, gave him a brooding attractiveness he had lacked in healthier times, a Byronesque quality that some find irresistible. On this occasion his ardor and passion, his musical feelings and the warmth with which he played overwhelmed his audience, and Maria, who had always found his art moving, now felt something within her stir, something not entirely the result of his music. When he finished she rushed up to him with what at first appeared to be merely heartfelt congratulations. The violinist thanked her politely. At this total misinterpretation of her sentiments she grasped his hand. "No, no!" she whispered urgently, her eyes flashing. "Can't you see I love you?"[6]

From that evening they were lovers.

Stendhal once remarked that "a great singer is essentially a creature of *nerves*; a great violinist, on the other hand, needs a radically different quality."[7] He might have been anticipating the union of Charles de Bériot and Maria Malibran, for Maria's cheerful exuberance and inexhaustible nervous energy contrasted with what was usually termed de Bériot's "coldness" or even "apathy." Maria preferred to call him shy.[8] The violinist did not lack personality; on rare occasions he could even show uncharacteristic vivacity, but as long as he was with Maria Malibran, he remained in her shadow.

The lovers' sojourn in Belgium was brief; Maria was engaged at the music festivals of Chester, Gloucester, and Birmingham in September and October, as well as for concerts in Bristol, Manchester, and other cities later in the fall. Perhaps the separation was best, at least for the present, for their relationship had to be kept secret lest disgrace and dishonor destroy her assiduously cultivated image of perfect virtue. Not even Mme. Naldi could know. She and de Bériot parted, arranging to meet in early October when they were both engaged in Birmingham.

---

*At this juncture of Malibran's life dates are difficult to establish, but a clue is provided by a letter written on Wednesday, July 29, presumably from London, in which she states, "I have been quite sick, but at present I am infinitely better and I will be well enough to leave next Sunday [August 2] for Brussels, where we [she and Mme. Naldi] will stay for two weeks at the Hotel Bellevue" (MS Sibley Music Library, Eastman School of Music, University of Rochester).

The English festivals offered Maria the opportunity to reveal herself as a concert singer. Although her greatest impact was sometimes said to be on the operatic stage where she had the advantages of plot, costume, and character, there is evidence to the contrary, for her versatility lent itself to any musical situation. In concert, according to a critic, "she seems to consider the audience as a multitude of friends for whose certain pleasure she is about to manifest her skill." Never affected or insincere, she expressed her delight naturally, and, in combination with a vulnerability and femininity that communicated itself to each individual in the audience, made each want to please her in return. That unique sense of "a certain intrepidity, yet joined with a courtesy and a delight" made her seem more than a paid performer, just as her listeners became more than a crowd paying to be amused.[9] They felt emotions they did not know they possessed as Maria revealed "glances of a purer, brighter world which they had forgotten, but to which her divine tones summon them to return," in the words of Lady Blessington, who also wrote that "the sound appears to emanate from a soul thrilling with sublime emotion; and its deep harmony causes mine to vibrate. There is something mysterious, something magical in its influence on me. It haunts one for many succeeding hours."[10]

Her effect on the public during the applause was vividly described by one who experienced her spell in person. "Delight beamed from her eyes; there was an indescribable joy in her whole look; it was certainly the happiest moment in her life. And was it not also the happiest of mine? I shared in her delight as well as in the acclamation of the others."[11]

A report from the Birmingham festival indicates that Maria's personality, apart from the roles she assumed, could exert considerable power over an audience.

The star of the evening was again the inimitable Garcia. She accompanied herself upon a miserable square untuned piano-forte; and sung with the most admirable naivete a Spanish song composed by her father, "Bajelito Nuevo".* Her jocose playfulness and characteristic manner were so immediately brought in contrast with her tragic dramatic performance, her classical and finished singing of "O Salutaria" and "Ah Parlate", and several other varieties not yet reviewed, that the whole audience were unanimous in esteeming her the most extraordinary and versatile creature that ever appeared in an orchestra. Her Spanish song, we need scarcely add, was enthusiastically encored. She sang another instead of it. Her performance was interrupted by shouts of laughter, elicited by the vivacious archness of her manner, although her auditors understood not one word of the matter.

Her singing of Handel's "Rejoice Greatly," considered a complete failure when she attempted it four years earlier, was now "the best exhibition of the song perhaps ever witnessed" and incorporated an

---

*Her own "Bajelito Waltz" appeared in England at about this time. Wherever she traveled, songs from her pen were regularly published.

ascending scale of two octaves to high B flat which "was given with the most pure and perfect intonation, and a rapidity of execution unparalleled."[12] But perhaps the most striking example of her musicianship was a feat fully in the style of those her father had once exhibited, although Maria's was less a deliberate stunt than a necessary correction in the performance of "Una voce poco fa."

Written in the key of E, the aria had often been transposed up into F by lighter sopranos such as Sontag, and the orchestra was accustomed to performing it this way. Maria may have had absolute pitch, for as the orchestra began its prelude to the piece she immediately realized that it was being played a half-tone high. At its conclusion she stepped quickly forward, murmured "in E" to the conductor, and proceeded to sing in that key. Whether the musicians could transpose on such short notice is doubtful, and one can only wonder what the piece sounded like, but an astonished reviewer reported the feat as "an attempt for its boldness, talent, and novelty without precedent. This we know to have been the general feeling and unbiased opinion of the artists present."[13]

After concerts in Manchester, Bristol, and other cities, Maria departed for Paris. If Pasta had not been utterly vanquished as a rival, the more astute musical authorities were appreciative of the odds against which Malibran's English successes had been won as well as her present state of accomplishment, which was considered beneath what her genius would eventually acquire. "It is in the grasp of the whole—in the expressive power, and in the beauty and force of the contrasts, the lights and shadows of her art that her pre-eminence consists," wrote one. "In Desdemona and Ninetta, in Tancredi, Semiramide and Zerlina, the adaptation of her vocal style and her dramatic manner is alike excellent. Dignity, force, and pathos are equally, as it appears to us, at her command . . . we have no hesitation in asserting that if Madame Malibran be not already the finest actress and singer combined in Europe, her certain occupation of that high place depends upon the continuance of her health and faculties alone. She has all the endowments, all the acquisition, and above both, all the devotion and concentration of mind common to those strong and gifted individuals who rise to pre-eminence, whatever the nature of their pursuits."[14]

In the fall of 1829 Paris witnessed a return perhaps even more interesting than that of Maria Malibran, who had, after all, become a familiar artist in the city. Garcia again accepted an engagement at the Italien, and "The Old Lion," as he was now affectionately called, reappeared in late September as Almaviva, opposite the Rosina of Henriette Sontag. An immense crowd came to hear him, with a predictable effect on the receipts. But Garcia was now fifty-four years old, and although he still sang with charm, taste, and enthusiasm, he had to force his weakening voice, which now showed doubtful intonation in the high notes and loss of quality and power throughout its range. Declared a reviewer flatly, "Garcia, formerly the most wonderful tenor who ever sang . . . has lost a part of his powers."[15]

On November 6 his daughter returned to the stage of the Italien in *La Gazza Ladra*. For the first time in Paris the music of the prison scene was included, and Maria made of it a tour de force with its rapid changes of mood from girlish innocence, to fury at unjust persecution, to recollection of earlier joys, to despairing resignation. Her singing was considered equal to her acting: she sang the andante with touching sadness and then dashed so boldly into the allegro that she seemed to defy fate with her rapid leaps from the lower to the upper notes.[16] The public cheered her performance and critics praised it, although they regretted the drama's threat to the preservation of her voice.

On November 23 the Théâtre-Italien presented father and daughter together for the first time in Paris in *Don Giovanni*, a stellar evening that included Sontag as Donna Anna and Sabine Heinefetter as Donna Elvira. This tactful choice of opera allowed Garcia the leading role while his daughter took a lesser one. But the critical notices were harsh, with one reviewer writing that "Garcia is still a great actor: in the last scene with the commanditore he was . . . at least equal to what he once was, but as a singer he is no longer even a shadow of himself. . . . When one has saved the memory of a great talent it is painful to see only ruins remaining."[17]

Public response, however, led him to continue performing the roles he had once made his own—Almaviva, Otello, the Don—frequently opposite his daughter. This combination regularly outdrew every other theater, and, according to *Le Figaro*'s daily reports of the receipts for Parisian theaters, they often outdrew all the theaters in Paris combined.

By December 1829 Charles de Bériot had returned to Paris, not only to fulfill his musical engagements, but secretly to join Maria, whose public reputation was at stake. Suddenly Mme. Naldi, the "guardian angel" who had assured Eugène Malibran that no scandal or harm would come to his wife, was a nuisance, a "dragon of virtue" who disapproved of illicit love and adulteresses and gave her adopted daughter endless lectures on the grave consequences of her actions. Maria listened politely and moved into a house at 46 Rue de Provence where, for the first time, she dared to live alone.

As Maria Malibran stepped into a love affair, Henriette Sontag emerged from the results of hers, which included social disgrace and the death of her baby daughter. The constant references to her thin, haggard appearance spoke of the shame endured by the poor woman, but in early January 1830 the leading newspapers announced the end of her misery: she would become the Countess Rossi. The explanation finally fabricated for the world cleared the way for a respectable marriage. It was declared that she and her lover had been married in Berlin in 1827, but because marrying a stage performer could jeopardize the Count's career, the union was kept secret. The birth of their child, however, had made divulgence of the marriage necessary, and now the Sardinian court sanctioned a second marriage on the condition that Henriette retire from the stage forever.

Why a second marriage was needed if a first had taken place was blithely overlooked. As for her station in life, King Friedrich Wilhelm proclaimed her "née de Launstein" and retroactively noble from birth, thus evading the unpleasant reality of her true parents, who had been itinerant performers of the lowest sort. The prospective Baronness von Launstein heaved a sigh of relief and made plans to earn as much money as possible in the remaining weeks of her career. And Laurent, determined to squeeze the last franc possible out of a public faced with losing its Henriette, began announcing the first of her many final performances.

On January 2 a jammed theater heard Sontag in what was feared to be her last appearance, and Maria was so moved she handed her rival all the flowers at the final curtain, no doubt thinking that this would be the last time she would have to do so.[18] Performances continued until her last final appearance on January 18. Three days later she was heard at a concert for the poor in which de Bériot played, and then on January 24, in another benefit for the poor, she sang the second act of *Tancredi* with Maria, the first act of *Don Giovanni* with the Garcias, and scenes from other operas. Even Charles X attended, and for the last time the voices of the two women joined in "those ravishingly executed duets." "It was fantastic, ideal, perfection" exulted a critic.[19] "The effect it produced is indescribable," echoed another.[20]

On January 26, 1830, Henriette Sontag left Paris for an extended European tour, and Maria Malibran, finally without rival, continued her performances with the Italien. On April 3 she took her own benefit: Bonifacio Asioli's *Pygmalion* reduced to one scene and the entire opera of *Tancredi* with Laure Cinti of the Opéra. The gross receipts of 10,000 francs almost equaled the combined ticket sales of the seven other theaters as reported by *Le Figaro,* despite some disappointment in this program, since she backed out of a scheduled appearance in Rossini's *Matilde di Shabran*.* Thus her performance as Matilde could not be compared with Sontag's, but she was grudgingly praised for her courage in abandoning a part already in rehearsal and for substituting an opera in which everyone had already heard her. The Asioli work, despite its beauties, was considered more appropriate for the salon, and, because of lack of rehearsal time, was punctuated by unfortunate accidents.

---

*Maria would plan to sing Matilde every so often but always avoided it at the last moment. For one thing, Sontag was a great success in the role; for another, the tessitura was particularly high and would have required extensive reworking for Maria to sustain it through an entire evening. Changes were made by any singer performing a role not written for her specific talents, but Matilde apparently offered Malibran unusual problems. Obviously dissatisfied with herself in the work, she never sang it publicly.

Some disgrace surrounded the performance for, unknown to the audience, a dandelion crown was supposedly thrown at Malibran during a curtain call by certain parties who, at the singer's request, had not been allowed backstage during rehearsals. This insult, if it happened, was lost among the bundles of flowers heaved at Maria by her adoring audience and had it not been for *Le Figaro,* the incident would have remained unknown (10 April 1830).

A stage accident also marred the evening. Just before the performance Maria fell through a trapdoor in the stage, and had she not been wearing Tancredi's helmet, she might have been severely injured. Still, she bruised her face and hurt her arm badly enough so that it bothered her for several weeks afterward.[21] The press, in reporting the incident, blamed the stage manager and his crew, who immediately countered that Mme. Malibran had fallen down a staircase leading to her dressing room. A heated discussion was conveniently postponed for a few days until her departure for London made verification of either story impossible, but her brother, in a letter to *Le Figaro,* stated that she fell through the trapdoor (15 April 1830). Music journals from England to Italy reported both the fall and the dandelions; for every incident of la Malibran's life, no matter how insignificant, was important to the music lovers of Europe.

On April 9 Maria set out for England again to fulfil her engagements in London. Music connoisseurs of Paris felt that her performances of the current season had been "consistently inferior" to those of the preceding year.[22] But many found this her most brilliant season, and the last years of the decade were already becoming legendary. Years later Marie d'Agoult would comment, "Never, I think, will one encounter a more extraordinary gathering of first rank talents."[23]

As she traveled to London Maria was no longer accompanied by Mme. Naldi, but by Mme. Sevestre, a servant lent to her by her friend the Baron Denie. Charles de Bériot could not be with her, for engagements took him to St. Petersburg. The separation caused a quarrel between the lovers, for although Maria considered him her husband, she would not risk publicly admitting their relationship. Sontag's disgrace made her see even more clearly the price of advertising her love; canceling her English engagement to follow Charles to Russia would be the source of gossip from one end of Europe to the other.

For a few days neither spoke to the other; Charles annoyed at her fears, and Maria furious that he could be so unconcerned about her reputation. The disagreement was eventually settled: he would go to Russia without her, and they would meet in England in June. As a token of their reconciliation, he sent her a harp in recognition of her ability to accompany herself on that instrument in Desdemona's Willow Song. Maria wrote Mme. Merlin of her happiness:

It is with the greatest pleasure that I promise to visit you this evening. . . . I am
so happy! Everything has been successful since yesterday, and this reconciliation
is a good omen for everything else. . . . I was sure that a good friend like you
would be enchanted with what has just happened. As soon as *he* comes in, I will
show him your letter, which is very obliging for me and for him, and I am sure
that he will have 36 pockets in which to put 36 violins, if he has them, and will
bring them to you with his best wishes.[24]

Although the lovers would not see each other again for months, they would
not be separated again.

Because of bad weather in Calais, Maria remained there for several
days. Immediately asked to do a concert, she agreed, provided it was a
benefit for the poor. Because of the hasty arrangements, the concert was not
announced until 2:00 in the afternoon of the day of the performance.
Despite this short notice the event grossed 387 francs from subscribers
alone, and that did not include what was collected at the door. "That's
enormous!" she exulted to the Baron Denie. "These poor people have
suffered so much!!! I am happy to be able to procure them some bread all
by myself."

The concert gave her pleasure too, despite an uncultured audience.
She described it in detail to the Baron.

After the first part, I made the offering; after the offering the mayor came before
the audience, and in a loud and intelligent voice presented me with a crown of
flowers, then a bouquet, all the while making me a eulogy, very pleasing, in a
most persuasive, penetrating, moving tone. Then he read some verses written in
my praise AGAIN. The public accepted everything enthusiastically, screaming,
stamping, applauding. In short, my friend, I was overcome to be able to be good
to the poor of Calais, who have been beleaguered, who have suffered, who have
been so very unfortunate. The public was so enchanted with me that even after
the offering was finished they applauded me as I traveled back to the hotel.[25]

Two days later the weather cleared, and with Mme. Sevestre Maria
embarked for Dover.

CHAPTER 9

The Adulteress

Maria Malibran arrived in London with time to spare, for her engagement at the King's Theatre was not to begin until early May. Thus she had the chance to assess the musical scene of which she would soon be a part. Her main curiosity concerned Henriette Méric-Lalande. With Sontag's retirement the King's Theatre needed another soprano, and Lalande was the choice. A former pupil of Garcia's, she had once possessed a magnificent voice of phenomenal agility and great beauty of tone. Gaetano Donizetti wrote his *Elvida* for her in 1826, and Vincenzo Bellini chose her to create the leading roles in no less than four of his six operas, including the highly successful *Il Pirata* and *La Straniera*. London eagerly anticipated Lalande's arrival because of the triumphant premier of *La Straniera* at La Scala.

Unfortunately Lalande, at the age of thirty-two, was developing serious vocal problems, in particular a tremolo in her upper register. She would create yet another work, Donizetti's *Lucrezia Borgia*, in 1833, but the end of her career was imminent. Because her reputation led the English to expect much of her, disappointment was all the greater at her failure. On April 17 Maria heard the new singer make her London debut as Imogene in *Il Pirata*, and her letter to de Bériot, although amusing, shows that her charity did not always extend to her rivals.

Mon bon, mon meilleur ami,

I was only going to write you when I had something interesting to tell you, but I am breaking the ice and writing without any purpose, except, however, the idea of making you read my scribbling a little, which, I don't doubt, will make you thrill with joy and happiness for several days. . . .

Let's see if I can dig up some news. Let's speak of the debut of Mme Lalande.

I went to the theater with Lady Flint, her daughter, and her husband. There I am, my lorgnette aimed, beady-eyed, motionless, waiting, after the overture, for the pirate, played by Donzelli, to make his appearance. The overture . . . hum! comme çi, comme ça. It doesn't make much of an effect. The curtain went up. Pretty scenery. The overture was applauded. A good set designer is most important for the success of an overture. . . .

The pirate arrives. . . . An aria well bellowed, well howled, earning him undeserved applause which he received while making 36,000 bows and nods until he was right in the wings. The aria isn't bad, it has originality.

"Enter the beautiful Italian!" said I to my little self,* very impatiently. "At last there she is," I said, and leaned forward over the edge of the box to see better. Imagine a woman around forty, blonde, the face of a laborer, with a bad expression, bad figure, having in common with me the ugliest feet in the world, badly coiffed, and the same for her dress.

The recitative began . . . Her voice shook so badly that I could not judge whether it was sour, sweet, or otherwise. I patiently awaited the cavatina so I could judge. Begins the cavatina. . . . She spun out a sound like ⌒⌒⌒ . There I was, pitying this unfortunate woman who could not find her courage. She finished her aria, which is very pretty and which she consistently sang with that bad wobble. She was well applauded. A thousand curtsies, the custom in London only, earning her prolonged salvos.

Next came the beautiful duet, which you know. She sang this coldly and always with the tremble. To make a long story short, she finished the opera the same way she began it. She has a beautiful aria at the end in the mad scene. Her husband and her lover have both just been killed. She arrives with a little child, who is yawning, because he would prefer to go beddy-bye than to hear a lachrymose aria which has to be sung, and especially acted, in a manner completely opposite to produce an insane effect. The result of this was that she didn't make the least effect. However, she was called for after the curtain, coming out to the most anonymous applause, the most unanimous applause I mean, that has ever been given, because the consensus is that she wasn't good. But I didn't want to judge her right off the bat, like everyone else. I waited.

"Now comes the best" as Susanna says. I have discovered that this manner of singing and the sound like ⌒⌒⌒ is an unchangeable trait, fixed, eternal! You can guess how well our voices will go together . . . two by two like three goats. Her middle notes are like a taut wire, producing a sound that is rather rusty, piercing, and little or not at all pleasant.

The opera isn't bad, it works, but there are a lot of weaknesses. There is a magnificent trio between the two rivals and the wife who is so faithful a lover to the Pirate, that the rival and husband throws himself at the feet of his wife, who will not consent to follow him despite his humble attitude. Someone else could have explained this scene in a more intelligible manner. But as I know who I am writing to, I won't take the trouble to dispel the gloom that generally hangs over all my descriptions.[1]

The critics concurred, finding Lalande "unquestionably past the culminating point of personal and vocal attraction."[2] Such criticism did little to enhance her appeal, and, even worse, notices of her performances appeared directly above the statement "Madame Malibran is arrived, and will shortly make her first appearance this season." Small wonder the new Henriette failed to hold her own.

Maria kept Charles abreast of the situation.

April 29, 1830

I am making my debut early because Laporte is in a difficult position. Mme Lalande's lack of success has disappointed him; he is losing money, and he is awaiting me like the Messiah to pull him from the mire, in which he is up to his

---

*Lalande was neither beautiful nor Italian; Lalande was fat, Maria was not.

neck. You know that chimney sweeps always come out on Mayday, dancing in the streets dressed in bedsheets and painted with rouge! . . . I'm glad I don't have to appear on that day, for fear of comparisons. There will be so many others to make without that one! . . . You can tell that I am so shaken with fear that it is making me sick. But enough of this. I'm going to lunch. Tonight after the opera you will learn how I made out.[3]

That evening Maria sang her first performance of Angelina in *La Cenerentola* before the clamoring English public. The previous summer one critic had stated, "We hesitate not to predict that she will ultimately become a second Pasta."[4] But the English no longer could compare Malibran to Pasta; she had become a personage in her own right, an imitator of none. "Her reception was cordial in the extreme," observed a reviewer, "and the talent of her performance justified the enthusiasm with which every part of it was greeted . . . her variety of talent is so great that but a tithe of it would be appreciated on a first or second hearing."

Madame Malibran's conception of the part is, as usual, very clever, and the execution of it very spirited. She is one whose ideas are sure to be original, and, from the abundance of her resources, there is no fear of any poverty or weakness of performance, or that any two performances will be composed of materials so alike as to smack of mannerism;—for she has variety even in the constancy of her high spirits; and though her interpolations spring from the same invariable cause, yet they differ from each other in every part of the same character, and even at every repetition of the same part.[5]

Another critic concurred, finding her "improved in health as well as in voice, science, and execution. . . . She has already found ample opportunities of displaying the versatility, nay, the universality, of her histrionic genius."[6]

Maria passed the news on to de Bériot.

April 30, 1830

There's one labor over with. I debuted last evening in *La Cenerentola*. My friend, I made what is called a *furore* in England, although in Paris I would have taken my success for a half-failure. However, my first appearance went well. They called me back at the finish, and I can say I was thoroughly applauded by the whole house, from the boxes to the pit. They say my voice is more powerful than last year. They are enchanted with my petite figure, which is equally improved. I tell you this only because I always tell you everything. I am also considered to be in good health and resources, which is very true. I have shown great cooperation in consenting to debut on Thursday, which is an unfashionable day when no one goes to the theater, or I should say, when only benefits are given. Also, despite the fact that the house was not completely full, the number of people who did come was astonishing; and since it was because of me that they came, that makes me terribly *à la mode*. . . . Tomorrow I again sing the same role, and all I know is that I will sing it better.[7]

Despite the light tone of Maria's letters, she was depressed while in England. Missing her lover, she found herself unusually susceptible to annoyances, among them the caste system that placed her, as a performer, at the bottom of the social ladder. In a letter to a friend, perhaps Constance de Bériot, she wrote of her feelings and dreamed of a more peaceful life, far from "the enchanted palaces" of the theater which separated her from Charles.

I will then be more at ease to give myself to the sweet ways of a tranquil life, to the charm of friendship, to the happiness that it brings, the source of which is pure, and which continually gives life to its two plants which, in growing old, are continually rejuvenated. Then I would no longer fear that the name of actress, said with scorn, with curled lip, would disturb the calm of my existence. . . . Don't believe that I *scorn* my art; but it is so painful to find oneself mixed, pell-mell, with people who would give the word *actress* only the most revolting and unfavorable connotations—I don't know why I always return to a subject that is so painful to me; despite myself my pen traces my daily thoughts. After all, it is my profession, and I have to do it. . . . I hope that I have not annoyed you too much with my reflections! I can't write otherwise; I have to say what I think, or I really couldn't put two words down next to each other. Pardon me, I beg you; I feel relieved every time I think I can dare to put an intimate thought on a bit of paper.[8]

In two letters to the Baron Denie Maria described an incident of social discrimination, fortunately with a happy ending.

London, May 2, 1830
I dine tomorrow at the home of Mme . . . . What a strange woman! What a strange manner in which to receive someone who is carrying a letter of recommendation from her daughter! . . . What a strange manner in which to ask an artist to give four concerts, obliging the artist to offer his services for nothing rather than stoop to bargaining . . . all this obliging the *strange* woman to invite me for dinner tomorrow.

Do you know what happens when milk is poured on oysters? . . . Dissolve. I believe I experienced the fate of the unfortunate oyster when I went into the dining room. . . . I was *dissolved* by the *milk* of the repulsive *lady of the castle*. She had a severe look, and cold disdain. . . . I am going again tomorrow, trembling, to her house . . . what an agreeable family dinner![9]

May 4, 1830
I didn't dine at Mme. . . . .'s. I was too afraid of her. I sent an excuse and went later in the evening. She was more pleasing this time. She was very respectful to me. I sang a little. Then I went to the Duchess of Canizarro's. Mme Lalande was there. I made all the money and got all the *fanatisme*. They were standing on the chairs to see me. The Duke of Wellington came to take my hand, which he shook for ten minutes and practically crushed. He was charming. All the ladies invited me to visit them, asking my address so they could come see me. All in all, you would have been happy with the way they treated your *little girl*, your second spoiled child.[10]

During the summer in England she took the first step to escape the disgrace that continually threatened her—the specter of public denunciation as an adulteress—by turning to her good friend, Louis Viardot, a writer and influential man in Paris. Maria trusted Louis from the moment she met him at a soirée, seeing that he would not applaud her for a charade that everyone else seemed to enjoy. "They want to flatter you," he told her. "I really respect you, and therefore will tell you the truth, even at the risk of offending you."[11] Maria valued Viardot's special friendship.

She wrote of her plan to Charles, her "dear husband," shortly after arriving in England.[12]

April 30, 1830

I have written in my despair to Viardot, who has done everything he can to console me. I was so miserable that I told my good friend Lady Flint what was the matter. She spoke of it to one of her friends, an excellent man, who told me that in a similar case he had himself been saved from difficulty by consulting one of his friends, an old nobleman (seventy years old) who, it seemed, knew the laws like the palm of his hand. This morning at noon Sir George Warrender, who is *the old friend* of the *even older one*, is coming to speak to me about this. As I risk nothing in seeking information, I will tell him as much as is expedient (nothing more) to get him to give me advantageous counsel, which will ease my oppressed mind a little. If you were near me and I could talk to you, I would look elsewhere to cheer myself up.

In a burst of misery and passion, she continued,

Do I have to tell you again that you are everything to me? You know it better than I. It is to you that I owe the little happiness I now have, and that I had in Paris. You are so good! Thus I wear a ring which is the perfect symbol of our friendship: a knot which cannot be untied; the more you pull it, the tighter it gets. Isn't it the symbol of the most durable and pure friendship? Yes! The more I think of it, the more I understand the eternal nature of this friendship, for it seems to me that we will meet again after death, and that I will still love you the same. Eternity is beautiful in this case, but there are things in this world of death and misery that will last forever.

She looked forward to seeing him again.

But my friend, I beg of you, don't surprise me. When the happy day comes when I can see you again, tell me a long time in advance so that I can enjoy, in advance, the happiness whose source I will soon have. Yes, you are the only source of that; you alone are able to lift the head of this flower which is drooping toward the ground; you make it reborn; you make it recover, by your soul, all its strength, all its vigor . . . the pansy [pensée—thought]! . . . and that flower is one that will never leave you, that is all yours, because you are good, because you know how to console the afflicted, because you give the advice of a father, because you are their brother, because you are mine, and because . . . because. . . . Ah! My goodness, I would never finish with all my *becauses*, if I had to do them all it would be in front of M. le . . . .

Now I leave you. I am going to dress to receive my man, *friend of old friend*, and then I am going to my rehearsal. Goodbye, papa, mamam, brother, sister, you are all of them to me.[13]

In the midst of all her problems and work, she found time to tell Charles about her second performance of *La Cenerentola.*

May 1, 1830

I have had people here all day for rehearsal. I haven't been able to write you, my good friend; the coach is below, waiting to take me to the theater, or it will leave me just like my slipper, if I delay; my coachman will turn into a fat rat, my footman a squirrel, my horses a beautiful pair of mice. I will write you about the outcome of this evening, a fashionable night in London for our theater.

I have just performed, my good and honest friend; never, my dear, never, in the whole season, has there been a fuller house. They came in great numbers. I sang better than Thursday. All my colleagues were thrilled with me and seemed to love me infinitely. They came to congratulate me afterwards, and as they left they were saying: "That is what you call singing! . . . There is a true artist. . . . What talent!" . . .

That made me very happy. At the same time I am a little upset that this has to be, for the pain it may bring others. But that's the way it is.[14]

Maria poured her energies into her hectic schedule, often traveling to the provinces for concerts whenever she had a day off from the King's Theatre. She repeated her roles of Rosina, Fidalma, Tancredi, Zerlina, and Desdemona, and introduced her Arsace to the English public in a performance that presented Lalande as Semiramide. She added to her repertoire the part of Orazia in Cimarosa's *Gli Orazi* on June 17, and on July 26 the trouser role of Don Diego in Severio Mercadante's *Donna Caritea,* an opera being produced in England for the first time.

In Paris Joaquina Garcia anticipated her daughter's activities and was disturbed enough to write the Baron Denie, for she knew that Maria would be far more inclined to listen to him than to her mother.

May 1, 1830

Convinced, Monsieur, that everything you can tell Maria will be listened to, I beg you to try and persuade her to spare herself for the theater and not to accept dinner invitations in the city. You know that Mme Lalande did not make a good impression, and consequently Maria will have to appear before the time of her engagement. It is possible that she will have to sing quite a bit more than her engagement intended, and if she takes care of herself this can be a golden year for her; but if she wears herself out and overexerts herself as she did in Paris, you can understand that she will throw the fortune out the window.[15]

If the Baron acted on Mme. Garcia's request, his advice went unheeded. Maria's creative drive admitted no human limitation, and as long as crowds applauded and threw flowers, she sang. On May 26 she reported, "Lalande having failed, I am up to my neck in work. A concert in the morning, two or three more in the evening, and the same thing over again the next day, not even excepting the nights I sing at the opera."[16] She planned to sing that Wednesday in a London concert, leave immediately for

Bath where she would arrive at 9:00 in the morning, sing two songs, depart for Bristol at 1:00 in the afternoon, be there by 2:00 and play the third act of *Otello* with Donzelli, pocket her 120 guineas, and arrive in London the next morning to start all over again at the theater.

She could still say, "I never enjoyed better health. I am now quite strong. My voice is as clear in the morning as in the afternoon, it is never hoarse or husky."[17] But her recklessness, her careless disregard for her health became more apparent and a doctor often was needed to repair whatever damage her frenetic life inflicted on her occasionally unwilling physical resources. She barely ceased complaining of a bad pain in her arm, a result of her fall through the stage in Paris, when the Baron Denie received a letter about her most recent accident, perhaps a fall from a horse.

I just missed making a visit to the *ancestors of bouillon consommé*; but the devil said: "She is kind, she is unfortunate, she deserves to live." Vivat! He turned the path away from the bed, and death was nicely tricked; believing himself at my head, he found to his great astonishment that he was at my feet. That's how the old horned one spared me from eternity at one of the extremities of the other world.[18]

Her performances frequently mirrored her physical ailments, provoking comments such as one made by a critic after a concert: "Mad. Malibran appeared and pretended to sing, but she was not audible. If she were really *so* ill as she appeared to be, it was madness in her to come forward, and cruelty in those around her to permit her to do so."[19]

Appearing in *La Cenerentola* on June 15, she was obviously sick throughout the first act. When the curtain fell the manager announced that Mlle. Blasis, who had been noticed in a box seat, would take over the title role for the remainder of the performance, but just as the new Angelina prepared to step on stage, Maria suddenly declared herself recovered and insisted on continuing. "But how?," wondered an incredulous reviewer. "We sincerely advise this gifted young lady to be more careful of herself, and not to ruin her powers by overstraining them."[20]

The introduction of her Don Diego in the Mercadante work was postponed several times by illness, but her first portrayal of the part earned her the highest praise.

It showed in its full lustre a combination of vocal and dramatic perfection, of skill, deep feeling, acute and strong intellectual discernment which it is in the nature of human things to find but rarely in one individual. Madame Malibran, perhaps owing to a fluctuating state of health, is not always equal in her exertions; but there are fortunate moments of inspiration when she has it in her power to convince us that she stands aloof in her art, without the fear of any one rival. We refrain from entering upon a minute survey of Madame Malibran's representation of the part of Don Diego; the whole was a masterpiece from beginning to end. Her recitativo and aria at the first entry will forever remain indelibly imprinted on our memory; nothing we heard before made such a powerful impression on our mind, never did we witness deep pathos and unrivalled skill so happily blended and carried to so extraordinary a degree of perfection. Passages the most audaciously ventured, and for the success of which we sat in anxious suspense, came beautifully clear and finished upon our unaccustomed ear, and plunged us, and all the audience, in a trance of delight; they were not merely the vocal feats of mechanical dexterity, it was a Promethean fire, a sensitive soul breathing in every note.[21]

But the greatest acclaim of all went to her Desdemona, the part in which she had been found inferior to Pasta during the preceding summer. Her first performance of it was described as "magnificent in the extreme." "In point of vigor, and force, and variety, and the skillful union of dramatic and vocal excellence, this character will, we believe, rank pre-eminent amongst the representations hitherto given to us by Madame Malibran; and we are not sure that any of her predecessors in it have done it equal justice. The beauties of the performance studded it so thickly, and with such lustre, that we are almost dazzled to select any, and despair of being able to enumerate all." The critic praised her unique acting style, which was "more marked, but more controlled and judicious than formerly" and surrendered to the spell of her vocal artistry.

There is a wonderful beauty in the flow and undulation of her voice in ornamented passages which we do not know how to describe; it moves with the lightness of the feet of a greyhound gamboling on turf—and yet far more lightly, and with wider range, and a more elastic movement. It is rather like some happy bird floating at will in the air,—and carried here and there, higher and lower by the currents as they reach it, or now and then stretching out its wings and taking a vague but rapid flight with many turnings as it goes—rising and sinking and baffling the eye with its uncertain track. Others conform, or seem to conform, to a certain pattern or rule, whose directions may be at all times anticipated: Mad. Malibran darts away from all precedent and leading-strings, and surprises the ear with a combination of notes that seems new and untried; prompted by a similar character in the music that leads to it, and not otherwise to be accounted for than by giving her credit for an independence and originality which are almost the same as the creative faculty. Under this impression, we shall not be surprised if, at sometime hereafter, this very talented person becomes the chief of a new school—a revolutionist in style—which, whether for better or worse, will, at any rate, be her own.[22]

With the conclusion of Malibran's engagement at the end of July, the English sadly anticipated musical life without her. "Parting, even for a few months, is not such sweet sorrow when such a being is in question; for, with all her faults, we must love her still. Malibran is a genius, and has fallen into that error incident to almost every genius—extravagance; but we excuse the fault for the cause, and are better pleased to occasionally see the modesty of nature *overstepped* than that it should be totally *overlooked*. . . . She is an extraordinary woman; for to be a Malibran is not the lot of one out of every million vocal aspirants."[23]

Charles de Bériot, now in England, had been praised since mid-June almost as extravagantly as had Maria. "Paganini may do great things," asserted a reviewer, "but we would back de Bériot in *real* music against *him* or *any* one."[24] At the conclusion of her engagement with the King's Theatre, Maria and her lover traveled to Bath for a brief vacation in August. From Sidney's Hotel she wrote the Baron Denie, "I am very idle," assuring him, "I am now quite well. Bath agrees with me. I remain until the 25th of August. Thanks to my excellent and sincere friend Dr. B[elluomini], I am in a completely restored state of health. I now continually display, as you say, the pink and white in my complexion. You must love this man, who has saved my life as much by skill and promptitude as by *fatherly* kindness."[25]

Several armed conflicts among various powers occurred during the summer of 1830. All affected Maria Malibran. France and Algeria disputed the enormous debt incurred by the French in the Egyptian expedition. Hassein, the Dey of Algiers, impatient to receive his money, wrote the King of France, who replied, "The King of France holds no correspondence with the Dey of Algiers."[26] At this, the furious Dey declared war. Manuel Garcia, still wandering in pursuit of a profession, became a soldier, and Maria, through her influence with the Baron Denie, secured him a position in the military hospitals of the army. On May 11, 1830, he sailed for Algeria with the Baron. "Send me some little jewel, as big as a bedouin's head, or something like that to adorn my Seigneurie Malibranienne," wrote Maria gaily, confident of the safety of her brother and friend.[27]

The Revolution of 1830, which broke out in Paris in the last weeks of July, affected her more immediately. Because of acute and widespread economic depression, as well as quickening social change and popular unrest, such revolutions flared up easily. After three days of civil war the Bourbon King Charles X was driven from power and the Duke of Orleans assumed the throne under the name Louis Phillipe, making France a state in which the wealthier bourgeoisie exercised political power.

In the spring of 1830 Maria heard rumors about revolution. In early May she wrote a nervous letter to the Baron Denie expressing her fears and wondering whether she should remain in England, where a similar uprising might occur, or whether she should return to France. "Although I try to elevate my ideas, whether it be here or there—it's all the same thing to me— it doesn't rid me of my fears: thus I am careful," she told him.[28]

Once the revolution was over, however, she had no difficulty being a vicarious heroine, as she proudly professed to Ernest Legouvé.

Norwich, August 1830

I am happy, proud, vainglorious, vain totally, to belong to the French! You cry from having been away from home? There isn't a day that I haven't been grieving, me, a woman, not to have broken a leg in the melée of that golden age cause! Is it not the real golden age that revolted for liberty and to reject, at the same time, even the appearance of a usurpation of other people? I assure you in thinking of Paris I feel my mind elevated! Do you think that soldiers armed with guns would have been able to stop me from crying "Vive la liberté"? They tell me that everything is not yet peaceful in France. Write me about it; I will come! I want to share the fate of my brothers! Well ordained charity, they say, begins by itself. Well, others are my "by itself." Vive la France![29]

France's example inspired Belgium, long under the yoke of Dutch rule, to rebel against Holland, and on August 25 rioting broke out in Brussels. Troops sent in to restore order had little effect, and on October 4 Belgium declared its independence. This conflict ended Charles' title of Violinist to the Dutch King as well as the small pension it carried, but except for this minor loss neither he nor Maria suffered from these revolutions. Maria asked a friend to find them a house in Paris; henceforth they would have less reason to be apart, and, perhaps inspired by the revolutionary fervor sweeping Europe, less desire to hide their affair.

More than a year earlier it had been announced that as of October 1, 1830, Edouard Robert and Carlo Severini would become joint directors of the Théâtre-Italien. These gentlemen immediately set out to contract Maria Malibran, for the Vicomte de Laferté, a government official involved in underwriting the theaters, advised them that la Malibran intended to end her Paris engagement and travel to Italy. Severini informed the Vicomte that he would offer Maria exactly what Laurent was paying her, 1,000 francs per performance.

Meanwhile Robert, advised by Rossini, wrote to Severini from Bologna, "We must have her at the best price possible, and if that can't be, we'll have to give in to whatever she wants, otherwise we are ruined."[30] Severini did his best, but Malibran wanted 1,075 francs per performance, plus exclusive rights to most of the roles in her repertoire, and, in addition, she demanded that the theater supply her with costumes and props, a burden that always fell on the performer.

While Severini haggled over this "extravagant and unprecedented insolence," Robert wrote him impatiently, "Keep in mind, mon cher, that she is absolutely essential to us. Otherwise we are beat from our first year. . . . Try to tie this up with la Malibran. We absolutely must have her, and at whatever cost, for in the end she will do us three jobs, dramatic soprano, buffo, and contralto, and as for talent, you must get it into your head that she is unequaled in all the world."

Maria, with the Vicomte as intermediary, gave not an inch, and Robert wrote a despairing letter to the official, pointing out that his subsidy had been reduced 20,000 francs from the amount Laurent received, and that under the circumstances he could not afford to raise Malibran's salary. In fact, he told the Vicomte, he had originally planned to offer her 800 francs per performance, "a very considerable sum in itself, but more in harmony with my subsidy."

To Severini Robert wrote, "One may indeed haggle when one demands too much in such an indecent manner," reiterating, "We urgently need that rapacious blood-sucker to get through these hard times." But Maria merely pointed out that Italian engagements would give her more than she was asking in Paris, and Severini was forced to "drink hemlock." "You are right, of course," responded Robert, "they are as thick as thieves, but we must bend or be broken."

In the last week of October 1830, Maria returned to Paris for her new engagement with the Théâtre-Italien, to begin on November 6.

CHAPTER 10

Lafayette

For a few days the lovers were separated, Maria returning to Paris for her performances with the Italien, Charles traveling to Brussels to visit his sister Constance and to check on his property. His letter to Maria of November 1, 1830, indicates that they considered themselves partners in a marriage that lacked only legal sanction.

Ma chère Maria,

Last evening I was thinking of leaving by mail coach when I learned by newspaper from the Netherlands that the Dutch troops were bombarding Anvers and that the town was already in flames. The article in the journal added that the company of the Infantry of Chasteleer, in which Joseph de Franquen [Constance de Bériot's fiancé] is enlisted, was the first into the city. This bad news has thrown poor Constance into despair, and I can't think of leaving her. I prefer to wait for more reassuring news on the fate of our prospective brother-in-law. Today the journal gives some details on the ravages caused by the wretched, the vile, Dutch; it didn't say a word about the volunteers, which makes us hope that nothing has happened to Joseph. He is so well known that it would be mentioned if anything had happened to him. Constance is a little happier today and I hope that tomorrow I will be able to get on my way. I will not be far away when you get this letter, for it precedes me by only a few hours. To hold up my departure when I am anxious to rejoin my darling Marietta is without doubt the greatest proof of fraternal affection that I can give to my little sister. I am burning with impatience for some positive news from Anvers. Constance assures me that you would be upset with me should I abandon her in her state of suspense. Until tomorrow, my darling wife,

Ch. de Bériot[1]

Incapable of further hypocrisy and deceit, Maria finally ceased hiding her love affair; subterfuge had proved too uncomfortable for one so candid. With Baron Denie's help she and Charles rented a house on the Rue Blanche, but she soon found social opinion difficult to ignore. Many doors were slammed in her face and the slights she suffered for her breaking of the moral code deeply wounded her. Neither her old friend Mme. Naldi nor the Countess de Sparre would have anything to do with her, nor would many others of the aristocracy and the bourgeoisie with whom she had once ingratiated herself. Polite society found fault with her for being a mere actress, despite her refined manners, her talent, and her achievements. She was once more the opera singer, "the slave they pay to give them pleasure."

Her father turned against her, and coarse remarks from the pit made her resent her profession. Pretending to enjoy the soirées, she was painful to watch, and sympathetic individuals pitied her.

Maria began seeking a solution to her problem. Obviously Charles should become her legitimate husband, and she pursued this goal with the same zeal she brought to the stage. The outcome of her meeting with George Warrender and the English lawyers is not known, but in Paris she hired a staff of legal advisers to help her obtain a legal separation from Eugène Malibran, whether in France, which did not allow divorce, or in the United States. Her principal lawyers were Messieurs Cottinet, Plé, Marie, and Labois. There were doubtless others. The first three researched the French laws for a legal quirk that would dissolve her marriage, while Labois sought a solution in New York. Louis Viardot helped coordinate this legal staff.

Alarmed by gossip from the Chastelains, as well as by his wife's silence, Eugène Malibran arrived in Paris toward the end of November and went straight to the Rue Blanche to demand his rights as Maria Malibran's husband. The date and details of this confrontation are not known, but on December 2 Maria sent him a short note. "Since you have my happiness at heart, *leave at once*, or, if you remain, stay only for the purpose of consenting to the divorce, do you understand? It is the only way left for you to prove what you say. In regard to this I beg you to go to M. Labois, #40, rue Coquillière. *Tell him who you are*, he knows of my intentions. Consent and thereby find a little gratitude left in the heart of Maria (née) Garcia."[2]

Madame Merlin believed that Maria had paid Eugène a substantial sum of money not to live with her,[3] an agreement that, as Maria well knew, would not have been legally binding. This arrangement seems unlikely, but Maria no doubt considered such a move, and many others as well.

Her legal staff was not initially encouraging. The French courts refused to judge formalities contracted in America, and American authorities declared themselves unable to rule on a marriage that had been conducted before a French consul.[4] While her lawyers mulled over this impasse, Maria sought more potent aid. In late November she was introduced at Court to General Lafayette, one of France's most venerated heroes, powerful in the Chamber of Deputies as well as the entire French government, and seizing this opportunity she wrote to the General. Her letter has an evenness of composition unlike the impulsive scribblings she dashed off to her friends, and several drafts probably preceded the final communication Lafayette received. Similarly, her handwriting, often a mad scrawl of misspellings and canceled words, is elegant and unusually graceful.

November 27, 1830
Rue Blanche no. 28

Monsieur le Général,

Having had the honor of being presented to you at Court, I dare to hope that you would be willing to pardon the indiscretion that I take in asking you to have the extreme goodness to give me a word of recommendation for the person here responsible for the affairs of the Government of the United States, and from whom I would desire to obtain some information on some affairs that I have in New York and which are of the greatest concern to me.

I would fear, Monsieur le Général, to involve you with a matter of such little importance in the midst of the great matters that occupy you, if I didn't know that without any hope of glory you like to concern yourself with the happiness of each individual, after having assured that of an entire nation.

M. F. Malibran[5]

Her letter succeeded beyond her wildest hopes.

To Madame Malibran
Rue Blanche No. 28, Paris
Tuesday, November 30, 1830
Permit me, Madame, to offer you my thanks for the kindness you have to address yourself to me; but the proof of your goodwill encourages me to ask of you another favor; that is to please make me responsible for your American affairs if I can be of any help in them. I have a great desire to do my part before contacting my friend, Mr. Rives, the United States ambassador, for his help. My duties ordinarily keep me busy here until eleven or twelve o'clock. Thursday I have to go to the town hall to receive an Irish deputation at noon. But if tomorrow, Friday, or Sunday is convenient for you, I should have the honor to come to your house, or I will wait for you here, rue de Montblanc, between twelve and one o'clock. I would be happy to receive your instructions and renew for you the expression of the feelings which have made me attach a great value to the occasion, long desired, of meeting you. Please accept my sincere respect.

Lafayette[6]

Thus began an affectionate, almost father to daughter, relationship, which would continue until Lafayette's death. "Maria Garcia is my last love; I don't think anyone will supplant her," he laughingly told Mme. Merlin.[7] Maria answered him the same day.

What have I done, then, mon Général, to deserve so great a sign of your goodwill! My happiness overflows—I had not, in the beginning, addressed myself to you for you to concern yourself with the affairs which occupy me, but then, with that angelic goodness which characterizes you, you put me in a position to chat with you. I will come tomorrow to see you before eleven o'clock to thank you a thousand and a thousand times for this sign of interest which I have no right to expect, and to explain to you in a few words what is involved.

You may be convinced, mon Général, that my appreciation is boundless, and that this favor will be eternally written in the heart of

M. F. Malibran[8]

Despite his duties with the Chamber of Deputies, Lafayette gave Maria his greatest attention. "I am doubly happy with your trust and with your friendship," he told her. "You will find everywhere worthy admirers of your incomparable talents and excellent qualities, but you will rarely find a friend who appreciates you as much, who sympathizes as completely with you, as your old and no less affectionate tutor."[9]

Henceforth they addressed each other as "tutor" and "pupil," nomenclature that Lafayette introduced and which Maria quickly adopted. On Sunday, December 5, he reminded her that they were to meet with the ambassador, Mr. Rives, who had offered to help the General in any way he could. The interview was arranged for three rather than noon as originally planned, because another of Maria's recurrent illnesses had brought out an affectionate concern in the old General for his new "pupil." "I saw last night that you were unwell," he wrote to her. "I was even told the sad cause of your suffering. Surely you don't doubt the affectionate sympathy that I feel for your misfortune. There was something instinctive in my first feelings of concern for you, but now that I know you, chère Madame, I can't explain all the affection that you inspire in me, and how happy I would be to provide some consolation or some remedy for your sorrows. You were kind enough to choose me for your tutor; I beg my dear pupil to accept my affectionate friendship."[10]

Meetings and interviews followed. A conference with the French barrister de la Grange, the barrister most informed in American law, yielded valuable new knowledge. "The details of our meeting give me hope," wrote the General to Maria, "but for the divorce it is necessary that your husband consent to be unfaithful; abandoning without notice would be a cause; also the rite of marriage without parental consent. I don't see that that applies in your case."[11]

Leaving no avenue unexplored, he took a group of Americans, including James Fenimore Cooper, to the opera. He knew that Cooper was from New York, but the author had little advice to give. Lafayette reported, "There is a motive for divorce which is something unto itself, but which is not for your use, my dear young friend, even as supposition." Maria could only reiterate her gratitude with the wry comment: "While awaiting another name, I am, always, Malibran."[12]

With no intention of committing adultery for the purpose of a divorce, Eugène Malibran expressed his desire for a reconciliation when he met with the General in December. Undaunted, Lafayette prepared a long letter for the stubborn husband, attempting to persuade him that a reconciliation was impossible and that he had nothing further to lose by consenting to a divorce. First, however, he sent it to Maria for her approval, and at the same time he gave her some cogent advice.

> Paris, January 1, 1831
>
> I wish you a happy new year, my dear pupil, and I am sending you my letter to your husband who can't be treated as nimbly by me as by you. He seems to me to have asked his questions very flatly. Yesterday you found me more preacher than tutor. The fact is that you have inspired in me an indefinable sentiment and concern which would be almost the same, I think, were you without beauty and talent. Don't surrender yourself, dear pupil, to the vivacity of your imagination. It could be a bad adviser. You have given me all your confidences, even the least reasonable. I do not ask that you follow my advice, but to consult me before making up your mind what you want to do. We will see how M.

Malibran will respond. Send my letter back to me. My dear pupil will permit
me to embrace her here with all my heart.

Lafayette

It is superfluous to tell you that the preliminary communication of this letter
ought to stay a secret between you and me.[13]

In the letter for Eugène the General spoke gallantly, if untruthfully, of
Maria's "pure conduct" and "presently untouched virtue," as well as
Eugène's "still unsullied name." He presented three alternative courses of
action: a reconciliation, a separation of properties, and a divorce, attempting to convince Eugène that divorce was the only practical option. At the
same time he tried to gain Eugène's trust by appearing not to take sides.

You know the character of my new pupil, and whatever may be her affection
and deference for me, you know that her passions are lively and her wishes
strong.
    Her very first emotion on entering my house was the fear of encountering
you there, and then, after having heard everything that I could tell her about
your desire for a reconciliation and the reasons she would have in order to
consent to it, her refusal was so pre-emptory that no chance remained for me to
use my influence, and I would lose it uselessly for you if I attempted to argue
with her. If some means remains to me to serve both of you, it would be because
of some change in the situation. . . . I don't know what legal recourse would be
necessary for you, but in struggling thus with such a strong minded woman, you
risk embarrassment for yourself and great ill for her.

And he mentioned the separation of properties, for Eugène had legal
claim to all her belongings, her fortune, and whatever money she would
earn at the theater. This, contended the general, would be a "wiser path"
than the pursuit of a reconciliation, but even better was a divorce, "which
would be on your part a generous action that public opinion would
appreciate" and which "gives you the merit of a noble sacrifice without
depriving yourself of any real happiness, since I have been told emphatically that a reconciliation is absolutely impossible." And he expressed
his belief that if both parties consented to a divorce, some legal means to
obtain it could be found.
    In conclusion Lafayette assured Eugène, "I will speak with you about
this as much as you want; her resistance on the point under consideration
seems to me invincible, at least for me; for other plans it would be possible
for me to serve you both. I wish it with all my heart."[14]
    This masterpiece of diplomacy did not weaken Eugène's resolution,
and on January 11, after having met with him again, Lafayette was obliged
to tell Maria, "Your husband has come to see me to signify that he will not
consent to the divorce. I begged him to reflect on that some more." But all
was useless. Eugène Malibran would not be an infidel in order to give his
wife grounds for divorce and told Lafayette so flatly. His only concession
was a willingness to live with her platonically.[15]
    Lafayette now intended to push a divorce law through the Chamber of

Deputies and to hope for ratification by the Chamber of Peers. "So long as all this isn't finished, I shan't exist,"[16] Maria told him. Reading Victor Hugo's "Esmeralda," she was struck with the description of the heroine's being taken from the poet Pierre Gringoire "not innocent, but pure," and thereafter she compared Esmeralda's marriage to her own.[17]

On November 6 la Malibran reappeared at the Italien as Desdemona. The next day *Le Figaro* proclaimed her "The première lyric tragedienne of the universe," adding, "We pity the dilettanti who were not present on this remarkable evening." Tickets were sold at top prices, the theater doors were scenes of mob disorder until they were opened, the seats were taken "by assault,"[18] and the theater was filled more than an hour before curtain time. The critics found her vocal powers improved, especially in the contralto register, which had gained in fullness and freedom. Her soprano voice was as sonorous as formerly, but on sustained high notes it seemed occasionally to reveal an incipient tremolo that she cleverly countered with successive accents.[19]

An unhappy private life seemed to inspire her to express the impossible in dramatic and musical emotion. More than ever she pushed herself to the limit, bringing the operatic art to unparalleled heights. "Her talent has acquired all its power, and despite her youth, one can say that in her the admirable virtuoso, the great actress, the compelling woman, are completely matured," wrote a reviewer. "The critics blame her, not too unjustly, of exaggerating her acting, but on the stage she seduces, she fascinates, she captivates even those who reproach her for this after the curtain has fallen."[20] Obviously she could not long perform at this level, and an observer commented, "As the riches dissipate she is prodigious with the treasures that she could have saved for the future. We might as well enjoy her largesse now; she alone will regret it later."[21]

No matter how many times Maria repeated her roles, the opera lovers of Paris came out to hear them again. Her *Cenerentola* earned special praise from a reviewer who noted that "in the aria di bravura which terminates the opera she reminded us of Mlle Sontag by the prodigious flexibility of her voice, and surpassed her, if we dare say so, by the grace and the exquisite taste which characterized all her embellishments."[22]

On November 30, the day Maria received Lafayette's first letter, her Ninetta was so inspired that Fétis wrote:

Perfection is rare: one could say that it has been encountered in the performance of *La Gazza Ladra* which was given November 30. The role of Ninetta is one of those that Mme Malibran acts and sings the best. Her entrancing verve, her prodigious facility of improvisation, and that nervous caprice which form the principal characteristics of her talent reached their highest point of development in this role; but never did these qualities produce more of an effect than in the performance in question, even though her voice appeared to be touched by the beginnings of a light cold. The enthusiasm of the public could not be contained after the curtain was lowered, and the admirable singer was obliged to come forward again to the cries of the audience.[23]

In the three years since her first appearance in Paris, Maria had progressed from being a captivating new singer, to a rival of the established favorites, to an incomparable performer in her own right, and she was now beyond mere success. Even while she continued to appear on the familiar stages of Paris and London, she became legendary as a leader of "the romantic age." Witnessing one of her performances, George Sand wrote, "I have seen Madame Malibran in *Otello*. She made me weep, shudder, in a word, suffer as if I were present at a real-life scene. This woman is the première genius of Europe, beautiful as one of Raphael's virgins, simple, energetic, naive, she is the foremost singer and the foremost tragedienne. I'm crazy about her."[24] Sand also wrote, "The curtain falls, the illusion is destroyed, but the deathly impression lingers. The heart-rending voice of Malibran and Otello's dagger follow you long after you have left the theater."[25]*

A German writer who saw la Malibran perform this winter sent home a description of her effect on the public, an effect that was nothing if not supernatural.

What wouldn't you have felt if you had heard la Malibran? It seemed my heart had been changed into a harp on which the angels were playing. My ears were listening from within it. . . . I hung onto the earthly note with real anxiety so as not to be spirited away by these ethereal sounds. God has given Malibran his signed blue-print, no one can imitate it. It was like a countryside flowered with every human emotion: tenderness, pride, calm, heroism, sweetness and bitterness, with a profusion of colors. . . . She didn't sing only with her mouth. Every limb of her body sang. The sounds shot out in sparks from her eyes, from her fingers: they streamed from her hair. She was singing even when mute.[26]

As a fixture of French culture, Maria was being immortalized in literature, appearing as herself in various novels.[27] But her fame had spread well beyond European borders. Two young Indian chiefs of the Ouwothiees tribe traveled to Paris from Baltimore to see "the better of the republics," and in particular its two most famous citizens: General Lafayette and Maria Malibran.[28]

She attracted individuals and organizations eager to take advantage of her fame. The Saint-Simoniens, for example, spread the word that Maria Malibran was one of their followers, which she refuted in a letter to a journalist: "It is of great concern to me to deny these rumors, which are completely false."[29]

Unimpressed by all this attention, Maria reflected, "If life is not a crime, it is at least an expiation."[30] In the throes of one of her depressions she wrote to Ernest Legouvé:

---

*According to Curtis Cate in *George Sand*, pp. 505-6, Malibran was the inspiration for *Rose et Blanche* and *La Prima Donna*, Sand's first published works.

April 1831

How many women envy me! What do they envy me for? It is this unfortunate happiness. Do you understand? My happiness is Juliet! It is dead like her, and me, I am Romeo, I mourn it. I have in my soul a stream of tears whose source is innocent; they will water the flowers of my tomb when I am no longer of this earth. Perhaps the next world will give me recompense up there! Let's get rid of lugubrious ideas! At this moment they are cadaverous. . . . Death is at the head of them, soon at mine. . . . Pardon me, I digress; I am weeping and it relieves me to make you a recipient of my most secret thoughts. . . . You don't hold it against me? No, you can't. Come tell me yourself that you sympathize with me. Come right away,—We will chat, we will be in the other world. I will close my door to this one.[31]

"She always said that she would die young," wrote Legouvé in his memoirs. "Sometimes, as if she had felt all at once I don't know what cold breath, as if the shadow of the other world had fallen across her imagination, she would fall into frightful fits of melancholy, and her heart would be plunged into a deluge of tears."[32]

Wondering whether she would ever free herself of Eugène Malibran made Maria miserable. To escape her morbid thoughts she kept up a frantic pace that made her more vulnerable to illness. Forced to cancel appearances, she ruminated on her situation even more, with the additional disadvantage of sickness. In this vicious cycle, spurred on by unhappiness and thoughts of death, she raced onward in a pathetic attempt to outrun the fate she never doubted. Her reliance on Madeira led to rumors that she was a drunk, gossip that infuriated her, and against which her friends invariably defended her.

Occasionally this and other stimulants, combined with her natural energies, made her impossible to control as she jumped over the furniture and tried out gymnastic and balancing acts. Worried friends attempting to calm her would be told, "You don't know my nature. I can't make up my mind to rest, it must come from fatigue. I can't economize my energies, I have to use my life as much as I have the faculty for it, otherwise it would suffocate me."[33] At other times her exuberance for life, her effervescence, natural or induced, would vanish for a few days and give way to calm and silence. Then she could sit for hours, gazing into space. Legouvé described these states as "demi-sleep." Her imagination lay dormant until some circumstance, not always apparent to others, would wake her, and with the abruptness of a thunderclap her enthusiasm would return.[34]

The directors of the Italien, plagued by her frequent cancellations, reprimanded her for not taking greater care of her health. She took no heed. Severini had no doubt come to dread the sight of an envelope bearing Malibran's handwriting, which could only mean that she was once again going to substitute Rosina, not a taxing part, for whatever work had been scheduled. On one occasion there was no substitution at all.

Neither I nor my work are anything, with or without the least comparison to the immense eternity of our God! However, absolute God that he is, he needed a day of rest after six days of creation. I have worked, I have created, only for one miserable day, and while you may very well think so, one day does not suffice to rest me. I am not like Penelope, I can't in one day throw off the fatigue of the preceding day. I am even the complete opposite: the preceding day I am not sick, but the day after I am exceedingly so. In returning home yesterday evening, I was very sick. Today I can hardly move, or, to say it better, I am stiff in every joint. It took me all the trouble in the world to scribble these few words.

Therefore, my dear Severini, no Malibran at all tomorrow. I can't even play Rosina!!!

Have pity on the poor cripple!
Wednesday Evening.[35]

If Severini pitied anyone, he pitied himself.

One evening she had promised Mme. Merlin to sing at a party, when Robert approached her about a benefit scheduled for that night at which she was expected to appear. An argument ensued and management won. "Very well," acquiesced the disgruntled singer. "I will sing at the theater because I have to, but I will sing at Mme. Merlin's because I want to." She kept her word. After singing Tancredi she arrived at the party, sang several songs for the guests, and partied until dawn. Returning home she slept until noon, rode horseback all afternoon, and appeared at the theater again that evening. No sooner was she in costume as Arsace than she fainted from exhaustion. The Italien panicked for nothing revived her. Finally Robert, both furious and frantic, applied ammonia to her lips, and she regained consciousness, but her mouth was badly blistered. With the audience waiting, it was too late to change the program. Rising from her couch Maria examined the damage in her mirror, "Don't worry," she said calmly. "I'll fix this." Picking up a pair of scissors she carefully broke the blisters and cut away the dead skin. A few moments later she was onstage, singing Arsace to Lalande's Semiramide.[36]

Although it was rumored at the close of every season that she had accepted an Italian engagement for the following year, Maria, who annually announced she would take the summer off and never did, turned down all contracts, and at the conclusion of her engagement she left with Charles for a vacation at the de Bériot home in Brussels. The newspapers, which had noted her chronic illnesses, as well as the change in her voice toward the end of the season, feared "the blade is wearing out the scabbard" and earnestly hoped she would carry out her intention.[37] A journalist admonished her, "If art has its inspiration, and if brilliant success has an ineffable charm, nature has severe laws, and one must obey them."[38]

The trip to Brussels was not without incident. In a letter to Virginia Cottinet Maria wrote,

Namur [May] 1831
My good friends, we have been here since yesterday. Finding a red-hot bullet in your soup would not be more astonishing than our presence here. The trip is going wonderfully, we are almost always on the forward seat, both very happy.

But do you know that there is a revolution in Brussels? At this moment they are giving the alarm here, we hear the gun shots. Adieu.

On Monday, May 23, she described the minor skirmish that had kept them up until three o'clock in the morning and which was still in progress. "The volunteers behaved like cowards; some of them were crying! . . . What men! As for me, I hadn't a shadow of fear. The first thing that I did was to get two pistols. I imagined that they would come to attack Charles."[39]

This time Maria took a vacation; she and Charles spent their summer and fall far from the public eye overseeing the building of a magnificent new mansion in Ixelles,* just outside Brussels. But the restful summer led to complications; Maria became pregnant. Having once relished Henriette Sontag's predicament, she now faced the same trials herself, and she would suffer no less.

With the advent of autumn and the commencement of the opera season, she considered not returning to Paris, where her condition would certainly be discovered. She wrote Severini a letter explaining that for reasons of health she would not be able to perform for an unspecified duration of time.[40] The directors were dismayed at this news; they had no replacement for her nor did they have a prospect of one. Pasta had been reengaged at the theater, but her stay would be short. Wilhelmine Schröder-Devrient and Maria Caradori-Allan would also sing in Paris, but they did not have Malibran's appeal. In a desperate move they summoned Louis Viardot, who journeyed to Brussels to reason with their recalcitrant prima donna. At first she did not give in, but a compromise was finally reached. She would return to the Théâtre-Italien at a fee of 1,250 francs per performance on condition that she be allowed to leave before the end of the season.

She expressed her black mood in a letter (written in English) to Sir George Smart, the English conductor with whom she had become friendly on her many tours of the English music festivals.

October 15, 1831

Dear Sir George Smart—You are good, I know it & therefore dont tremble before you as I ought, if I were to remember that I have not written to you as I said I would—You know, or you dont know perhaps, what have been my misfortunes ever since I have left London—they have broken my head, and worried me so, that I would have given my existence for a pin, or nothing—It has made me forguet every thing on earth—Things dont go much better now, and I am not a bit calmer than I was—Dont be angry therefore, & be enough my friend to take all my troubles into consideration, & to pity and pardon me for this kind of negligeance that has made me silent so long—

I had however thought a great deal of you and had ready for you a letter with a little snuff box, very simple but nicely made, and opening curiously—I

---

*Around the turn of the century this elegant home had been turned into a hotel and a nearby street was named for Malibran. Now it is the town hall of Ixelles, and in it hangs a portrait of the singer.

have got it still, & I shall do my self the pleasure of sending it to you by the first opportunity—I know you [are] too much my friend to refuse such a trifle—it is unworthy of your merits, but the intention is good for it is a very little souvenir—God bless you my good Sir George Smart believe me your sincere friend Malibran. . . . Write to me at Brussels, No. 4—Rue Leopold.[41]

In the two and one-half months she remained at the Italien, Maria attempted only one new role, an unfortunate but precedented stunt and the only personal failure of her career. On November 20 she, like Pasta before her, played Otello in Rossini's opera. When Pasta essayed this part, in London in 1829, a performance Maria may have seen, the opera had been shortened by omitting the first act. With her ever-competitive spirit, Maria chose to perform all three, although with cuts and numerous transpositions. Not one reviewer was impressed, and not even the audience appeared interested in this unusual attempt at versatility. Malibran was considered less masculine than Pasta had been as the Moor, and the whole performance was pronounced "ridiculous."[42]

Frédéric Chopin, a habitué of the Italien this winter, offered his opinion of the performance, and of others he had seen. He wrote enthusiastically to a friend:

But I haven't mentioned the opera yet. Never have I heard the *Barbiere* as last week with Lablache, Rubini, and Malibran. . . . Malibran impresses you merely by her marvelous voice, but no one *sings* like her. Miraculous! Marvelous! Rubini is an excellent tenor. He sings true notes, never falsetto, and sometimes his ornamental runs go on for hours. . . .

Schröder-Devrient is here—but she's not such a sensation as in Germany. La Malibran played Othello and she was Desdemona. Malibran is small while the German lady is huge—it looked as if *she* would smother Othello! This was an expensive performance—all seats cost twenty-four francs—to see Malibran with a black face and not very good in the part.[43]

Two days later, in another letter, he spoke of the wonderful operatic productions being presented in Paris. "Briefly, it is only here that one can fully realize what singing is. Today, unquestionably, it is not Pasta but Malibran who is the leading European prima donna. She is fabulous!"[44]

Behind the scenes all was not well. Maria postponed some performances, canceled others only to show up at the last minute, and kept both the theater management and the public in suspense. Her strange behavior attributed to temperament, she lost some of her popularity, especially with ticket holders who expected la Malibran and found instead another performer or even another opera. And her pregnancy affected the luster of her voice in the upper register, while her breathing became shorter.

On some occasions she made extraordinary efforts to fulfill her engagements lest a cancellation lead to more gossip. On January 8, 1832, she and de Bériot, who was having a brilliant season, appeared together in concert despite a terrible cold that nearly ruined her performance. A music reviewer left an account of the event:

Mme Malibran was suffering badly, horribly choked up with a cold. The phrases of the recitative in her aria were coupled with fits of the most violent coughing to the point of making us think she would not be able to continue. There was throughout the hall a feeling of indescribable suffering and sympathy, but despite the grave deterioration of her voice, Mme Malibran was able to make those who heard it forget her suffering. At each phrase of song, pity gave way to admiration, while at each pause, the sickness took the upper hand and compassion was reborn. That alternation of anguish and pleasure lasted as long as Mme Malibran was before the audience. It was one of those victories that only a great artist can carry off, but which are fatal to those who triumph. Certainly for my part it convinced me more than ever that Mme Malibran is the first singer of our age, but Mme Malibran ought not to buy glory by perhaps ruining and sacrificing her future.[45]

To be helpful, some of Maria's friends suggested that she reconcile with her husband, thus legitimizing her unborn child and avoiding further disgrace. She refused vehemently. "Never! I'd rather confess my dishonor and suffer for it."[46] But she hoped not to suffer much longer: with Lafayette's influence the Chamber of Deputies passed a bill in favor of reestablishing a divorce law in France and sent it to the Chamber of Peers for ratification. In a surge of hope she wrote to Labois with new instructions: "Do you know, mon cher, that I see myself forced to drop your magnificent law suit against that bear M . . . ? I must put all my hope in that divorce law which, they say, or which (says General Laf . . .) is going to pass immediately, since the difficulties are infinite for our first plan, and since, in addition, the means to obtain the same result in New-York are almost impossible."[47]

Maria's last performance took place on Friday, January 20, 1832, as Desdemona. Excitement was at a high pitch, and rallying to the occasion she gave the Parisians a last glorious opportunity to experience her art. This performance was perhaps the one witnessed by the American writer and traveler Nathaniel Willis, who had heard her sing in America and who now compared la Malibran to the Maria Garcia New York had known.

Madame Malibran is in every way changed. She sings, unquestionably, better than when in America. Her voice is firmer, and more under control, but it has lost that gushing wildness, that brilliant daringness of execution that made her singing upon our boards so indescribably exciting and delightful. . . . Her acting was extremely impassioned; and in the more powerful passages of her part she exceeded everything I had conceived of the capacity of the human voice for pathos and melody.

Although he found her art improved, Willis was shocked by the state of her health.

The round, graceful fullness of her limbs and features has yielded to a half-haggard look of care and exhaustion, and I could not but think that there was more than Desdemona's fictitious wretchedness in the expression of her face. Still, her forehead and eyes have a beauty that is not readily lost, and she will be a strikingly interesting and even splendid creature as long as she can play. . . . She is just now in a state of health that will require immediate retirement from the stage, and indeed, has played already too long. She came forward after the curtain dropped in answer to the continual demand of the audience, leaning heavily on Rubini, and was evidently so exhausted as to be scarcely able to stand. She made a single gesture and was led off immediately, with her head drooping on her breast, amid the most violent acclamations.[48]

Her performance also affected those accustomed to seeing her frequently in all her roles. "We are happy to express to Mme Malibran all our admiration for the talent she deployed," wrote Fétis.

She has regained all her powers, the alteration of which has been noticeable for several months. Her voice was clear. Daring, genius, astonishing fecundity of imagination, surety of execution, all the brilliant qualities to which we have so often paid homage we found again this time, and she moved us to the highest degree. We cried with her tears; her melancholy made us grieve; we were surprised to find ourselves bursting with joy at her sudden joys; all her emotions were ours; and when the curtain fell between us to separate us, perhaps for a long time, we felt a great affliction.[49]

But Paris would never again hear la Malibran.

CHAPTER 11

Italy

Within hours of her final performance, Maria fled Paris and France. Accompanied only by a servant she traveled by coach to Brussels but remained there only a few hours. In disguise, she returned to Paris and a rented house at the end of the Rue des Martyrs—a name that could not have escaped her wry humor—where she and Charles awaited the birth of their child. She wrote to Constance de Bériot of this interlude.

I can't tell you what an angel Charles is. He is kind enough to say that he likes it here, that he isn't bored, and even that he would live here with me for the rest of his life! You know how I try to read his heart; he must mean what he says though, because for four or five days, you have no idea of the delightful things that come out of that head of his, put together like those that God wanted to endow with every excellent quality. We haven't had the tiniest argument; the most perfect harmony reigns between us and I must tell you that this kind of daily routine is not at all boring. On the contrary. . . . Goodby little angel, you know how much I love you.[1]

Meanwhile the Théâtre-Italien, loath to admit Malibran was not singing, continued to announce her name in a variety of operas. She occasionally ventured out from the Rue des Martyrs, and on January 31 she was seen in the box of the Dey of Algiers at a meeting of the Chamber of Deputies. At the news of her presence all legislative eyes turned toward her. "It was almost a feature of the debate," commented a journalist.[2]

Her happiness ended when her baby girl died almost immediately after birth. Sadly the couple returned to Belgium.

Although she had vowed never to sing in Paris again until she was Madame de Bériot, Maria's pledge would have meant virtual retirement from the Italien because of the machinations of the French judicial process. By the second half of February offers from the theater were coming through that always helpful diplomat Louis Viardot, and Charles negotiated for a reengagement. In a letter dated February 24, 1832, he explained to Viardot that Maria would contract herself for the entire month of April at a fee of 1,500 francs per performance.[3]

By this time Maria had made at least one tentative step toward resuming her career; on February 21 she appeared with Charles at a concert given before Leopold I of Belgium. But she apparently was in no hurry to return to the stage. Her zest for life, and for the frantic pace of Paris, had abated, and she drifted into one of her "demi-sleeps." She seems not to have minded when plans to return to Paris were ended by the outbreak of cholera in France and the inauguration of quarantines between the two countries.

The virulent outbreak resulted from unusually warm weather conditions that favored the spread of the bacillus, and in three months 20,000 people died in Paris. At first the disease was confined mostly to the lower classes, and the wealthy did not immediately face the imminent horror. Expensive entertainments, not frequented by the poor in the healthiest of times, continued unabated. At a masked ball in the Théâtre des Variétés a crowd estimated at 2,000 people in costumes and fancy dress mocked the disease with a cholera-waltz and a cholera-galopade, and an immensely tall man costumed as The Cholera himself, with skeleton armor, bloodshot eyes, and other symptoms of the pestilence, was the evening's most spectacular success.

But by Mardi-Gras the epidemic had touched nearly every family in the city, even the Royal Palace, and all who could fled to the country. A visitor to the Hôtel Dieu, a hospital that stood in the shadow of Nôtre Dame, described a patient. A litter carried into the hospital, when uncovered, revealed "a young woman of apparently twenty-five, absolutely convulsed with agony. Her eyes were started from their sockets, her mouth foamed, and her face was of a frightful, livid, purple. I never saw so horrible a sight. She had been taken in perfect health only three hours before, but her features looked to me marked with a year of pain. The first attempt to lift her produced violent vomiting, and I thought she must die instantly."[4]

Maria and Charles were safer in Brussels, which had not yet been infected. Occasionally a concert diverted their routine. One given at the Théâtre de la Monnaie on March 24, in which they both performed, earned Maria praise from a Belgian reviewer who wrote, "If one hadn't heard la Malibran, he couldn't possibly imagine all the marvels of her voice, so full, so deep, so imposing, and all at once so sweet, flexible and flute-like."[5]

Toward the end of May, Luigi Lablache left London and traveled south for engagements in Italy. On his way he visited the de Bériot mansion for an evening. Delighted to see him, Maria and Charles begged him to spend more time with them, even though it was eight in the evening. He explained that he would be rising at dawn to continue his journey to Italy and so could not visit longer.

This venture excited Maria, and in an instant her dormant imagination awoke as she remembered all the engagements offered her by Italian impresarios. So far she had triumphed only in France and England, cultured lands to be sure, but the home of Italian opera was Italy. What successes lay before her in that country, known to be far more demonstrative and enthusiastic than any of its northern neighbors! "We're going with you!," she announced, at once forgetting her plans for a tour of Germany. Lablache, knowing that the two could not possibly make the necessary arrangements for such a trip on a mere evening's notice, told them they would have to be at his hotel by six in the morning.

The next morning at five he was awakened by the sound of horses and a carriage beneath his room. Thinking his own gear was being readied and annoyed at having overslept, he jumped out of bed and threw open the window. There were Maria and Charles. In half an hour the party was on its way to Italy, across France and through Switzerland, but in their haste neither Maria nor Charles had stopped to think about passports, and when they reached Chiavenna on the Italian border only Lablache had the necessary documents. No amount of arguing convinced the border police, and three days passed before the entry permits were granted.[6] On June 5 the travelers arrived in Bologna, and on the following day they left for Rome.[7]

For years the management of the Théâtre-Italien had lived in fear that Malibran would desert Paris for Italy. Every season closed with the rumor that she had accepted an Italian engagement. Through a letter to the Vicomte de Laferté in 1829, Robert attempted to discourage her from such an undertaking. "Heaven preserve her from the theaters of La Scala or San Carlo," he cried.

One must sing six times a week, four times at the very least, in addition to the rehearsals that take place on the very day that one sings. . . . If you could see how harsh the conditions of engagement are! And in those vast halls one can't sing but must scream at the top of his voice. . . . They only applaud screaming there. . . . What would become of our dear Madame Malibran in those theaters, and with a public so barbarous and vandalous! With her energy and burning soul she would have ruined her throat in no time, and her powers could not withstand such fatigue. . . .

"It is in her own best interest that I speak thus," Robert told the Vicomte, "so that she may conserve the power to finish out the brilliant career that she has begun so well."[8] And yet, in spite of the kernel of truth in his allegations, that brilliant career was barely a prelude to what awaited Maria in Italy.

At the news of Malibran's arrival, Italian impresarios rushed to secure her services, offering her enormous fees, sums greater than any artist had ever received there, as much as the equivalent of 4,000 French francs per performance. For this amount, in advance payment, she accepted an engagement with Giovanni Paterni of the Teatro Valle in Rome for twelve performances beginning June 30. "Soon a city will be offered for a cavatina and a province for a rondo," joked a journalist.[9] She was first seen in Rome on June 11, when, with Charles and Lablache, she attended the opera.[10]

As she was rehearsing the role of Desdemona for her Italian debut, Maria learned of her father's death on June 9 in Paris. Despite the constant friction between them, the news was a terrible blow; she felt real affection for him and never forgot that it was he who had developed her talents. In her grief she even forgave his brutal treatment of her as a child. "If my father had not been so severe with me I would not have done anything well," she admitted. "I was lazy and stubborn—a real gypsy."[11]

In a letter to Louis Viardot she poured out her anguish.

> [Rome, 45 Piazza della
> Minerva]
> June 21, 1832
>
> If only the cholera or the revolution had carried off *the other one* [Eugène Malibran]. . . . Tell me I don't have to weep for the death of my poor father. . . . I await news from you as one in convulsions who has not ceased crying waits for a little relief from her sorrows. I am not able to break an engagement I made here to play one month three times a week, twelve days. The director has undertaken great expense, the costumes are done, and the sets too, and he has engaged several people for all this. You know my heart, do not blame me. The day after St. Peter's day I debut in *Otello*. The company is bad.
>
> Embrace for us my mother, my sister, my brother, and. . . . It isn't possible, the newspapers have lied! You should be able to embrace him for me!![12]

Alarmed at Maria's grief, her mother, as she had once written to the Baron Denie, now wrote to Lafayette, "Console my poor daughter, I beg of you."[13]

The "Old Lion" was given a magnificent funeral in Paris, attended by the greatest artists of the day, but neither Maria nor Manuel was present. Fétis and Castil-Blaze read eulogies, and Garcia's many musical accomplishments were enumerated. "Console yourself, Garcia," concluded Castil-Blaze. "Immortality is promised you."[14]

Maria continued preparing for her appearances at the Teatro Valle, which were to be followed by engagements in Bologna and Milan. The Rome company was not, as she had indicated, bad, but there were censorship problems because of the Austrian occupation of Rome. The censors wanted to remove from *Otello* lines that might inflame a large crowd, such as the passage "Ti maledico" ["I curse you"], sung by Desdemona's father. Maria refused to sing the incomplete opera, and the pressure of public enthusiasm forced the censors to give in, lest a greater disaster ensue.[15]

Reports about the success of her first performance on June 30 differ. Supposedly the public disapproved of quadrupled prices, and the commoner King of Rome hissed Maria while applauding a "detestable" tenor.[16] But Italy's leading music journal indicated otherwise in its review, finding her "an outstanding actress and singer."[17] On July 11 she sang her first *Barbiere* at the Valle, and the audience applauded until the lesson scene, in which she had inserted a French song, "Bonheur de te revoir." The Italians expressed nothing but scorn for this piece: the "ah! ah! ah!" of the final passage reduced the audience to hilarity and cries of "ah! ah! ah!" echoed from the pit. Bravos followed her return to Rossini's music.[18]

But neither Maria nor Charles enjoyed their sojourn in the eternal city. Depressed since the death of her father, Maria was touched neither by the applause of the Roman public nor by the interest of the ancient ruins. She visited the Roman Forum and saw the heaps of soil and broken pillars resulting from recent excavations. The triumphal arches of Septimius Severus and Titus, the three lonely columns marking the remains of the temple of Jupiter, the ivied skeletons of Caesar's palaces—all left her more downcast than ever. Nothing built by human toil endured, no matter how great or beautiful. All that remained of Rome itself was ruined traces of forgotten glories. Even the excavations were already overgrown with grass.

Charles suffered from more mundane persecutions, as he indicated in a letter to Constance.

> I long to leave Rome. I am haunted by my admiration for the antiquities since I am chewed up by fleas! You laugh, but I am not laughing at all myself. . . . I could weep from anger; I am suffering like a martyr, I am furious. I can sleep here neither night nor day! I have a chest cold! They say that in Naples it's even worse. . . . That's possible, but at least I will take care to find a house more appropriate than this stable we're living in here.[19]

Whether by choice or by renegotiation of a contract that was bankrupting Paterni in spite of her popularity, Maria sang only six performances in Rome rather than the twelve she anticipated. She then continued on to Naples to sing eight performances of three works that would display her vocal and dramatic versatility: *Otello*, *La Cenerentola*, and *La Gazza Ladra*. She had last known her impresario, the indomitable Domenico Barbaja, when her father was singing in Barbaja's opera houses with Isabella Colbran. Barbaja already had one prima donna to contend with, Giuseppina Ronzi-de Begnis, whose illness and subsequent trip to Naples had helped put Maria Garcia on the stage of the King's Theatre in 1825. With Ronzi drawing well at the Teatro San Carlo, Naples' premier opera house and one of Europe's largest, Barbaja did not pit his prima donnas against one another but, ever-mindful of profits, placed Malibran in the Teatro del Fondo. Whether Maria would sing later at the San Carlo was not yet certain. An observer of the musical scene picturesquely wrote:

> It is not yet known if she will sing at the Theatre, Barbaja being hardly disposed to it. It seems to me that he knows, by quite correct reasoning, that in the case of a great success, she would overwhelm his ordinary troupe, would throw the apple of discord into his seraglio, and would blunt the public for this winter, for she is engaged later in Milan. Whereas in the case of a fiasco, (not entirely improbable, considering the capricious humor of our aristocracy and their presumption which kicks against foreign reputations) poor Barbaja could very well, in that dead season, remain buried in his expenses.[20]

Nothing was certain yet, and Maria would find the tenor Gilbert Duprez' evaluation correct: "The Neapolitans are the most demonstrative public on earth, and at the same time the most capricious."[21]

On August 6 she made her Neapolitan debut as Desdemona before so large an audience that, despite doubled prices, the ambassadors of Russia and Austria were forced to share a box on the fourth tier where their view was blocked by a chandelier.[22] Maria did not disappoint her audience, and further performances only increased the enthusiasm. After her fourth appearance a reviewer wrote, "The teatro del Fondo is the most brilliant on the evenings when Malibran sings here. All the critics agree in saying that la Malibran is as great in singing as in acting, and superlative in expression. . . . This artist astonishes in every scene, and holds the audience in suspense for new surprises."[23]

But la Malibran did not reserve her surprises for the stage. Maria learned that in Naples it was customary for singers to request the King's presence at their debuts. This meant nothing, but she was also told that audiences did not applaud in the presence of royalty unless the King set the example, a convention that greatly upset her since royalty and rulers of state were not known for displays of enthusiasm in the theater. To complicate matters, Ronzi was rumored to be King Ferdinand's mistress, and he might not want to offend her by applauding a rival. There was only one possible course of action, and Maria requested an audience: ushered into the royal chambers, she presented a strange appeal.

"Sire," she said, "I come to ask your Majesty to please not come to the theater tomorrow."

The King, astonished, asked why this singer did not want him to visit his theater. "I would have thought that you would have asked me to come," he responded.

Maria explained her fears, and Ferdinand, amazed at her daring, and liking her for it, promised to set the example for the audience. Not entirely sure of his word, however, she left nothing to chance and the next night stationed herself between the side scenes where he could see her from the royal box. Just before her entrance she caught his eye and mimed the action of clapping. He had not forgotten, and at her entry she received an enthusiastic welcome from the crowd.[24] Unfortunately, the King would be less reliable in the future.

Whatever Barbaja's reservations about presenting her at the San Carlo, Maria's success was such that she could demand, in her reengagement for ten additional performances, to play at that theater. To Ronzi's displeasure, she first appeared there on September 7.

Word of her Italian successes reached Paris, and Maria received a note from Lafayette dated August 13.

Your continuous engagements in Italy sadden me a lot, my dear Maria. I am so happy to see you, to admire you, to receive the expressions of your affection for your old tutor! Be sure, nevertheless, that if I don't see you, I do think constantly and tenderly of you, and that the great interest of your life [the divorce] will no more be neglected than if we were speaking of it every day.[25]

The news of the divorce proceedings in Parliament was not good. After its passage by the Chamber of Deputies in December 1831, the bill passed to the Chamber of Peers, a group of very conservative gentlemen. There, on March 12, 1832, Count Portalis gave an extremely long speech, stating that the Deputies had acted rashly and that a divorce law could not be passed so quickly, and that so grave a move would require lengthy reflection. "It should not be free to husband and wife to break their marriage when it pleases them" he told the Peers, and when the vote was cast on March 28, the bill was defeated seventy-eight to forty-three.[26]

But Lafayette had not given up. "They say that the Chamber will not reconvene before the 5th of November," he told Maria. "Others say that it will be the first of October. I hope that M. de Schonen will take it upon himself to renew his proposition. If not, it will be done by others. One speaks of an addition to the Chamber of Peers which will change the majority."

The general also wrote of her family's reservations about her situation. "I would like to add that there was cordiality for the future husband," he told her, "but sentiments on the divorce, and consequently on the new marriage, appear to me to be always in accordance with their [Catholic] convictions."[27] This lack of enthusiasm was primarily Joaquina Garcia's, for Lafayette later reported that "[Manuel] shares my impatience to see the advent of the divorce law and the consequences that should result from it for you." He added, "You can be sure that the interest of this cause will not be neglected, and although the plans of the assembly don't always come true, I foresee it in this way for the next session. It is superfluous to tell you that I am putting all my efforts into it."[28]

Maria continued to hope, but reiterated to Mme. Merlin, "I regret very much not being in Paris, but I will never return until I am married to de Bériot, not because of the public, which is always disposed to pardon those who entertain them, but because of my relatives and friends, etc."[29]

The Neapolitan aristocracy generally shunned Maria, but she was a great favorite with the students and younger members of the haute monde. She at last began throwing off the depression that had cast a shadow over her spirits since her father's death, and with her new friends she explored the Neapolitan countryside. The group climbed through the foothills, ignoring the no trespassing signs on the property of the Prince of Capua, and were nearly murdered by his guards for their daring. They danced in the trattorias and swam in the Bay of Naples; they traveled to the top of Mount Vesuvius, sloughing through the knee-deep ashes to reach the summit, where Maria was yanked back from the crater's edge by the less adventurous Charles.

Picknicking near a monastery, they were suddenly interrupted by the sound of a bell tolling the death of a friar. The funeral procession emerged from the monastery, and as the superstitious Neapolitans fearfully watched, Maria approached the door, above which was written "Women Forbidden." Although she hoped her male attire would allow her entrance, the friar at the door was not fooled and refused her request to tour the monastery. Perhaps she thought of Father Malou.

One of the more interesting people Maria met in Naples was Guillaume Cottrau, a distinguished French composer and publisher who recorded his relationship with Malibran in letters to his brother in Paris. On August 31, 1832, he wrote of his first impressions of the singer, impressions colored by jealousy, not only for her musical success and a self-confidence capable of ignoring the criticisms he gave her, but for the effect she had on his wife Jenny and sister Lina, who were far more enchanted with la Malibran than with their lord and master. His resentment grew, and he eventually came to dislike Maria, but in the early stages of their friendship he allowed himself to succumb.

I have spent almost two days with the famous Malibran, who has been extremely affable toward me. . . . I was surprised to find more vocal charm, more dash, and more artlessness in her performance, more facility in her roulades, etc., than I had at first been forced to admit . . . forced, I say, because I confess to you that Smargiassi [probably a family friend] told me a little vaguely that Lina had felt obliged to complain to him of the manner in which he received Malibran. I was nothing less than favorably disposed toward this singer, of whom my wife is positively crazy to excess—to the point of refusing to see all those who dare to make the least derogatory remark about her, and without making an exception for her very honored master and spouse, who allows himself to find that this admirable actress never forgot to be one and, although self-serving with the utmost taste, spirit, and an astonishing mobility of physiognomy, with all the resources of the dramatic art, never let herself be carried beyond one of those sudden inspirations which come straight from her heart. However, in this regard it is Mme Malibran herself who has confirmed to me how much she seeks to analyze her roles. She makes fun of those who vaunt so much their pretended improvisations of song and acting, actually prepared in longhand and in some way numerated on paper for a given number of performances.

I noticed first hand that her voice was rather rebellious and was trained only by force of the most difficult studies; eh bien! Not only have I had a chance to learn this for myself, in hearing her practice a duet with Mme Fodor, but she has taken pleasure in confessing it to me herself, adding that she was proud of it. Such a victory over obstacles seemed to her preferable to the most beautiful gifts of nature, and in this chat she told me that she has studied the rondo from *Cenerentola* for six years and isn't through yet.

We have had some discussions on several details of her performances in *Cenerentola* and *Gazza*, discussions that she sustained with an infinity of spirit and even of good sense and tact, in a manner often convincing to me. But I have not yet dared to offer her any more important criticism than this: it seems to me that from the force of wanting to show Desdemona's passion for Otello, she loses, especially in the scene of the killing . . . that nuance of yet virginal modesty (for in the Italian piece she is not yet married) that I would like to see there in place of those wanton caresses which are even more than passionate, and which seem to me more appropriate for Cleopatra or Armida than for the pure and naive Venetian girl.

As an actress, her most magnificent role is Ninetta in *La Gazza Ladra*.[30]

Despite the praise that Maria received from the critics, she bridled at the custom that prevented applause in the presence of the court and an undemonstrative King. Since the court always attended her performances, and since Ronzi had put an end to King Ferdinand's earlier cooperation, the plaudits were neither what she expected nor needed. "I have succeeded well here, but I am not pleased about it," she wrote to Mme. Merlin. "I have reasons to think that I am appreciated, but they don't applaud at the theater, and I need it like the spark of life. How can I sing without it? . . . It is said that they are deaf. Why is that? Because I sing badly? Not at all. It is very simply because I am too thin. Do you understand what I'm trying to say? . . . No. Well, so much the worse, for I will tell you nothing more."[31]

Maria's fear of mail censors prevented her from writing that Ronzi, the King's favorite, was very fat. As the composer Donizetti noted succinctly, "The balance weighs in her favor, for to tell the truth, she has more ass to help add weight, and even more flesh elsewhere."[32] Thus neither the King nor the audience applauded. La Ronzi had a powerful lover.

Even so, the rules became increasingly difficult to obey, and Maria's final performance on September 29 swept away all traces of court protocol. Cottrau's description of the last days of Maria's engagement may sound exaggerated, but future events would prove its accuracy. Indeed, such frenzy, such public excitement, would soon accompany every Malibran performance. "These are details that no one, I am very sure, will contest in any way," he wrote to the Parisian publisher Eugène Troupenas.

October 6, 1832
To Troupenas, Paris
At first our public, to be truthful, resisted in some degree such a colossal reputation, and held itself in a restraint like that of a French Court. But soon, recovered from the kind of shock experienced at such an unconventional talent, a talent as sublime as a natural force, the public overflowed with an uncontrollable enthusiasm the likes of which our theatrical annals offer no parallel, according to our oldest music lovers. Seventeen performances, almost always sold out, were given at doubled prices, and were of the old operas such as *Otello, Cenerentola,* and *Gazza Ladra* (three presentations that could not be more unfavorable in a country where there is no affluence, where the subscribers comprise a very spiteful caste, and where, long blasé to the beauties of Rossini, they are greedy for novelties). The performances, given in quick succession, offered Malibran a series of triumphs. But the bouquet was reserved for the final performance last Monday, in *La Gazza Ladra.* The wildest imagination, even considering the descriptions of the Roman Circuses, couldn't give any idea of the electrifying spectacle which the immense hall of the San Carlo offered, filled up to the roof and resounding with applause, acclamations, stamping and enthusiastic cries. The object of this unanimous rapture, and twenty-five curtain calls during the course of the opera, was called back six times after the curtain fell by an idolatrous multitude unable to bear the idea of a separation that might be permanent. She could get out of her costume only by throwing kisses to the audience and indicating, by an expressive and gracious gesture, her

exhaustion at the conclusion of such a fatiguing role and especially after such intense acclaim. But that isn't all. The most enthusiastic ones formed a numerous crowd at the stage door, and hardly had they escorted her to her home amidst noisy acclamations which echoed their emotion throughout the Rue de Toledo, when they acclaimed her with even more energy in the courtyard of the Barbaja Palace while she ascended the steps. But this is a further indication, perhaps, of the extraordinary impression Mme Malibran has made on the public here and the tremendous progress she has made in her art in so little time.[33]

Cottrau was not writing under the impression of the moment; he drafted his letter a full week after Malibran's final performance.

As Cottrau had predicted, the Neapolitans were numb to further musical pleasure. Donizetti's *L'Esule di Roma*, given two days after Maria's departure in a masterful performance featuring Ronzi and Lablache, resulted in "the coldest reception you can imagine. . . . Nothing is left but apathy. The brilliant meteor has disappeared and here we are again, plunged into a twilight that our feeble eyes will have to adjust to gradually, but which is now unbearable after such bursts of light."[34]

On October 3 Maria departed for Bologna, leaving the people of Naples with the hope that the government would make her brilliant offers to return. She had performed three days beyond the terms of her contract, and since her engagement in Bologna did not begin until October 13, she offered to continue at the San Carlo for an additional fee, but her demands were not met. The jealous Ronzi, using all her influence, made sure of that.

The Bolognese eagerly awaited Malibran despite the additional taxes that had been levied on the populace to meet the immense fee [3600 scudi (36,000 French francs)] promised her for eighteen performances by the directors of the Teatro Comunale.[35] On October 7 Maria and Charles arrived, lodging at the Pensione Svizzera on the Piazza de Porta Ravegnana. Two days before Maria's first scheduled performance, a newspaper proudly announced the coming event: "*La Gazza Ladra* will have its first performance on Saturday, the 13th. Every music loving soul awaits this delightful evening. The name alone of the incomparable Malibran electrifies. Our magnificent theater is worthy of her: it is very vast, but suitable to her gigantic fame."[36]

Even though the Bolognese expected more than a miracle, Maria's performance was generally considered a success. Her few detractors were disappointed that her voice was not superior in tonal quality to many other celebrated singers, that she did not provide the constant surprises they had read about, and that her graceful movements better suited a ballerina than an opera singer. A local conductor who had seen her perform in London declared her voice slightly inferior to what it had been when he last heard her, and Isabella Colbran, now living in Bologna and never known for complimentary largesse, claimed that she had lost range in the soprano register and gained in the contralto.[37] But the audience, the only barometer important to Maria, indicated that her engagement would be a success.

On October 27 Maria undertook for the first time the part of Romeo in Bellini's *I Capuleti e i Montecchi*, the second opera in which she had interpreted that character. She did not, however, sing his work as written, but replaced the last scene with that of Nicola Vaccai's *Giulietta e Romeo*, which suited her voice better and had a more dramatic conclusion. In addition she interpolated music by Mercadante, Filippo Celli, and other composers throughout the score.* Unusual even in a period when improvisation and substitution were common, this mélange succeeded overwhelmingly. Commented a journalist, "All this made a stew, a sauce, a fricassee marvelous to hear, and la Malibran, as beautiful as Circe, magician that she is, presented this ragout at the theater . . . and the auditors, abandoned by Reason, tasted this stew and were dazzled out of their minds . . . like Ulysses' companions."[39]

Mme. Merlin left a description of her acting in the last scene, the interpolated Vaccai piece:

Silently approaching the inert form of Juliet on her tomb she touched her head, her arms, her shoulders, her neck, her eyes, and then suddenly cried "Juliet!" in a stifled, broken voice that seemed to come from the depths of her soul. This word had a magical effect on the spectators. A glacial shiver spread over everyone even before she had said it, and on several occasions in Bologna women were carried fainting from the theater.[40]

During the second performance excitement reached its highest pitch: the boxes were stuffed with as many as ten patrons each, and the singers obligingly repeated whole sections of the opera. So compelling was Malibran's performance that several wastrels paid by another impresario to hiss her instead applauded.[41] The clapping, the stamping, the yelling so

---

*Malibran's adaptation of Bellini's *I Capuleti* was so successful that it became standard performance practice for the work, even until the present day. Ricordi's modern score includes Vaccai's last scene with the notation, "To be substituted, as is generally done, for the final scene of Bellini's opera." But in 1834 Giuseppina Ronzi-de Begnis set out to rectify the situation, and her success was such that she could not resist taunting la Malibran behind her back in a letter to Francesco Florimo written on June 18, 1834.

"Yesterday evening, first performance of *Capuleti*. Everyone feared for the undertaking because they had presented it some time ago and it hadn't entirely pleased. Yesterday evening, however, they saw that where there is a Romeo like la Ronzi they needn't worry! (Modesty!) In sum, they wouldn't have recognized it. Introduction, good; Romeo's cavatina, two curtain calls; duet, curtain call; and finale, furore. What do you think of that?

"Second act: Juliet's aria good; and duet also good, but no furore.

"The third act should have fallen flat, but didn't. Here it was said that Vaccai's was better and it was wished that la Ronzi had done the *pasticcio alla Malibran*, but I put back together the sections of the original opera: if it will be a fiasco, it will at least be all Bellini! I assure you that I was trembling, because the Florentines have a reputation for not listening, and you know that in that third act there is nothing that wakes up the ear. To taste the beauties of it, both of the music and of the declamation, a religious silence is needed. This was obtained, and the public, as soon as it saw me, remained motionless. In sum, to make it short, it pleased greatly and afterwards we were called back onstage.

"It seems to me that things are going well; now I am truly content. To tell the truth, it would displease me should this opera fail; and I am so much more happy with this because it is Bellini's entire opera. There are people who have asked you, 'why is it that Malibran changes the third act?' It seems to me that as one who is considered just as much an actress as a singer, she ought to be content with it, don't you think? Does this seem a small triumph to you?"[38]

intensified that a government official present pointed out these infractions of the law to the President of the Deputation of Performances, who politely replied that the rules governing the stability of worldly things did not apply to the divine.[42]

A condition of Malibran's Bologna contract was that de Bériot be allowed to use the theater without charge for two concerts of his own, concerts in which she would also perform. The Marquis Francesco Sampieri, director of Bologna's excellent Philharmonic Society, was eager to join the famous pair on these evenings, and arranged to appear with them, but Maria objected to Charles' being paid a fee less than her own. A few days before the concert she declared herself ill, and de Bériot sprained his thumb.

Isabella Colbran saved the day. While walking down the street, she heard from an open window the sounds of an excellent violinist practicing his instrument. Making inquiries she learned that the musician was a twenty-two-year-old Norwegian named Ole Bull who so far had had no luck in launching his career. Through Colbran's efforts, Sampieri engaged the young violinist to replace de Bériot; his success was immediate and emphatic.

Maria was furious that Charles could be so easily replaced, and Bull's success did not mollify her feelings. Although de Bériot graciously congratulated his rival, Maria would neither see nor hear him. But because Bologna was small, she could not avoid her peers forever and eventually permitted her introduction to him. To be polite, she asked him to play something. After the first few notes from his violin she flushed, and when he had finished his piece she exclaimed, "Signor Ole Bull, it is indeed your own fault that I did not treat you as you deserved. A man like you should step forth with head erect in the full light of day, that we may recognize his noble blood."[43]

From that time they were fast friends and the Norwegian became a frequent guest at the de Bériot lodgings. Maria even compared him to Charles, and after a soirée commented to her lover, "He has a much sweeter tone than you, de Bériot."[44] Charles replied that the difference was probably in their instruments, but she was not convinced. And Bull became an ardent fan of Malibran's. He loved her hilarious impersonations of other singers and of aristocratic amateurs, and he liked to recite an incident of her great musicianship: she boasted to him that she could sing anything after having heard it once; putting her bravado to the test, he played an intricate caprice and was astonished to hear her sing it right back to him without error.[45]

Like most contemporary musicians, Bull considered her the greatest female singer he had ever heard, but he was shocked to discover that the spontaneity, the remarkable impulsiveness for which she was so famous, was very much under her control by this stage of her career. Standing in the wings one night while she performed, he was so completely overcome by her "ravishing" voice and intense dramatic powers that tears ran down his face. Catching sight of him, Maria turned from the audience for a split second, gave him a ridiculous grimace, and was instantly back in character before a public convinced she was living her role. On being confronted with Bull's awful discovery, she commented gaily, "It wouldn't do for both of us to blubber!"[46]

In becoming friendly with Malibran, Bull made himself accomplice to one of her eccentric pranks. Maria invited him to supper one evening after a performance and hurried him away in her carriage to the Pensione Svizzera; before he knew what had happened he was in an old cape and bonnet, heavily veiled, and pushed into a chair in the corner. Cautioning him to be silent, Maria received her guests, introducing each one to "my aunt, just arrived from the country." During the evening she snatched up a riding whip and attacked her "aunt" while her friends looked on in disbelief. As Ole Bull was revealed from beneath the disguise she laughed uproariously at her joke.[47]

Maria Malibran and Ole Bull encountered each other many times during their concurrent tours of Italy and remained good friends for the rest of her life.

Two days before she sang her first note in Bologna a newspaper announced that la Malibran would be unable to fulfill her contract with La Scala.[48] The agreement she signed with Teodoro Gottardi contained a cancellation clause for conditions of "grave illness," which is how Maria classified her second pregnancy. Indeed, her planned appearances there would find her close to term. But Gottardi, not wanting to lose an engagement with the prima donna who was a gold mine at the box office, chose to believe that pregnancy was not a grave illness. Maria, seeing his situation better than he saw hers, offered to sign an agreement binding her not to sing in any other city after Bologna, and to give preference to Milan for all performances after the birth of her child. Gottardi could not accept this; if Malibran was gravely ill with pregnancy for Milan then she was gravely ill with pregnancy for Bologna, and as far as he was concerned she could prove her allegations to his satisfaction only by canceling her engagement with the Teatro Comunale immediately. The furious impresario even traveled to Bologna with his contract to defend his rights, as he saw them, and to terminate Maria's performances. She immediately engaged two Bolognese lawyers who assured her that her pregnancy constituted grave illness for Milan, but not for Bologna, telling her to continue singing in their city. Gottardi's attorneys turned to the Governor of Milan for justice, and the struggle between the two cities dragged on for two years until the director's successor, eager to engage Malibran for La Scala, dropped the suit.[49]

Maria's first visit to Bologna concluded happily with her benefit performance on November 25. To secure seats for this occasion, the more determined citizens set out for the theater in early afternoon, and by 4 P.M.

all the upper galleries and a section of the parterre were occupied. At curtain time a crowd of 1,700 filled the house. Flowers and laurels from Florence decorated the theater and prints of the singer were distributed to all the boxes. A column in the illuminated foyer bore escutcheons with the inscription: "This woman flies like the eagle, obscuring every star before her."[50]

She played the last three scenes of the Bellini/Vaccai *I Capuleti* and finished with the final scene of *La Cenerentola*. The audience called for an encore, but just as Maria was about to repeat the rondo she burst into tears and could not continue. The acclamations lasted for over an hour; she received twenty-four curtain calls, and the flowers and sonnets rained upon the stage. That evening her bust, sculpted in marble by Cincinnato Baruzzi, was unveiled in the foyer, and a plaque set into the theater wall praised the sublime art that the Bolognese had applauded. The cheering crowds accompanying Maria back to the Pensione Svizzera would not disperse until she showed herself on the hotel balcony.

For three weeks she rested in Bologna while her lawyers attempted to dissolve her contract with Gottardi. On December 19 she and Charles left for Brussels via Turin, arriving at the de Bériot mansion on January 1, 1833. She left behind her the reputation of being "a musical phenomenon," the possessor of "a talent perhaps unique in her art."[51]

CHAPTER 12

London: Bunn and Bellini

In Brussels the travelers were met by Constance de Bériot and her husband, as well as Joaquina and Pauline, for Maria's family had gone to live at the de Bériot home after the elder Garcia's death. And on February 12, 1833, Maria gave birth to a son, Charles Wilfred de Bériot, who was, as his illegitimate grandfather would have been the first to point out, a bastard.*

Lafayette sent no encouraging news about the divorce law, and although he fully expected the proposal to be brought up again in the Chamber of Deputies, he warned Maria against expecting too much from the Chamber of Peers. "I cannot give you new conjectures in this regard," he told her, "but I doubt that this plan is well founded. Your principal affair finds itself embroiled in political circumstances from which it ought to be separated."[1] But he assured her that de Schonen and Barrot would be working on it.

Bavoux reintroduced the proposal in the Chamber of Deputies on December 22, 1832, and on March 5 it was again converted into a project of law. As the General predicted, the Deputies passed it by a large majority on March 23; he wrote to de Bériot: "This majority is so imposing that it would be difficult for the Chamber of Peers to turn down the law. They will certainly try to take advantage of the delays while the Peers discuss it. Nevertheless it will certainly be necessary to get at it there, and the number of voices in our chamber gives me good hope."[2]

But the upper chamber let the proposal die without a discussion. Wasting no time the Deputies again presented the bill, adopted it by the largest margin to date on May 25, and passed it for the third time to the Peers, who commented on the deep division between the two governing bodies.[3]

Eugène Malibran had not been sitting idle in Paris. His own legal staff obtained a royal ordinance on October 6, 1831, that permitted him to live in France as a reinstated citizen, a victory that brought ever closer his right to sue not only for his wife's property, but for her return to his household.[4] Maria could no longer afford to wait for the French Parliament to help her. On April 1, 1833, while the Chamber of Peers set up a committee to discuss the proposed divorce law for the second time, her lawyers took the first step

---

*The baby was left in Belgium to be raised by Joaquina Garcia.

toward an anullment and solicited the Civil Tribune for a separation of properties.[5]

Maria had been ill since her son's birth, but on her recovery she made plans to resume her career in London. Her constant absences from Paris disappointed Lafayette, and although he knew their cause, he still hoped she would accept a contract with the Théâtre-Italien. Just before her departure he wrote her a farewell letter: "I received your affectionate and very touching letter, my beloved pupil. Your misfortune was unknown to me. I share your sadness with all my soul. I didn't know about your sickness. It is very painful to love you so much and to be separated from you like this, my dear Maria. . . . I will enjoy your triumphs and I request all the details which multiply those enjoyments. . . . I love you and embrace you with all my soul."[6]

In London she and Charles set up housekeeping on St. James Street and were first seen at the opera on Saturday, April 27, where the glittering audience included Pasta, Rubini, Paganini, the composers Vincenzo Bellini and Nicola Vaccai, the pianists Johann Hummel and Henri Herz, as well as Wilhelmine Schröder-Devrient and singers from the German opera company. The newspaper delicately reported de Bériot as Maria's "husband."[7]

Her contract was for fifteen performances at the exorbitant fee of 2,000 pounds sterling (50,000 francs), and Alfred Bunn, her impresario at the Drury Lane Theatre, fervently hoped her drawing power would keep him solvent. The engagement commenced on May 1 with Bellini's *La Sonnambula*, in which Maria assumed the role of Amina for the first time.* Originally written for Pasta, the opera was first performed in March 1831 in Milan to great acclaim. When Pasta introduced it to London a few months later, however, the English were unimpressed and there was little enthusiasm for the work. The score, prepared by Henry Bishop for the new Drury Lane production, featured a translation by Samuel Beazley so that the plight of the sleepwalker would not be lost to English ears. Malibran's diction, always exemplary, must have been severely tried, especially when the words were to the coloratura flights of "Ah, non giunge!": "Do not mingle one human feeling/With the rapture o'er each sense stealing."

Although Dr. Belluomini treated Maria for a sore throat at the beginning of the evening, her Amina was a complete success. At the conclusion Bunn led her back onstage to a standing ovation with waving handkerchiefs, hats, and the cheering that had long since become a part of her appearances. The critics without exception found her superlative. The *Athenaeum* spoke for the consensus:

We hardly know in what terms to write of Madame Malibran's performance of this part—and the difficulty is the same whether we turn to her singing or her

---

*Maria had been announced to sing it in Paris the winter of 1831–32, but, because of her pregnancy and early leave, did not.

acting; to our mind she is the most perfect actress and singer that the Italian, or any other stage has ever produced. Taking her requisites altogether, nature has done more for her than it has ever yet done for any other performer, and art worked, we must think, by steam at its highest pressure, has been brought to bear upon her natural gifts in such manner as to command an acknowledgement that perfection is at last attained. We well remember the grand and inspiring notes of Catalani, we are familiar with the liquid sweetness and brilliant execution of Cinti, and we can dwell with delight upon a recollection of the intensity, the feeling, and the expression of Pasta, but the sweets of all these, and twenty other flowers, have been extracted and combined to form the musical bouquet called Malibran. . . . She was perfection. [no. 288 (4 May 1833), p.284]

"Her voice is one of the most touching sweetness, full of soft and luxuriant melody and managed with the most perfect science," added another. "To these she unites considerable power and perfect flexibility."[8] "In its low notes especially [it is] instinctive with the very soul of feelings which 'lie too deep for tears,' "[9] proclaimed yet a third. Even her embellishments, perhaps extravagant, were "so nicely executed that they seduce even the best critics and lead them to applaud what in their sober senses they could not but disapprove."[10] "We regard her as the first singer in Europe,"[11] declared the *Spectator*, ignoring Pasta's presence in London.

Despite the tongue-twisting text, Maria gave "a distinctness of expression to the words of her songs which some of our English singers would do wisely to imitate, if they can."[12] Her impersonation of the peasant girl was considered daring: in the sleepwalking scene Amina appeared in nightgown and nightcap, with stockings so sheer that her feet showed.[13]

Although one reviewer remarked that "Madame Malibran's performance of Amina was . . . so excellent that it might have made an opera far inferior pass off well,"[14] critics agreed that few inferior operas existed. Consisting of "flimsy," "worthless" music,[15] it was "the most stupid" opera ever heard.[16] And yet the critic from the *Times* wrote, "If anything has the power to bring audiences to the theatre, we should think that *La Sonnambula*, played as it was last night, is more calculated to effect that objective than any performance that has lately been seen."[17]

Perhaps the most meaningful praise came from Bellini himself, who had been in London since April and had attended her first performance of his work, and many subsequent ones as well. The thirty-one-year-old Italian, tall, slender, delicately blond, dressed in tightly fitted, expensive clothes and carried a little cane. Although his studied elegance irritated men, many women found his childish personality and romantic appearance irresistible and the leading hostesses of London lionized him. On May 1 the Duchess of Hamilton took him to Drury Lane to hear his *Sonnambula* performed by Maria Malibran.

Bellini described his first acquaintance with Malibran and her art in a letter to a friend in Naples.

The day after my arrival in this great country *of gray skies*, which have been
called, with great wit, *leaden skies*, I read on the theater posters (which are
carried through the streets here) the announcement of *La Sonnambula*, translated
into English (protagonist Maria Malibran). Being eager to hear and admire the
diva with whom the musical world is so absorbed, and knowing her only by
reputation, I did not miss a chance to go to the theater where I had been
invited anyway by one of the grander women of the high English aristocracy, the
Duchess of Hamilton. . . . I lack words, my dear Florimo, to tell you how my
poor music was tortured, torn to shreds, and, as the Neapolitans say, *flayed* by
these . . . Englishmen, especially since it was being sung in that language of
birds, namely parrots, and of which I don't understand so much as a syllable.
Only when la Malibran sang did I recognize *La Sonnambula*. In the allegro of the
last scene, especially on the words: "Ah! m'abbraccia"* she put so much feeling
and expressed the phrase with such realism that I was at first surprised, and
then felt such delight that, forgetting the social conventions as well as the
respect that I owed the lady at my side, whose box I was sitting in, and further,
putting aside any modesty (which an author should always show even when he
doesn't feel it) I was the first to cry at the top of my lungs: "Viva! Viva! Brava!
Brava!" and to clap my hands as hard as I could.

Bellini's exuberance attracted attention, and soon the excited Italian
in the Duchess of Hamilton's box was identified. He was dragged to the
stage by a group of young admirers, one of whom was the son of his hostess.
"The first person who came to meet me was la Malibran, who, throwing her
arms around my neck, sang to me my four notes 'Ah! m'abbraccia' in an
indescribable transport of joy and said nothing more. My emotions were as
high as the roof. I thought I was in paradise. I couldn't say a word, I was
stunned. I don't remember what happened next."

Malibran and Bellini, hand in hand, were called to the front of the
stage to greet the tumultuous applause. "All I can say is that never in my life
shall I be able to feel a greater emotion. From that moment I have become
very close to Malibran. She shows me all the admiration she feels for my
music, and I show the same for her immense talent. I have promised to write
her an opera on a subject befitting her genius. That's a thought which
electrifies me already, my dear Florimo."[18]

Bellini's excitement about writing an opera expressly for Malibran
almost equaled her own excitement at the prospect of such an honor. In
addition to marrying Charles de Bériot, Maria's abiding interest was the
immortalization of her art through an opera by a great composer. Her
ambition was heightened by Pasta's success in creating roles written
especially for her own talents. Not only had Pasta inspired Bellini's *La
Sonnambula*, *Beatrice di Tenda*, and, of greater importance, *Norma*, she had also
created Giovanni Pacini's *Niobe* and Donizetti's *Anna Bolena*. Maria spared
no effort in maintaining Bellini's interest in this project, to the point where
rumor linked the two as lovers. Pasta, who saw him constantly this summer,

*"Ah! Embrace me." Malibran was singing in English, but Bellini knew which words of
the original libretto would fall on the notes being sung at that point.

joked, "Bellini, you will not leave London without having had a duel with
M. Bériot!"[19]

Bellini, puzzled over Malibran's love for the "sad and funereal Charles
de Bériot," told Lablache that he would bet his life that Maria did not love
"that insipid man." "Marietta is too intelligent, is too alive, and that's why
she can't be content in the company of that macabre being. When I see la
Malibran and Charles de Bériot together, I seem to see life and death in
company with one another."[20] But he assured Pasta that he was not head
over heels in love with Malibran. She merely replied, "Your love can be read
in your eyes."[21]

Perhaps she was right. To Francesco Florimo the composer confided,
"How not to love that devilish Malibran? Tell me, my dear Florimo, you
who know how weak I am with women, especially when they are beautiful. . . . And this one, who is prettier than all the others, and sings divinely
and possesses such beautiful feelings that only to see her and feel her, not
even the hardest man on this earth could remain frozen in the presence of
such a miracle."[22]

Always true to Charles, Maria did not love Bellini other than as a
friend. A letter he sent her at the end of May, however, indicates where
things stood between the determined prima donna and the smitten
composer.

May 29, 1833

Amatissima Maria,
    I have a damned cold that has been bothering me for three days and which
has prevented me from seeing you, and imagine what a cruel blow it has been
for me to be in such an unfortunate state. [line lost] You cannot imagine with
what great pleasure I received from Signora [illegible] the piece that you sent
me, and with what joy I have learned about your feelings and your beloved
regards. I have pressed many and many kisses on the music written by your
beautiful hand [line canceled]. I cannot begin to describe to you the feelings
that I experienced, my adored one, the other evening in the home of maestro
[canceled] next to you. Do you remember it? I had *les larmes dans les yeux** (do I
write it correctly?) [two lines missing] and you must still recall the grimace on
the face of Signora Bunn when she found us in the entrance to the salon with
our hands entwined one within the other. My heart was in a tumult, and I was
on the point of squeezing you closely to my chest, and if it were not for the
appearance of that old witch [three lines gone] Patience, my enchanting Maria!
I long for the moment and it will definitely be tomorrow that I see you. [A long
cancellation] . . . in order to give you a million kisses? I find myself confused in
thinking about you . . . . Your Bellini[23]

But Maria longed for the opera Bellini had promised her, and he did
not begin its composition as quickly as she would have liked. The composer,
never a fast worker, seemed always to require external motivation, which

---

*"I had tears in my eyes." Bellini's letter is in Italian, but to please Malibran he
attempted a little French.

Maria was willing to provide. She hinted that perhaps he could compose just a song for her while she waited, and, more boldly, even offered to pay him to write the opera.[24]

Meanwhile Maria was having contractual difficulties with Alfred Bunn, surely one of the most amusing and personable impresarios it was her misfortune to know. Rushing off to the concerts that filled those hours of her day and night not actively devoted to the theater, she suddenly found herself in violation of the terms of her engagement, which assumed that those who could hear Malibran sing free would not be likely to pay for the same privilege. Pointing out this breach of contract to his dismayed prima donna, Bunn gave her the choice of eliminating the concerts or giving, at no charge, an extra performance for the benefit of Drury Lane. His intransigence infuriated Maria, who stood not only to suffer pecuniary loss but to forgo the social advantages of the soirées. Clearly Bunn's second alternative coincided more with her interests, despite her denial.

St. James Street
May 6th, 1833

Mon cher Monsieur Bunn,

Permit me to continue my correspondence with you in French. Perhaps I can explain myself more clearly in that language. In response to what you told me relative to the rights that, according to you, I do not have, to sing in any concert given in the locality of a theater, I will tell you that all the judges on earth, be they English, French, Turk, or Chinese, will tell you that I *have* according to my contract *the right* to sing in any concert hall—HALL FOR CONCERTS—no matter in what locale it may be situated or built. But neither rights nor judges are concerned here; I am answering you in this fashion only to make you understand, my dear director, that if you had a hundred thousand devils in your body you would not have the brains of one Spanish head. Thus I prefer your second alternative, it will prove to you at least that my own interests are the least consideration, and that I desire nothing so much as to preserve between us these amicable relations that have been in evidence up until today. I propose then, to give one more performance than my contract requires, for the benefit of the administration of Drury Lane, on the express condition that you will put no obstacle, not the least obstacle, to any kind of concert that presents itself to me. Now I will stop here. . . . I declare to you that this is for the *first time in my life*!! and I give myself some credit for it, because I think you are a little *hard* on me.[25]

For unknown reasons Bunn refused her conditions, and for the remainder of her engagement she appeared in no extra concerts. At this time Maria corresponded with Bunn almost daily. Whatever their differences she clearly enjoyed sparring with her portly impresario. In another letter she imitated his annoying manner of underlining every other word, facetiously quoting his own admonitions. She also resumed writing in English.

[May 14, 1833]

It is *so long* that I have not written to you, that I am sure you *must* want to hear from *me*. I have a great mind to scold *you*—but I shall not do it, because you can repair the *gross mistake* that has been made. *First of all,* be so good as to give de Bériot's name at the door, and Bellini's, so that when they do me the honour (I mean Bellini) to come and witness my seventh appearance in the same opera of *his composition,* him and *t'other* should *not pay* at the door, as they both have *done last time.* I am *sure* that *you* were not aware of *this;* and now that *I have* told *you* the *fact* (which Bellini himself told me last night) I am *sure* you'll put on all your squints and smiles in a beautiful letter, addressed both to Bellini and your humble servant, and offer them a box very gracefully, besides two tickets for the pit or stalls, just as it may suit your convenience. What do you think of that? Really you *owe* me that as a reparation for the immense sum of money that he has laid forwards to see me. I mean to be very particular, since YOU are so TOO, with a miserable pair of stockings that I wanted, and that you most *sweetly* refused!!! Hee? What do you think of that? No excuse for to-night, for I have given my word, being sure, before hand, that Mr. Brutus Bunn, or rather Mr. *Pilato* Bunn (on account of his washing his hands at all things) would not be so ungallant as to refuse what now I beg and *command* him to do, for his most *obedient* (when he has nothing to command) *servant,* and in expectation of being obliged . . . . . . *Amina* Sir, can please you. You, as one seldom pleased, what do you think of——

The favour of the *boxes* and tickets is requested, if your *immense* occupations should *prevent* the *event* of all your sweet squinting smiles and ferotious compliments, au bas de la *lettre.*[26]

At this time the King's Theatre was presenting a wide selection of operas, with Pasta appearing in *Anna Bolena, Medea, Tancredi, Pirata, Norma,* and other works. But at the Drury Lane Theatre two operas played with unrelenting frequency, and at some point the theater could no longer continue with only Schröder-Devrient's *Fidelio* and Malibran's *La Sonnambula.* Bunn wanted Maria to sing the male role of Count Belino in Horn's *The Devil's Bridge,* a part she had performed in New York. He also attempted to persuade her to learn the part of Orlando in John Braham's *The Cabinet.* Maria had little interest in Count Belino and none whatsoever in Orlando. She wanted to play Adele (Daughter of Monsieur and Madame Roulade, intended for the stage) in Hyppolite Chelard's operetta *The Students of Jena.*

The clue to Maria's insistence lay in Chelard's subtitle: . . . *or the Family Concert.* This concert offered her an almost unparalleled opportunity for showing off her ability to sing songs in different languages and styles; indeed, it could be rewritten to fit anything she had in mind, and, as always, Maria wished to display her versatility. She apparently discovered the work through its librettist, James Planché, whose box at Covent Garden she often borrowed, and who was more than happy at her interest. She soon approached Bunn with the idea of staging it at Drury Lane. "Mr. Planché has just been reading to me his delightful little opera, and I think, sans meilleur avis, nothing can be better; therefore I am satisfied complètement; but that is only harlequin's marriage, if my advice stands single, and is not ratified by yours. I remain, Your Columbine, Malibran."[27]

Bunn considered the work too short to waste on one earning Malibran's enormous salary, and thus a battle of wills ensued. "I cannot give you a decision at once," she wrote him in regard to Orlando. "I must see the role, to know if it suits me. I am only sorry that you propose something else, instead of the piece by Chelard, which I know *almost by heart*, which is an immense advantage for learning the part quickly." Bunn had insisted that she live up to the letter of their contract; now she pointed out that he was not keeping his end of the bargain. "When I set out for London without receiving the remittance from Mr. Rothchild* directly," she told him, "I then expected to receive in London the first payment on the second of May, as is stipulated in my contract,—that condition has not been fulfilled.† I attribute the omission to the immense occupations the Theatre causes you; nevertheless, I am not provided with the necessary funds to wait longer. I beg you to dispatch to me, as quickly as possible, a draft on the banker with whom the first deposit of *one thousand pounds* has been made. Believe me, my dear Mr. Bunn, that there is no ill temper on my part, still less want of confidence, but truly a problem with my purse." And having advised Bunn that her performances would cease unless she was paid, she once again requested a response about the Chelard operetta.[28]

Bunn maintained enough aplomb to send the score of *The Cabinet* to his prima donna, who replied disdainfully, "I regret to have to tell you that this role doesn't please me at all and that, as for the music, I will never sing it. It is in a style completely different from mine, and which consequently doesn't suit me in any way. I am therefore returning the score to you and ask you not to speak to me about it any more. Such is my *response*, positive and negative." As if she had not made her point sufficiently clear, she added, "Have the kindness, therefore, when you have an opera to submit to me, have the kindness I say, to choose something which suits me and which is within my capabilities, and not beyond the limits of the few abilities I possess."[29] So much for Orlando.

On the matter of Count Belino she was almost as adamant. "I cannot promise to play the part of Cont Belino," she wrote him. "The music is exeedingly week, and after the sunnambula, I am not capable of singing *baby's music*; however, I dont say *positively no* until I see both the *music* and *the pice* again, for it is about 8 years that I have not even herd of the part— therefore be so good as to send the whole to me & I shall give you a

---

*Her payment was guaranteed by a bank.

†A receipt in the New York Public Library, Lincoln Center, indicates that she received payment on June 9, 1833.

consientious answer quite à la Malibran."[30] In a letter addressed "To A Bunn!!!!!! Esquair!!!!!!," she made one last attempt on the Chelard work.

Again and again, alwais me, and eternally me, my dear Mister Bunn. I have been tormenting poor Chelard out of his wits. I want to have my part to practise it, know it, and be able to play it in 10 days the latest. I am sure if you give proper orders for the copy of the parts, *we* shall be all ready, at least I will be ready in 8 days . . . . . . but——rehearsals, parts, rehearsals, parts, orders, rehearsals, no rehearsals without parts, no parts without orders, and no orders without my eternal hints, and my never ending letters, since it appears you will not do me the high honour of comming at my house for a quarter of an hour to have a little settling chit-chat. However it may be, I wait your pleasure, noble cousin, and humbly beg for an answer when it may suit your Majesty. Nonsense apart, pray say YES or no, for it would be too late to give orders for the copies in a few days. We should not have the necessary time for learning.[31]

They reached a compromise. Maria sang her first Count Belino on May 20 and got her way with the Chelard work on June 4. Neither was particularly successful. The *Athenaeum*'s critic wrote of Belino: "Madame Malibran's performance was, as far as anything she does *can* be, a failure."[32] The critic for the *Times* thought otherwise, no doubt impressed by the half-dozen extraneous songs Maria introduced into the piece. "Her acting was remarkably skillful, and infinitely too good for the sad stuff of which the part is composed," concluded the reviewer (21 May 1833).

Opinions also differed about *The Students*. The *Harmonicon* proclaimed it "a decided failure," while the *London Literary Gazette* hailed it a "complete success."[33] But whatever judgment was passed on the work itself, Malibran received unanimous praise in the family concert scene, where she interpolated songs in German, French, and Italian. "She was a native of each country for the time being," wrote a critic, "and such is her talent, that if it happened to suit her to become a Chinese, we have no doubt that the Emperor himself would be deceived—claim her for a subject, and take no denial."[34]

Both works had disastrous moments of sufficient distinction to be reported in the *London Literary Gazette*'s "Unrehearsed Stage Effects" column. During an early performance of *The Devil's Bridge*, the red and green curtains, customarily raised and lowered in rapid succession to provide a dramatic change of color, became entangled, and the red curtain was torn to a height of eight or nine feet before the accident was discovered. That same evening Malibran, as Count Belino, rushed at her deadly foe Toraldi crying in her exotically accented English: "Yase, detasted villaine, I am Toraldi!"[35]

In *The Students*, her moment of reckoning came during an interpolated dance. Maria loved to dance, although in Mme. Merlin's opinion her passion apparently precluded any desire to move in time to the music. But she considered herself accomplished, and whenever possible she danced on stage, almost always unsuccessfully. Unfortunately she attempted too much this time, for as she danced, sang, and shook a tambourine, she tripped and fell with a crash "in a very dangerous looking attitude." The other performers immediately forgot their roles, and Mr. Seguin ran to pick her up. Quipped the *London Literary Gazette*, "An ordinary dancer would have jumped up without his aid, and even pretended not to have tumbled at all; an ordinary singer would at once have begged leave to faint in his arms; but Madame Malibran totally refused his aid, and went on gaily singing and playing the tambourine on the ground, without altering in the least the extraordinary position in which the accident had thrown her."[36]

Maria chose John Templeton, a young Irish singer in his second season with Bunn, to be her tenor this summer because his voice had great range, power, richness, flexibility, and an exceptionally fine falsetto.[37] But Templeton, or "Tempe," as his prima donna called him, remained a simple, unsophisticated individual, one who thoroughly lacked not only temperament, but the self-confidence to state his will and demand that it be done. Too timid even to protest Bunn's impossible scheduling, which through a dreadful oversight required that he sing at both Covent Garden and Drury Lane on the same nights, Templeton swallowed his unstated objections and carried out his director's wishes, amusing everyone but himself. To save time in the rush from one theater to the other, he retained the makeup and costume of his performance at Covent Garden and was whisked through the streets to Drury Lane wrapped up in a large cloak. The cloak slipped at least once, provoking such comments from startled passersby as "Look at that man who has painted his face!"[38]

On another occasion Templeton arrived late to find a restless audience listening to the overture for a third time and was pushed on stage still breathless and so dripping with perspiration that his false moustache loosened and slipped into his mouth as he sang. In a rage he tore it off and threw it into the orchestra pit where it stuck tenaciously to the strings of the first violinist. The dramatic effect was so magnificent, and so uncharacteristic of the phlegmatic singer, that he was given an ovation.[39]

Under ordinary circumstances Templeton's lack of temperament precluded any display of drama, and Maria decided to teach "Tempe" to act. In *La Sonnambula* his character was to react passionately to hers; Maria gave him definite thoughts and feelings to relate his acting to. Failing this, she tried to get a reaction from Templeton himself.

"You are cold, inanimate! Are you a man? Do you have a wife? And do you love that wife?" Templeton nodded in the affirmative. "Then," she continued, "would you, if she were in such trouble, stand so far from her and look at her with such indifference? Come closer to me, and seem very sorry for my situation." Templeton moved closer. "Come to me," she urged. "I won't bite you!"[40]

Templeton, annoyed at her constant needling, did the biting. "Ah, Mr. Templeton," she told him one day, "you are a very fine, tall man, but you are a very bad lover. I would rather have Mr. Woodleg for my husband." She indicated the prompter, Mr. Wilmot, who had a wooden leg, and the rehearsal was reduced to laughter at Templeton's expense. As they continued he put so much passion, or anger, into the love scene that he bit Maria on the neck and was this time firmly admonished for his realistic acting. "That's not really necessary," she told him sternly.[41]

Maria treated Templeton as though she were a mischievous older sister heckling her little brother. During one performance when his acting dissatisfied her, she pinched him sharply in the rump, causing him to jump suddenly and kick his leg. Annoyed at this disrespectful treatment on stage, he went to Mr. Bunn for advice. Bunn suggested that he call on Malibran, let her know what was on his mind, and ask her what he had done to deserve "such a total want of good breeding." Templeton took his director's advice; the next morning he confronted her in Bunn's presence. Maria could barely keep from laughing, and she replied facetiously, "I thought you wanted, Sir, to kiss me."

Bunn was stunned at the tenor's response. "At this moment, when she was the idol of the people, 'the admired of all beholders', when peers would have given their coronets to press only the tips of her fingers, and the world at large was sighing at her feet, imagine the phlegmatic songster exclaiming: 'Gude God, is that all? Mak your mind easy, I would na' kiss you for ony consideration', and shaking hands, he left the house."[42]

But Maria could sympathize with her easy prey and attempted to reconcile herself with her colleague. Unfortunately she chose a way that jeopardized yet another performance of *La Sonnambula*. On her knees in the second act, telling her lover of her faithfulness and begging his forgiveness, she reached up in a supplicating gesture and tickled Templeton so hard under the arms that the poor man could barely keep from screaming.[43] But despite all that he suffered, both his acting and singing progressed noticeably with Maria's tutelage. For his improvement she gave him a ring, her favorite choice of gift.

At the conclusion of Maria's fifteen performances, Bunn attempted to negotiate another contract for the month of June. Unable to afford her at the previous fee, he appealed to her to accept a lower salary, observing that her performances had not always sold out at the doubled prices he was obliged to charge. In an unprecedented act, Maria acquiesced. A primary factor may have been Bellini's presence in London. With his promised opera ever on her mind, she was in the midst of painting two miniatures for him: one of him, and a self-portrait.* Furthermore, her engagement in Naples did not begin until mid-November, and she would not sing in Paris.

---

*These are now in the Museo Belliano, Catania. The self-portrait is set into a small gold brooch with a looped gold ribbon surrounding it; it shows her with her right hand raised to touch her long hair. Bellini often used it to pin the knot of his cravat.

Whatever her motives, she signed the new contract—which paid her just over half of the previous one—with the comment, "For God's sake don't tell anyone that I accepted such a sum!"[44] Her written acceptance arrived shortly thereafter.

A Melancholy Engagement of £1000 for Twelve Performances!

Madame Malibran is hereby engaged to perform at either the Theatre Royal Drury Lane, or Theatre Royal Covent Garden for the month of June, to perform three times per week, for the sum of 1000 £ sterling, on the conditions of her previous engagement; except that she is at liberty to sing at all the concerts, provided they do not interfere with the performances or rehearsals of the said theatres.

Monsieur De Beriot is also to have a concert at one of the said theatres, and is to be entitled to a clear two-thirds of the receipts of the evening.

London, May 24, 1833   M. F. Malibran[45]

Many critics believed Bunn's financial difficulties stemmed from mismanagement. He chose a questionable repertoire, he presented opera at a theater usually associated with drama, and he paid his prima donna sums that practically guaranteed bankruptcy. A particularly deplored tactic was Bunn's habit of announcing "on this one occasion only," followed by "for one night more" on the day after the performance in question. In the case of Maria's first engagement, to conclude with *The Students of Jena*, the *London Literary Gazette* remarked sarcastically, "Malibran, having been advertised all *last* week as the *last nights* of her engagement, *of course* played the principal character in the novelty of *this* week; because people ought to understand that in the Drama, being finished means being about to begin again; and taking leave only continuing a more intimate acquaintance."[46]

Although particularly brilliant for London, the season was inconsequential to Maria's career, except for the addition of *La Sonnambula* to her repertoire. For the only time during their careers, Malibran and Pasta appeared together in a staged opera, an abbreviated version of *Semiramide* presented at the King's Theatre on July 18. Wrote the *London Literary Gazette*: "A most brilliant audience assembled to witness Madame Pasta and Madame Malibran shine out two suns in one sphere: but comparisons in such cases are principally odious because they are impossible—the styles of the two are so utterly different. . . . Their mutual reception was as enthusiastic as it deserved, and more it is impossible to say."[47]

Between performances Maria made quick trips to outlying cities, Oxford and Cambridge in particular. And she filled in between the acts of comedy and vaudeville productions singing a ballad by Horn entitled "The deep deep sea," which never failed to elicit the greatest enthusiasm from audiences amazed by her trilling on her lowest contralto notes, an effect described as "the variation of a growl."[48] An impressed critic wrote that "her almost boundless voice ebbed and flowed alternately—sometimes dying away in soothing murmurs, and then suddenly advancing in an irresistible volume and lashing the various cliffs at pleasure. This gifted creature's voice is surely the American sea serpent of music. It is to be met with in folds, in coils, in wreaths; but nobody seems to know where either the head or tail of it is to be found."[49]

Somehow Maria found time to enjoy the company of some of Europe's foremost musicians, many of whom were in England this summer. They invariably found la Malibran intriguing. Among those who made her acquaintance was James Planché, translator of the libretto for *The Students of Jena* from the German. Perhaps co-translator would be a better term, for whenever Maria did not like the English words he had given her to sing, she would return the music to him marked "betterer words here," and Planché would rework his phrases.[50]

According to Planché, he spent some of his most enjoyable evenings in the company of "that brilliant and fascinating woman."[51] One evening that he never forgot, Bunn, Malibran, de Bériot, and Sigismond Thalberg—"le monstre pianist" as she called him—dined with him at Eagle Lodge, in Brompton.[52] After dinner Thalberg sat down at the piano and extemporized, while Malibran vocalized in harmony and de Bériot joined in with his violin. Charles countered his dour reputation later that night by hilariously imitating a woman he had once seen dancing on a tightrope while playing the French horn. Fastening a bunch of keys to the strings of his violin, he drew a chalk line on the carpet and went through all the gyrations of the dancer, imitating the French horn on his instrument "to perfection."[53] One tour de force suggested another, and by morning the little party was eating mulberries beneath an old tree. This could easily have been the day on which Bunn received a note from his prima donna, "My dear Mister Bunn—I am so horse that I am really afraid not to be able to sing to-night."[54]

At a party given by the Vincent Novellos, Maria renewed her acquaintance with Felix Mendelssohn, whom she had met in England four years before. On July 7 Felix's father Abraham wrote admiringly of the event that he chose over Mrs. Austin's concert, although he admitted that Maria had made "hardly any impression on me when I heard her for the first time on the stage." De Bériot opened the program, playing "very beautifully," and then Maria sang "some rather dull sacred music . . . with great simplicity and exquisite delivery." Warming to the occasion she then sang a Spanish song to her own piano accompaniment. Felix asked for two more, and as the evening continued Abraham was overwhelmed.

Although this lady commands four languages in her singing (Italian is a matter of course), that does not show, any more than I can describe it, with what flowing, glowing, and effervescing power and expression, what caprice and boldness, passion and esprit, with what assurance and consciousness of her means this woman, whom I now *do* appreciate, sang these ditties. From the same throat issued Spanish passion, French coquetry, with again a touch of primitiveness, English unpolished soundness, and also that somewhat frivolous but fresh and most characteristic individuality: she loved, yearned, rowed, and drummed with such wonderful self-possession, such bold command and lavish expenditure of her inexhaustible means, that one may truly say she sang songs without words. She sang sentiments, affecting situations. It was something quite new, and I wish you could have heard her![55]

The guests applauded this display, and Maria exhorted Felix, one of her most enthusiastic admirers, to play the piano. But Felix, "who justly, or at any rate wisely, refused to perform after her" (in his own father's words), had to be brought from another room where he had retreated. "Now Mr. Mendelssohn," she cajoled in her exotic accent, "I never do nothing for nothing; you must play for *me* now I have sung for *you*," and she forced him to the piano where he extemporized to everyone's delight, and to his father's satisfaction, on the songs she had just sung.[56]

While in England Maria received a letter from her mother telling her that the separation of properties sought by her lawyers had been granted by the French courts. "That's strange!," she wrote to Lafayette. "If the news is positive and official, how is it that Mr. Plé, who is my lawyer, did not inform us as is his duty! If, to the contrary, it is false, why has he not told me! I don't know what to think of all this."[57]

News from the French Parliament was not good: the Chamber of Peers had continued to reject the relentless propositions submitted by the Deputies, and although the lower chamber would continue to fight for the divorce law, it was obvious that Parliament would not dissolve her marriage. But she appreciated Lafayette's efforts. "You are really an angel of goodness," she told him once again. "You busy yourself ceaselessly with our happiness to the neglect of your whirlwind of affairs!! You have no children more grateful and more devoted than us—but then I don't have a voice for nothing: it can sing the praises of the best of friends."[58]

On October 15 Maria and Charles left England for Naples, where Maria's new engagement was to begin in mid-November. Hurriedly they passed through Brussels, where, for obvious reasons, the Garcias now warmly accepted Charles. "We were all together as one family," wrote Maria to Lafayette. "You can't believe how happy he was from all this, and how his family rejoiced—Charles' sister, her husband, and Charles' God-father wept for happiness."[59]

In Paris Maria and Charles went to the Théâtre-Italien on October 24 for Giulia Grisi's first *La Gazza Ladra,* and they were cheered when their presence in the theater became known. On November 2 they arrived in Bologna, making good time despite the difficult journey, and after an impromptu performance on November 5 at the Società del Casino, they departed for Naples, where Maria's first appearance was to take place on November 14.

The first week of her engagement involved festivals and galas for several members of the royal family: November 14 was the Queen's birthday, for which Maria sang an unfortunately abbreviated *Otello*; the following night she appeared in *La Prova* in honor of Prince Leopold, and on November 19 she sang *La Gazza* for the Queen Mother's birthday. On this occasion, and probably on other gala evenings, the interior of the San Carlo was decorated brilliantly: its lavish gold latticework reflected the light of 750 enormous wax candles arranged between the six tiers of boxes, those on the lowest level being about five feet tall, those at higher levels being of correspondingly lesser size. The pit was filled with officers of different military regiments dressed in splendid uniforms and arranged in rows according to the color of their jackets—blue closest to the stage, and red, greater in number, in the middle and rear—and the boxes were full of ladies, gentlemen, and officers in their most expensive attire. As she entered the royal box at stage left, superbly illuminated by the brilliant candles and reflected gold light, Queen Mother Maria Isabella received the only applause of the evening.[60]

But in spite of the silence demanded by social protocol in the presence of the court, and Maria's assertion that she could not sing into silence, she clearly put forth all her powers on this and similar occasions. And the audience, silent against its will, just as clearly enjoyed her performance. An English musician present described her as singing and acting "most astonishingly." "T'was in some parts really too much. What a splendid creature she is!—what a voice, what a mind in everything she undertakes! It is needless to add that everyone was in raptures with her."[61]

But Guillaume Cottrau's impression of this performance differed completely: "Madame Malibran has sung only three times," he wrote to his brother in Paris. "The enthusiasm has not relit to the same extent. I have pointed this out to her."[62] To Cottrau her performances were deliberately uninspired so that she could blame the lack of applause on Ferdinand's supposed dislike of her.

Cottrau made every effort to have her perform in Bellini's *La Sonnambula* and *I Capuleti* for the Neapolitans, who had not yet seen her in the roles that had brought her such unqualified success in London and Bologna. He hoped that she would perform the *Capuleti* as Bellini had written it, without the pieces by Mercadante, Celli, and Vaccai that she had previously interpolated. "I have told her some hard truths on this subject, over which she becomes angry, and we have been almost falling out for the last few days," he admitted, but he still hoped to change her mind on a few of her alterations.[63]

Maria confessed to him that she wanted nothing more than to sing an opera composed especially for her by Bellini, and she expressed her annoyance with the composer for not having kept his promise. Cottrau tried to persuade her to abandon the idea of paying him to compose it, pointing out that she had neither librettist, theater, nor opera company. He tactfully

refrained from explaining that rumor linked Bellini and Pasta as lovers,*
and that she who had already inspired three operas from him was not likely
to approve of his writing one for her greatest rival.

Bellini dragged his feet, but others, less exalted to be sure, were more
than willing to do what he would not.On November 30, 1833, Maria
appeared in *Irene, o l'assedio di Messina,* a work written for her by the well-
known composer Giovanni Pacini. The superlative cast, which included
Lablache, Giovanni David, and Giuseppina Garcia-Ruiz,† almost disguised the opera's mediocrity, and the composer was overwhelmed at
Malibran's performance. His response to her art is reminiscent of Bellini's
letter from London.

The unique genius of Maria Malibran sustained the principal role [Irene] in a
manner that the composer and the public marveled at. This splendid woman, so
full of talent, produced on me such an impression when I heard her for the first
time in *La Gazza Ladra,* that they had to drag me out of the San Carlo because I
was giving an additional performance in my box. Never, I can say quite
honestly, have I ever experienced such an emotion in hearing a singer. She was
thoroughly extraordinary.[64]

Irene was withdrawn from the repertoire, but Pacini, who lived in the
Barbaja Palace, as did Maria and other famous artists, became friendly
with her and left his impression of her in his memoirs.

Of an inexpressibly affable character, she made no distinction between the rich
and the poor, the noble and the plebian. She was familiar with five languages;
Spanish, Italian, English, French, and German, and was thoroughly schooled in
the history of belles lettres, in the art of design and painting, and furthermore in
everything that one could desire in a cultivated person. It was claimed that she
was irregular in her life, that she had the fault of getting drunk at the dinner
table; but as for me, who had the good fortune to live near that celebrated
woman for six months and more, as I was also living at the Barbaja Palace and
was eating at the same table as she, I can affirm the falseness of the rumors
which spread the malice. Ordinarily she was very frugal: only in the evenings
after having sung, did she like to drink a glass of champagne, which did not
seem to me to characterize her as an intemperate woman. She was a real
Amazon! She mounted a horse with a skill and perfection to match the most
expert swordsman. In sum she was a complete genius. . . . One can justly say:
"Nature made her, and then broke the mold."[65]

*It is not certain if Bellini and Pasta were living together in London during the summer of
1833. The composer told Florimo that he saw a great deal of her but gave no further hints.
Their addresses, however, were similar and may refer to the same domicile. Pasta was living at
"Old Burlington Square" and Bellini at "3 Old Burlington Street." Weinstock believes the two
were the same (*Bellini*, p. 142).

†This soprano, a pupil of the elder Garcia's in Paris, was no relation to the Garcias but was
constantly referred to in the Italian press as Malibran's "sister." Maria herself spoke of Ruiz as
"my sister" in her correspondence. This peculiarity has led some musical historians to suppose
that Pauline Garcia accompanied Maria on her Italian tours. I do not believe this to have been
the case.

As her public reception in *Irene* indicated, the capricious Neapolitan public was once again warming to Malibran. Toward the end of December Maria wrote to her "excellent tutor" to tell him, "I am getting along perfectly well in Naples" and to ask him to wish her and Charles a happy new year. "I hope then, that you will be wishing me a happy new year for the next hundred years—you see that I want to go on until then."[66] She told another friend, "My voice is *stentorian*, my body *falstaffian*, my appetite *cannibalesque*."[67]

On January 9, 1834, she attempted another new work, *La Figlia del'Arciere*, by Carlo Coccia, a composer of less stature than Pacini, but one whose operas she enjoyed. Coccia's work met with even less success than Pacini's and was withdrawn after three performances.

But if Naples was not providing an opera that would immortalize her art, and if the Ferdinand-Ronzi conspiracy sometimes prevented the applause for which she thirsted, the city at least offered an opportunity for revenge. In early January, as part of Carnevale, King Ferdinand announced that his people might amuse themselves by flinging sugarplums at each other, and at their noble ruler as well. This much anticipated event was scheduled for the mile-long Strada di Toledo, which on the appointed day held hundreds of thousands of people, all dressed in their brightest colors. Bands played amidst the confusion of costumed people, harlequins on horseback, and coaches full of masked revelers, and throughout this kaleidoscopic display rained a shower of candy, more specifically, hard sugared almonds that fell from the decorated balconies like hailstones and returned through the adroit use of blowtubes in a reverse flow that defied gravity.

The King and several noblemen joined the revelry in a long open carriage drawn by four horses and surrounded by masked riders. His heavily decorated conveyance, fitted with large troughs of the lethal sweets for His Majesty to fling at his subjects, was followed by similarly equipped carriages bearing other members of the royal family. This train proceeded up and down the street while candy flew in all directions at once. Sometimes in the crush of the crowd the King was forced to stop, whereupon the barrage became a desperate war that left him snow white with sugar and raised clouds of white dust that temporarily prevented people from directing their volleys.

On the balcony of the Barbaja Palace, which faced the Strada di Toledo, Malibran, de Bériot, and their friends threw as fast and furiously as their hands would let them. The King ordered his carriage to be stopped directly below Maria, so he could engage her in direct combat; in a position of power at last, Maria took her sweet revenge. Picking up a full basket of the rock-hard candies, she emptied its entire contents directly onto His Majesty's head. An immense roar arose from within the white cloud beneath her, the royal order of surrender was sounded, and the carriage, with its sugared occupants, retreated.[68]

Malibran's greatest triumphs in Naples always occurred at the conclusion of her engagements, when the court suddenly realized it was about to lose her. Significantly, these successes were in Bellini's *La Sonnambula* and *Norma*. Cottrau's success in having these presented became Maria's success, and Maria's became the city's. On February 5 she took her benefit in the role of Amina. It was one thing to sing this part in London, in English, where Pasta had not been heard effectively in the role, and another to perform it on Italian soil, where la Pasta's art was admired to the skies by her countrymen. But Maria thrived on challenge. Adapting the music to her voice, she challenged her venerable rival on her own ground and won, surpassing Pasta with the same effects in the same places, and, in addition, bringing all the power of her vocal and histrionic gifts to those areas Pasta had, of necessity, subordinated.[69]

To Francesco Florimo "Maria Malibran was the most sublime interpreter of *La Sonnambula*. She can be said to have given this role a second premier . . . the impression produced was so great and so profound that one could almost question whether the honors of the triumph belonged to Bellini . . . or to the exceptional artist who had interpreted it so well." The celebrated singer Girolamo Crescentini, then in retirement, was moved to tell Florimo that "the singers of former times would have been able to sing the andante from the scene 'Ah! non credea mirarti' as well as la Malibran, but no better than she. As for the allegro which follows, no one, even among past celebrities, could have stressed it with more feeling, with more intense passion, particularly in the phrase 'Ah! m'abbraccia.' "[70]

The public was no less overcome than were these erudite musicologists. The critic for Italy's leading music journal decided that no commendation was worthy of her. "How to find a way to praise her as highly as she deserves?," he wondered. "How to describe in words the sweetness that the heart experiences and that the soul feels from her admirable singing and masterful acting?" The audience called her back for ten curtain calls at the conclusion of the opera, and the applause was "universal and unanimous."[71]

Having made Pasta's *La Sonnambula* her own, Maria proceeded to perform the same miracle with Pasta's most demanding role, the Druid priestess Norma, which she first sang on February 23, 1834, at the San Carlo. The audience alternated between wild applause and—even more remarkable for the Italian public—eloquent silences in which breathing was barely tolerated. "It seemed that her mind overflowed," wrote a critic. "Never has there been such a unity of singing and acting. Her voice is most beautiful, as is her capability of overcoming every musical difficulty."[72]

Of her triumph Cottrau wrote to Paris; "Mme Malibran is delightful in that opera [*La Sonnambula*] but her definitive triumph is in *Norma*, in which she has had a success of unbelievable enthusiasm. Imagine: at her last performance day before yesterday, after having been applauded in all her arias with a frenzy, she was called back again in the final piece ten successive times by a frantic crowd of admirers."[73]

On having experienced her Norma, Hans Christian Andersen wrote, "Her singing and acting surpassed anything which I had hitherto either seen or heard," and he placed her "among my most sublime impressions in the world of art. Hers is not one of those brilliant voices that startle you, but rather a heart dissolved in melody."[74] She became the glorious but doomed singer Annunziata in his first novel, *The Improvisatore*. Taken to the opera to see the new singer, Antonio, in *The Improvisatore*, is stunned by Annunziata's apparition on the stage.

She stood there, a delicate, graceful creature, infinitely beautiful and intellectual, as only Raphael can represent woman. Black as ebony lay the hair upon her exquisite arched forehead; her dark eyes were full of expression. A loud outbreak of applause was heard. . . .

She sang the happiness of her love; it was a heart which breathed forth in melody the deep, pure emotion which, upon the wings of melodious sounds, escapes from the human breast. A strange sadness seized upon my soul; it was as if those tones would call up in me the deepest earthly remembrances. . . .

How astoundingly did she express all that which passed in her soul— astonishment, pain, rage; and when she sang her great aria it was as if the waves of the deep had struck against the clouds. How indeed shall I describe the world of melody which she revealed? My thoughts sought for an outward image for these tones which seemed not to ascend from a human breast. . . . There was a truth, a pain in the whole of her expression which filled my eyes with tears, and the deep silence which reigned around showed that every heart felt the same . . . her heart broke in melody.

A universal burst of acclamation resounded through the house. "Annunziata! Annunziata!" they cried, and she was obliged again and yet again to present herself to the enraptured crowd. . . . We were all beside ourselves with admiration for the glorious actress, her beauty, and her indescribably exquisite voice. [pp.93-95]

At the conclusion of the evening Antonio and a group of other students unhitch the horses from her carriage and draw her back to the hotel.

Andersen mentions Malibran's name only once, at the end of the story when the dying Annunziata, still young but deprived by illness of beauty and talent, is forced to sing so that she may maintain her miserable existence. Antonio again goes to the opera, a third-rate house in Venice, and contemplates the wasted figure before the footlights.

"Who is she called?" I asked at length.

"Annunziata," replied my neighbor. "Sing she cannot, and one may see that by her little skeleton! . . .

"She does not resemble," said I tremulously, "a namesake of hers, Annunziata, a young Spaniard who once made a great figure in Naples and Rome?"

"Ah yes," answered he, "it is she herself! Seven or eight years ago she was on top of the world. Then she was young, and had a voice like a Malibran." [pp.304–5]

Maria's last performance took place on March 12, as Norma, and the crush of admirers almost prevented her from leaving the theater. Cheering crowds followed her through the streets to the Barbaja Palace, refusing to disperse until she came out on the balcony. The next day she departed for Bologna, leaving behind her a reputation as the greatest singer in the world.

CHAPTER 13

La Scala

Malibran did not leave Naples without having arranged for her return, however, in a contract that would run from November 10, 1834 through March 3, 1835, at the fee of 2,000 francs per performance for forty performances.[1] She also accepted offers from many other cities, barely leaving herself time to travel from one to the next in a schedule so hectic that it was said she had only eight free days during the year.[2] Milan expected her in May, London in June, Sinigaglia in July, Lucca in August and September, Milan again in October, and then back to Naples to open the big winter season. This meant that she had to run across Europe "with the speed of a diplomatic messenger," in the words of a contemporary.[3] A friend admonishing her to take better care of her health met with the grim reply, "The public will kill you, either by their neglect or their exactions," and she continued her course unabated.[4]

Cities refused for lack of time included Turin, Padua, and New York. Maria intended to return to the scene of her first real successes in order to show the Americans the truth of their predictions for her; she enjoyed the thought that they would now find her "half woman, half nightingale."[5] But for now Europe offered too much for her to take the time to visit a country unimportant in the musical world. There was also the annulment of her marriage to think about; should her presence be required she wanted to be near Paris.

In Bologna she triumphed again as Bellini's heroines, introducing *La Sonnambula*, which had never been played in the city. A critic wrote, "This lady, who is the true model of art in regard to music and acting, did not portray one emotion that was less than perfection. She truly imitated nature. Every word, every note, dropped tenderly straight into the heart. Her very act, her silences, even her immobility, everything in her was a great thought providing much to be portrayed by the painter, the poet, the sculptor."[6]

Because Malibran, like the operatic art, inspired all artists, her previous epithet, "La Donna del Canto" [the first lady of song], was inadequate: "La Donna dell'Arte" suited her better.[7]

Critics and correspondents were still ransacking the Italian language for terms to describe the perfection of Malibran's Amina when it was announced with three exclamation points that on April 23 she would undertake the role of Norma.[8] People from outlying districts who had not yet journeyed to Bologna to hear her now did so, and with the crush of visitors, hotel accommodations were inadequate; guests stayed in private homes and innkeepers gave up their own beds. Her performances in *Otello* and *La Sonnambula* had inspired excitement, but *Norma* drove the populace into a frenzy. "Every spectator seemed to be not at the theater, but a witness to the love, to the jealousy, to the fury, to the sacrifice of Norma, so magical was the spell that la Malibran cast. . . . Ah, how this lady is a master of human emotions, and can govern them at her will!"[9]

On the evenings Maria sang Norma, mobs of admirers accompanied her home and serenaded beneath her window for hours on end. "La Donna dell'Arte" now seemed as inadequate as had "La Donna del Canto," and a new title was thought of, "La Regina del Canto" [the Queen of song].[10] The management of the Teatro Comunale now reported that ticket sales for Malibran's performances were the highest ever recorded in the archives of the theater.[11] The ubiquitous Nathaniel Willis happened to arrive in Bologna on an evening when Malibran appeared as the Druid priestess, and he left his impressions of the performance.

The divine music of *La Norma* and a crowded and brilliant audience enthusiastic in their applause, seemed to inspire this still incomparable creature even beyond her wont. She sang with a fullness, an abandonment, a passionate energy and sweetness that seemed to come from a soul rapt and possessed beyond control with the melody it had undertaken. They were never done calling her on the stage after the curtain had fallen. After six re-appearances she came out once more to the footlights, and murmuring something inaudible from lips that showed strong agitation, she pressed her hands together, bowed till her long hair falling over her shoulders nearly touched her feet, and retired in tears. She is the siren of Europe for me![12]

Her effect on the public began to concern the Austrian government, and the secret police sent reports of her activities to Vienna. These spies discovered that underground factions of the *Risorgimento* used the migrations of people to Bologna and other cities in which Malibran sang to conceal their meetings. The informers took note of two concerts in Ferrara and advised Vienna that "the liberals profit by the opportunity provided by Malibran's coming here for two evenings to hold secret meetings with p . . . ,"* and again, "all the principal factions of Bologna were seen there."[13]

Certainly Ferrara provided a perfect opportunity to hold clandestine meetings. Maria was engaged for one concert only, but the crowd at the Casino on May 1 was so large that many had to stand outside in the Piazza listening to the music echo from the auditorium. Thus another concert was

---

*Unfortunately, the file on Malibran was damaged in a severe fire and most of the notes on her activities are burned.

given the following night. The question of whether Malibran was better in a staged performance than in concert had long been resolved in France and England; now Italy reached the same conclusion.

Marvelous is la Malibran in *acting*, many affirming that it is to this, principally, that she owes her successes; but we have heard her in a concert hall where acting is of no use, and with no other support than just singing . . . and yet we have proclaimed her the great mistress of song; we have seen the genius of art, not visually, not adorned and supported by sister arts, but bare. . . .[14]

On May 8 she gave her last staged performance ever in Bologna, and four days later she left for Milan. Ole Bull, who had seen her in Bologna this season, never forgot what he experienced at her performances. Later, learning of her death, he wrote to his wife, "I can't believe it. A woman gifted with a soul of fire, full of the highest passion, a ravishing singer, her dramatic talent and declamation—ah! I remember how I wept in Bologna when I saw her as Desdemona."[15]

In Paris the Chamber of Deputies again proposed a divorce law, passing it on February 24, 1834, by an almost unanimous vote, and three days later they submitted it, for the fourth time, to the Chamber of Peers. Anticipating its success with the Deputies, Lafayette wrote to Maria on February 10, "We have done our annual proposition of law in the Chamber; it will pass with us, but the Chamber of Peers is worth no more than last year, unless by force of beating on the door it feels obliged to open." Once again the Peers ignored it, and the lower Chamber made no further attempts. Lafayette's plan had failed, but his love and devotion still remained.

I have chatted a lot about you and our dear Charles with your friend Mr. Viardot. He confides to me a hope that makes me more happy than I can express. I need to see the appearance of the sun, superior to all the planets; I need even more to embrace my dear Maria and our excellent Charles—Your Italian triumphs are worthy of you and I wish I could witness them, but it is here that I can have the hope of seeing you again, soon, and I live for that hope so dear to my heart. . . . Write me, my dear friend, and you too, my dear Charles, for I need to know everything that interests you. I have only your letters, your scrapbook, and another portrait of you that was given to me, and I would certainly like to see you in person and to chat with you on all your interests.[16]

Both Maria and Charles received this dictated letter with alarm; only the general's signature and a postscript were in his own hand: "Don't worry about me, I will be well in no time." Because of her travels and Lafayette's incorrect addressing of the letter it had been twice forwarded before Maria finally received it in April, and she responded immediately.

April 27, 1834

Mon cher et Bon Général,

You can't know how much pleasure you gave us with your first letter, and especially the second which is written entirely in your own hand.* The first made us weep with emotion and thanks for that angelic kindness which gave you the courage to dictate my letter while all suffering as you were and especially to add those words which well assured us on the state of your health. Nevertheless Charles couldn't help weeping in telling some friends what your goodness constantly does for us, who are ever devoted to you—The second letter made us feel joy in thinking that you were completely out of danger and in a condition to attend to your numerous affairs.

We are in Bologna. I am happy here, for the friendship of the people who surround us contributes to the happiness of existence, and the Bolognese want to demonstrate it to me in the most vehement manner. The evening that I arrived in Bologna, and that I was in the Theater, to greet me, I was saluted with cheering from the entire audience, which cried "Viva la Malibran!" Don't make fun of me, dear Tutor, it is not through vanity that I tell you this, but because I think it would give you the greatest pleasure. You are so good! I have done Otello—La Sonnambula, and Norma. This last one more than the others has excited the rages of fanaticism. I was called back 12 times in the present performance of the piece, and at the end five times, which is the height of success, I may say. The theater was full of foreigners, the city was full of them. I can give you no better idea than to tell you that I have been offered 200 thousand francs for next year, in the most beautiful climate in the world. God give me bis!

It is 2:00 AM—I am tired and I embrace you—Charles too.[17]

In a moment of prescience, Maria, who had never signed a letter to Lafayette with anything more final than "Your pupil," now added a final farewell. "Adieu, cher Tuteur, from your devoted pupil Maria Malibran" were the last words she wrote to the man who had taken such an interest in her life and career. Three weeks later General Lafayette was dead. "It is, after all, a fate which all of us must expect at any time, and which we must take philosophically,"[18] she had once written, but she and Charles grieved deeply over the death of their ever-willing benefactor and friend.

The Milanese considered Maria Malibran's debut at La Scala long overdue, but until Duke Carlo Visconti became manager of the theater she could not appear there because of the mutual lawsuits pending with Gottardi. Now Visconti, eager to bring her to La Scala and being rudely coerced by an impatient public, arranged for the legalities to be pushed aside. Her debut role would be Norma.

Norma had not been heard in Milan since its first performances in 1831–32. One reason was that Pasta, the first Norma, now performed sporadically and her voice, even at its best, had been tried by the difficulties

---

*I have been unable to locate this letter.

of Bellini's score. For another, the work was not a decisive success when first introduced. The singers were not in their best form on the night of the premier and Bellini himself described it as a "fiasco!!!fiasco!!!dismal fiasco!!!"[19] The performances improved, and *Norma* was finally pronounced a triumph, running for thirty-three more evenings. But since the critical reviews were of the first performance, people remembered the opera as a failure.

Pasta, who had made her own La Scala debut as Norma, was a favorite with the Milanese, who considered the newcomer bold, even arrogant, for daring to make her first appearance in a role written for her rival's "encyclopedic character."[20] So, instead of the "Sontagistes," Maria now vied with the "Pastists." And despite rumors that her life was being threatened,* she adhered to her plans. "I am not afraid of Pasta," she declared with determination. "I will live or die as Norma!"[21]

On May 15, the day of her debut, excitement reigned. One music lover, determined to obtain a seat for the event regardless of cost or effort, left a record of his experiences.

For that day, goodbye lunch, goodbye dinner. The fever and excitement dragged me to the theater. It was three o'clock in the afternoon. A ticket one scudo. (With Pasta it was only a florin.) For a box seat in the orchestra it cost as much as eight scudi. The price of seats absolutely fabulous. When I arrived a thousand and more people were already crowded around the theater entrance and were yelling "open up, open up!" I pushed my way into the crowd, pushing myself into that human hedge, and started to scream like a madman without knowing why. I received several punches and avoided several others. . . . Finally the doors were opened ahead of us, turning into a gulf between which we all rushed like demons to take the pit benches by storm with a clamor, an uproar, a brawl. . . . In this manner, entombed in the darkness, we lived from three-fifteen until eight o'clock in the evening. The boredom of waiting, the impatience to hear, the annoyance of the imprisonment reached to the brim. A hand like steel clenched my chest and cut off my breath.[22]

Finally the great chandelier was lit, blazing like a sun in the middle of the theater. The audience began to enter, among them the Viceroy and his wife, the brother of the Duke of Modena, and la Pasta herself, who received wild applause from the pit.

Maria arrived at the theater to prepare for the performance, but she was so nervous that she burst into tears. By the time she appeared on stage she had almost recovered, but it was evident that something had badly upset her. Her trembling was attributed either to another threat against her life or fear of failure. The audience greeted her with prolonged applause, followed by the most profound silence. Her nervous condition affected both her voice and her expressiveness throughout "Casta Diva."

---

*Not as unlikely as it sounds. Melba's life was threatened with grim determination before she made her La Scala debut. She sang and never returned.

Some knew of her Bolognese triumphs in the role and what la Malibran was supposed to represent in the way of surprise and emotion. Considering that she did little or nothing at all in this first scene, they recognized her only by the phenomenal range of her voice, its purity, and the extraordinary beauty of her lower notes.[23] But her voice alone was enough to bring forth the greatest applause, and she had to come forward several times to greet the cheering audience. At the first duet with Ruiz, "attention redoubled," and after the trio that concludes the first act "a universal cry of enthusiasm sprang forth from the entire theater."[24] In the passage "Trema per te, fellone" her powers returned and her sensitive features expressed the strongest and liveliest passions, bringing an unaccustomed realism to the part. At the conclusion of the act the audience gave her four curtain calls.

In the second act the duet between Norma and Adalgisa was "executed with a perfection very difficult to equal, never surpassed," and the audience demanded an encore. The last scene, Pasta's greatest, found Maria struggling against the overpowering impressions her predecessor had left. Because she succeeded before a public familiar with Pasta's interpretation, before an audience in which Bellini's first Norma was sitting, the critics agreed that no higher praise could possibly be paid her.[25] At the conclusion of the performance she received three curtain calls.

Although Maria considered this performance a failure in light of those that followed,* her success was decisive. The following day people discussed little else as new converts praised Malibran, and the Pastists defended their diva. One new admirer wondered if Maria had not been more brilliant on those evenings in Bologna than in her first Milan performance, but decided that even if she wanted to she could not sing badly and that what little or nothing she had done at La Scala was more than enough to turn Milan of the succeeding day into Bologna of the preceding season.[26]

The Pastists pounced on Malibran's weak acting, while the Malibranistes justly claimed that Pasta never sang the role as well as Malibran. The arguments, the disputes, the discussions continued. Although there were questions about Malibran's first performance, after she repeated the role at the height of her powers two days later, doubts disappeared. "What can I say?," wrote a correspondent to a Bolognese journal. "Milan no longer knows itself. The Milanese are out of their minds; they seem to me even . . . . , not even I understand how it is possible to have such a triumph. I would recognize la Malibran from the tears that run down the faces of all her listeners, from the thrill, from the yelling, from the indescribable excitement of the public . . . . All you hear now in Milan is: what singing! what power! what acting! We are stunned. They screamed bis, bis, bis, even for the recitatives. The last scene was something that I can in no way describe."[27]

---

*Manuel Garcia always described his sister's first Norma at La Scala as being less than well received. But since he had not attended the performance, that information could only have come from Maria. Other reports of the evening indicate a success.

Observers of the city's musical life said that her triumph was unprecedented in the annals of La Scala; that her success surpassed anything that had ever been imagined. Maria received sixteen curtain calls after the first act, and when she reappeared in the second the applause became a "veritable tempest."[28] So prolonged was the ovation that the chief of police obtained order only by threatening to evacuate the theater. After thirty curtain calls at the conclusion of the opera—an ovation abbreviated by the reappearance of the police—during which it rained flowers, poems, and other tokens of praise, she was accompanied back to the Visconti Palace by an estimated 20,000 people. At the brilliantly illuminated entrance to the palace she found a triumphal arch bearing complimentary inscriptions, as well as an orchestra and chorus to perform a cantata in her praise. She remained at her balcony to thank the crowd with gracious gestures, and when it at last dispersed, she wept.[29]

Comparisons between Malibran and Pasta had long disappeared in the wake of Malibran's maturing genius. Pasta was now seen to be the perfection of the classic style: the "walk of terrible grandeur," the noble gestures, her every movement accomplished with the full awareness that she was acting for an audience. Although her performances were always magnificent, they were always the same. There were no surprises: she had carefully memorized one musical and dramatical interpretation.

Malibran, in contrast, represented a new style, an emotional realism that replaced the accepted attitudes and gestures hitherto used to portray a character's sentiments. Her emotions, although carefully analyzed in advance, were felt rather than portrayed, and she varied her performances as new subtleties of her part occurred to her. That her reviews constantly refer to her "truth to nature" was no accident, for audiences were not accustomed to a more natural style. "She was always present for herself on the stage," wrote Delacroix of Pasta, and he meant it as a compliment. But Malibran "forgot to find herself before a public."[30] The painter attempted to defend Pasta at Malibran's expense, but he did not realize that of the two approaches Malibran's was the more modern, pointing the way to future conceptions of stage presentation. Pasta's style, great though it was, represented the stilted concepts of the past. Legouvé noted that "even in the works of Rossini, la Pasta expressed a dignity, a gravity, a nobility that bound her to the old school."[31]

Three days later Maria presented her famous Desdemona. The critics cautiously wondered how they could accurately describe the continued hysteria without sounding excessive to those who had not witnessed the performance, and without seeming cold to those who had. "Nature, in overwhelming Madame Malibran with her favors, would seem to have wanted to exhaust everything in the luxury of her gifts," raved one.[32]

During her Milan engagement Maria sang five performances in ten days which, for the Milanese, became a series of holidays, a festival in which the orchestra of La Scala played in the gardens of the Visconti Palace and crowds followed Malibran home from the theater every night. So many people had come to the city to hear her sing that, in the words of a journalist, "The streets of Milan, usually dull after midnight, have been transformed into the streets of Venice in the summer night festivals, and the crowds of every class of people are immense, all exultation and joy.—The name of Malibran resounds to the stars."[33] A music periodical declared her "almost deified." "She has excited an enthusiasm for which there is no precedent. . . . It is a fanaticism, a rage, which passes all boundaries."[34]

"Mariette will never be able to find anywhere else the delights of vanity that they give her here," wrote Charles to his sister. "In the streets they stop to watch her go by, the people of the lower classes follow her and greet her as if she were the Queen. . . . All this would turn the head of a lesser singer."[35]

On May 25 Maria left Milan, but not without first having signed a contract for fifteen performances the following fall as well as accepting engagements for the Carnivales of 1835 and 1836 at a total fee of 420,000 French francs. Visconti could afford to pay these enormous sums, because the demand to see la Malibran was so great that boxes at La Scala sold for as much as 1,000 French francs.[36] As she departed, the Count de Hartig, Governor General of Lombardy, presented her with a replica of the famous Lombard crown entwined with flowers. "The leaves and flowers are too ephemeral to be a symbol of our lasting admiration for your genius and talents," he told her. "Please accept this metal crown which holds them and wear it once in a while."[37]

En route to London, she and Charles stopped in Paris for a day or two, and spent several hours with friends who were amazed to see her sit down at the piano at eight o'clock in the evening and remain there until two hours after midnight. The improvement in her vocal powers since they had last heard her astonished these people. "Such is the revolution in her talent that she would hardly be recognized by those who are most accustomed to hearing her. Her voice has doubled in volume, and has become more sonorous, and more mellow. Her genius as a singer has grown in immense proportion, and her manner of executing her beautiful embellishments makes any comparison impossible."[38] The publication of this news disappointed the Parisians, for Malibran would not accept an engagement with the Théâtre-Italien.

From Paris the lovers traveled to Brussels to visit their families and then continued to London, where Manuel, now a voice teacher, was giving a concert. There Maria was immediately accosted by Alfred Bunn for a performance of *La Sonnambula*. Her reply was very businesslike; she did not even take the trouble to write in English.

Mon cher Monsieur Bunn—Pressed for time as I am, having but a few days to remain in London since I leave for Italy *before the end of the month*, I would willingly accept your offer to play *La Sonnambula* in English for one night, but on the terms of *two hundred fifty pounds sterling*, payable on the morning of the performance. I thought it right to let you know my intentions at once so as not to lose time in correspondence and meetings which would in no way change my mind.

With best regards,
M. F. Malibran

21 June
Saturday morning
P.S. Yes, or no, at once if you please.
In case you accept, would you please mention the terms contained in the present letter?[39]

Bunn did not consider *La Sonnambula* as big an attraction in London as it had been in Naples and Bologna. Stunned at her fee, and at her demand to be paid in advance, he did not accept her terms.

On June 30 Maria left London for Italy to perform in Sinigaglia and Lucca. As she traveled through the Italian countryside word of her presence spread, and in every village she was awaited as though she were royalty. Crowds pressed around her coach to catch a glimpse of her as she passed by, and the streets outside her hotel windows filled with people calling to her to sing. If they were too persistent she would sometimes come to the balcony and with de Bériot's accompaniment give them a song. Maria always declared that the appreciation of the simple folk at such impromptu performances meant as much to her as the greatest ovations in major theaters. She rarely missed a chance to sing to shepherds, farmers, woodsmen, or anyone else she encountered while riding or traveling. The open-mouthed astonishment of a peasant was as great a compliment to her as the homage of a king.

On July 13 the travelers reached Bologna, and on July 15 they arrived in Sinigaglia for the fair. A bout with heat prostration—Maria drove the coach herself—did not prevent her from beginning her engagement on schedule, or from making the expected furore, a fact that immediately put her at odds with the government. Because the Austrian government feared political uprisings, meetings or groups were not allowed, nor were demonstrations that might excite the populace. An ordinance forbidding a performer to receive more than one curtain call at the conclusion of a performance was tested to the limit at Malibran's first appearance; when the audience insisted on calling her back more than once, the police appeared and painted white crosses on the backs of the offending music lovers. When the theater at last emptied those so marked were taken off to jail.

Learning of this outrage, Maria immediately informed the city council that she would not tolerate curtailment of applause, and that if her admirers were not freed at once she would leave the city. Faced with the disastrous economic consequences of such a defection, not to mention popular anger at the loss of "La Regina del Canto," the government capitulated.[40] This was no doubt the wisest course of action: the Sinigaglians so loved Malibran that at the conclusion of her stay in their city, as her coach was seen departing across the fairgrounds, they unhitched her horses and would not let her continue until she sang for them one last time.

Maria was so successful in Lucca that the Italians tried to claim her as their own, discovering that previous rumors of her Spanish parentage were incorrect. She had been born twenty-six years before, near Lucca, the daughter of one Francesco Paolinelli.[41] Every social class adored her. One night during a performance the Duke of Lucca and his party were eating ices in his box, and he had a dish sent backstage for Maria. When the dish was later returned with her thanks, the Duke smashed it so that the young nobles, already fighting over it, could each have a piece of the cup from which la Malibran had eaten.[42]

The court in Lucca, presided over by its good-natured Duke, was undoubtedly the most informal in Europe, as a letter from Charles de Bériot attests.

August 31, 1834

Ma Chère Sœur,

We returned yesterday from the baths of Lucca, where we passed two days in a most beautiful fashion. It is impossible to find a sovereign more affable and more jovial than the Duke of Lucca. The same goes for the Queen Mother of Naples. The soirée which I told you about in my last letter took place at her home last Friday. Mariette sang a dozen different pieces, among them one by Coutiau, which made everyone laugh heartily. This was not laughing of the pinched and required type which etiquette demands in France, and even in Belgium, but of that frank gaiety of the bourgeoisie; for here one does not constrain himself at the court! One enters, one salutes the Duke and the Queen, one takes off his hat in a corner of the salon and does what he wants. I would become an enraged royalist if there were such liberty in all the courts. . . .

The day after this soirée the Queen sent us, through her secretary, a magnificent brooch of diamonds for Maria's forehead and a solitaire of great value as a ring to be worn on the little finger of my left hand, with which I am sure always to have a brilliant cadenza, and a very pretty ornament for Mariette's sister Pauline. And in addition to all this, a purse to cover the expenses of the trip. So you can see that things are going well.

We passed the rest of the evening with Prince Poniatowsky, in company with the sovereign Duke who was madly gay during dinner, over which he presided amidst the company with a little ruler at hand to kill the wasps which are numerous in this country; he didn't miss a one. After dinner he began to dance, sing, and jump, taking everyone by the hand. . . . Finally he played the piano and sang a buffo duet from *Le Mariage Secret*, in a piquant manner.

For one moment a little incident occurred to trouble the music, but it only made the evening more picturesque. Two bats, attracted by the light, were having fun fluttering and frolicking around our heads. All the women fled from the room, but the men, in the midst of which was His Royal Highness, armed themselves with sticks and whips and after two hours of combat, we succeeded in killing our enemies.

My letter, my dear Constance, has been interrupted by another campaign improvised on the spur of the moment. We spent two days at the baths, at the home of Prince Poniatowsky with His Royal Highness, who was as amiable as ever. I had brought a cane from Paris with a lead knob, which appealed very much to the Duke who took it and gave me his own in exchange, which is garnished with a knob of gold and is therefore worth twice as much to me.[43]

When Maria sang her last performance, her benefit, on September 7 Charles wrote to his sister that "the house was one vast field of laurels, and the escort [home from the theater] was armed with torches this time.[44]

She was seen in Bologna on September 23, and the next day she continued her journey to Milan where her new engagement of thirteen performances was to begin September 27. Still excited about Malibran's first series of performances the previous spring, the Milanese struck medals commemorating her visit. One side bore Maria's profile and the inscription "Maria Felicita Garcia Malibran"; the reverse read "Proclaimed Admirable in Acting and Singing, Milan 1834."[45] A Milan newspaper described Malibran in terms beyond those reserved for mere mortals.

La Malibran is a rather small lady, lively, fickle as a thought, heedless as happiness. She does not have desires because hers are all anticipated. Her eccentricities and monumental caprices are pardoned. Wherever she goes, Glory in human guise acts as her courier, and if she did nothing other than to give 30 of her days to 30 singing women, 30 reputations would be made. La Malibran is neither beautiful nor ugly; she has something not descended from Adam, something that is the result of what we wish and imagine. Everyone sees her differently. She has a face that is rather elongated, but delightfully so, a nose that is almost aquiline, a mouth immense in delight, and two great big flashing black eyes that a nail couldn't put out.[46]

She performed *Norma* first and continued with *La Sonnambula*, *I Capuleti*, and *Otello*. She was greeted as a deity, the "most resplendent and admirable star who could ever have risen on the theatrical horizon," eliciting "that furious applause which only her presence seems to excite," and she left at least one critic admitting that to describe her superlative singing and acting was "an undertaking beyond the limits of possibility."[47] At a performance of scenes from *La Cenerentola* and *Il Barbiere*, "each scene formed a complete composition, a finished representation of a complete character," and "the enthusiasm reached to such a point that in the annals of La Scala there is not to be found a like example."[48] At her last performance, on October 26, she again sang Norma, and was called before the curtain eighteen times. *"I said eighteen times,"* repeated one awed critic.[49]

The next morning she rushed off to Naples, where her third engagement with the Royal Theaters was to begin November 13. She and Charles reached Modena November 27 and Bologna November 28.

[undated]

To Counselor Parola, Milan.
I am writing you without knowing if the post will leave, but I cannot wait any longer to give you news of us. With our usual speed, we arrived in Modena the

same Monday at 9:00, in time to enjoy the show (Sonnambula) with our good friend the Marquise Carondini. After the performance, to bed.

Tuesday, at 11:00 we were flying by coach and at 1:00 we were in Bologna. Again this time we arrived in time to be present at the performance (Norma) and to enjoy it. I left, persuaded *more than ever* that all the rumors spread in Milan about the non-success of this opera are wrong. La Pasta was received with acclaim. After the cavatina (which she sang marvelously) she received five curtain calls. After the trio, two curtain calls. Always applauded at the end of all her scenes. Two times after the duet with Adalgisa in the second act. The duet with Donzelli was also repeated and well sung; at the end of the performance she reappeared two more times. It was nearly midnight when the performance was finished: the unanimous acclamations called Pasta back. It appeared that she had gone through too much emotion; she waited several times; she finally appeared, supported by Garcia and Zucchelli, with barely enough strength to express her thanks to the public, and particularly to the honorable spectators who had had the consideration not to leave until they had seen her again.

You see then, my dear Parola, that the fun they have had in saying that Pasta has not had a great success is impossible to believe after such facts, which, I assure you, are very true. Therefore, when you are told such idle rumors, read my letter and believe only me. In the intermission I went to see Pasta, who was extremely gracious to me. She asked me for news of the Duke and Duchess Visconti, adding that she thanked me on behalf of the Milanese people for my gift of singing there. You can see that no one could be more amiable than la Pasta. I beg you then to inform those who are always ready to spread bad news, that they are *very mistaken* about her, and that in my presence she made a furore.[50]

Just after the conclusion of the performance, Pasta wrote her mother a few words about the evening. "Here I am back from the theater, which was not filled. But the applause was beautiful, louder than usual. La Malibran appeared during Donzelli's aria in the company of the Countess Carondini. As soon as the act was over, she came to see me in my dressing room and the two of them showered me with compliments which were very much appreciated. . . . I thanked la Malibran for the favor she did me for my compatriots."[51]

Maria often was charitable toward her rivals, especially when it became apparent to her that she need fear no one—she had no real competitors. On her first trip through Italy she heard the soprano Caroline Ungher. "I stopped expressly to see Mlle Ungher. The time I spent in hearing her will not be lost for me. I have over her at present a notable advantage: I know the nature of her talent; she knows me only by name, and for that I am not sorry."[52] And yet, as Alfred Bunn observed, "The idea that the fame of any living *artiste* could approach hers was enough to eat her heart away."[53]

On October 30 the travelers continued on to Naples, arriving safely on November 5 after a harrowing journey via Florence and Rome. In a letter to Parola Charles wrote,

You have heard, no doubt, that [Alessandro] Lanari was cleaned out on the road from Rome to Naples, between Fondi and Terracina. He was with his wife and daughter. The robbers, having put a pistol to their throats, laid them on the ground and took everything they possessed, money, jewels, etc. These same bandits were captured by 25 gendarmes. There were four of them; three were killed, the fourth is to be executed shortly. They put up a stubborn resistance and a gendarme was killed by a gunshot. We passed over the same ground during the night, but with an escort of three men armed to the teeth.[54]

On November 13, 1834, Maria reappeared at the Fondo in the role of Amina, an occasion for tripled prices and predictable hysteria from both audience and critics. "Furore, sempre furore," reported the reviewer for *Teatri*, who praised her "perfect execution."[55] She followed *La Sonnambula* with *Tancredi* on November 19 and concluded the performance with a rondo Pacini had composed for her to interpolate. And on December 4 she repeated *Norma*. "Yes," wrote Cottrau to his brother, "la Malibran has had a colossal success in her reappearance! Truthfully, she is better than ever according to all reports."[56]

Many operas were to be written for Malibran during her Naples engagement probably because a new group, the Society of the Theaters of Naples, now managed the Royal Theaters. The Society was eager to make a brilliant impression, but from the beginning it had trouble. Meyerbeer, Auber, Donizetti,[57] and Bellini were busy with other projects when first approached in 1834, and although Bellini—hard at work on a new score for the Théâtre-Italien but sorely tempted by the thought of writing for Malibran—finally agreed to adapt his unfinished French opera for Naples, the Society had to turn to lesser talents for other new works. When Malibran arrived in early November, there were four new operas for her to learn this winter: *Amelia*, by Lauro Rossi; *Ines de Castro*, by Giuseppe Persiani; the Naples version of Bellini's *I Puritani*; and *Il Colonello*, by the brothers Luigi and Federico Ricci.

Amelia, first presented on December 31, 1834, delighted Maria especially since she had persuaded Rossi to include a mazurka for her. Naples, never having seen Malibran dance, eagerly anticipated *Amelia*, but the work fell flat. In spite of the lyrical and spontaneous music, the public did not like opera buffa at the San Carlo, a large theater associated with grand opera, and the production itself was poor. Cottrau reported that "la Malibran was badly seconded in it by Pedrazzi, Frezzolini and a crowd of second and third rate dogs, and the work was horribly mounted in old sets, used to death and out of place, not to mention the completely disparate costumes which were anachronisms and charades of the action. Add to that an unfortunate mazurka which that crazy Malibran wanted to dance in the second act with a dancer named Mathis! . . . It was enough to scandal our perukes! In brief, the opera, although applauded at several reprises in Malibran's four pieces, has not been a success and will not long be a part of the repertoire."[58]

Maria was disgusted with the Society, which allowed *Amelia* only a week and a half at the San Carlo because of upcoming productions. And she did not want to move the production to the Fondo, "what with the very horrible sets and the spite shown by the Society via Frezzolini, whom they never let sing because they are obliged to give 50 ducats per performance to Lanari. Frezzolini *pleases me very much* as an actor, and he is a good man."[59]

Maria was much embittered by this third losing attempt to create a great opera in Naples, following the ill-fated *Irene* and *La Figlia del Arciere* of earlier seasons. Now she would try again with *Ines de Castro*, which had music by Persiani and a libretto by Salvatore Cammarano. At first she refused the role altogether, and when she at last was persuaded to play it, she ridiculed the music bitterly. Gilbert Duprez, her tenor this winter, understood her emotional state but was annoyed at her behavior. One day when she let herself go in a "scoffing humor," he seized the score, sat down at the piano, and sang a fragment of it himself. "If you would sing that with conviction," he told her, "you would see that it is no laughing matter."[60] Delighted to see that someone else had confidence in the opera, she immediately began learning her part with all her usual intensity.

Duprez' confidence paid off: *Ines de Castro* was the greatest work Maria had created since *Clary*, and it would be played throughout Europe by other renowned singers, including the composer's wife, Fanny Tacchinardi-Persiani. During the opera's first performance, the theater was said to have quaked from explosions of applause that surpassed Vesuvius' strongest eruptions,[61] and when the hapless Ines was led to the block singing "Io non moro, vado in cielo i miei figli a ritrovar,"* people sobbed audibly, and several women were carried out fainting. On these words Maria was considered "superhuman,"[62] and before the evening ended, she was responsible for a new law in the city: only one curtain call per artist at the conclusion of an opera.

The critics declared the work "a complete success." Writing moments after the final curtain, a reviewer found it "full of good situations and beautiful verse." As for Malibran's performance, "We are incapable of finding new ways in which to praise her as she finds new passions with which to enchant us. When, in the terzetto, she embraces and blesses her sons, when, in the last scene she shudders before her phantom persecutor, when, in the cavatina she remembers the first joys of love, when, made wife, she consoles herself so as to be able to appear before everyone, who will doubt that she is divine? There was one signora this evening who denied it, but through tears."[63]

Charles de Bériot left his own revealing insights on *Ines*:

---

*"I do not die, I go to heaven, my sons to find." Excerpts from two of Malibran's arias were published in *Allgemeine Musikalische Zeitung* 37, no. 30 (July 1835): 500-501. They are extremely difficult.

Naples, February 3, 1835

Mon cher Parola,

Persiani's opera *Ines de Castro* had its first performance last Wednesday. I promised to tell you a little about it. I will act then as a reporter of that evening. This work is decidedly superb from beginning to end and has obtained a complete success, a success even more meritorious when you consider that in the last fifteen years it is only the third new opera to have succeeded, the other two being [Donizetti's] *L'Esule di Roma* and [Pacini's] *L'Ultimo Giorno di Pompeii.* All others have been hissed unmercifully.

Ines de Castro is an opera largely tailored for the effect of a big theater. There is not one weak piece; there is in particular a scene with trio in the second act which brings tears to the eyes. It is at the moment when Ines embraces her sons, whom she will never see again. The role of Ines is one of the most beautiful in Mariette's repertoire. The tenor part, which Duprez performed with much honor, is also very first rate. In sum total, it is a superb opera. But, my dear Parola, in a country where the chefs-d'oeuvre of Rossini have been hissed one after another, I question whether the merit of the composer alone is the cause to which one can attribute the success of a work. . . . No, without a doubt, and to explain to you the success of *Ines de Castro* I will tell you that if one were able to lift the veil which covers this mystery, one would see at the very beginning fifty ducats in the pocket of the conductor, without which that gentleman is incapable of favor for the author, of zeal, and of attention to the rehearsals, and finally of the ensemble and regularity of the orchestra.

One would see, in the second place, another sum likewise in the pocket of the chorus master, without which the choristers don't have lungs. One would see that even the costumer receives his little gift, without which the actors would be dressed like pigs and the opera held up by a month more. In a word, everything here is bought, because everything is up for sale. Friendship, favor, kindness, all are reduced to this balance: *"How much will you give me for that?"* Even silence is bought in the theater. Silence behind the scenes is a matter of negotiation here, and the poor author who doesn't pass all these conditions finds a thousand arms against him which will, without fail, kill him.

Persiani had the good sense to foresee all these obstacles. Also, one says that the poor devil entirely sacrificed the profit from his opera. Also, contrary to the custom of the San Carlo, there was ensemble in the execution, luxury in the costumes and sets, and as for Amelia, she was covered with rags while Ines de Castro was resplendent in gilt and richness.

All that, my dear friend, is very degrading, but it is the truth. I have such a distaste for it that I await the day when I will leave Naples, never to return, as the most beautiful day of my life. One more word on Ines. The success of this opera, which no one expected, has mortally wounded two parties: the Ronzists, because of Maria, and the Barbaistes because of the Society. What they have done to entirely paralyze the effect of the music! They decreed yesterday an order which prevents applause more than one time, and prevents more than one curtain call for the artists. As a result of this, the performance yesterday, which was the third time for Ines, restrained by several gendarmes, was reduced to an ordinary, everyday performance. Maria has been crying over this, for nothing is closer to her heart than to excite the enthusiasm of the public. That is, in effect, the only recompense for a true artist. As for me, I don't mind telling you that nothing can better prove a triumph than the necessity of employing force to restrain it.[64]

But the trying political intrigues of Naples did not depress Maria for she received promising news from Paris on the status of her pending annulment. On February 3 Charles told Parola, "I await constantly and with impatience a decision from Paris. Troupenas wrote me, but his letter told me nothing new. The thing will be judged shortly, that's all."[65] Any shred of hope raised Maria's spirits. To Legouvé she wrote, "I am the happiest of women! The idea of changing my name does me so much good! My health is perfect, and as for the fatigue of the theater, it is, for me, as refreshing as *sherbet!*"[66]

The third new opera written for Malibran was to be Bellini's new work for Paris, his *I Puritani*, commissioned by the Théâtre-Italien for a brilliant cast including Giulia Grisi, Rubini, Tamburini, and Lablache. As such the opera did not suit the Naples company, which lacked the two required basses. But even before signing his final contract with the Society in late November 1834, and even as he was writing the original piece for Paris, Bellini gave much thought to the changes necessary for a Malibran version in Naples.

On arriving in Naples in early November, Maria learned of the Society's negotiations with Bellini and voiced her fears that a role written for Grisi would not suit her.[67] But the composer had already told Florimo he would adapt the opera to Malibran and the rest of the company, "perhaps composing some new piece when I believe it necessary, in conjunction with Malibran, who will be consulted by me fully, and perhaps write a quasi-new opera which will be quite new by the changes that I will do for it. . . . In the opera there is no cavatina for the leading lady, and if Malibran wants it, I will write one for her. In the course of the opera I will get together with her so that she will be the principal column, whereas now there are four of them."[68]

On November 30 he rejoiced in Malibran's success in his *Sonnambula*, and in another letter to Florimo he sought to calm her fears about the new work: "Tell her that I will adapt *I Puritani* to her voice and that she need have no fear of the role because it is as passionate as *Nina,** and that it would provide some solo situations spoken in prose and played by her so that they will excite an immense appeal. Tell her also that I am waiting for, and that I long for, a chance to show her the vast extent of my admiration for her, an admiration that could even give umbrage to her dear Charles, whom I greet dearly."[69]

In this letter Bellini made clear the interest he took in revising his work for Malibran. Some revisions were even being incorporated into the piece as it would be played in Paris.

*Paisiello's *Nina, Pazza per Amore*, one of Pasta's favorite operas.

Dec. 21–22, 1834

These are the changes that I have made for Malibran. The situation for the cavatina is not in the libretto; therefore she will enter in a duet with Porto, and then in place of a small insignificant quartet I have written a piece so curious and so brilliant that she will be overjoyed with it, because it is the sort of thing she likes. This aria is worth more than ten cavatinas, because it is well placed, so much so that I will even give it in Paris, it being so effective.[70]

The piece was the aria "son vergin vezzosa," a great success. Thus if Malibran did not have an entire opera written for her by Bellini, she did have the great aria she so desired.

Bellini continued:

To her will go the finale, the largo will rest on her, there will be much action and especially in the *stretta*, where, since she doesn't have the principal motif, which, being the Puritani Anthem, belongs to the basses and the chorus, she will fill the stage with her insane, emotional cries, felled by the immense pain of fleeing from her lover, etc.—she can be admirable in this kind of expression, which is new to the stage.[71]

Malibran had so inspired the work that Bellini already thought of giving it with her in Milan, quite apart from the Naples contract.[72]

Under the terms of his contract Bellini was obliged to see that the first act of the score reached Naples by January 12 and the second no more than eight days later. He worked furiously to finish it in time to mail it to Marseille, where ships were due to leave December 31 and January 1 for Naples. But in early January 1835 he learned that because of the cholera quarantine, the steamships bearing the first parts of the work had been delayed, and he advised the Society of the problem. Perhaps foreseeing a futile outcome, he bitterly told Florimo that if the Society refused the score he would never again come to Naples, "not for all the treasures in the world, and the result of the first orchestra rehearsal of the first act of *I Puritani* this morning makes me hope that I will remain in Paris. The music has an admirable effect on me."[73]

"This work was a wonderful inspiration, and here Rubini does it like a God. La Malibran will do it even better, I do not doubt, but who knows whether it will be given. I see that if you start rehearsals on the 24th or 25th you could perform within twelve days. The opera is uncomplicated, without many complexities, and it stands completely on that little devil Malibran, who in the course of one night can learn a whole opera."[74]

But the event was not to be, for the ships reached Naples long after the deadline. Maria tried to convince the Society not to cancel the contract, but to no avail. On January 24, 1835, the very day of the enormously successful premier of *I Puritani*, the Society sent Bellini a letter stating that his opera would not be produced.[75] Annoyed that "that angel Malibran" had not been able to play his work for the Neapolitans, Bellini begged Florimo to "tell her that I will love her always, always, even at the risk of incurring the hate of her Charles. Her behavior in these last circumstances makes me want to go right down to Naples and cover her with kisses in spite of everyone. But tell her I hope to meet her again some day, and there is no telling what will happen on my part."[76]

Paris, February 27, 1835

Madame Malibran, Venice

My dear and good friend,

I cannot help myself from thanking you personally and directly for the affectionate manner that you showed me on the final circumstance of receiving the score of my *Puritani* on behalf of the Society of the Theaters of Naples. Florimo writes me that one of my lovers couldn't show me more concern, and I believe it, and I will always believe that you love me, because I adore you, and I have always adored you and your truly miraculous talent as well as your truly delightful and animated self, and also your three souls* (because you must have that many of them and not just one like all other women). From now on, *I want* to write to you from time to time. *I want* you to answer me, and *I want* our friendship to be a fraternal one full of concern and love, and to say so, and that our friendship be founded upon true esteem, and to become very dear. Therefore, from now on, whatever la Malibran imposes, Bellini will accomplish!

I wish frankness and sincerity, even at the cost of momentary displeasure, but I don't want any feelings which would destroy the most solid friendships. Therefore, write me if you accept my affection with your heart, an affection which is the offspring of the highest regard, sympathy, and gratefulness. Write to me and count on me for everything I can do without any reservations. My kindest regards to the dear Bériot and here is a letter to him from our common friend Aubry, the most amiable of men. Addio my little angel. I hope that it will be you who will give *I Puritani* in Milan, and I hope that that miser Duke Visconti gives me much money to write an opera especially for you. Addio, addio, I hope your Charles permits me to send you a kiss of gratitude.

Your most affectionate Bellini[77]

Had fate permitted, such an opera probably would have been written.

The fourth new work written for her was *Il Colonello* by Luigi and Federico Ricci, but an accident ended her participation in its presentation. One evening she was returning from a shooting contest in the open calèche of a young French doctor named Thibault, on her way to dine with Madame Lagrange. The coach proceeded through a crowded stretch of the Strada Toledo, a section being repaved and thus muddy and uneven, when the vehicle became bogged down in the mud. As the horses slowly pulled it through, a hog which was about to be slaughtered in the street—usual procedure in Naples—became excited by the fire being prepared and escaped, running madly between the legs of the horses, which charged, tearing off the front of the carriage and throwing Maria and the doctor into the street. Thibault, uninjured, carried Maria into a nearby cabaret where he set her dislocated wrist, and then took her the short distance to Mme.

---

*See Lamartine's verses on her tomb (p. 230), although Bellini is due precedence.

Lagrange's mansion where the hostess and her guests placed her on a sofa in front of the fire and saw that she received a proper sling. Maria suffered only a sprained wrist and a few cuts, but her concern turned to de Bériot. "Don't let Charles know how bad this was," she told her friends. "I know how upset he will be."[78]

All Naples discussed the incident. Many imaginative and inaccurate drawings of the accident appeared in the papers; friends and strangers offered condolences. The next day the King sent his personal physician to bleed her, but she accepted only homeopathic remedies, in which she had great faith. Her mishap did not keep her out of society for long, however, as a letter from Charles indicates.

I had put on a chinese costume to go to the ball of the Marquise de Lagrange and Mariette went as a chinese woman, with her poor little arm in a sling. I have never seen her as pretty. The Marquis de Lagrange went as Mother Goose with twelve feet. The ball was the most brilliant given in Naples this year. What a wonderful woman Mme Lagrange is! During the whole time of the accident, not to say of Mariette's illness, we have lived with her and she has treated us like children.[79]

On February 23, eight days after her fall, Maria reappeared as Amina, somewhat hampered by her arm, which was still in a sling. The audience applauded her vehemently, so much so that the police once again were called in to enforce the ordinances. Perhaps thinking the acclaim was solely the result of her performance rather than sympathy for her battered arm and happiness at her return to the stage, Maria commented to an actor friend, "I've learned a good lesson from this. Perhaps I used too much action before: the accident kept me almost immobile, but even so, I never received more applause."[80]

Meanwhile *Il Colonello*, along with *I Puritani*, lost its chance with Malibran, whose engagement ended in the first days of March. Caroline Ungher performed the work three weeks after Maria left Naples for Venice. To the surprise of all it was a resounding success. Maria declared her intention of singing the work in an English translation during her engagement in London, and at La Scala, but the plans never materialized.[81]

On March 4, 1835, crowds of admirers followed Maria Malibran to the outskirts of Naples as she departed from the city for the last time. "The crowns, the medals, the monuments of marble and letters, are rewards of our time, but the pleasures enjoyed recommend themselves to posterity" wrote a journalist in a published "addio." "And when we live in memories, recalling how nature and art lavished on you their utmost powers, we will have that memory with which to embitter the youth of our children. Addio . . . may your life be long and glorious and most happy. Addio . . . addio."[82]

CHAPTER 14

Venice: Il Teatro Malibran

To alleviate the long and tiring journey from Naples to Venice Maria and Charles intended to stop in Bologna for a few days rest. Just before they reached the city, however, their coach broke down in Arezzo, and they stopped for repairs.

While the work was being done, the travelers toured the town. In the process they visited an insane asylum. Maria spoke with the director, who tried to explain to her the nature and treatment of the patients' problems. Never one to overlook a charitable cause, she asked if any of them might like to hear her sing. The director thought that a young man, whose madness had been caused by his having fallen in love with the Queen, would enjoy her singing. He loved music but was so sexually frustrated that he would rave at the sight of a woman. Maria decided this would cause no problem, for she was dressed in male attire, and at her request was led to the madman's room. When she entered he stared at her curiously. She walked to a piano and sang the Willow Song from *Otello*. Her listener was rapt. "Is this divine?," he asked, and became violently excited. "No!," he cried, answering his own question, "this is the voice of a woman!," and fell into hysteria.

The director quickly dragged her from the room, tactfully thanking her and assuring her that she had done worlds of good for his patient. She needed little encouragement to leave and was hurrying out of the building when she was stopped by a group of inmates who asked her if she would like to hear them sing. Unwillingly, but politely, she listened as this madmen's chorus turned into a truly unforgettable performance. As soon as she could she fled, leaving a large donation with the director.[1]

On March 8, 1835, at three in the afternoon, she and Charles arrived in Bologna, where, over the next ten days, she sang three unscheduled concerts. There she and her lover learned that on February 20 and 27 Maria's suit for the annulment of her marriage had been judged by the Tribunal de première instance de la Seine. Monsieur Marie, one of her legal contingent, presented the case: Eugène Malibran was born French but had long been absent from his native land and had become an American citizen, thereby renouncing his French citizenship; Maria Garcia, on the other hand, was the daughter of a Spaniard who, although he had immigrated to France, had never become a French citizen and therefore could not pass this privilege on to his children: thus the marriage, which had been performed before the French consul, was void, since a French official had no authority to marry a Spaniard and an American. As for the question of who could judge the case, Marie pointed out that the French courts were able to do so, for Eugène Malibran had returned to France and claimed his French citizenship, while Maria Garcia lived in France and had taken out naturalization papers.[2] This questionable logic was accepted by the Tribunal, and on March 6, 1835, the marriage between Eugène Malibran and Maria Garcia was declared null and void. The annulment carried two stipulations, however: the divorced parties could not remarry for ten months, and to do so they had to prove residence in Paris at the time of the remarriage. These vexations could be tolerated after so many years of uncertainty.

In learning the good news Maria nearly became ill from joy. To Virginia Cottinet she wrote: "In the midst of all my fluctuations of hope and of fear, I thought of you, and it gave me courage. . . . Never in my life will I forget those dear people who took as much interest in me as if I were their own daughter! Am I not almost your daughter? And at the same time your sister? And at the same time your friend? Everything together! Ah! It is good just to tell you so!"[3]

On March 19 the couple left Bologna for the last time. In the opinion of a Bolognese writer, "Her singing was what no pen will ever be able to describe: unknown melodies, new expressions, and tones that came from heaven."[4]

Two months earlier Maria had signed a contract with the impresario of the Gran Teatro La Fenice in Venice for an engagement of no less than six performances of three operas: *Otello, La Cenerentola,* and *Norma.* The announcement of her contract, and of the enormous sums being paid for her eleven-day engagement, met with a degree of rancor from the Venetian press, which observed that "an age infatuated with female singing throats is a very strange age, if not worse" and wondered if so much love, indeed, so much money, might not be put to better use in helping the poor and discouraged.[5]

Published during the weeks before her arrival was a book of verse entitled: "For the arrival of the eminent Singing Artist - MARIA GARCIA MALIBRAN - in Venice," forty-six verses celebrating the coming of Malibran, written by Carlo Cambiaggio, a performer at the Teatro Emeronittio. Cambiaggio anticipated not only the "exquisite enjoyment" that would be provided the Venetians, but the influx of tourist money. He concluded his work by wishing Malibran "health and happiness for a hundred years, far from misfortune and harm,"[6] a vain hope for only days after the publication of his booklet she was thrown from her carriage in Naples.

On March 18, 1835, a notice appeared in the *Apatista:* "LA MALI-

BRAN A VENEZIA: the enthusiasm that we all feel for the arrival of Signora Garcia-Malibran, foremost singer, as they say, of the universe, is extraordinary. . . ." Even at this point in her career people could still imagine new ways to publicly honor Maria Malibran. She could not have been prepared for her reception in Venice. The entire city awaited her arrival as though Caesar were returning in triumph from his wars. On the morning of Friday, March 20, boats were sent out into the lagoon to watch for her approach from the mainland. At 12:45 the word came back: la Malibran was nearing the head of the Grand Canal. At that moment all work and business abruptly stopped as people ran through the narrow streets shouting "She's coming! She's coming!" Her gondola entered the canal as brass bands trumpeted her arrival, great crowds cheering along the waterway. The crowds and bands followed as she passed slowly through the city. At St. Mark's Square police had to make room for her to disembark and then lead her and Charles through the backways to their lodgings at the Barberigo Palace.

It had originally been announced that she would appear first as Desdemona on March 24, her twenty-seventh birthday, but because of political difficulties her debut was postponed until March 26. Whatever the Venetians had expected, they were not disappointed. Charles wrote to Cottrau: "Mariette made her debut yesterday in Otello. . . . Immense success! The first cavatina repeated—then the enthusiasm continued to increase until the end of the third act, after which she was called back more than ten times. The Venetian public has shown a feeling and intelligence perfect to the last detail."[7]

Two days later Maria repeated the work with equal success, and she wrote of her satisfaction to a friend in Paris.

The devil, or rather the emperor (God bless him!) has upset us; for we had been up in the air until the famous decision permitted us to appear onstage the 24th. Right away we took the road to Venice. To describe to you the enthusiasm which preceded me would be long in the telling.

I want, however, to tell you about an incident which happened before we got here. You know that they play the lottery in Venice, as they do in Naples, for the lower classes. Well! my dear papa, the people of the lowest class amused themselves by playing: 10, the singer;* 17, the day when my debut was announced; 24, the day of my debut; and 6, the six performances that I would be playing. . . . Would you believe that *the four numbers won*, and that the lowly winner won 900 Austrian pounds?

The Venetians have therefore said that I was a *good omen*, and consequently they follow me like little dogs, mastifs, pugs, greyhounds, toutous, and some bipeds, according to whether the person is of a lower or higher station. Fortunately, pigs don't run all over the place here like they do in Naples. Lithographs have been made of me and my fall, my departure from Naples, and my arrival in Venice. . . .

*Ten letters in *cantatrice* (singer).

I couldn't debut until the 26th instead of the 24th because of a fête that was being honored here. I will not tell you of the enthusiasm which I have had the good fortune to have. Yesterday I gave the second performance of Otello.[8]

But she made her mark in Venice with more than music. A fifteenth-century Venetian law ruled that gondolas could be painted only black, and this hardly fit Maria's ebullient spirits. In violation of the decree she designed a gondola that immediately became a scenic attraction.

"I have introduced a novelty here that will make an epic in my good fortunes," she wrote a friend.

I have scored a coup d'état. I have revolutionized the reflections of the canals and the boats. I have a gondola which I have decorated with a gray exterior, with buttons and balls of silk and gold. The gondoliers have scarlet jackets, hats of pale yellow with black ribbons around them, pants of navy blue with red borders, and black velvet sleeves and collars. The interior of the gondola is scarlet with blue curtains. As a result, whenever I pass, everyone knows who it is. The fact is I could not bury myself alive in one of those gondolas that are black inside and out.[9]

On March 29 she introduced her Angelina, which met with the same reception as had her Desdemona. In this part her acting was considered "admirable," her singing "of extraordinary excellence," and the admiration of the audience "indescribable."[10] Four days later she sang an unscheduled role, Rosina, instead of the planned Norma, and played Norma two nights in a row, April 4 and 5. Wrote a critic, "Such universal applause, such unanimous fascination has never been engendered by anyone, and it is unlikely that anyone ever will again."[11] Another commented, "If you had been in the theater, you were finally satisfied how in one evening, even in three hours of one evening, it is possible in good conscience to earn, or better yet to deserve, 3000 francs."[12]

The Venetians criticized only Maria's interpretation of Norma, in part because of circumstances beyond her control. Three years before they had heard Pasta sing the role at the Fenice; those who had accepted Pasta's interpretation as the only one possible compared Maria unfavorably.

> La Malibran è basta
> Ma per la Norma
> Ghe vol la Pasta*

went the rhyme.[13] One critic stated that Malibran distorted the intentions of both composer and librettist, a clear indication of the great differences between the interpretations of the two prima donnas. Little did he know how the composer would have disagreed with him. Bellini had asked Cottrau to have Malibran sing Norma in Naples the preceding winter, and he hoped that she would introduce his opera to Paris.

*La Malibran is good enough/but for Norma/one wants la Pasta.

During Maria's engagement at the Fenice, Giovanni Gallo, manager of the Teatro Emeronittio, approached her for help in saving his nearly bankrupt theater. In desperation he begged her to sing two additional performances at 3,000 francs each. Maria was not initially enthusiastic about the idea, but unable to desert a colleague in need she succumbed to his pleas. Arrangements were made to present *Il Barbiere* at the Fenice on April 3 with Gallo taking half of the net, and *La Sonnambula* at the Emeronittio on April 8. The *Barbiere* brought the impresario 2,875 francs,[14] not an enormous sum, but the *Sonnambula* netted him 4,125 francs after expenses—or would have. When the grateful director approached Maria after the performance with the 3,000 francs due her, she expressed surprise. "I don't want your money," she told him. "Keep it." Gallo was stunned. "M'abbraccia," ordered Amina, "and we will consider everything even."[15]

On the evening of the *Sonnambula* the theater was a virtual garden.[16] The flowers hung in garlands and festoons from the boxes and tiers, and in addition Gallo had decorated the hall with banners and flags of every description. From the moment the doors were opened, every seat was taken and many disappointed people drifted away in their gondolas. The first act unrolled before a rapt audience. The tenor singing the role of Elvino suffered a memory lapse during the first duet, but no one cared as la Malibran sang both parts. At the end of the act the audience began to scream "bis" tearing the flowers from their places and heaving them at the stage. Flowers fell from the boxes into the parterre, from the parterre into the orchestra, from the orchestra onto the stage. Franz Liszt counted thirty-six curtain calls, although *L'Apatista*'s critic reported only thirty-five (9 April 1835). "We have no idea of the mania with which the Italians call back artists to the stage," Liszt commented, perhaps a bit enviously.[17]

The second act met an "even greater" success. The banners were raised, and from the heights of the theater rained poetry, pictures, white pigeons, and song birds. The storms of applause following the thrice encored finale "Ah! non giunge" lasted a full half hour, and when the curtain finally fell Gallo announced the renaming of his theater: Il Teatro Malibran.[18]*

Near Malibran's distinctive gondola outside, flotillas of boats lit with torches waited to accompany her back to the Barberigo Palace, but because of her exhaustion, she slipped away in another. People in the waiting gondolas, discovering her absence, chased after her, their torches shooting along the reflecting waters like meteors through the night. Many overtook her and by the time she reached the Palace, all of Venice seemed to be there. After she entered, a group of gondoliers sent a gilt chalice of wine with a request that she drink from it. Graciously consenting, she stepped out onto the balcony and, illuminated by the flickering torchlight, drank for them all to see. The vessel was then returned to the gondoliers, who toasted la Malibran's health from the cup that had just touched her lips.[19]

*The theater is still known by this name today.

On the following day Maria departed with a diadem from the Venetians, and five medals depicting the roles she had performed in their city.[20] Barely twenty-seven years old, she was the world's most famous performer, and the greatest singer who had ever lived. Asked if the idolization she inspired did not make her proud, Maria answered, "The harsh ordeals of my childhood and the disappointments of my early youth made me bitter, but success has made me happier."[21]

Maria arrived in Paris in mid-April. During her brief stay Bellini saw her, "always with her miraculous talent and extraordinary lunacy: can you believe that having been invited to dinner in a house, she sang from 8:00 in the evening until 1:00 in the morning, without any rest, and did all this in a stentorian voice?"[22] He wrote to Florimo, "With la Malibran I have behaved with much love, and thus I will do at her return from London."[23]

Her presence in the French capital immediately revived hopes that she would accept a contract with the Italien, and rumors spread that she had done so for the following season. Bellini wanted her to introduce *Norma* to the French, and he was especially eager for Malibran to do so rather than Giulia Grisi, who had attempted it in London "malissimo."[24]* But Maria's primary reason for being in Paris was not only to personally thank the judges and lawyers who had enabled her to dissolve her marriage, but also to use her influence to get around the ten-month legal delay before she could marry Charles. Many of her friends believed she would be back in France in July 1835 to marry her lover.[25]

After a week in Paris she traveled on to Belgium, and then to London, where she was due by May 15, according to the terms of her new engagement with Alfred Bunn. Of her "peculiar" contract, Bunn commented with his characteristically dry humor, "I had entered into a perilous engagement with Madame Malibran—doubted by many—believed by few—its results apprehended by all."[26] Although no one had forced him to accept Malibran's demanding terms, he, contending with the financial problems that would eventually send him into bankruptcy, had decided opinions about their contract.[27] "Nineteen nights, at 125 pounds each, amounts to the sum of 2,375 pounds, to be paid in the space of six weeks! 375 pounds for only three nights in a week, payable every Monday morning IN ADVANCE!" he shrieked, noting with horror that Templeton, who had received 121 pounds per week for the entire season, now demanded 301 pounds per week for his performances with Malibran.[28]

From the moment of her first appearance on May 18 in *La Sonnambula*, Maria made it plain that this was her greatest season yet in London. On her entrance the audience rose en masse with deafening shouts and cheers, and

*Although Grisi's first Norma may not have been successful, future years would find her a truly great interpreter of the role.

the reviews unanimously praised her performance. The comments by the *Athenaeum*'s critic were remarkable only for their brevity.

Covent Garden—This house re-opened Monday with Bellini's opera of *La Sonnambula* for the reappearance of Madame Malibran. She has been absent two years; and one has heard this great singer, and that great singer, and been captivated with each in turn. But Malibran comes back, and one feels in a moment not only the force of *her* song, but the force of that which says "On court de belle en belle/ Mais on revient toujours / A ses premiers amours". First among the first to our thinking, she was and is. The greatest compliment that can be paid to her singing is to say that it is equal to her acting; the greatest to her acting that it is worthy of her singing. Both are close upon perfection, and taking the extraordinary combination of the two in one person into consideration, her performance may, on the whole, be described as reaching it. We cannot say more, we dare not say less. We may review other performances— *hers* we have only to record; for criticism, whose province it is to teach others, goes to school to learn of Madame Malibran. The house was full and so were the hearts of those who heard this gifted creature sing. [395(23 May 1835), p. 396]

But amid the extravagant praise was a note of warning. The life that Malibran led, "the life of a horse," as she had once described it, was not conducive to vocal health or a long career. During the preceding season the young Giuseppe Verdi, while pronouncing her "a very great artist, marvelous," noted that her voice was sometimes shrill on high notes and that her technique, long a model of perfection, was "not always correct."[29] After her first two performances in London a critic wrote,

Her lower notes are as fine as ever, but the upper ones, especially in the loud parts, are occasionally harsh and out of tune, as if they had already begun to suffer from the wear and tear of theatrical engagements. Her enthusiasm is so great that she never spares either her voice or her strength when the occasion demands extraordinary exertion; and we tremble for the consequences to an organ which is naturally sweet, but not naturally powerful in the upper part of the scale. We earnestly hope our fears may prove groundless, and, in the meantime, would advise Madame Malibran to be less lavish of those ornamental passages which give needless exertion to the higher notes of her voice. It is quite natural that she would wish to display the originality and fertility of her resources in this way, but it is "paying too dear for the whistle" to run the risk of doing the smallest injury to her physical resources for that purpose. With her impressive vocal elocution, if we may be allowed so to speak, she may dare to be perfectly simple, without incurring the smallest chance of being outshone.[30]

In London in 1833 Maria had observed with great interest the soprano Wilhelmine Schröder-Devrient's interpretation of Beethoven's *Fidelio*, as well as the German singer's popular and critical success in the work. No two singers could have been more different in style and training than Malibran and Schröder, although each, in her own way, made innovations in the operatic art. As Malibran was more modern than Pasta; so was Schröder more progressive than Malibran, and by an even wider margin. Malibran brought superb acting to beautiful singing; Schröder carried acting to lengths that all but precluded singing as it was known in her century.

The German singer began her career as an actress in such roles as Racine's *Phèdre*, Luise in Schiller's *Kabale und Liebe*, and Ophelia in *Hamlet*. Her first operatic role, at age eighteen, was Pamina. In spite of her scant vocal training, she did not immediately disqualify herself from her new profession, but Schröder had not learned to sing. "A man whose fingers cannot control the strings would hardly have a second hearing did he attempt instrumental music," pointed out Chorley. "But a woman, supposing she can correctly flounder through the notes of a given composition has been allowed, too contemptuously, to take rank as a singer. . . . Her tones were delivered without any care, save to give them due force. Her execution was bad and heavy. There was an air of strain and spasm throughout her performance, of that struggle for victory which never conquers."[31]

But even Chorley admitted that "within the conditions of her own school she was a remarkable artist."[32] She had pale features and an intense, expressive German face. Her figure was large and well-proportioned, and she used her profuse blond hair for dramatic effect. Her voice, despite its lack of training, had an inherent expressiveness, great power, and a true metallic ring. As such it did not suit the Italian or French repertoires but was perfectly adapted to Beethoven's *Fidelio*, an opera which had not made much of an impression until she first sang Leonora.

Her moment of truth came during the first performance of the Beethoven work, in the pistol scene, which had not seemed right to her during rehearsals. She began to tremble and nearly fell as she sang the line: "One more step and you are . . . ," and then, to her own amazement as well as that of the audience, ceased singing and declaimed the final word ". . . Dead!" At that instant a new era, a new style of operatic performance, was born. Henceforth Schröder willingly sacrificed the beautiful sound for the dramatic effect, undoubtedly the first singer to do so consciously, and her declamation became almost a mannerism.

Schröder's great contribution was yet to come. Richard Wagner stated that his life was changed the evening he first heard her sing, and he wrote her a letter that very night telling her so. She was to become the inspiration for his "music of the future" and would create many of his leading roles.

But if Schröder was willing to sacrifice the beautiful note for the meaningful sound, Malibran was not. Her art demanded that in the event of a conflict between voice and drama voice took precedence: never did it lose "that velvet which made it so bewitching in tender and passionate pieces."[33] Inspired by the challenge, she set out to prove that she could equal Schröder as an actress without sacrificing vocal technique and, undertaking the role of Leonora, turned to a musical style that required powers other than those she had exploited in any of the thirty-two roles in her repertoire.

On June 12 at Covent Garden Maria entered the stage looking like neither a good-natured peasant nor a jailer's servant, nor a woman disguised. To one of her viewers it was "almost incomprehensible" how her simple costume—grey frock, grey trousers, black leather belt—could conceal her feminine form so entirely. Exhausted by her labor she sank down onto a seat, and when she raised her eyes to greet Rocco and Marcelline, she smiled with "such an indescribable look of the profoundest suffering, the most dignified melancholy" that even before she uttered a word tears came to the eyes of her beholders. Throughout she portrayed "the long-suffering, the heartwearing anxiety, the dubious mind; till at length the strength of her heart and her love overcome all anxieties and doubts," yet never once did she fall into a manner of whining sentimentality.[34] She threw more horror into the vault scene than had Schröder, and the scenes in which she rushed between the dagger and her husband, and pointed the pistol at Pizarro, were "among the most striking and effective that have perhaps ever been attempted."[35]

Malibran succeeded with the general public, but memories of Schröder's Leonora lingered, and many reviewers found it difficult to judge a different conception of the role on its own terms. Nevertheless, her defenders outnumbered her censurers. "Malibran has at length found a character worthy of her unrivalled powers," trumpeted the *Spectator*, calling her performance "one of the most perfect exhibitions of singing combined with dramatic action that we ever witnessed."[36] "Madame Malibran's execution of the vocal part of the performance was in her happiest style," wrote another critic. "The beauty and richness of her voice, and her graceful and energetic style of singing were displayed in all their most enchanting force."[37]

Although Chorley lists *Fidelio* (with *La Sonnambula* and *The Maid of Artois*) as one of the three "real stage triumphs of Malibran's English tours, he had reservations about her assumption of this dramatic soprano role. "She delivered Beethoven's music wondrously, considering its unsuitability for her voice, making changes and adaptations where they were inevitable with such musician-like science that not the protest of a solitary purist could be raised against them, but the effect produced in the opera by a singer incomparably inferior to her, Madame Schroeder-Devrient, was far deeper and more moving."[38]

Her use of two pistols in the prison scene bothered several observers. Certainly she understood the theatrical effect of pulling out two guns instead of one, but then Malibran's life carried into her art. Four years earlier she had written Virginia Cottinet during the night of the soldier uprising, "The first thing that I did was to get two pistols. I imagined that they would come to attack Charles."[39]

As the season continued with Maria's performances in *Fidelio* and *La Sonnambula*, sometimes alternately, sometimes together on the same night (surely an unequaled tour de force), Bunn and his prima donna continued their furtive correspondence.

June 18, 1835

My dear Mr. Bunn, I have just received a letter from persons living in the country who desire to know if I play *Fidelio* and *Sonnambula* the *Monday* after next week, and *the Tuesday* also; or else Wednesday the same opera as Monday. I said I thought I would finish with *La Sonnambula*—and that Monday June 20 would be *Fidelio*. Did I say the right thing? As for the rest, I told them that I was going to write to you. I beg you then, to give me a response *right away*, so that I can send it to them, for they desire *especially to know* if I play TUESDAY, for the last time, *Fidelio*, for they are not able to come and then they would like to know the other days.

Pardon my importunity

Malibran[40]

But Bunn caught her on this one. "The reader will perceive how particularly anxious she is to know if she plays on the *Tuesday* (strongly marked twice), merely for the information of her friends in the country, *who could not come that* NIGHT! The fact is, she had an enormous offer to sing THAT VERY TUESDAY at the Oxford Music Meeting, of which I had been apprized; and the *fin contre fin* was therefore the order of the day. This is but a solitary instance of the many similar tricks to which a manager is exposed— who, to be in only comparative security, should be many-eyed and many-eared too."[41]

"The season in London is magnificent this year," wrote Charles to a friend.

Never have there been so many concerts. The theaters are making a fortune, especially the English Theater, which is always filled when Maria plays *La Sonnambula*. Maria is well, despite the unprecedented work that she endures. Here is her schedule three or four days a week: morning rehearsal at ten o'clock, after a good hour of piano practice. Concert from 1:00 until 4:00. Opera from seven until 10. Then, one or two private concerts to finish the evening; and poor Maria has hardly returned to rest before it is daybreak. And that is the existence that she leads in London. All this is against my will, for I oppose with all my strength her acceptance of these concerts after the performances, and I refuse a large part of them although she doesn't know it; for you know that little Spanish head. She would kill herself if she were permitted.

Happily the greater part of the work is done. She performed yesterday in *Fidelio*, in English, for the first time, with immense success. They made her repeat the final scene. Grisi has also had a great success in *I Puritani*. She gets along marvelously with Maria and often sings with her in private concerts. Since the days when Sontag was performing one has not heard such perfect duets from two women. They are to sing a duet from *Semiramide* together at my concert, which will be June 29, and as it is the first time that they will appear together in public, I have taken care to announce the duo with a poster three yards long and letters a foot high. I'm counting on a full house.[42]

A critic spoke glowingly of the duet from *Semiramide* which the two prima donnas sang together at Charles' concert. "Grisi and Malibran have left an impression on our minds so strong, that even now we cannot write of it with anything like sober critical calmness . . . this magnificent performance awakened in us feelings which we had almost thought, and *feared*, we were too hackneyed in pleasure ever to experience again."[43]

According to Bunn, Maria's remarkable contract was filled "to the letter," and a renewal of seven nights was arranged at the Drury Lane Theatre, also under Bunn's management.[44] She accepted this additional engagement for two reasons: there were contractual problems with Lucca, where she was to sing in early August, which prevented her departure from London; also, she and Charles had learned in early June that they would have to wait the ten-month delay prescribed by the law for widows before they could be married. Thus there was no point in returning to France in July. "This bothers us a lot," Charles admitted, "but even if we are able to surmount this obstacle there remains the further problem of the domicile that neither of us has in Paris, and it is necessary that we be married there, the judgment having been granted by French laws, etc."[45]

At the last performance of her initial engagement, a marathon evening on which Maria sang a double bill of *La Sonnambula* and *Fidelio*, she returned to her dressing room after the final curtain to find on her table a jewel case containing a bracelet and ring of rubies and diamonds. On a silver plaque set into the case was engraved the following inscription:

> To Madame Malibran,
> The most distinguished Artiste
> The Theatres of Europe have ever possessed,
> This trifling token of esteem is presented,
> By Alfred Bunn,
> Lessee of the Theatres Royal Drury Lane, and
> Covent Garden.
> London, July 1st, 1835.[46]

Bunn described the reception of this "trifling token of esteem": "Madame Malibran was a creature of so much impulse, that with all her inordinate love of money (and it would be sheer humbug to say she had not that passion), an attention of this nature was sure to enchant her. It was a costly trifle, though a mere nothing compared with what she had received from me *argent comptant*; but she prized it as if it were a principality just settled upon her—she hugged it as a mother would her child, or a child her doll; she was excited beyond measure; and absorbed in a dream of *bijouterie*, thought no more of the public and their plaudits and shouts, whose echoes were even then floating between the auditory and her dressing room. Such was the nature of this extraordinary creature."[47]

The additional engagement brought the total number of performances to twenty-six and was filled as scrupulously as the first. For these twenty-six performances Maria received the astronomical sum of 3,463 pounds, but Bunn still found the money to throw a farewell supper for his diva on July 18, "to which above a hundred patrons and friends of the dramatic art were invited to meet the gifted illustrator of it. Though she had played that very night the two arduous parts of *La Sonnambula* and *Fidelio*, Madame Malibran stayed at that table until the hour arrived for her to put foot into the steamboat, and many of the guests escorted her to the Tower stairs, whence she embarked."

As she left Bunn's party after a night of intensive performing and partying, her host watched her board the boat with a sense of foreboding. That evening, and the sight of her departure, remained in his memory, and he would have reason to recall them in the future. "The energy of her character eventually destroyed this astonishing woman; and the only wonder to me is that the melancholy and premature event did not take place sooner. The powerful and conflicting elements mingled in her composition were gifts indeed, but of a very fatal nature—the mind was far too great for the body, and it did not require any wonderful gift of prophecy to foresee that, in their contention, the triumph would be but short, however brilliant and decisive."[48]

Maria was engaged for another tour of Italy, but since a cholera epidemic raged in that country, neither she nor Charles was eager to fulfill their contracts. As early as June Charles had feared "the Lucca affair will not be settled without our being forced to visit that city," and he was correct.[49] They reached the city in the first week of August and found the populace in a panic over the cholera. But interest in the opera could not be totally squelched. After Maria's final performance on September 2, a group of students unhitched her horses and pulled her carriage from the theater to her hotel, begging from her her bouquet, her gloves, and any other souvenir. They would not leave until she appeared on her balcony, where she was cheered while a military band played a piece composed especially for the occasion.

But her mind was not on the performances, as she indicated in a letter to the Marquis de Louvois.

> September 2, 1835
>
> Come quickly to Milan, for we are all escaping from here, not from the actual cholera but from a beautiful prospect of that charming malady which makes so many precautions necessary, which has caused so many quarantines and roadblocks to be put up, and which, consequently, has ruined my poor *impresario*. *Not to mention us*; enough! It is better not to think about it.
>
> The Duke has bravely deserted Lucca. The pious Duchess too, without leaving any arrangements or funds for these poor people in case of a cholera attack. *So be it*. Wisely they save themselves for the love of God and their confessors, and then for fear of the proverb which says "He who bites off more than he can chew. . . ." I will leave it at that and let the misery run its course!
>
> It appears that my Duke Visconti has a dreadful fear of the cholera, and thinks it would have been better not to engage me. However, they say that I am awaited in Milan with *devotion*, being persuaded that my apparition will *camphorize* [i.e., disinfect] the partisans and propagators of the cholera. As for me,

I have no fear of it; I tremble only at the idea of singing to empty benches. Oh! How annoying that is! There is only one thing to do, to give a lot of parties, to distract oneself, to laugh, to eat homeopathically; for the rest, one must leave that to Providence. . . .

I am in a bad mood, for everyone speaks only of death, sickness, cholera, the devil, hell and purgatory, and I'm up to my neck with that. Thus, not wanting to annoy you further with my complaints, I leave you in anticipation of the pleasure of seeing you soon in Milan.[50]

Maria was due in Milan by September 12, 1835, but roadblocks and quarantines almost prevented her arrival. All Italy was in a state of alarm over the cholera. On reaching Carrara Maria and Charles were told that the disease had broken out in Genoa and that all routes to and from that city were blocked. Even worse, the cholera had made its first appearance in Carrara itself, and soon no one would be permitted to leave the city. Maria learned that it was possible, if inadvisable, to travel over the Appenines on an unused mule trail through the treacherous Spolverina pass and to connect with the route between Modena and Milan on the other side of the mountains. This rocky trail apparently was impassible with a carriage, but undaunted, she decided to leave Carrara regardless of the difficulties.

She hired approximately twenty-five men, along with eight oxen and six mules to draw the two coaches up the mountains. The little caravan assembled in secrecy and in the dead of night the travelers silently began their journey. In the first two days the carriages proceeded only nine miles, and on succeeding days they covered even shorter distances slowly overcoming rivers, ravines, cliffs, and boulders as big as houses. In some places only one set of wheels was supported by the narrow trails; those on the far side of the coach were suspended over the abyss by strong ropes held fore and aft by men and mules. The muleteers themselves often complained that the trip could not continue, but Maria was not discouraged. She rode on horseback, leaving the coaches to Charles and the others, who were less adventurous. To maintain morale she sang, she joked, she pretended that the trip was not so difficult. If she, a woman, could do it, so could they. When a muleteer was thrown from his animal she dressed his wounds, and when he refused to remount, she gave him her own horse and rode the mule.

Danger and inconvenience accompanied the caravan. Robbers in the mountains quickly organized in order to take advantage of travelers. Ruthless and untraceable, they vanished once their work was done. Food also became a problem. Neither Maria nor Charles had supposed they would be unable to buy it on the journey. And the poor countrypeople encountered along the way feared that the travelers might be carrying the plague. Small-town authorities frequently read the bill of health to them before allowing them to pass through, telling them to make no human contact, however indirect, and not to stop until the coaches has passed well beyond the village limits. Occasionally they cajoled isolated peasants into selling them bread or meat; one brave soul would approach the carriages holding rags to his face, and, lest he come too close, would throw the food at them. Peasants accepted money only in bowls of vinegar and they thoroughly washed the coins afterward.

With few places to stop the travelers often journeyed for twenty-four hours at a time without nourishment or sleep. When too tired to continue they slept in the coaches or out in the cold and wet, which became more severe as they climbed upward through the mountains. If they found a deserted shelter, rats or other animals made rest almost impossible.

But in spite of the "indescribable" hardships, the party crossed the Appenines. Before the unbelieving eyes of the people of Castelpoggio, the battered caravan with its dirty and exhausted travelers pulled into the streets of the town, safe at last.[51]

CHAPTER 15

Madame de Bériot

Maria remained in Castelpoggio long enough to give a concert for the awed populace, and on September 8 she reached Milan. Four days later she began a six-month engagement at La Scala with a performance of Rossini's *Otello*, one of eight operas she would perform during the winter season. Her reception in this city, which was not yet affected by the dreaded cholera, compensated her for her travels across the mountains.

During the first weeks of her engagement she learned of the death of thirty-three-year-old Vincenzo Bellini on September 23, near Paris. This shock threw her into a state of depression. Sending 200 francs to the subscription raising money for a monument to the composer in Catania,[1] she wrote Florimo: "That fatal day, the 23rd of September, will be remembered as a sad and tragic day in the annals of the Italian theater!!!"[2] Malibran thus wrote her own epitaph, for in exactly one year, Bellini's fatal day would become her own.

Maria's most controversial role this winter was the Scots Queen in Donizetti's *Maria Stuarda*, an opera that met the same fate as its famous protagonist. Donizetti had originally written it to be performed in Naples in 1834, and rehearsals began in September of that year. Anna del Serre and the eternal Giuseppina Ronzi-de Begnis, two singers who abhorred each other, played Elisabeth and Mary. As they rehearsed the confrontation scene between the two Queens, Ronzi, as Mary, advanced toward Elisabeth, accusing her of being a "vile bastard," an "obscene, unworthy whore," "la figlia impura di Bolena." Del Serre, who had reasons of her own to be sensitive on these subjects, took the well-acted insults personally. According to one journal, she grabbed Ronzi by the hair, slapped her, bit her, and nearly broke her own foot kicking her.[3] Initially stunned at this attack, Ronzi nevertheless rallied and took the offensive so viciously that del Serre fell unconscious to the stage.

Matters did not end there. "You are aware of the fight between the two women," wrote Donizetti to a friend, "but I don't know if you heard that Ronzi slandered me. Thinking me out of hearing range she said: 'Donizetti is protecting that whore Del Serre!', and I surprised her by answering: 'I am not protecting either of you, but those two queens were both whores, and you two are whores. Now, admit you are embarrassed or hold your tongue!'

She said nothing more, the rehearsal continued, she sang, and the matter carried no further."[4]

Preparations for the presentation of *Maria Stuarda* continued under great strain. The worst blow came at the dress rehearsal, to which Maria Cristina, Queen of Naples and the Two Sicilies, was invited. In such politically troubled times it was unthinkable for royalty to be portrayed in distress before countless impressionable citizens, and as Mary was led to the block to be beheaded, Maria Cristina was carried fainting from the theater. Within hours Donizetti received orders to cancel the premier of his opera.

On October 7, 1834, the composer wrote naively: "Stuarda has been forbidden, heaven knows why! but better not to ask, as the King himself has forbidden it."[5] Donizetti then hastily revised the work, setting the music to another libretto. This was presented at the San Carlo on October 18 as something called *Buondelmonte*. *Buondelmonte* sank without a ripple to the bottom of the operatic stream, and there, for the time being, it lay.

On November 5, 1834, shortly after this debacle, Maria arrived in Naples. Although she could not have seen either the work or its rehearsals, she somehow developed a passionate desire to perform it in its original form.[6] At about this time Ronzi was urging Donizetti to have the opera produced for her at La Scala, but the composer, aware of her unreliability and the capricious Milanese public, rejected the idea. He would, however, try Malibran, and by May of 1835 accepted the plan of having *Stuarda* produced at La Scala with her. On May 3 he indicated to Ricordi that if Malibran would sing *Stuarda*, he would write a new overture, a "sinfonia," for the opera.[7] During the summer she visited Westminster Abbey to sketch the costumes of Mary and Elisabeth and wrote Visconti that she was studying her part.[8]

Maria had already been singing in Milan for two months when, on November 12, 1835, the Austrian censors approved the libretto with no changes, complete with the phrases and scenes so upsetting to the Queen of Naples. Rehearsals began in the last days of November, and by early December Donizetti arrived, only to find the opera company in complete disorder. Sofia Schoberlechner, the Elisabeth, had resigned, considering her part unworthy of a prima donna, and worse, inferior to Malibran's role as Mary Stuart. As of December 9 Maria expected *Stuarda* to premier on December 26, but just before the work was to be presented she fell ill.[9] On December 28 Donizetti himself had no idea when his opera would be put on.

Stuarda was finally performed unsuccessfully on December 30. The composer declared that Maria was "voiceless," and he believed that she performed only to avoid a 3,000-franc cancellation penalty. In his words the evening was "painful from start to finish."[10] Maria's vocal condition improved in later performances, and the work was more favorably received, but after the third the censors demanded changes.[11] They would not tolerate the word "bastard" or kneeling in the confession scene.[12] Maria refused to perform this watered down version, rightly believing that the changes weakened the drama. Consequently, on four additional evenings the first act of *Stuarda*, in which Mary Stuart does not appear, was followed by the last two acts of *Otello*, in which la Malibran scored further triumphs. And thus ended the history of *Maria Stuarda* at La Scala for 130 years.

Despite the fiasco many considered Maria's performance worthwhile, and one of them blamed *Stuarda*'s failure on its author. "Certainly this drama did not have favorable results, and the merits of Mad. Malibran were not sufficient to sustain it. It is a musical work which lacks color, variety, inspiration, and the composer should not take offense if we place it among the least fortunate of his works." The reviewer praised the cast, especially Malibran: "She is always the great singer, the grand actress, and she spared nothing for the success of this Queen of Scots."[13]

Yet another new role this season was Lady Jane Grey in Vaccai's opera of the same name, which was written for Maria to perform at La Scala and which met with a fate similar to *Maria Stuarda*'s. Maria wrote of this work to the Baron Perignon in Paris:

We performed yesterday evening Vaccai's *Jane Grey*. It is claimed that the opera is tolerated out of respect to me, that is boring to endure, that everyone yawned so much that they couldn't hiss it, despite their good will. I did everything I could, and for what it's worth, I again swam in that muddy sea and acquitted myself *as well as I could*. The fatigue that I feel from all this today deprives me of the courage to write more than one letter. I play again tonight the same *Jane Grey*.[14]

Although the composer considered the performances a success, his work was withdrawn after being played four times.

On March 20, 1836, Maria Malibran gave her last performance of the season, and her last that Milan or Italy would ever see. Two days later she left with Charles for Paris. The Milanese expected her in the autumn of 1836 for an engagement to run through March 1837 and again in the fall of that year. For decades afterward her last season at La Scala was called "the glorious year."[15]

Maria had not sung publicly in Paris since the time of her departure in 1832, but the French still hoped to see their favorite perform again at the Théâtre-Italien. Toward the end of December 1835 she wrote to the Baron Perignon of new offers:

Milan, December 14, 1835

Aimable monsieur, mon cher juge,

Alas! You have made my mouth water by speaking to me of performing in my dear Paris. It is very true that I have been made offers through our friend Troupenas for the month of April for twelve performances. I guess you don't know then that by the end of March I will have done sixty-five performances since September 15, and that I will only have had in all that time just one month of rest, traveling included?, that there is a season in London to do, the most fatiguing of all, for I will have two new operas to perform in English, and two others to get into my head? And certainly I want, when I reappear on the stage in Paris, to return with all my powers, and not all blown out as I would surely be if I were reappearing after two seasons as fatiguing as those in Milan and a trip across those frozen mountains, those rocks loosened by the rains, which result in avalanches and ruined roads, the problems with the coaches, not to mention the fear of a few nice thieves. One hears every day of some new conquest, some charming murder on their part.

No, no, the dear Parisians will hear me when my heart will not have had any other emotions for a month than those caused by the pleasure of finding myself among them again, no other fear than that of not pleasing them as much as formerly.

So you wouldn't want me to, would you? I am thankful for the rumors which run through Paris of my engagement, for they have brought me a delightful letter from my judge.[16]

But Maria underestimated her winter; she had sung not sixty-five but seventy performances in Milan, an average of one every two and one-half days, and she did not have a month's vacation. It was just as well that she refused the Italien's offers and was traveling to Paris only to fulfil her dream of nearly seven years—to make Charles de Bériot her lawfully wedded husband.

Once long ago she had written him, "I wear a ring which is the perfect symbol of our friendship: a knot which cannot be untied; the more you pull it, the tighter it gets. Isn't it the symbol of the most durable and pure friendship?"[17] Certainly she proved her devotion through years of disagreeable tugging on the knot: the self-righteous indignation of the aristocrats, the public insults, the fear that Eugène would claim his legal rights as her husband. But now the ten-month wait required by French law had passed, and she and Charles hurried to Paris to establish a domicile that would qualify them as citizens.

On Tuesday, March 29, 1836, at four o'clock in the afternoon, Maria Malibran became Mme. de Bériot in a ceremony performed by the mayor of the second arondissement of Paris. Witnesses included Ernest Legouvé, the Marquis de Louvois, Baron Perignon, and other close friends. As the magistrate read the lines, "Do you promise to love, honor, obey," she shrugged her shoulders slightly and made so droll an expression that even the official smiled. She left him 1,000 francs for the poor in Paris.

After the ceremony the newlyweds and their guests went to the home of Eugène Troupenas, Maria's publisher, on the Rue Saint-Marc, where they were joined by other friends for a soirée in their honor. The pianist Sigismond Thalberg promised to come, because he had never heard Malibran, nor had she met him. When he arrived she went straight to him and asked him to play something for her.

"Play before you, Madame?" he replied. "Impossible! I would much rather hear you!"

"But I'm tired", she told him. "I would be abominable."

"So much the better. It will give me courage."

She went to the piano and began to sing. Her voice was hard, her manner uninterested, her performance so bad that even her mother reproached her.

"What do you want, Mamam?" she cried angrily. "You only get married once!" Turning to Thalberg she said, "Now it's your turn."

Thalberg played, and as she listened to him, Maria's expression changed. Her eyes became animated, her color returned, and when the pianist had finished she cried, "Admirable! Now it's my turn!," and rushed to the piano. Fatigue and disinterest vanished. Thalberg was stunned; he could barely believe it was the same woman or the same voice. When she finished he could only murmur "Oh Madame!," and then, inspired by her example, he jumped up and cried, "Now it's my turn!" and played as he had perhaps never played before. Toward the end of his piece, Maria burst into tears and was carried from the room. In a few moments she reappeared and ran back to the piano demanding, "Now it's my turn!" This musical duel went on for hours.[18]

In the first days of April the de Bériots traveled to their villa in Ixelles, where the bands of the Royal Guards, the orchestra of the Harmonic Society, and the Vocal Society greeted them. Although intending to rest before moving on to London, they gave two concerts in Brussels, one for the Polish refugees, the other for the poor. Both netted great sums. At the first of these, on April 9, Maria's aria from *Ines de Castro* drove the audience wild and so moved the Queen of the French that she sent Maria a magnificent clip of pearls. At the second concert several days later, young Pauline Garcia, not quite fifteen years old, sang a duet with her sister.

On April 19 they left for London where Maria was under contract to Alfred Bunn. While the carriage was being unpacked, she sat down in the hall of their rented home at 59 Conduit Street to write her impresario a note. "I have just arrived, at your service and even in good health. I would like very much to go to the theater, in the dress circle or in a box. Do you think I could go? A word of response and my role, if you please. In haste, Maria de Bériot."

"I signed it de Bériot," she later told him, "to tell you myself that I was married."[19]

Maria was engaged to sing three works in London this spring: *La Sonnambula*, *Fidelio*, and a new opera, *The Maid of Artois*. She performed the first two with the expected success. "In that rare art, the power of exciting the emotions of the audience, she is without rival," wrote a journalist, "unless Signora Pasta is to be reckoned as still on the stage; and even compared with her, Madame Malibran may safely encounter the rivalry."[20] One year before, a critic had warned Maria about her vocal condition, but his fears proved groundless. The same reviewer now found her voice "in fine order, the upper notes having now restored more than their pristine beauty."[21] Maria never stopped working to improve her powers. One who had heard her earlier London successes remarked that passages she had not even attempted when she first came to England she now executed with ease.[22]

Maria's third role of the season was *The Maid of Artois*, with music by Michael Balfe and libretto by Alfred Bunn. Balfe met Malibran in Venice and Milan where he and his wife Lina sang with her in *Il Barbiere, La Sonnambula*, and *Otello*. With her prophecy that he would become "Il Rossini Inglese" he returned to England in the summer of 1835, and to Bunn's libretto wrote *The Siege of Rochelle*, which ran for seventy nights.[23]

His second collaboration with Bunn was to be *The Maid*, a work tailored to Malibran's talents. The plot was based on the Abbé Prévost's romantic novel *Manon Lescaut*, but with changes and shifts of emphasis the entire opera focused on Malibran's character of Isoline. Thus the still virtuous Manon-Isoline of Malibran implored the wealthy Marquis to save her lover, the Des Grieux-Jules of Templeton, who had been tricked into joining his regiment. She sailed to French Guinea, disguised first as a sailor and then as a nun, to save Jules; rescued him from prison in a vivid escape scene; revived him out in the desert; and wound up the opera with a brilliant finale after the repentant Marquis forgave her and her lover. Throughout this convoluted tale she had the flattering pleasure of repulsing multitudes of characters intent on seducing her, and of wearing a wide variety of costumes, both male and female.[24]

The Maid of Artois had a difficult birth, but as Bunn admitted, "The effect produced by Mme Malibran upon the town in the character of Isoline made amends for every indignity and for every pang that had been endured."[25] No small character in this tragicomedy was the Shakespearean actor William Macready, who had long resented Malibran's operatic invasion of Drury Lane Theatre, an establishment formerly reserved for the Drama. Not since Mr. Cooper in New York had called the Garcia troupe "a foreign influenza" had dramatic actors appreciated operatic competition, and Macready felt no differently. "It is most unjust that a foreigner should be brought into a national theatre to receive enormous terms at the expense of the actors of the establishment," he declared bitterly and professed to find "much satisfaction" at every imagined setback to Malibran's career.[26] But if he hated Bunn and the operas put on at Drury Lane, he could not quite make himself hate Malibran. And if he considered *La Sonnambula* "the very excrement of trash," he admitted that Amina was "a creature of genius."[27]

Not as successful as he believed his talents warranted, Macready was in a constant state of frustration. Unable to analyze his own feelings, he bitterly poured them into his diaries, replete with glaring contradictions. His attitude toward Maria Malibran provides a perfect study of his character, for although he loved her, he felt obliged to dislike her for her success, especially when they competed for performance time at the Drury Lane Theatre. His opinion of her varied according to his self-esteem and the strength of his ego. Sometimes he imagined that she loved him. Maria was always friendly toward Macready, even affectionate, but whether she really knew his sentiments toward her is doubtful.

Macready directed his ire toward Alfred Bunn. Desiring to perform *Richard III* at Drury Lane, he was infuriated by Bunn's plans to stage his own poetry in the form of *The Maid* rather than Shakespeare's verses. For the final blow, Bunn attempted to make Macready agree to change his contract, which stated that he would not perform in "after pieces," and as incentive threatened to have the actor appear at half-price on Malibran's off nights. "The miserable scoundrel," howled Macready. "What can his insane and stupid spite hurt me?"[28]

Bunn reasoned that "the genius of the Shakespearean actor was totally unequal to the task of attracting an audience that would meet (or anything near it) the expenses of the establishment; while the said 'poetry' was warbled by the exquisite tones of a *real* child of genius, who filled the theatre every night she performed. Pray let it not be supposed that my 'poetry' had anything to do with this—Malibran would have done the same with the 'London Primer', and could have done no more with the sublimest of Shakespeare's verses."[29]

But he underestimated Macready's anger and paid dearly for his duplicity. One evening while sitting in his office, which was darkened except for a shaded lamp on the desk, the door crashed open. The cry of "there, you villain, take that—and that!" rang out, and Macready threw himself onto the unsuspecting impresario, fists pounding. Bunn dramatized the story more with each retelling.

I was knocked down, one of my eyes completely closed up, the ankle of my left leg, which I am in the habit of passing round the leg of the chair when writing, violently sprained, my person plentifully soiled with blood, lamp oil, and ink, the table upset, and *Richard the Third* holding me down. On my naturally inquiring if he meant to murder me, and on his replying in the affirmative, I made a struggle for it, threw him off, and got up on my one leg, holding him fast by the collar, and finally succeeded in getting him down on the sofa, where, mutilated as I was, I would have made him 'remember ME', but for the interposition of the people who had soon filled the room.[30]

To his discredit Bunn gloried in the drama of the incident, deliberately delaying the production of his opera, claiming blindness in one eye and complete physical incapacitation. When he could walk again he attended rehearsals with a cane and limped around feebly. He also took legal action against Macready.

Macready, on the other hand, was terribly distressed and embarrassed by his own actions. At his trial he spoke of "a series of studied and annoying and mortifying provocations, personal and professional. . . . Suffering under those accumulated provocations, I was betrayed, in a moment of unguarded passion, into an intemperate act for which I feel, and shall never cease to feel, the deepest and most poignant self-reproach and regret."[31]

As usual, Macready's feelings about Malibran were confused, while she, unaware of his resentment, continued to treat him as a friend. Walking one day down a London street to the Garrick Club, he was reflecting on his gloomy situation when a carriage whirled by. He instantly recognized it, and as it drew abreast of him, Malibran, dressed entirely in white, leaned from the window to wave. Just as quickly the coach disappeared, and Macready, stunned, was left more despondent than ever. She had seemed "bridally attired," and her image as she waved from the window remained in his thoughts all day. That night, in a burst of self-pity, he recorded the incident in his diary. "How different her lot from mine! She, with fame, affluence, idolatry on every side; I, poor, struggling to maintain a doubtful reputation . . . God *help me!*"[32]

Rehearsals for the *Maid* commenced. The composer considered Maria's embellishments of the aria "Yon moon o'er the Mountain" so strange that he asked her to sing the song as written. La Malibran, however, had her heart set on her changes and declared graciously that he could have his way with anything else in his opera. They argued; Maria offered to bless Balfe if he would only let her have her way this once. He gave in, she sang all her cadenzas, and the piece fell flat. Maria then decided that the darkness of the stage ruined the effect, so daylight was supplied for "Yon moon." The results were still disastrous, but rather than give in she omitted the song.[33]

Meanwhile she had found another aria she liked. As the cast came together for rehearsals she first heard Henry Phillips, as the Marquis de Chateau Vieux, sing his song "The light of other days is faded." This was considered one of the best pieces in the opera and Maria was enchanted with it.

"Oh," she said in delight, "that is beautiful! I must have it in my part!"

Balfe, Bunn, and the stage manager all assured her that this was impossible.

"Don't tell me," she responded confidently. "I shall speak to Phillips. He is very good natured and I am sure if he knows I prefer it in my role he will let me have it."

Phillips, good natured, but no fool, refused to part with his song and was rewarded for his generosity by being twice encored on opening night. Greatly annoyed at this rebuff, Maria half-heartedly declared that she would no longer perform in the opera.[34] Her threat was taken in good humor, and preparations continued.

The day before the dress rehearsal, Balfe, more and more dissatisfied with the finale of his work, decided to compose another despite the objections of his prima donna, who considered the original "brilliant." Tired, he went home and tried to sleep on his sofa. At midnight he awoke with an inspiration and composed the new piece. The next morning at eight o'clock he drove to Conduit Street where he found de Bériot practicing his violin in the drawing room. Maria, uncharacteristically, was still asleep and became most indignant when awakened to hear the new song. Undaunted,

Charles and Balfe picked up a small spinet piano and carried it upstairs to her bedroom. After Balfe played a few bars of the music, the unwilling listener raised herself on one elbow, her face growing ever brighter, and at its conclusion she praised it enthusiastically, promising to sing it at rehearsal that morning if the composer would leave her a copy. When she appeared several hours later to try it, even the orchestra applauded.[35]

Bunn's problems persisted until the last moment before the performance, for not even the "star of the evening," as he liked to call her, was above reproach in her professional conduct. At the next to last rehearsal she slipped quietly out of the opera house without saying a word to anyone and disappeared for an hour and a half. The rehearsal, of course, stopped. Meanwhile, on the other side of London, Mr. Holmes apologized for Malibran's late appearance at his morning concert, for which he had offered her twenty-five pounds. She arrived before its conclusion, and although out of breath, sang "una voce poco fa," acquiring strength as she continued and finally astonishing her listeners with a profusion of new and original ornaments. The piece was encored and the second try was considered even better than the first. Maria finished, snatched her twenty-five pounds, and ran back to Drury Lane where Bunn furiously reprimanded her for a thoughtless indiscretion clearly in violation of her contract.[36] (Perhaps this was the occasion on which he earned the nickname "Good Friday" from his prima donna, for she sometimes accused him of being a "hot cross Bunn."[37])

The day before the first performance of *The Maid*, Maria invited a group of people, including Lablache and Templeton, to her house for the rehearsal. All went well, despite the discomfort of the intensely hot weather. The group considered it unwise to open the doors or windows for fear of "alarming the natives," but at the conclusion of the session everything was thrown open and Malibran served champagne. She then announced that she would cool her guests in the South American way, which meant rubbing one's head with handfuls of cologne. She began with the nearest scalp.

When Templeton's turn came, he bobbed his head inexplicably up and down, but Maria finally steadied him and poured cologne over his head. To the shock and merriment of all, the tenor's wig dropped to the floor, where it remained for an instant until both parties dived for it. Maria emerged from the scuffle with the hairpiece and refused to return it until Templeton allowed her to rub cologne over his balding head. With no choice he submitted, and after completing the ritual, she dropped the hair on his head—backward so that the curls hung into his face—with the remark: "My dear Mr. T., I'm deceived. I didn't think there was anything fake about you."[38] Everyone was amused but poor Templeton, once again the butt of Maria's humor.

But the first performance on May 27, 1836, compensated for whatever the cast, and Bunn, had suffered at the hands of Macready and Malibran during the preparations for the new work. *The Maid of Artois* surpassed the combined hopes of everyone concerned, becoming one of the most successful operas ever staged in England.* The work received some small criticisms—it was considered extremely eclectic—but Malibran did not.

The *Morning Post* published an extensive review (28 May 1836). An awed critic discussed every act, every scene, and every note in detail, observing that the opera was "acted by Malibran with that giving up of her whole soul to the actual situation which so peculiarly characterizes her." In its entirety, this extraordinary "rave" review would fill a volume in itself.

The reception of Madame Malibran, as may be supposed, was very great, and her presence was felt to be a decided impetus to the interest. She left little time for comment on her appropriate costume. The masterly light and shade in her singing of the recitative, her intense and refined expression, and the novel and musician-like graces and ornaments which she introduced in the succeeding passages, brought down a torrent of approbation. Her clear and powerful voice, her wonderful skill in executing roulades, chromatic phrases, and shakes, the richness and volume of her contralto notes, and the precision, brilliance, and variety of her cadenzas, defy all description and set at naught all criticism. To hear her in this scene sing the phrase, "I'd dash the bauble down," is of itself a memorable point of recollection. The intonation and whirlwind of notes on the word DASH, for grandeur of purpose and dignity of musical sentiment, were never surpassed in vocal or histrionic effect. This alone would have stamped her as a woman of extraordinary genius. Of the composition itself we cannot now pretend to write. Our faculty of thought, by Malibran's electrifying execution, was taken from us, and in that respect we were only in the same position as the whole audience, for her astounding compass left them the only choice of cheering vehemently.

The reviewer described the finale of the first act, as Jules, having wounded the Marquis in a duel, is taken away to be sold into slavery. "There was a fearful reality in her exertions, which proved the utter self-abandonment of the actress to the delusion of the scene. In the midst of this she has to sing, and does sing, some complex music to wind up the act. The curtain fell amidst overwhelming applause, and Malibran was unanimously called for."

Bunn, who knew that Maria was exerting herself to her limit, visited her in her dressing room. "She had borne along the first two acts . . . in such a flood of triumph, that she was bent, by some superhuman effort, to continue its glory to the final fall of the curtain," he wrote in his memoirs. "I went into her dressing room previous to the commencement of the third act, to ask how she felt, and she replied: 'Very tired, but' (and here her eye of fire suddenly lighted up) 'you angry devil, if you will contrive to get me a pint of porter in the desert scene, you shall have an encore to your finale.'"

Bunn thought twice about granting such a request, "but to check *her*

---

*Bunn recorded the receipts of the most popular operas he presented: [39]

16 Sonnambula in	1835	311 pounds
10 Fidelio	1835	330
9 Sonnambula	1836	333
4 Fidelio	1836	317
16 Maid	1836	355

powers was to annihilate them. I therefore arranged that behind the pile of drifted sand on which she falls in a state of exhaustion towards the close of the desert scene, a small aperture should be made in the stage; and it is a fact that, from underneath the stage through that aperture, a pewter pint of porter was conveyed to the parched lips of this rare child of song, which so revived her, after the terrible exertions the scene led to, that she electrified the audience, and had the strength to repeat the charm with the finale to *The Maid of Artois*."[40]

The audience, unaware of the source of Malibran's seemingly incredible energy, wondered how she finished the opera with so much strength—and then repeated the finale. The *Morning Post* concluded that

It would be useless for us to enter at any length into the matchless display of Malibran. . . . We cannot say she reserved herself for the end, for she was transcendently grand throughout; but she gave the finale, "The Rapture Dwelling" with inexhaustible fire and energy, and the furore of the audience was at its height. Three octaves did Malibran call into requisition in this masterpiece of execution, reaching E in alt, and making a prolonged shake, if we mistake not, on B flat in alt.* It was, in sooth, a wondrous burst, and it was cruel to demand it a second time. The curtain however drew up, and she again went through what would on the score appear an almost incredible task. A storm of cheering summoned her, after the act-drop fell, and Templeton led her forward. The waving of hats, handkerchiefs &c., could not be exceeded even at La Scala.

The *Times'* critic added that "the finale, which Madame Malibran sang, must be heard; —to describe it adequately is impossible. It is one of the most delicious, thrilling pieces that has perhaps ever been heard on the stage, and is executed with surpassing skill" (28 May 1836).

Maria was thrilled by *The Maid*'s success and so amused at the novelty of drinking port during a performance that Bunn arranged during subsequent evenings for the negro slave at the head of the governor's procession to carry it in a gourd around his neck so that she could imbibe as Isoline lay dying in the desert.[41] Unfortunately, the public, which already had heard rumors of Malibran's intemperate drinking, found out about this. And Mr. Berkeley, the music critic for a leading London newspaper, constantly referred to it, hinting that Maria was more than a little addicted to Barclay and Perkins Porter, her favorite brand, and that in the last act of *The Maid* there was "more beer than bier."[42]

One day Maria's friend Lord Lennox, while praising her to Mr. Berkeley, offered to introduce him to Malibran in her dressing room at Drury Lane. The uneasy Berkeley knew very well that Malibran suspected him of writing the diatribes, but he accepted anyway and was taken backstage.

"Allow me," began Lord Lennox to Maria, "to introduce Mr. Berke-

---

*Henry Phillips said it was on high C "and was one of the most extraordinary vocal efforts I ever heard" (vol. 1, p. 219).

ley." At his words Maria leaped up from her dressing table, ran to the nervous Berkeley, and with the utmost sincerity told him, "Oh monsieur Barclay, I shall never drink another glass of *Barclay and Perkins* without thinking of you!"[43]

On May 11, 1836, Ignaz Moscheles gave a concert at the Italian opera house in London, which de Bériot and Malibran attended. Maria had known the pianist since her first concerts in 1825, and she had already inspired several of his compositions, in particular his transcriptions for piano of her cadenzas entitled "Gems à la Malibran." During the summer of 1836 they renewed their friendship, and his diaries tell of many hours spent in the company of "her sparkling genius, sunny cheerfulness, and never-failing spirit and humor. . . . Other singers may captivate by their art, and gifted and amiable women by their manners and conversation, but Malibran had magic powers to lead us captives, body and soul." The Moscheleses accepted her as a family member. The children considered her their own, for only she knew how to play with dolls—a passion she had never outgrown—and only she had an irresistible black silk bag which contained a paintbox, paper, and brushes. Within moments of her arrival she would be down on the floor painting pictures with the children, wholeheartedly sharing their youthful delight.

The pianist's diary describes June 12 as a day spent with the de Bériots.

We had great fun the other day when she and de Bériot joined our early dinner. The conversation turned to Gnecco's comic duet [from *La Prova d'un Opera Seria*], which Malibran sang so frequently and charmingly with Lablache. Man and wife ridicule and abuse each other, caricaturing alternately each other's defects—when she came to the passage: "La tua bocca e fatta apposta pel servizio della posta;"* "just like my mouth," said Malibran, "as broad as you please, and I'll just put this orange in to prove it." One must have known de Bériot to appreciate his amazement and agony at seeing his wife open her mouth wide, and discover two beautiful rows of teeth, behind which the orange disappears. Then she roars with laughter at her successful performance.

She came at three o'clock; with her were Thalberg, Benedict, and Klingemann. We dined early, and immediately afterwards Malibran sat down at the piano and "sang for the children", as she used to call it, the Rataplan† and some of her father's Spanish songs. For want of a guitar accompaniment she would, while playing, mark the rhythm now and then on the board at the back of the keys. After singing with exquisite grace and charm a number of French and Italian romances of her own composition, she was relieved at the piano by Thalberg, who performed all manner of tricks on the instrument, snapping his fingers as an obbligato to Viennese songs and waltzes. I played afterwards with reversed hands, and with my fists, and none laughed louder than Malibran.

At five o'clock we drove to the Zoological Gardens, and pushed our way for

---

*"Your mouth is made expressly for the service of the mail."

† Both Maria and her father wrote pieces titled "Rataplan."

an hour with the fashionables. When we had had enough of man and beast we took one more turn in the Park, and as soon as we got home Malibran sat down at the piano and sang for an hour. At last, however, she called out to Thalberg: "Come play something, I need to rest," her repose consisting of finishing a most charming landscape in water-colors (an art in which she was self-taught). Thalberg played by heart, and in a most masterly way, several of his etudes. . . .

We had supper afterwards; there again it was Malibran who kept us all going. She gave us the richest imitations of Sir George Smart, the singers Knyvett, Braham, Phillips, and Vaughan, who had sung with her at a concert given by the Duchess of C.; taking off on the fat Duchess herself, as she condescendingly patronized 'her' artists, and wound up with the cracked voice and nasal tones of Lady——, who inflicted "Home Sweet Home" on the company. Suddenly her comic vein came to a full stop; then she gave in the thorough German style the *scena* from *Freyschutz*, with German words, and a whole series of German songs by Mendelssohn, Schubert, Weber, and my humble self. Lastly, she took a turn with *Don Giovanni*, being familiar not only with the music of Zerlina, her own part, but knowing by heart every note in the opera, which she could play and sing from beginning to end. She went on playing and singing alternately until eleven o'clock, fresh to the last in voice and spirits. When she left us we were all rapturous about her music, languages, painting; but what we liked best was her artlessness and amiability.[44]

But despite her "artlessness and amiability," her talents and her charm, some fashionable people still discriminated against Maria. In the summer of 1836, she wrote to the Marquis de Louvois of one such incident.

I ran into M. and Mme Crown . . . but they hardly recognized me, since they would have dropped a notch in the good opinion of everyone (and especially the Duke of Devonshire, at whose home I met them once again for the first time) if people had been able to believe that M. and Mme Crown had condescended to come chez moi to have a good time with me in Naples. One condescends to know certain people only when it means they will have a good time, but after that, you are, that is to say I am, visible, but only from a great distance.

I confess that I have had the stupidity to become upset over this sudden change, which is even more absurd when you consider that she came to my home and received me at hers.[45]

Over the years Alfred Bunn had developed a real fondness, even a fatherly concern, for this strange girl whose superhuman exertions seemed so self-destructive, this "extraordinary creature," as he called her, who would not or could not admit to human limitations. During this last season in London he paid particular attention to her arbitrary behavior and tried to reason with her. In his memoirs he recounted one such occasion: what he did not know at the time of this incident was that Malibran had suffered a fatal accident, and had little more than two months to live.

I was leaving the theatre one evening, and going into Malibran's room I found her, after the performance of *La Sonnambula*, dressing for an evening concert. I remonstrated with her, pointed out the inroads she was making on her constitution, and urged her to send an excuse. She promised to do so, and in a belief that she would keep that promise I bade her good night and drove home to Brompton.

I was reading in bed about half an hour after the midnight chime when the bell of the outer gate was rung violently and on its being answered I heard a voice say, "Tell Mr. Bunn not to get up - I am only come for a little fresh air in his garden." I dressed, and found in one of the walks Madame Malibran, Monsieur De Bériot, and Monsieur Thalberg, from whom I learnt that despite all my injunctions she had been to TWO concerts, gone home afterwards to undress, and dress, and had taken a fancy to this slight country trip at such an extraordinary hour. I had supper laid under a huge walnut tree which overshadowed the entire southern aspect of the house; and beneath its umbrage some viands, especially aided by a favourite beverage of hers—home brewed beer—and ONIONS. . . . She pulled them fresh from their beds, and, thus humbly entertained, she seemed to be as happy as possible. She warbled as late as three into the morning some of her most enchanting strains, and wound up saying, "Now I have had my supper, I will go and steal my breakfast"; and running into the hen-house, emptied every nest and started off to town.[46]

Bunn was sitting beneath the walnut tree—where Maria had eaten his onions—when he learned of her death.

CHAPTER 16

The End

Even though she had been pregnant since May and had scheduled many performances and concerts, Maria continued to pursue her athletic activities in London. When Lord Lennox organized a hunting party in early July and invited the de Bériots, she immediately decided to go. Charles refused the invitation and disapproved of his wife's decision, but as he well knew, objections were pointless.

On the morning of the hunt Maria disregarded the advice of her friends and chose the most spirited mount in the barn, a horse called "King of the Stables." Nervous but unwilling to admit an error in judgment, she insisted on joining the hunt. King of the Stables lived up to his reputation; even Maria was alarmed by his energy and speed as he took the bit in his teeth and set out across the English countryside at a gallop. Her alarm soon became fear, and she gestured to a gatekeeper on the road ahead to close the turnpike gate that she was fast approaching, but misunderstanding her signal, and unaware of an imminent catastrophe, he threw his hat at the excited horse. A moment later Maria felt her foot slip through the stirrup and become entangled in it. A second turnpike, unattended, came into sight; the open gate, a single bar that lifted up, extended across the road at a height of about twelve feet. In a bold, desperate attempt to extricate herself from her predicament, Maria threw down the reins, and as the horse charged through the gate, she jumped from the saddle and grasped the extended bar with both hands. But as she did so the tangled stirrup gripped her ankle, tore her from her hold, and threw her headfirst to the ground. Now hanging from the runaway animal she was dragged brutally across the road, her head dashing against the stony soil.

Her horrified friends, having seen this lurid sight, chased after her and found her bloodied body lying a distance down the road. The stirrup had finally broken, dropping her to the ground, and King of the Stables had vanished. She was still breathing, a heartbeat was detected, and the party carried her home, where, to the immense relief of all, she regained consciousness. Her first words were: "Is my husband home?" Once assured of his absence, she immediately rose, despite protests, and went to the mirror where she washed the blood from her face and arranged her hair to conceal as many cuts and bruises as possible. Her friends attempted to move her back to bed, but she resisted. "Not for anything," she told them. "I'll be better in no time. All I want is for this to be kept a secret from de Bériot: he will be miserable if he finds out about it."[1] She seemed afraid not only for him, but of him.

"But," pointed out Julius Benedict, "when he sees you he will know what happened."

"No he won't," she retorted. "And I will sing tonight as planned."

"You're mad."

"Maybe, but I'll do it anyway."[2] She continued disguising the effects of the accident, and by the time Charles returned most of the damage was concealed. When he questioned her she told him that she had tripped on her riding gear and fallen downstairs. A letter had already been dispatched to Lord Lennox begging him to keep the incident a secret.*

That night she sang at the theater as she had said she would. The audience did not suspect her condition, but when a chorister brushed against her she cried out in pain, so bruised was her whole body.[3] Nevertheless, she did not concede physical frailty and continued to perform. Madame Merlin believed that many of Maria's strange whims and irrational actions resulted from her belief that she was destined to die young, and that when she slowed her pace or stopped enjoying her childish pleasures she would die.[4]

On the night of the accident, certainly no more than a day or two later, Maria attended Moscheles' concert. "Malibran and De Bériot appeared at eleven o'clock," he wrote in his diary. "She looked weary, and when she sang one scarcely recognized Malibran so voiceless was she. We only heard subsequently that she had been thrown from her horse when riding in the park. Although suffering no injury she had not yet recovered from the violent shock. She was soon herself, however . . . . When my wife showed some anxiety lest she should over-exert herself, she replied, 'My dear lady, I would sing for you until the extinction of my voice.' "[5] The de Bériots remained at the party until three o'clock in the morning.

In spite of Maria's determination to ignore the accident and continue her life as before, the effects of her fall were becoming increasingly obvious to those around her. At first, her friends attributed the changes in her temperament to her pregnancy, but as time passed it became apparent that only serious injury could explain them. Her moods, always extreme, became manic-depressive. Acute headaches racked her, and her usual

---

*Maria's efforts to conceal her accident, or barring that, to change the circumstances of it, resulted in another story which has often appeared as a separate anecdote in various biographical sketches. This second story involves a hypothetical riding trip in either Regent's or Hyde Park, during which she was recognized by a crowd of people who cheered her. Her horse, unaccustomed to such demonstrations, bolted, and was finally brought under control by a passerby who grabbed the reins. In this version and its variations, Maria was thrown against a railing and was injured only slightly (Merlin, *Memoirs*, vol. 2, pp. 67–68, and other sources). This story was initially accepted as truth, later as an additional incident, but subsequent events indicate that it is a bowdlerized version of the accident.

nervous attacks repeated themselves with greater severity. Between these seizures she would become hyperactive, but her extravagant gaiety seemed more an unnatural excitement than real cheerfulness. Regardless of whether she had been singing the night before, she arose at five or six in the morning to vocalize and practice poses before the mirror, and by the time anyone else was awake, she would be off on horseback galloping over the countryside. If she had spare time, she would paint pictures, draw caricatures, or write rhymes and music.

One of the songs she composed at this time was set to a poem called *La Morte,* by the Italian poet Benelli. She dedicated it to Lablache, who had sent her the verses.

Ton, ton, chi batte là?
Ton, ton, sono la morte.*

On July 16 Moscheles heard her sing it and left an account of the occasion. "She sang us a comic song that she had just composed: a sick man weary of life invokes death; but when death, personified by a doctor, knocks at the door, he dismisses him with scorn. She had set this subject so cleverly, and sang the music so humorously, that we could scarcely refrain from laughing; and yet we couldn't endure to lose a single note."[6]

Maria's altered disposition alarmed her friends. One day she and a group of singers tried out a new organ in a small town near London. Giulia Grisi chose to sing the rondo from *I Puritani,* the piece Bellini had written for Maria. Not to be outdone, Maria went to the organ and sang an aria by Handel, "effacing Grisi," in the words of one present. But in the middle of the piece her voice began to fade, her hands fell from the keyboard, and she stopped, a vacant look in her eyes, lost in thought.[7] Her condition prompted the consultation of two doctors who decided that she should be bled. Although opposed to such practices, Maria finally gave in to the demands of friends and relatives. Afterward she was less excitable and appeared to improve.

Meanwhile she continued her stream of performances at Drury Lane, often singing night after night without a break in her busiest musical schedule ever. On July 5 she renewed her contract for eight more performances. On July 16 she finished her engagement with *The Maid of Artois,* the last act of *La Sonnambula,* and a stirring rendition of "God Save the King" that brought down the house; the following day she sailed with Charles from London to Anvers. Many engagements loomed in the future: she was under contract to Bunn for three nights a week beginning in May of 1837; there were two years remaining in her La Scala contract; Mr. Caldwell in New York had offered her 10,000 pounds sterling for a year in America,[8] and there were offers from Vienna, Paris, and Prague as well as a possible

*Rap, rap, who is knocking?/Rap, rap, I am death." Benelli died two months after writing the poem, Malibran two months after setting it to music.

tour of Edinburgh, Dublin, Liverpool, and other English cities with the Drury Lane troupe.

Although her headaches became more severe, Maria could still write letters in the cheerful tone of happier days. On July 28 she wrote to the Marquis de Louvois.

Oh! Of all the naughtiest and untruthful men. What? You make our mouths water and then . . . nothing! No more father Louvois at all! You witness the fact that I am writing you; thus if you do not take the coach to come see us in Brussels upon the receipt of this letter, I won't speak to you again for life, and I will be very sullen towards you. That will upset my stomach a little, but no matter, I will pout. We're staying here until the 14th. That is to say that on the 14th there will be a concert in Liège, and we will perform there, and I will scream away. It is the 28th today, thus you can still spend from ten to twelve, to fourteen to sixteen days with us. It is the very least that father Louvois can do to add to the happiness of his adopted children.[9]

At approximately the same time she wrote a letter in a different mood to another friend, perhaps Lamartine, requesting verses to set to music for Adolphe Nourrit, "who is my companion in musical misfortune and stormy childhood." In an almost pathetic tone she asked: "Is it true that Rossini is writing an opera for me? I have been assured that he wants to make me that surprise! I would sell my soul to him for such a thing." In closing she added, "I'm not at all well—since my fall I have [remainder of letter missing]."[10]

On August 14 the de Bériots and Pauline Garcia, now fifteen years old, appeared together in the concert at Liège. Pauline sang with her older sister and also demonstrated her gifts as a pianist. Then, at the request of the King of Prussia, Maria traveled to Aix-la-Chapelle (now Aachen) for two performances of *La Sonnambula*, which she sang in Italian while the rest of the cast performed in German. As she left the theater after the final evening of this brief engagement, the King's guard, in full uniform, presented arms, an honor hitherto reserved for the royal family.

At the time of these performances Maria's headaches became so intense she could not even stand up. Although she never complained, her appearance often betrayed her suffering and she finally had to tell Charles what had happened. But she did not tell him the whole truth; swearing Pauline to secrecy Maria told her sister that she knew she had a blood clot in her head and would soon die. True to her word, Pauline kept the confession to herself, but she regretted her promise for the rest of her life.[11]

From Brussels the de Bériots moved to Roissy, on the outskirts of Paris, where they had bought a small chateau. Charles hoped that the fresh air and calm life there would help Maria's health, but she lost all interest in her athletic pursuits and spent many hours at the piano, composing. She wrote several songs dedicated, as she had promised, to Adolphe Nourrit, among them "Noce du Marin" and "Au bord de la mer,"* often holding the pen in

*For Hector Berlioz' critical review of these songs, see Appendix.

one hand and her throbbing head in the other. As her physical strength declined she resorted more and more to those stimulants she had always relied on, a glass of champagne, wine, barley water, coffee, anything that might provide a temporary surge of energy. Her emotions reached new extremes; hours of weeping alternated with hysterical euphoria.

Occasionally flashes of her former energy returned. At Roissy the gardeners found several subterranean caves. Everyone in the chateau explored these caverns, which were several feet below ground level and which were reached by climbing down ropes. Charles forbade Maria to join in the explorations and despite her arguments, she was left at home. Shortly before dawn the next morning, she crept from the house, and going to the gardeners' quarters awoke several men to accompany her down to the caves. Having explored them she returned to bed. When the others awoke and went to breakfast she told them she dreamed she had visited the caves, describing them vividly to her amazed friends. Finally confessing the truth, she laughed uproariously at her joke.[12]

In the last days of August she and Charles traveled back to England for the provincial festivals. Alfred Bunn saw her at the Théâtre des Variétés on August 31, and around that time she wrote Ernest Legouvé a letter similar to one she had sent him several years earlier: "Come see me right away! I am suffocating from sobbing! Every mournful idea is at my bedside, and death at their head."[13]

On Saturday, September 10, they arrived in Manchester, where the music festival was to begin on September 12. Traveling lightly and with only one servant, they stopped first at the Royal Hotel but moved the next day to the Mosley-Arms where Lablache and the other singers were staying. She seemed in good health, but when a member of the festival committee visited her Sunday afternoon, she complained of shivering and a headache. When he informed her of the exact schedule of singers and events organized by the committee, she attempted to change them to better suit herself, and in failing this she became so upset that Charles could barely calm her. But she delighted in seeing her friends again, particularly Lablache, with whom she and Charles spent the evening laughing and performing. She played and sang her latest compositions, including "La Morte," which she dedicated to the bass and which he was eager to hear. But in singing this piece, Maria became so overwrought that Lablache and Charles finally persuaded her to go to bed.

On Monday, September 12, the festival began, but complaining of ill health, Maria did not attend the morning rehearsal. She did not seem particularly unwell, but no one questioned her decision. In the evening she considered herself well enough to perform, but the effort so exhausted her that she had to support herself against the piano to keep from falling. On Tuesday morning she ate her usual breakfast, oysters and port with water, and left for the church, where she was to perform in the morning concert. When she heard the organ she burst into tears but was calmed in time to sing her pieces. Although visibly sick, she sang with her unique intensity and depth of emotion. The evening performance passed without incident, but the festival committee, alerted to her health, counseled her to seek immediate medical attention. She ignored their advice.

On Wednesday Maria vomited her breakfast but insisted on going to church for the morning concert. Mrs. Richardson, proprietress of the Mosley-Arms, tactfully suggested that perhaps the port did not agree with her.

"What can I do?" she replied. "I have to take something for my voice, and this seems to be the best thing for it."

On this day she laughed hysterically when she heard the organ, and was so weak she could barely stand to sing. Her performance of Handel's "Sing ye the Lord" was considered fine and impressed the festival audience, but many noticed that she was not well. After the performance she was carried back to the Mosley-Arms and slept for the remainder of the day.

When she awoke, she found Maria Caradori in her room with Lord Lennox and asked them what time it was. Told that it was six o'clock she replied: "Tell them we will sing tonight." Ignoring all protests she repeated, "I will sing tonight," and although barely strong enough to rise from her couch, she prepared to leave for the concert. She bribed the doorman at the theater to allow the hackney coach to enter a forbidden area immediately adjacent to the entrance, so that no more than two or three steps were necessary to enter the building. Even so, she required assistance. But once before the audience she seemed sustained by an inexplicable strength. Although she looked pale and ill, her voice had never sounded more full or powerful as she sang the music of Haydn, Mozart, and Handel, followed by the quartet from *Fidelio,* which was encored.

The next piece on her program was a duet from Mercadante's *Andronico* that she and Caradori would sing. They had planned the embellishments at rehearsal, but the ambitious Caradori now decided to add further ornaments without advising Maria, who now faced both the audience and her rival's challenge. As she had once vanquished Velluti, she now made up her mind to triumph over this impertinent partner and further embellished her own part, "in which she displayed most wonderful execution," according to her conductor, Sir George Smart. Rising a third above Caradori she held a trill for a remarkable length of time, and the astonished audience gave her an ovation. Once in the wings she heard the cries for an encore reverberating through the hall.

"If I sing it again it would kill me," she told Smart.

"Then do not," he replied. "Let me address the audience."

For a moment she considered excusing herself. But had her father ever allowed her the unforgivable words "I cannot?" She had carved the most brilliant operatic career in the world through disregard of the impossible, through an absolute refusal to admit physical limitations. The cheers and applause continued. Her cheeks flushed and her tired eyes shone feverishly.

"I will sing it again," she declared with determination. "I will annihilate her!"[14]

Although the drama that evening in Manchester led to an exaggeration of Maria's success, all reports indicate that her last performance was brilliant. All her powers of improvisation were let loose, and her voice followed with power, beautiful tone, and unfailing accuracy. At the conclusion of the duet she repeated the trill on high B, holding it for an enormous length of time, and when she finished the audience rose in an ovation for la Malibran, perhaps no more enthusiastic than on previous occasions, but it was the last.[15]

Maria was practically carried by Caradori to the wings where she collapsed and lost consciousness. De Bériot, whose performance followed hers, was unaware of what happened and went onstage from another entrance. As he played, two English doctors, Worthington and Beardsley, prescribed bleeding. Lablache, knowing that Maria did not believe in it, and fearing the therapy would only aggravate her condition, attempted to prevent it. The doctors told him to concern himself with singing and not healing.

"Let them do what they want," Maria finally told her friend. "It doesn't matter anymore."

After the bleeding she again lost consciousness, but not before having sent a message to Smart that she would sing again in the second part of the concert. An announcement was made that she could not continue, and she was carried on a stretcher back to the Mosley-Arms, since a coach was too rough for her. At the hotel she recovered long enough to ask, "How did Charles play? Was he much applauded?" Upon being assured that all had gone well she smiled and fainted. De Bériot immediately sent to London for Dr. Belluomini, whom he trusted more than Worthington and Beardsley.

On Thursday morning Maria regained consciousness, but she complained to Mrs. Richardson of violent pains in her head. Although vomiting a cup of coffee—her only sustenance—she wanted to sing again in the concerts that day and became so excited when the doctors tried to dissuade her that they decided it would be better for her to sing than to suffer a nervous trauma. Mrs. Richardson helped her to dress, and then Charles helped her into the parlor where she had another attack of vomiting. The seats of the carriage summoned to take her to the church were covered with sheets and towels as a precaution. She was so weak that she was almost carried to the coach and crept into it on her hands and knees.

With de Bériot and Mrs. Richardson, she set off to the church but complained of pains in her head, chest, and abdomen. Once at her destination she became hysterical and was immediately returned to the hotel, where she rested more comfortably in the parlor with the remark, "Oh how I wish I could have sung, for I was never in finer voice." The doctors issued a certificate stating that she would be unable to perform in the festival for an undetermined period of time.

For the next few days Maria hovered on the edge of life. On Sunday, September 18, Dr. Belluomini arrived from London at seven in the evening. On seeing her old friend Maria threw her arms around him with the feeble cry, "I am saved! He has known me from childhood and loves me like his own daughter!" Belluomini was not so sure. Having known her for years he knew her strange constitution and even before departing from London had wondered aloud if he would find her alive. At his arrival she was delirious, a state the doctor diagnosed as a "grave nervous fever." Her pulse was very weak, and for four days a constant dry cough had prevented her from eating or sleeping. Belluomini dismissed her doctors and gave her an effective remedy for the cough. That night she slept for the first time, and by the next day the fever and delirium had diminished substantially. Belluomini began thinking he might actually save her, and Charles, grasping at this favorable turn, wrote to Lablache and Ivanoff, who had departed for engagements in Paris, that she was now out of danger. "No one would believe this wonderful change if they had seen her," he told them. "Maria was out of bed, doing her toilet, and wanted to go for a walk."

Malibran's illness caused a sensation in Manchester. The leading citizens inquired about her, and crowds formed beneath her windows wanting to know the latest developments. Daily bulletins on her condition were issued and published in the newspapers. The strong affection between the de Bériots was commented on, for Charles had not left her room since she first returned from the fatal concert; in her coherent moments she asked how he was, turned her head to see him, and held his hand. "If he had had any faults," she told Mrs. Richardson, "I should have known about them by now, but there never was such a man. I am certainly blessed with a most affectionate husband; and that, I am afraid, few people can say." She continued to fear that the public would think her illness just another manifestation of the famous Malibran "caprice," or even worse, the result of her rumored drunkenness.

Before the day was over, the fever and delirium returned. Her sickness continued to be aggravated by her inability to eat anything but a few raisins or a little peach juice, and for the next four days the periods of remission became ever shorter. Charles became more and more depressed and at last realized that she would not recover. He was advised to keep his spirits up for his wife's sake but replied despairingly, "Oh no, she will never get better, it's impossible." On September 22 Dr. Belluomini saw indications that his patient was getting worse and consulted a gynecologist, who thought the child Maria was carrying was dead. For the duration of the night she was comatose, only occasionally turning her head. The next morning her condition deteriorated more rapidly; her hair was cut off and compresses of hot water and vinegar were applied to her head and body to provoke a physical response, but to no avail.

That night, recognizing that nothing could save her, Belluomini turned his attention to de Bériot's health. At about ten he persuaded Charles to rest in another room, but half an hour later found him getting up to return to Maria. To spare him the agony of seeing his wife die, the doctor told him she was already dead. Charles' reaction was violent: Maria had judged his character well on those many occasions when she had shielded him from her accidents and illnesses. "I cannot describe his tears, his despair," wrote the doctor in his journal. From this moment he made all of Charles' decisions, and had the bereft husband sign an authorization granting Mr. Beale, a member of the festival committee, responsibility for the funeral arrangements. "I judged that he had nothing better to do than to immediately leave this desolate place, where, to my mind, he would have become severely ill himself, succumbing, as he would have, to ten or eleven days of fatigue, sleeplessness, and anguish. Knowing that on Sunday, the 25th, a steamboat was leaving from London to Anvers, I hastened our departure so as not to miss this boat, and not to waste any time in reaching Belgium where he would find consolation and all the assistance he would need in the bosom of his family."

As Belluomini rushed to make these arrangements, Maria showed few signs of life. So peaceful were her final hours that she had been dead for several minutes before the fact was discovered. The doctor pronounced her dead at 11:40 P.M., Friday, September 23, 1836. The doctor and Mrs. Richardson packed her belongings and called a coach for the trip to London. Another committee member, fearing that de Bériot was in no state to travel so soon after his wife's death, offered him the use of his home, but Belluomini dissuaded him. "In precipitating this departure, I followed the practice of several civilized countries in Europe, where the relatives of the deceased are taken away to their homes, while friends charge themselves with the execution of the funeral ceremonies," he wrote in his journal.

As news of Maria Malibran's death spread through the night several artists petitioned for the right to draw bedside sketches and to make death masks. One was selected*—perhaps by Beale—and the others were dismissed with the explanation that Malibran's husband wanted no likeness made of his wife's body. When the coach arrived Charles was so grieved and exhausted that it was necessary to carry him to the conveyance. Shortly before 2:00 A.M., September 24, barely two hours after Maria's death, he and Belluomini left Manchester.[17]

---

*This was a secret so well kept that until the present day the existence of a death mask was all but unknown. According to the Central Library, Manchester, the man who made it was William Bally, a sculptor. Further evidence indicates that Charles de Bériot may have owned it, or a cast from it, for it is believed that he used it in modeling the crowned bust he made of his wife after her death. This was his only sculpture and was not considered to be a good likeness, or even a good bust. Charles mentioned it in a letter to Alfred Bunn dated January 22, 1839, in which he promised to make a copy of it for the impresario.[16]

The mask next surfaced in New York in the early 1860s when it was discovered near Tompkins Square by the writer and critic Laurence Hutton, who believed it might have been brought to America by the phrenologist George Combe. Hutton's comments (in his book *Portraits in Plaster*) raise far more questions than they answer, but they are, for better or worse,

By morning couriers had announced the tragic news to a shocked world. The death of Maria Malibran shook Europe as the death of no other performer ever had before. At first the reports were not believed. Even in Manchester many considered her to be in good health; either her condition was an act or she suffered from alcoholism. No one offered a definite diagnosis of her illness and Charles requested that an autopsy not be performed, that Maria's body not be disturbed except for the actual funeral arrangements.

Mr. Beale and the festival committee planned the Catholic funeral service for the following Saturday. The committee tried to write Charles de Bériot to request his presence as chief mourner, but no one knew where he was. In his absence a group of leading citizens was chosen as pallbearers. These included Sir George Smart and Alfred Bunn, whose desire to be at the ceremonies led him to postpone the opening of Drury Lane for a week so he could travel to Manchester.

On Saturday morning at 8:00 the muffled bell of the Collegiate Church began to toll. At the Mosley-Arms Hotel, where all was draped in black, the funeral party assembled around the remains of Maria Malibran, sealed in a triple nest of oak and lead-lined coffins. On the lid of the outermost casket lay an ivory crucifix; at each side stood silver candelabra bearing lighted candles. A brass plate fixed to the top bore the inscription:

Maria Felicia de Bériot
Died September 23, 1836
Aged Twenty-Eight Years

At 10:30 A.M. the hearse, drawn by four black horses, arrived at the entrance to the hotel. The pallbearers placed the coffin inside and covered it with a black cloth. A half hour later the funeral vehicle, followed by six mourning coaches, each drawn by four black horses, departed on its circuitous journey to the Collegiate Church. About sixty Manchester gentlemen, dressed in mourning, walked three abreast ahead of the procession. They in turn were led by the Deputy Constable of the city and his administrators, their staves of office covered by black crepe. Private coaches containing citizens of the town, and many people who had journeyed from London to pay homage, followed in a long line. Silent crowds, estimated at about 50,000 people, lined the streets of Manchester for the entire route between the hotel and the church. Flags were hung at half mast, and the interior of the Collegiate Church, including the pulpit and reading desks, was heavily draped in black. When the cortege arrived,

---

all that exists on the subject. His large collection of death masks was willed to Princeton University, and it is there, in the Theatre Collection, that the Malibran mask may now be found. It is a gruesome object, revealing nothing of Maria Malibran other than her lifeless features.

the church quickly filled with everyone who could squeeze or push himself in, and many attempted to buy admittance.

The music played on the organ during the funeral service included "Holy, Holy" and "O Lord have mercy upon me, for I am in trouble," two pieces with which Maria Malibran had electrified her listeners only days before in this very place. After the ceremony the coffin was taken to a vault beneath the foundations of the church. Candles burned at the head and foot of the grave, and for the duration of the day, and many days following, thousands of mourners filed silently through the church for a glimpse of Maria Malibran's tomb.

Charles de Bériot was much criticized for leaving his wife immediately after her death; many people suspected that his prime motivation in doing so was to secure for himself her estate, estimated at 700,000 francs. Fueling these rumors was his acceptance of the committee's offer of the entire sum Maria would have earned for the festival had she completed her engagement. Whether he received this on the night of September 23 or whether it was sent to him later is not certain, but before his departure he did leave twenty-five pounds sterling for the poor of the city. The public was slow to accept the fact that he barely knew what he was doing on the night of Maria's death and that Dr. Belluomini had made all his decisions. Belluomini pointed this out in a letter to the *Times*. "If the act of leaving Manchester so quickly is a reprehensible act, then the blame falls entirely on me, and not on Beriot, who at that moment was too depressed to cold-bloodedly determine the best means of satisfying the English public" (4 October 1836).

Alfred Bunn, whose letter of consolation was answered by Constance Franquen, also proved to be a friend.

October 14, 1836

Monsieur, For several days my brother has wanted to respond to your good letter, but he is still so unhappily overwhelmed by the misfortune that has struck us, and from the results of all that he suffered in Manchester, that the least emotion is disastrous to his health. I avoid as much as possible anything that might renew his sorrow. Let me tell you on his behalf how much he appreciates your remembering him, especially in a circumstance where he needs friendship so much.

I decided not to give your letter to Charles at the moment when I received it; he is unaware as of yet of the infamous calumnies spread about his character, about his heart. His soul is too pure for him to have suspected, and in the condition he was in, it was my duty not to tell him of this. I have prudently kept him from knowing a part of it, so that he would judge his true friends well. He is happy, monsieur, to count you among them.

Please accept, monsieur, the expression of my personal recognition of the

affection that you had for my poor dear sister, and that you feel for my
unfortunate brother.

C. de Franquen, née De Beriot

P.S. Charles will save for you the souvenir that you requested.[18]

"The postscript," noted Bunn, "refers to my request for a ring of
trifling value, as a memento of one it were impossible to forget."[19] In his
memoirs he remembered Maria as "the greatest vocal genius, in my humble
opinion, the world has yet possessed," and added bitterly, "lying in her path
[was] a forest of laurels yet ungathered, and a mine of gold yet undug. Petty
farce this life!"[20]

Like all her friends and acquaintances, William Macready remembered the moment he learned of Malibran's death—on September 27 in
Shrewsbury—and left a vivid account of his reaction to the news.

I asked for the newspaper. I had read three pages of it, and one or two columns
of the fourth—it was the *Standard*—when my eyes struck on the words: *"Malibran
is no more!"* The loudest clap of thunder in the calmest sunshine could not have
given me a greater start. I felt as if my mind was stunned; it was a shock that
left me no power to think for some time. I read on, when recovered from the
horror and surprise of the news . . . of one—in youth, so rich in talent, once so
lovely, with so much to enchant and fascinate, and so much to blame and
regret—suddenly taken from a world so full of delight to her, and to which she
was so frequently a minister of delight. I once could have loved her, and she has
since said that she loved—"was in love with"—me. Had I known it for certain I
might have been more miserable than I am . . . . This world is a sad loss to her,
and she to it. Poor Malibran! [pp. 343–44.]

In the public press Maria Malibran was mourned across Europe as one
unique and unprecedented in an era remarkable for its great singers, one
whose loss was "irreparable."[21] One English journalist wrote:

It is with bitter sorrow that we record the death of Madame Malibran. We have
heard singers in years gone by of whose powers we cherish a vivid and grateful
recollection, and we look around among those who are living for some of present
excellence and greater promise; but in Malibran were united all the powers and
capabilities, all the gifts and graces that were scattered among her predecessors
and contemporaries. She was the very impersonation of the vocal art, every
depth of which she had fathomed—every elevation attained. Nature had been
most bountiful to her: her voice was unrivalled for compass, volume, and
richness; her mind was powerful, her penetration quick, her talent wide and
large. Whatever she undertook to do, she did well; and the rapidity with which
she grasped at and attained acquirements of various kinds was marvelous. She
had an innate perception of beauty and grace in every art . . . .

Her impetuosity and ardent temperament, combined with her extensive
and sound musical knowledge and her unrivalled voice, rendered her singing
more varied than that of any performer we ever heard. With most singers the
mode in which a song shall be sung is an affair of deliberate study and trial—it
is always the same: but with Malibran it assumed every possible variety of

colour, as she happened to be excited or depressed—as she found a sympathizing and discriminating or a dull and ignorant audience. Sometimes her spirits would effervesce in passages of the most joyous and sparkling character, at others she would make the same song a vehicle for the display of her intimate knowledge of harmony in a series of elaborate cadences: it was just as the impulse of the moment prompted. And where was ever heard the artist who could achieve all this? Who ever possessed, like her, the fancy to prompt, the genius to invent, the knowledge to guide, and the voice to execute? We end as we began—she was the very impersonation of the vocal art.[22]

Another journalist added,

Both as a singer and an actress she was distinguished above all her contemporaries by versatility, power, and liveliness of conception. She could play with music of every possible style, school, and century. We have heard her, in the same evening, sing in *five different languages,* giving with equal truth and character the intense and passionate *scena* from *Der Freischutz* and those sprightly and charming Provençal airs, many of which were composed by herself. The extensive compass of her voice enabled her to compose the whole range of songs which is usually divided between the contralto and soprano. She was, it is true, often carried away by the tameless vivacity of her spirits into flights and cadences which were more eccentric than beautiful; we have heard her in the very wantonness of consummate power rival the unvocal *arpeggi* of De Beriot's violin, and execute the most sudden shakes and divisions upon those highest and deepest notes of the voice which less perfectly trained singers approach warily and with preparation. But those know little of the dignity Madame Malibran could assume, or of the unexaggerated expression she could throw into music, even the plainest and least fantastic, who are not familiar with her Oratorio performances . . . .

In short, upon the stage, though often extravagant, she was always *rivetting;* and few among her contemporaries could go home and sit in cool judgement upon one who, while she was before them, carried them as she pleased to the extremities of grave or gay . . . . It is difficult to write calmly of these things, and the thousand recollections that crowd upon us warn us to stop, lest we pass our wonted boundaries. It is enough to say that in the lyric drama of Europe, she who has died has left no peer behind her![23]

Her fellow performers invariably remembered her as the greatest singer they had ever heard, and much more besides. "She was an adorable woman," wrote Duprez, "a great artist, admirably gifted as to both voice and intelligence, an elite and very cultivated individual; and at the same time original, almost eccentric ."[24]

"Malibran was undoubtedly the greatest singer that lived in my time," concurred Henry Phillips, who lived to hear every great singer from Angelica Catalani to Jenny Lind and Adelina Patti. "Her mind, her energy, her knowledge of languages, were surprising, and her register of voice *amazing . . . .* In fine, she was a prodigious genius, possessed of marvelous power, and of an intellect that rarely falls to the lot of any human being."[25]

In 1838 Mme. Merlin made the prophetic remark: "Her death has created a void in the worlds of music and the stage that may never again be filled: and to have seen Malibran in even any one of her various triumphs will be, among her contemporaries, an event ever to be remembered with pride and rapture."[26] Toward the end of the century an elderly writer echoed Mme. Merlin's words with the comment, "The only singer who has at all approached her, and that one only in part, has been Jenny Lind . . . . Forty years after the grave closed over her, her reputation is the brightest of all the Daughters of Song."[27]

In 1862 Henry Chorley wrote of Maria Malibran's inimitable quality, and of her lack of successor:

Of a woman so bright, so kindly, so ill-starred . . . it is impossible to think without a strange and affectionate regret. Of the artist it must be recorded that, boundless as were Malibran's resources, keen as was her intelligence, dazzling as was her genius, she never produced a single type in opera for other women to adopt. She passed over the stage like a meteor, as an apparition of wonder, rather than as one who, on her departure, left her mantle behind her for others to take up and wear. [pp. 9–10]

But if she lived and was remembered as a public performer, she died the wife of Charles de Bériot—Maria Felicia de Bériot, as the plate on her coffin identifies her. No sooner had Charles reached Dr. Belluomini's home in London than he directed a letter to Mr. Beale and the festival committee requesting that Maria's remains be returned to Belgium for burial. The officials of Manchester, aware of the honor the city would acquire as Maria Malibran's resting place, refused this and subsequent requests. After the funeral seven hundred citizens signed a petition and submitted it to the faculty of the College of Manchester, demanding that the city government deny an exhumation because the Collegiate Church's burial grounds were out of usual jurisdiction and beyond de Bériot's purview. The petition also claimed that her divorce from Eugène Malibran was not legal and thus de Bériot had no claim on her remains, and that their religious feelings would be offended by an exhumation.

Charles countered this arrogant resistance by sending his cousin, a noted lawyer in Brussels, to Manchester to unravel the legal difficulties. The struggle soon became worldwide news, popular opinion in Europe decidedly favoring the bereft husband. Joaquina Garcia, making the long trip from Brussels, finally broke the impasse. The English could quibble over legalities and technicalities, but their laws could not deprive a mother of her daughter's remains, and at the sight of this elderly woman all opposition vanished. On December 17 she was given full possession of the body provided that she pay the 1,200 pounds in funeral expenses.

To avoid crowds the exhumation was accomplished in secrecy. At five o'clock on a December morning twenty-six people working by moonlight and torches attempted to lift the coffin from its resting place, but the lead lining made it too heavy to remove from the vault. Three cords snapped in turn before beams were found to raise it. From the church it was taken once more to the Mosley-Arms Hotel and from there shipped to London and finally to Anvers. From Anvers a military escort accompanied la Malibran's remains back to Brussels, arriving at the black-draped de Bériot mansion, Rue Leopold, on January 3, 1837. Charles, unable to stand his emotions, had fled to the home of an uncle, and once again the funeral proceedings of his wife were conducted without him.

Several years later he erected a mausoleum in the cemetery at Laeken to mark the grave. Inside was placed a statue by Geefs of Malibran as Norma; illuminated by the light from a cupola she stands fixed in eternal youth, arms outstretched, gaze heavenward, as though singing "Casta Diva." On the base of the monument are inscribed four lines by the poet Alphonse Lamartine, for whom Maria Malibran, "drunk with verse, music and inspiration," had once sung until three o'clock in the morning.[28]

> Beauté, génie, amour furent son nom de femme
> Écrit dans son regard, dans son coeur, dans sa voix.
> Sous trois formes au ciel appartenait cette âme.
> Pleurez, terre, et vous, cieux, accueillez-la trois fois.

> Beauty, genius, love, were the name of this woman
> Written in her glance, in her heart, in her voice.
> In these three forms her soul belongs to heaven.
> Weep, o earth, and you, o heavens, welcome her three times over.

"She was music, or even better, poetry in the form of a woman," he wrote in his *Portraits*. "On earth she was called *la Malibran*; in heaven she is without doubt the Saint Cecilia of the nineteenth century."[29]

EPILOGUE

Less than two months after Maria Malibran's death, a French newspaper reported the death of Eugène Malibran on November 12, 1836.

M. Malibran, the first husband of the celebrated singer recently mourned by the musical world, has himself just died in Paris, aged 54 years. Saturday morning he had made several visits, and appeared to enjoy good enough health. He was seized with a violent headache toward 3:00 in the afternoon, and in spite of a copious bleeding to which he had recourse, succumbed in the night to an attack of apoplexy.[1]

Another journalist allowed himself to be a little more sarcastic: "M. Malibran, he who had the honor [honneur] of giving his name to the celebrated singer the loss of whom we mourn, and who had not had the good fortune [bonheur] of seeing her keep it, has just died in Paris."[2]

Charles de Bériot did not return to public life for more than a year after Maria's death. He reappeared at the official debut of Pauline Garcia as a singer in her own right on December 15, 1837. He became director of the violin classes at the Brussels Conservatory until 1852, when he developed paralysis in his left arm and lost his sight. De Bériot's compositions, particularly his *Violin School,* were published in several languages and used extensively by students; his widely known concert pieces survived well into the twentieth century. Several of his pupils, among them Henri Vieuxtemps, became famous violinists. Charles died at the age of sixty-eight on either April 8 or 13, 1870, and is buried near his second wife in the de Bériot family plot.

In 1841 Charles married Marie Huber, the adopted daughter of Prince Dietrischten Preskau, and they had two sons; one, Fritz, was a violinist of great repute. Charles Wilfred de Bériot, the son of de Bériot and Malibran, became a pianist and taught at the Paris Conservatory. He had little ambition for a public career and was described by a contemporary as "an impeccable pianist who gave but little pleasure. His interminable sonatas were somewhat dreaded. One could but wonder that Malibran, that marvel, that creature of fire, of passion, of tenderness, could have been mother to so correct, so impassive a being." In the salons of his aunt Pauline he seemed to be "at least as old as she, dried up, gray, dusty looking."[3] Charles Wilfred died in 1914; his two daughters were both pianists.

Manuel Garcia, Jr., became the most famous singing teacher of his age, carrying on the principles his father had learned from Ansani in Naples. One of his most outstanding pupils was Jenny Lind. The "Garcia Method" is still known today and has a record of impressive successes: both Beverly Sills and Joan Sutherland can trace their artistic ancestry back to Garcia, as have countless others including Nellie Melba and Emma Eames. Manuel died in 1906 at the age of 101, vigorous and alert until the very end.

One day Maria was talking to Legouvé when a coach went by and a little girl leaned out blowing kisses. "Who is that child?," asked the writer. "She is someone who will eclipse us all," replied Maria. "It's my little sister Pauline."[4] Pauline Garcia made her operatic debut in London on May 9, 1839, as Desdemona. The *Athenaeum* hailed the evening as "the most remarkable one in this season's musical chronicle . . . . Long and bright be the career thus remarkably begun!"[5] Her voice was at first so similar to Maria's in tonal quality that some felt they were listening to Malibran returned from the dead. Alfred de Musset recounted the story of a young girl taking a voice lesson from Lablache: having been told how la Malibran sang "Casta Diva," the girl stood at the piano, about to begin, when she suddenly heard the faraway sound of Malibran's voice singing the very aria. She stopped, struck with amazement, and fainted. She had heard Pauline Garcia, who lived in the same building and was herself practicing the aria.[6]

But despite the initial similarity of voice, Pauline's style of performance proved very different from Maria's uninhibited spontaneity. Several operas were written for Pauline and her career was a great one, but it never reached the heights of her sister's. She married Louis Viardot, Maria's close friend, and they had four children, three of whom were musically inclined. She died in 1910 at the age of eighty-eight.

REVUE CRITIQUE

Dernières Pensées Musicales
de Marie Félicité Garcia de Bériot

Such is the title of a collection, curious in more than one respect, which has just appeared in Paris and London. One need not confuse this interesting work with the multitude of *Dernières Pensées* which are published at the death of great musicians and which do not always do extreme honor to the illustrious names with which they are adorned. Of concern here are compositions for song and piano actually owed to the pen of the celebrated virtuoso the premature loss of whom the musical art deplores, and which are also truly remarkable for their charming originality, which reflects the profound sensitivity and impetuous character of the author. In this work from a singer who was concerned almost entirely with Italian music, one is completely astonished at the bizarre turn of the melody and with the perhaps excessive liberty of the harmonic progression. This results quite often in great difficulties in the execution of the vocal part; and if any other than Mme de Bériot had allowed herself to write phrases like these, one would not refrain from saying that the author did not know how to write for the voice. Here such a reproach would be rather ridiculous; as ridiculous as saying that Paganini or Liszt did not know how to compose for the violin or piano. However, I believe that at more than one point the difficulties of intonation are not motive enough for the unreasonable demands of the style. One could see at these points less the artless result of spontaneous inspiration that a course deliberately taken through painful research. Thus in the first ballad (*La Fiancée du Brigand*), the unaccompanied phrase on the words "Il savait bien que sa compagne resterait fidèle au malheur" ranges from low A to high E, and is in a color so savage, and a burst so vigorous, that it appears to us as being forced and unnecessarily difficult. The second reprise, to the contrary, is of a great sincerity; and the phrase "Mon fiancé, si fier dans la disgrâce, n'a pas un cœur plus indompté que moi" produces a very grand and favorable effect by the melodic expression and the choice of harmony. In the romance (*le Message*), a modulation in A major, superior third of the principal tonic, introduces a song of a very sad mood, which the harmony gives an extreme originality. I like *la Prière à la Madone* less. The sailors' hymn has charm and truthfulness of expression. But a little chef-d'œuvre of artless verve, as it seems to us, is *la Noce du Marin.* This piece alone is enough to assure the success of the collection. The next one, *au Bord de la Mer,* is a delightful reverie; one regrets only that some movements of the bass produce with the vocal line *successive diatonic fifths* which are very difficult to justify. This remark is further applicable to many other passages of this collection. We are far from believing in the infallibility of the old rules of harmony, but we think that their infraction ought to be at least as well motivated as their observation. To our mind, the use of harmonic movements forbidden by the rules of musical theory ought to have at all times an evident purpose, and resemble neither the gropings of an inexperienced hand, nor the cynical bravado of a musician who mocks his listeners by his art and by himself. In certain progressions of the harmonies of the work which is here in question, we believe to discover, in particular, inexperience rather than ambitious desire to put oneself above the rules, and probably, if the sublime virtuoso were living at the time of the publication of her work, she would have corrected the faults that we have indicated after getting the advice of some great master. We would make an exception only of the two fifths from the very dramatic ballad *des Brigands,* on the words "du silence" where it would be a great pity to eliminate them, because, for us at least, the intention and the effect are excellent. This song, dedicated to A. Nourrit, shines especially in the expressive movement of the accompaniment and by the penetrating accent of the measured recitative on which the words are uttered. It is of a captivating verve. The verses of most of the pieces that we have just cited are facile, gracious, and well suited to the music. One will be less astonished by this exception to the general rule which makes an album of romances a collection of more or less silly and dull pieces, when one learns that the pen of M. Émile Deschamps supplied them.

We refrain from praising the printing and the edition in general of the *Dernières Pensées* of Madame de Bériot. I regret only one thing, that the editor felt obliged to *illustrate* by such ravishing vignettes from drawings whose author's names and intrinsic merit should have escaped the humiliating patronage of lithography. If there are music lovers *bourgeois* enough to buy this music because of the *pretty pictures* that go with it, it must be that their commendations are of a rather mediocre value and it would be in good taste to disdain them. But it is the custom, and the editor would have no doubt incurred the reproach of stinginess in dispensing with them, though his aim in doing so be completely artistic.

H. B[erlio]z.

Revue et Gazette Musicale, 2 July 1837

ADDITIONAL LETTERS

From Maria Malibran to Monsieur Cavalier. Probably January 1829.

I am having some bad luck! I am in a state of embarrassment, more than ever. It's that Mrs. Maubinne, who was to play the role of the chevalier in the fad of proverbs, can no longer do it, and me, I'm at bay.

There would be only one way to save us . . . . . . Can you guess it? Oh, would I become completely indiscreet? Ma foi, I'm taking the risk, and I run that of appearing to be the most importune woman—Would you, could you, do me the pleasure . . . . . of learning . . . . the role (Ah! mon dieu, I'm afraid) the role . . . . . of the . . . chevalier? The word went off like a bomb; there's no way to get it back now.

It is on you that the success of my proverb now depends.—I am living in faith and hope. I am awaiting from you *la charité*.

Malibran[1]

From Maria Malibran to Virginia Cottinet.

. . . Now, it is a question of knowing if *Mother Fret* and the so affectionate father would accept a little feat of strength, that is to say: me, to go for two hours to take them for a drive, nowhere in particular, and then from there straight to the inn for a little refreshment. Say yes, and the fatherland is saved. The chinese cap greets his venerable masters and kisses them very respectfully on the ends of their noses.
P.S. The Mercury of the said cap awaits your response on one wing.[2]

To the composer Daniel François Auber. Brussels, April 5, 1832.

Monsieur,

Although not having the pleasure of knowing you personally, what I have heard about you from several friends who are fortunate enough to know you well emboldens me to make a step, no doubt indiscreet, but which obtains for me the pleasure of expressing to you for the first time all my admiration for your works, which I always hear with new pleasure each time that I can seize the occasion for doing so.

On the point of traveling through Germany to give some concerts and to renounce for a period of time, consequently, a part of the repertoire to which I owe the applause that I have had the good fortune to receive in Paris, I can't help envying the luck of the French singers fortunate enough to sing airs that, like yours, are destined to obtain equal success on the stage and in the salons. Would it be, Monsieur, too much to presume of your good will that you would consent to write for me an Italian air in the style of those of the Court Concerts? Independently of the use a piece of this type could have for me, I would have a double motive for thanking you for it, since your willingness would be proof that you have not judged me unworthy of serving you as interpreter. [Here Malibran has written out five bars of music, presumably Auber's] It is in this hope that I await the moment when I will be permitted to go to thank you personally in Paris.

M. F. Malibran[3]

No. 4, Rue Leopold.

To the soprano Sofia Schoberlechner, Malibran's Giulietta in *I Capuleti.* Bologna, 1832.

Ma chère Sophie,

I just this minute learned that you don't want to do the last act of *Romeo* tonight.

I will begin by telling you that the management, seeing that the *Barbiere* would not attract much of a crowd, either because it is too familiar or because the weather is such to keep the public away rather than to attract it, has begged me to do the third act of *Romeo*. You know that I am ordinarily rather stupid, and for the good of the theater, I accepted. It never entered my mind that this might not be agreeable to you, and believe me, if the thought had occurred to me, I would have refused flatly. But now, dear Sophie, it is too late to change the announcements, the public is informed, and you would not want to see your Romeo in the arms of another, in the arms of la [Teresa] Ruggieri! Please then, be good to me; and do it just this once. I will do the same for you, whenever you want, and when the occasion presents itself you can prevail on me and be sure in advance of giving the greatest pleasure to your faithful Romeo.

Malibran

P.S. Just consult your heart, and I am sure you will do me this favor.[4]

To Alfred Bunn. 1833.

MAY I HAVE A BOX FOR TO-MORROW, TO GO AND SEE THE SONNAMBULA?

My Dear Mr. Bunn,

As I left the theatre last night I received this letter* which I send to you, not knowing what to do with it.

Do you know that it strikes me, if you let this letter go to the *Times,* it will only make things worse? For it seems to me that the writer takes too much notice of the King's Theatre being *well attended,* as I believe he says.

What do you think of that?

*Bunn failed to include the letter in question; one can only surmise its contents from Malibran's comments.

I think, if you were to answer in my name, that I would prefer that he should not take any notice of me, or if he did, not to say anything about the Italian Theatre, nor of my losing popularity in the credit of the aristocratic folks. What do you think of that?

I never take any notice of these things; but this time, as it so happens that my opinion is asked upon the question, and as I am afraid that such an article in the newspaper, *Times,* might have some bad influence upon the mind of the tender feet, *thick ancles,* and *read elbows* of the suprematy of high ranked, curled up, *tittled noses,* I think it exceedingly wise, prudent, and *circumspect* to pop into your room my letter enfolding the enclosed, upon which you must *ruminate* and deliberate, and *muse* the whole of to-morrow morning, until your ideas will be expounded on the pretious subject, and upon the many *ortographical* mistakes made, both in writing and in spelling.

By your most obedient

Scribbler and nonsense-teller

Maria, &c. &c. &c.

Monday, after having been delighted with the German singers.[5]

The Chronology of
Maria Malibran's Operatic Career*

1813 (?)
    Naples.   Paër: *Agnese*.

1818–1819
    London.   Family performances, both public and private.

1822 (winter)
    Paris.   Garcia's Cercle de la Rue de Richelieu.

1823 (November)
    Paris.   Rossini: *Penalver Cantata*.

1824–1825
    London.   Chorus King's Theatre; concerts.

1825 (11 June–13 August)
    London.   Rossini: *Il Barbiere di Siviglia* (debut as Rosina 11 June); Meyerbeer: *Il Crociato*.

1825–1827 (29 November 1825–29 October 1827)
    New York.   Arne: *Love in a Village*; Boieldieu: *Jean de Paris* (English translation); Garcia: *L'Amante Astuto, La Figlia dell'Aria*; Horn: *The Devil's Bridge*; Mozart: *Don Giovanni* (in English and Italian); Rossini: *Il Barbiere, La Cenerentola, Otello, Tancredi, Il Turco in Italia*; Zingarelli: *Romeo e Giulietta*.

1828 (14 January–1 July)
    Paris.   Rossini: *Il Barbiere, La Cenerentola, Otello, Semiramide* (Semiramide); Zingarelli: *Romeo e Giulietta*.

1828–1829 (2 October 1828–2 April 1829)
    Paris.   Halévy: *Clary*; Mozart: *Don Giovanni*; Rossini: *Il Barbiere, La Cenerentola, La Gazza Ladra, Otello, Semiramide* (Arsace), *Tancredi*; Zingarelli: *Romeo e Giulietta*.

1829 (21 April–18? July)
    London.   Cimarosa: *Il Matrimonio Segreto*; Mozart: *Don*

*Excludes concerts. The dates given are those of her first and last performances unless otherwise indicated.

Giovanni, *Le Nozze di Figaro*; Rossini: *Il Barbiere, La Gazza Ladra, Otello, Tancredi*.

1829–1830 (6 November 1829–3 April 1830)
Paris.

Asioli: *Pygmalion*; Cimarosa: *Il Matrimonio Segreto*; Halévy: *Clary*; Mozart: *Don Giovanni, Le Nozze di Figaro*; Rossini: *Il Barbiere, La Cenerentola, La Gazza Ladra, Otello, Semiramide* (Semiramide), *Tancredi*.

1830 (29 April–31 July)
London.

Cimarosa: *Il Matrimonio Segreto, Gli Orazi e Curiazi*; Mercadante: *Donna Caritea*; Mozart: *Don Giovanni*; Rossini: *Il Barbiere, La Cenerentola, Otello, Semiramide* (Arsace), *Tancredi*.

1830–1831 (6 November 1830–8 May 1831)
Paris.

Gnecco: *La Prova d'un Opera Seria*; Mozart: *Don Giovanni*; Rossini: *Il Barbiere, La Cenerentola, La Gazza Ladra, Otello, Semiramide* (Semiramide and Arsace), *Tancredi*.

1831–1832 (8 November 1831–20 January 1832)
Paris.

Gnecco: *La Prova d'un Opera Seria*; Rossini: *Il Barbiere, La Cenerentola, La Gazza Ladra, Otello* (Desdemona and Otello), *Tancredi*.

1832 (30 June–? July)
Rome.

Rossini: *Il Barbiere, Otello*.

(6 August–29 September)
Naples.

Rossini: *La Cenerentola, La Gazza Ladra, Otello*.

(third? week of September)
Rome.

Rossini: *Il Barbiere*.

(13 October–25 November)
Bologna.

Bellini: *I Capuleti e i Montecchi*; Rossini: *La Gazza Ladra, Tancredi*.

1833 (1 May–5 August)
London.

Bellini: *La Sonnambula* (English Translation); Chelard: *The Students of Jena*; Horn: *The Devil's Bridge*; Rossini: *Il Barbiere, La Cenerentola, Semiramide* (Arsace).

1833–1834 (14 November 1833–12 March 1834)
Naples.

Bellini: *I Capuleti* (?), *Norma, La Sonnambula*; Cimarosa: *Il Matrimonio Segreto*; Coccia: *La Figlia del' Arciere*; Pacini: *Irene, o l'Assedio di Messina*; Rossini: *La Gazza Ladra, Otello, Semiramide* (Semiramide).

1834 (31 March–8 May)
Bologna.

Bellini: *Norma, La Sonnambula*; Rossini: *Otello*.

(15 May–24 May)
    Milan.   Bellini: *Norma*; Rossini: *Otello*.

(19 July–? August [Malibran left the city the 10th or 11th])
    Sinigaglia.   Bellini: *I Capuleti, Norma, La Sonnambula*; Rossini: *Il Barbiere*.

(17 August–7 September)
    Lucca.   Bellini: *I Capuleti, Norma, La Sonnambula*; Rossini: *Otello*.

(27 September–26 October)
    Milan.   Bellini: *I Capuleti, Norma, La Sonnambula*; Rossini: *Otello*.

1834–1835 (13 November 1834 3? March 1835 [Malibran left Naples the 4th])
    Naples.   Bellini: *Norma, La Sonnambula*; Persiani: *Ines de Castro*; Rossi: *Amelia*; Rossini: *Tancredi*.

1835 (26 March–8 April)
    Venice.   Bellini: *Norma, La Sonnambula*; Rossini: *Il Barbiere, La Cenerentola, Otello*.

(18 April–18 July)
    London.   Beethoven: *Fidelio*; Bellini: *La Sonnambula*.

(15 August–2 September)
    Lucca.   Persiani: *Ines de Castro*; Rossini: *La Cenerentola*.

1835–1836 (12 September 1835–20 March 1836)
    Milan.   Bellini: *I Capuleti, La Sonnambula*; Donizetti: *L'Elisir d'Amore, Maria Stuarda*; Rossini: *Il Barbiere, Otello*; Vaccai: *Giovanna Grey, Giulietta e Romeo*.

1836 (2 May–16 July)
    London.   Balfe: *The Maid of Artois*; Beethoven: *Fidelio*; Bellini: *La Sonnambula*.

(Mid-August)
    Aix-la-Chapelle (Aachen). Bellini: *La Sonnambula*.

The Operatic Repertoire
of Maria Malibran
(complete performances)

Arne
>   *Love in a Village*
>   Rossetta   New York, 23 January 1827

Asioli
>   *Pygmalion*
>   Galatea   Paris, 3 April 1830

Balfe
>   *The Maid of Artois**
>   Isoline   London, 27 May 1836

Beethoven
>   *Fidelio* (English translation)
>   Leonora   London, 12 June 1835

Bellini
>   *I Capuleti e i Montecchi* (with Vaccai's last scene)
>   Romeo   Bologna, 27 October 1832; Lucca,
>   Naples (?), Milan, Sinigaglia
>
>   *Norma*
>   Norma   Naples, 23 February 1834; Bologna,
>   Lucca, Milan, Sinigaglia, Venice
>
>   *I Puritani** Special version written for Naples, never sung.
>   Elvira
>
>   *La Sonnambula*
>   Amina   London, 1 May 1833 (English
>   translation); Aix-la-Chapelle
>   (Aachen), Bologna, Lucca, Milan,
>   Naples, Sinigaglia, Venice

Bertin
>   *Fausto** (rehearsed but never sung publicly)

*Role written for Malibran

Boieldieu
    Jean de Paris (English translation)
    The Princess of Navarre   New York, 29 October 1827

Chelard
    The Students of Jena
    Adele   London, 4 June 1833

Cimarosa
    Il Matrimonio Segreto
    Fidalma   London, 16 July 1829; Paris,
                              Naples

    Gli Orazi e Curiazi
    Orazia   London, 17 June 1830

Coccia
    *La Figlia del'Arciere**   Naples, 9 January 1834

Donizetti
    L'Elisir d'Amore
    Adina   Milan, 27 September 1835

    Maria Stuarda†
    Mary Stuart   Milan, 30 December 1835

Garcia
    *L'Amante Astuto**
    Rosalia   New York, 17 December 1825

*La Figlia dell'Aria**
    Semiramide   New York, 29 April 1826

Gnecco
    La Prova d'un Opera Seria
    Corilla   Paris, 27 April 1831; Naples

Halévy
    *Clary**
    Clary   Paris, 9 December 1828

Horn
    The Devil's Bridge
    Count Belino   New York, 15 January 1827;
                              London

Mercadante
    Donna Caritea
    Don Diego   London, 26 July 1830

Meyerbeer
    Il Crociato
    Felicia   London, 30 June 1825

    †Role created by Malibran

Mozart
> *Don Giovanni*
> Zerlina

New York, 23 May 1826; London,
Paris

> *Le Nozze di Figaro*
> Susanna

London, 11 June 1829; Paris

Pacini
> *Irene, o l'Assedio di Messina**
> Irene

Naples, 30 November 1833

Persiani
> *Ines de Castro**
> Ines

Naples, 27 January 1835; Lucca

Ricci
> *Il Colonello** (never sung)

Rossi
> *Amelia**
> Amelia

Naples, 31 December 1834

Rossini
> *Il Barbiere di Siviglia*
> Rosina

London, 11 June 1825; Milan, New
York, Paris, Rome, Sinigaglia,
Venice

> *La Cenerentola*
> Angelina

New York, 27 June 1826; London,
Lucca, Naples, Paris, Venice

> *La Gazza Ladra*
> Ninetta

Paris, 6 November 1828; Bologna,
London, Naples

> *Matilde di Shabran*
> Matilde (rehearsed, but never
> performed publicly)

> *Otello*
> Desdemona

New York, 7 February 1826;
Bologna, London, Lucca, Milan,
Naples, Paris, Rome, Venice

> Otello

Paris, 20 November 1831

> *Semiramide*
> Semiramide

Paris, 14 January 1828; London,
Naples

> Arsace

Paris, 23 March 1829; London

> *Tancredi*
> Tancredi

New York, 31 December 1825;
Bologna, London, Naples, Paris

Il Turco in Italia
Zaida   New York, 14 March 1826

Vaccai
Giovanna Grey*
Jane Grey   Milan, 23 February 1836

Giulietta e Romeo
Romeo   Milan, 17 November 1835 (*see*
                                               Bellini: *I Capuleti e i Montecchi*)

Zingarelli
Romeo e Giulietta
Romeo   New York, 20 July 1826; Paris

Chapter 1 Beginnings

1. Viardot-Garcia, 1915, p. 526.   2. Mackinley, *Antoinette Sterling*, p. 150; Héritte de la Tour, p. 9; Levien, p. 12; and other sources.   3. Manuel del Popolo Vicente Garcia, pp. 98–99, letter dated 30 May 1807.   4. Cited by *La Revue Musicale* 12 (1832): 172.   5. Fétis, *Biographie Universelle des Musiciens*.   6. *La Revue Musicale* 12 (1832): 172.   7. Castil-Blaze, *L'Académie*, p. 170.   8. *Times*, 16 August 1824.   9. *Examiner*, 7 June 1818, p. 363.   10. Ibid., 13 January 1819, p. 78.   11. Mackinley, *Garcia*, pp. 35–36.   12. Marix-Spire, p. 24.   13. Fétis.   14. Desternes, p. 31.   15. Legouvé, p. 63.   16. Merlin, *Memoirs*, vol. 1, p. 45.   17. *New Monthly Magazine* 48 (1836): 303 fn.   18. Legouvé, pp. 63–64.   19. Pougin, p. 12.   20. Fétis.   21. Legouvé, p. 62.   22. Desternes, pp. 160–61.   23. Clayton, p. 334.   24. Desternes, photo of letter following page 96.   25. Merlin, *Memoirs*, vol. 1, p. 9.   26. Legouvé, p. 76.   27. Merlin, *Memoirs*, vol. 1, pp. 10–11.

Chapter 2 The Debutante

1. Ebers, p. 139.   2. Stendhal, pp. 101, 221.   3. *Harmonicon*, May 1824, p. 101.   4. *Quarterly Musical Magazine and Review* 10 (1828): 324.   5. Stendhal, p. 370.   6. Hogarth, p. 411.   7. *Times*, 26 April 1824.   8. *Quarterly Musical Magazine and Review* 6 (1824): 222.   9. Ibid., p. 218.   10. *London Magazine*, June 1824, p. 672.   11. *Quarterly Musical Magazine and Review* 6 (1824): 223.   12. *London Magazine*, August 1824, p. 204.   13. Ms. New York Public Library, Lincoln Center.   14. Ms. New York Public Library, Lincoln Center. See also Giulini, pp. 66–69.   15. Merlin, *Memoirs*, vol. 1, pp. 28–29.   16. *London Literary Gazette*, no. 438 (11 June 1825): 380.   17. Ebers, p. 162.   18. *New Monthly Magazine* 15 (1825): 296–97.   19. *Morning Post*, cited by Arundell, p. 317.   20. *Quarterly Musical Magazine and Review* 7 (1825): 272 fn., and others.   21. *New Monthly Magazine* 15 (1825): 345.   22. Chorley, p. 6.   23. *New Monthly Magazine* 15 (1825): 390.   24. Ms. New York Public Library, Lincoln Center.   25. *Harmonicon*, October 1825, p. 181 fn.   26. Ibid., p. 177.   27. *Quarterly Musical Magazine and Review* 7 (1825): 437.   28. Ebers, p. 162.   29. *Quarterly Musical Magazine and Review* 7 (1825): 188–91.   30. Giulini, p. 83.   31. Ibid.   32. *Harmonicon*, October 1825, p. 194.

Chapter 3 New York

1. The details of the voyage are taken from Owen, pp. 230–33.   2. *Evening Post* and other newspapers, 17 November 1825.   3. Francis, p. 259.   4. Unless otherwise noted, all references to the first performance of *Il Barbiere* are quoted or paraphrased from the comments in the *Evening Post*, 30 November 1825.   5. *Albion*, cited by Mackinley, *Garcia*, pp. 63–64.   6. Francis, p. 258.   7. *New-York Review and Atheneum Magazine,* December 1825, pp. 80–81.   8. Ibid., February 1826, pp. 233–35.   9. *Evening Post*, 27 January 1826.   10. Ibid., 1 February 1826.   11. Mackinley, *Garcia*, p. 84; Merlin, *Memoirs*, vol. 1, pp. 31–32; Legouvé, p. 65; and others.   12. *Evening Post*, 9 February 1826.   13. Giulini, pp. 87–

88.   14. Ms. New York Public Library, Lincoln Center.   15. Owen, p. 230.   16. Wilson, p. 329.   17. Ms. New York Public Library, Lincoln Center.   18. Teneo, p. 445 ff.   19. *Longworth's American Almanac, New-York Register, and City Director* lists only one Pelletier in New York City, a wine merchant living at 91 Grand Street.   20. Malherbe, p. 247.   21. Ritter, p. 188.   22. Malherbe, pp. 247–48.

Chapter 4   Madame Malibran

1. Cited by the *Evening Post*, 12 August 1826.   2. Ibid.   3. Giulini, pp. 83–84.   4. *Evening Post*, 2 October 1826.   5. Ibid., 17 October 1826.   6. *Times*, 27 January 1827.   7. Cited by Krehbiel, *More Chapters*, p. 223.   8. Benson, p. 34.   9. Macready, p. 306.   10. Teneo, pp. 448–49.   11. Ibid., pp. 449–50.   12. Cited by Curtis, p. 132.   13. *Philadelphia Gazette*, 20 January 1826.   14. Armstrong, p. 14.   15. Teneo, p. 450.   16. Ibid., letter dated 18 June 1827.   17. Ibid., p. 451, letter dated "Monday night, 1827."   18. Ibid., pp. 451–52.   19. Ibid.   20. Ibid., p. 452, letter dated July 1827.   21. Ibid., p. 451, letter dated "Monday night, 1827."   22. Ibid., p. 452, letter dated July 1827.   23. Moore, 18 May 1935, p. 6.   24. *Le Moniteur Universel*, 13 April 1833, p. 928.   25. *New-York Enquirer*, 9 October 1827.   26. Cited by Ritter, p. 195.   27. *Albion*, 3 November 1827.

Chapter 5   Return to Paris

1. Teneo, p. 453, letter dated 12 November 1827.   2. Ibid.   3. Ibid., letter dated 20 November 1827.   4. Ibid., pp. 453–54, letter dated 25 November 1827.   5. Ibid., p. 455, letter dated 29 December 1827.   6. Ibid., p. 454, letter dated 13 December 1827.   7. *Le Moniteur Universel*, 3 December 1827, p. 1658.   8. Merlin, *Memoirs*, vol. 1, pp. 36–37.   9. *Quarterly Musical Magazine and Review* 10 (1828): 328.   10. Ibid., p. 329.   11. Merlin, *Memoirs*, vol. 2, p. 123.   12. *New Monthly Magazine* 48 (1826): 303.   13. Merlin, *Memoirs*, vol. 1, p. 97.   14. *Quarterly Musical Magazine and Review* 10 (1828): 329.   15. Merlin, *Memoirs*, vol. 1, pp. 37–38.   16. Teneo, p. 455, letter dated 29 December 1827.   17. Ibid., p. 454, letter dated 13 December 1827.   18. Ibid.   19. Ibid., p. 455, letter dated 29 December 1827.   20. Legouvé, p. 56.   21. Pleasants, p. 194; Bauer, pp. 290–91.   22. Merlin, *Madame Malibran*, vol. 1, p. 68.   23. Castil-Blaze, *L'Opéra-Italien*, p. 430.   24. *La Revue Musicale* 2 (1827–28): 588–90.   25. Ibid., p. 589.   26. Ibid., pp. 588–90.   27. Fétis.   28. Teneo, p. 457.   29. Stendhal, p. 7.   30. LaForêt, p. 67.   31. *La Revue Musicale* 2 (1827–28): 541–42.   32. Teneo, pp. 460–61, letter dated 7 February 1828 to Eugène Malibran.   33. *Nouveau Journal de Paris*, 14 April 1828.   34. Teneo, p. 448, letter dated 6 February 1828.   35. Ibid., p. 463, letter dated 8 May 1828.   36. Ibid., p. 459, letter dated 6 February 1828.   37. Ibid.   38. Ibid.   39. Ibid., p. 463, letter dated 3 March 1828.   40. Ibid.   41. Ibid., pp. 459–60, letter dated 6 February 1828.   42. Ibid., p. 461, letter dated 7 February 1828.   43. Ibid., p. 462.   44. Ibid., pp. 462–63, letter dated 3 March 1828.   45. Merlin, *Memoirs*, vol. 1, p. 44.   46. Teneo, pp. 462–63, letter dated 3 March 1828.   47. Ibid.   48. Ibid., p. 464, letter dated 8 May 1828.   49. Ibid., pp. 462–63, letters dated 7 February and 3 March 1828.   50. Ibid., pp. 463–64, letter dated 8 May 1828.   51. Castil-Blaze, *L'Opéra-Italien*, p. 430.   52. Teneo, pp. 462–63.   53. Ms. New York Public Library, Lincoln Center. See also Giulini, pp. 116–17, which contains several errors in transcription.   54. Castil-Blaze, *L'Opéra-Italien*, p. 430.   55. *La Revue Musicale* 3 (1828): 268–71.   56. Paraphrased from Legouvé, pp. 64–65; Castil-Blaze, "Revue," p. 143; *Le Figaro*, 7 May 1828.   57. *La Revue Musicale* 3 (1828): 301.   58. Ibid.   59. Merlin, *Memoirs*, vol. 1, pp. 164–65; Legouvé, p. 66.   60. Teneo, p. 464.   61. Ms. New York Public Library, Lincoln Center. See also Giulini, p. 117, which contains several errors in transcription.   62. *La Revue Musicale* 3 (1828): 447.   63. Ibid., p. 448.   64. *Le Figaro*, 23 June 1828.   65. Ibid.   66. Teneo, pp. 467–68, letter dated 25 June 1828.   67. Ibid.   68. Merlin, *Memoirs*, vol. 1, p. 64.   69. Ibid., p. 65.   70. *La Revue Musicale* 3 (1828): 543.   71. Teneo, p. 466, letter dated 24 June 1828.   72. *La Revue Musicale* 3 (1828): 496.

Chapter 6   The Actress

1. Teneo, p. 466, letter dated 24 June 1828.   2. Ibid., p. 469, letter dated 2 August 1828.   3. Legouvé, pp. 71–72.   4. Ibid., pp. 72–73.   5. Merlin, *Memoirs*, vol. 1, p. 264.   6. Paraphrased from Merlin, *Memoirs*, vol. 1, pp. 67–70.   7. Ibid., pp. 70–72.   8. Teneo, p. 465.   9. Ibid., pp. 468–69, letter dated 2 August 1828.   10. Ibid.   11. Ibid., p. 471, letter dated 8 September 1828.   12. Ibid.   13. Bauer, p. 329.   14. Teneo, pp. 470–71, letter dated 8 September 1828.   15. Ibid.   16. Ibid., pp. 472–73, letter dated 11 October 1828.   17. Cited by Pougin, p. 47.   18. Teneo, pp. 472–73, letter dated 11 October 1828.   19. Cited by Pougin, p. 48.   20. Mackinley, *Garcia*, p. 91.   21. *Le Figaro*, 8 November 1828.   22. *La Revue Musicale* 5 (1829): 38.   23. *Le Figaro*, 17 November 1828.   24. *La Revue Musicale* 4 (1828): 468–73.   25. Merlin, *Madame Malibran*, vol. 1, pp. 91–93.   26. Ibid., vol. 2, p. 247.   27. Prod'homme, "The Baron de Trémont," p. 378.   28. Cited by Lanquine, p. 38.   29. A photograph of this letter appears in the pictures following page 96 in Desternes.   30. Paraphrased from Merlin, *Memoirs*, vol. 1, pp. 84–85.   31. Desternes, p. 108.   32. Merlin, *Memoirs*, vol. 1, p. 93.   33. Maynard, p. 310.   34. Teneo, pp. 473–74, letter dated 31 January 1829.   35. Mackinley, *Garcia*, p. 123; Husk, p. 50.   36. Prod'homme, "The Baron de Trémont," p. 378.   37. Merlin, *Madame Malibran*, vol. 2, pp. 291–93.   38. Merlin, *Memoirs*, vol. 2, pp. 64–66.   39. Legouvé, p. 77.   40. Paraphrased from Pontmartin, pp. 2–15.   41. Merlin, *Memoirs*, vol. 1, pp. 54–55.   42. *La Revue Musicale* 5 (1829): 102–3.   43. *Le Figaro*, 18 February 1829.   44. Merlin, *Memoirs*, vol. 2, p. 124.   45. *Le Figaro*, 18 February 1829.   46. Sainte-Beuve, vol. 4, p. 148.   47. Teneo, p. 474, letter dated 31 January 1829.   48. Ibid., p. 474, letter dated 25 March 1829.   49. Ibid.

Chapter 7   England

1. *La Revue Musicale* 12 (1832): 174.   2. Fétis.   3. Viardot-Garcia, vol. 1, pp. 526–30.   4. Teneo, p. 475, letter dated 8 April 1829.   5. Quicherat, p. 7 fn.   6. Teneo, p. 475, letter dated 8 April 1829, pp. 476–77, letter dated 14 July 1829.   7. Ibid., pp. 476–77, letter dated 14 July 1829.   8. Ibid.   9. Nathan, p. 46.   10. Ms. University of Chicago, Regenstein Library, letter dated 15 December 1833.   11. Pougin, pp. 71–73.   12. Escudier, p. 291.   13. Teneo, p. 474, letter dated 25 March 1829.   14. Ibid., p. 475, letter dated 8 April 1829.   15. Castil-Blaze, *L'Opéra-Italien*, p. 452.   16. Viardot-Garcia, vol. 1, p. 380.   17. Teneo, p. 476, letter dated 27 June 1829.   18. Giulini, pp. 120–21, letter dated 22 September 1828.   19. Clayton, p. 262.   20. Merlin, *Memoirs*, vol. 2, p. 121.   21. Paraphrased from *Quarterly Musical Magazine and Review* 10 (1828): 323–30.   22. Chorley, p. 8.   23. *Harmonicon*, 1828, p. 122.   24. Chorley, pp. 6–8.   25. *Athenaeum*, no. 79 (29 April 1829): 270.   26. *London Literary Gazette*, no. 641 (2 May 1829): 292.   27. *Athenaeum*, no. 83 (20 May 1829): 317.   28. *Quarterly Musical Magazine and Review* 10 (1828): 325 fn.   29. *London Literary Gazette*, no. 643 (16 May 1829): 324.   30. Teneo, p. 476, letter dated 27 June 1829.   31. Devrient, p. 76, letter dated 18 May 1829.   32. *Athenaeum*, no. 86 (17 June 1829): 380.   33. *Quarterly Musical Magazine and Review* 10 (1828): 300–301 fn.   34. Clayton, p. 306; and others.   35. Devrient, p. 77.   36. *New Monthly Magazine* 27 (1829): 298–99.   37. *Examiner*, 7 June 1829, p. 356.   38. *London Literary Gazette*, no. 649 (27 June 1829): 428.   39. Merlin, *Memoirs*, vol. 1, p. 58.   40. *New Monthly Magazine* 27 (1829): 346.   41. Teneo, p. 477, letter dated 14 July 1829.

Chapter 8   Charles de Bériot

1. Phipson, p. 168.   2. Lahee, *Famous Violinists*, p. 141.   3. Prod'homme, "The Baron de Trémont," p. 378.   4. Ibid., pp. 380, 387.   5. Teneo, p. 454, letter dated 13 December 1827.   6. Merlin, *Madame Malibran*, vol. 1, p. 98.   7. Stendhal, p. 344–45.   8. Ms. University of Chicago, Regenstein Library, letter dated 15 December 1833.   9. *Quarterly Musical Magazine and Review* 10 (1828): 323–26.   10. Perugini, pp. 242–43.   11. Andersen, *The Improvisatore*, p. 95.   12. *Athenaeum*, no. 103 (14 October 1829): 648.   13. Ibid.   14. *Quarterly Musical Magazine and Review* 10 (1828): 324–30.   15. *Le Figaro*, 26 September

1829.   16. Merlin, *Memoirs*, vol. 1, p. 76.   17. *La Revue Musicale* 6 (1829): 424–25.   18. *Le Figaro*, 5 January 1830.   19. Castil-Blaze, *L'Académie*, p. 214.   20. *Le Moniteur Universel*, 25 January 1830 (?), cited by Quicherat, p. 13.   21. Jullien, p. 312, letter dated 6 May 1830.   22. *La Revue Musicale* 7 (1830): 310.   23. D'Agoult, p. 302.   24. Merlin, *Madame Malibran*, vol. 1, p. 195.   25. Ibid., vol. 2, pp. 254–55, letter dated 12 April 1830.

Chapter 9   The Adulteress

1. Merlin, *Madame Malibran*, vol. 1, pp. 128–34.   2. *New Monthly Magazine* 30 (1830): 201.   3. Merlin, *Madame Malibran*, vol. 1, p. 135.   4. *London Literary Gazette*, no. 640 (25 April 1829): 276.   5. *Athenaeum*, no. 131 (1 May 1830): 269.   6. *New Monthly Magazine* 30 (1830): 241.   7. Merlin, *Madame Malibran*, vol. 1, p. 136.   8. Jullien, pp. 309–12.   9. Merlin, *Madame Malibran*, vol. 1, pp. 157–59.   10. Ibid., p. 160.   11. Merlin, *Memoirs*, vol. 1, pp. 104–5.   12. Jullien, p. 312.   13. Merlin, *Madame Malibran*, vol. 1, pp. 136–40.   14. Ibid., pp. 141–42.   15. Ibid., vol. 2, pp. 260–61.   16. Ibid., vol. 1, p. 161. See also vol. 2, p. 263.   17. Ibid.   18. Ibid., vol. 2, pp. 264–66, letter dated 11 August 1830.   19. *Athenaeum*, no. 140 (3 July 1830): 413.   20. Ibid., no. 138 (19 June 1830): 380.   21. *New Monthly Magazine* 30 (1830): 379.   22. *Athenaeum*, no. 132 (8 May 1830): 284–85.   23. Ibid., no. 145 (7 August 1830): 494.   24. Ibid., no. 138 (19 June 1830): 381.   25. Merlin, *Madame Malibran*, vol. 2, pp. 264–66, letter dated 11 August 1830.   26. Cited by Mackinley, *Garcia*, p. 98.   27. Merlin, *Madame Malibran*, vol. 2, p. 266.   28. Ibid., vol. 1, p. 159.   29. Legouvé, pp. 112–13.   30. Teneo, pp. 477–80; Soubies, pp. 44–48.

Chapter 10   Lafayette

1. Malherbe, pp. 164–65.   2. Teneo, p. 480.   3. Merlin, *Memoirs*, vol. 1, p. 102.   4. Ibid., p. 152.   5. Ms. University of Chicago, Regenstein Library.   6. Ms. Library of Congress, Music Division; Lafayette, *The Chesterian*, p. 147.   7. Merlin, *Memoirs*, vol. 1, p. 103.   8. Ms. University of Chicago, Regenstein Library.   9. Ibid.   10. Desternes, a photograph of this letter appears following page 96. The manuscript is in neither the Library of Congress nor the University of Chicago collections.   11. Ms. Library of Congress, Music Division; Lafayette, *The Chesterian*, pp. 147–48.   12. Ms. University of Chicago, Regenstein Library.   13. Ms. Library of Congress, Music Division; Lafayette, *The Chesterian*, p. 148.   14. Teneo, pp. 480–81, letter dated 2 January 1831.   15. Ms. Library of Congress, Music Division; Lafayette, *The Chesterian*, pp. 148–50.   16. Ms. University of Chicago, Regenstein Library, letter from Malibran to Lafayette dated 7 February 1831.   17. Merlin, *Memoirs*, vol. 1, p. 269.   18. *La Revue Musicale* 9 (1830): 23.   19. *La Revue de Paris* 20 (1830): 256–57.   20. Michaud.   21. *La Revue Musicale* 9 (1830): 24.   22. *La Revue de Paris* 22 (1831): 125.   23. *La Revue Musicale* 9 (1830): 120.   24. To Casimir Dudevant, 28 January 18–.   25. To Emile Regnault, 13 June 1831.   26. L. Boerne, cited by Pougin, p. 101 fn.   27. Mme. S. Gay, *Le Moquer Amoureux*, vol. 1, p. 35, cited by Bailbé, p. 48.   28. *Le Figaro*, 21 May 1831.   29. *Revue des Autographs*, no. 178 (June 1895): 11.   30. Bordeaux, p. 281.   31. Legouvé, pp. 110–11.   32. Ibid., p. 100.   33. Merlin, *Memoirs*, vol. 2, p. 90.   34. Legouvé, p. 82.   35. Castil-Blaze, *L'Opéra-Italien*, p. 452.   36. Merlin, *Memoirs*, vol. 1, pp. 135–37. Mme. Merlin's anecdotes, always based on truth, often confuse the details. This incident seems to involve a performance of *Tancredi* (not *Semiramide*) on March 21, 1831, which was for the benefit of Lalande, and which was followed on March 22 by a performance of Arsace to Lalande's (not Sontag's) Semiramide.   37. *La Revue de Paris* 24 (1831): 257.   38. *Le Moniteur Universel*, 30 April 1831, p. 902.   39. Cottinet, p. 96.   40. Merlin, *Memoirs*, vol. 1, pp. 145–46.   41. Ms. British Museum, Add. 41771. Reproduced by permission of the British Library Board.   42. *Le Figaro*, 22 November 1831.   43. To Titus Woyciechowski, 12 December 1831.   44. To Joseph Elsner, 14 December 1831.   45. *La Revue Musicale* 11 (1832): 394.   46. Merlin, *Memoirs*, vol. 1, p. 154.   47. Tiersot, *Lettres*, vol. 2, pp. 248–49.   48. Willis, pp. 70–71.   49. *La Revue Musicale* 11 (1832): 411.

Chapter 11   Italy

1. Malherbe, pp. 197–98.   2. *Le Figaro*, 1 February 1832.   3. Heron-Allen, p. 3.   4. Willis, pp. 121–29.   5. *Courrier Belge*, cited by Pougin, p. 105 fn.   6. Merlin, *Memoirs*, vol. 1, pp. 159–61; vol. 2, pp. 129–30.   7. *Teatri Arti e Letteratura*, 7 June 1832, p. 310.   8. Teneo, p. 479; Soubies, pp. 46–47.   9. Derwent, p. 130, citing an Italian critic.   10. *Teatri Arti e Letteratura*, 22 June 1832, p. 146.   11. Schoen-René, p. 114.   12. Merlin, *Madame Malibran*, vol. 2, pp. 271–73.   13. Ms. University of Chicago, Regenstein Library; Prod'homme, "Lafayette and Maria-Felicia Malibran," p. 19.   14. *La Revue Musicale* 12 (1832): 160.   15. Merlin, *Memoirs*, vol. 2, p. 131.   16. Cottrau, pp. 15–16.   17. *Teatri Arti e Letteratura*, 12 July 1832, p. 169.   18. *La Revue de Paris* 41 (1832): 53–54.   19. Malherbe, p. 197.   20. Cottrau, p. 16, letter dated 25 August 1832.   21. Duprez, p. 113.   22. *La Revue Musicale* 12 (1832): 239.   23. Ibid., p. 288.   24. Merlin, *Madame Malibran*, vol. 1, p. 210.   25. Ms. University of Chicago, Regenstein Library.   26. *Les Archives Parlementaires*, vol. 76, p. 316; vol. 77, p. 55.   27. Ms. University of Chicago, Regenstein Library, letter dated 13 August 1832.   28. Ibid., letter dated 13 September 1832.   29. Merlin, *Madame Malibran*, vol. 1, p. 217.   30. Cottrau, pp. 17–18.   31. Merlin, *Madame Malibran*, vol. 1, p. 216.   32. Zavadini, p. 295, letter from Naples 18 August 1832.   33. *La Revue Musicale* 12 (1832): 309.   34. Ibid.   35. Trebbi, p. 52.   36. *Teatri Arti e Letteratura*, 11 October 1832, p. 52.   37. Paraphrased from Trebbi, pp. 48–49.   38. Florimo, vol. 3, pp. 192–93.   39. *La Gazzetta Piemontese*, 18 January 1836.   40. Merlin, *Memoirs*, vol. 1, p. 218.   41. Trebbi, p. 54.   42. Ibid., p. 55.   43. Bull, p. 59.   44. Ibid., pp. 59–60.   45. Ibid., p. 295.   46. Ibid., p. 60.   47. Ibid., pp. 60–61.   48. *Teatri Arti e Letteratura*, 11 October 1832, p. 52.   49. Trebbi, pp. 47–50.   50. Ibid., p. 65; Merlin, *Memoirs*, vol. 2, pp. 141–42; *Teatri Arti e Letteratura*, 29 November 1832, p. 112.   51. *Teatri Arti e Letteratura*, 6 December 1832, p. 122.

Chapter 12   London: Bunn and Bellini

1. Ms. University of Chicago, Regenstein Library, letter dated 25 October 1832.   2. Ms. Library of Congress, Music Division, letter dated 23 March 1833.   3. *Les Archives Parlementaires*, vol. 85, p. 261.   4. *Le Moniteur Universel*, 9 March 1835, p. 477.   5. Ibid., 3 April 1833, p. 928.   6. Ms. University of Chicago, Regenstein Library, letter dated 10 April 1833.   7. *Morning Chronicle*, 29 April 1833.   8. *Sunday Times*, 5 May 1833.   9. *Examiner*, 2 June 1833, p. 343.   10. *Harmonicon*, 1833, p. 140.   11. *Spectator*, 11 May 1833, p. 426.   12. *Times*, 2 May 1833.   13. Finck, p. 89.   14. *Times*, 2 May 1833.   15. *Harmonicon*, 1833, p. 140.   16. *Spectator*, 11 May 1833, p. 426.   17. *Times*, 2 May 1833.   18. Bellini, pp. 363–65, undated letter.   19. Ibid., p. 366.   20. *La Gazzetta Italiana*, 5 September 1838; cited by Ammirato, pp. 179–83.   21. Bellini, p. 366, undated letter.   22. Ibid.   23. Ricca, p. 93; Bellini, p. 527 fn.   24. Cottrau, p. 22, letter dated 22 November 1833.   25. Bunn, vol. 1, pp. 100–101.   26. Ibid., p. 245.   27. Planché, p. 194.   28. Bunn, vol. 2, pp. 118–19, letter dated 10 May 1833.   29. Ibid., p. 115, undated letter.   30. *Autographic Mirror*, London 18–, p. 45. See also Bunn, vol. 2, pp. 114–15, but with errors in transcription.   31. Bunn, vol. 1, p. 101 fn.   32. *Athenaeum*, no. 292 (1 June 1833): 348.   33. *Harmonicon*, 1833, p. 160; *London Literary Gazette*, no. 855 (8 June 1833): 364.   34. *Athenaeum*, no. 293 (8 June 1833): 364.   35. *London Literary Gazette*, no. 833 (8 June 1833): 364.   36. Ibid., no. 857 (22 June 1833): 396.   37. Husk, p. 5.   38. Ibid., p. 6.   39. Ibid., pp. 6–7.   40. Nathan, p. 48.   41. Ibid., p. 48–49.   42. Bunn, vol. 1, pp. 243–44 fn.   43. Maynard, p. 259.   44. Bunn, vol. 2, p. 112.   45. Ibid., pp. 116–17.   46. *London Literary Gazette*, no. 855 (8 June 1833): 364.   47. Ibid., no. 863 (3 August 1833): 493.   48. Ibid., no. 865 (17 August 1833): 525.   49. *Athenaeum*, no. 303 (17 August 1833): 577.   50. Planché, p. 194.   51. Ibid., p. 193.   52. Bunn, vol. 3, p. 13.   53. Planché, p. 194.   54. Bunn, vol. 2, p. 117.   55. Hensel, pp. 301–2.   56. *Musical Times*, 1 September 1901, p. 587.   57. Ms. University of Chicago, Regenstein Library, undated letter received by Lafayette on 10 August 1833.   58. Ibid.   59. Ibid., letter dated 15 December 1833.   60. Description of the theater paraphrased from Parry, pp. 163 ff.   61. Ibid.   62. Cottrau, pp. 22–23, letter dated 22 November 1833.   63. Ibid.   64. Pacini, pp. 68–69.   65. Ibid.   66. Ms. University of Chicago, Regenstein Library, letter dated 15

December 1833.   67. Legouvé, p. 109.   68. Incident paraphrased from Parry, pp. 185–
89.   69. Castil-Blaze, *L'Opéra-Italien*, pp. 450–51.   70. Florimo, vol. 3, p. 256.   71.
Teatri Arti e Letteratura, 20 February 1834, p. 212.   72. Ibid., 13 March 1834, pp. 18–
19.   73. Cottrau, p. 25, letter dated 14 March 1834.   74. Andersen, *The True Story*, p. 120;
Stirling, p. 150.

Chapter 13   La Scala

1. *Teatri Arti e Letteratura*, 6 March 1834, p. 16.   2. *La Revue Musicale* 16 (1834): 176.   3.
Castil-Blaze, "Revue," p. 63.   4. Bull, p. 89.   5. Merlin, *Memoirs*, vol. 2, p. 61.   6.
Teatri Arti e Letteratura, 10 April 1834, p. 58.   7. Ibid., 17 April 1834, p. 61.   8. Ibid., 10
April 1834, p. 56.   9. Ibid., 24 April 1834, p. 78.   10. Ibid., 10 May 1834, p. 92.   11.
Ibid., 3 May 1834, p. 89.   12. Willis, pp. 427–28.   13. Morgulis, p. 380, note dated 7 May
1834; note dated 4 May 1834.   14. *Teatri Arti e Letteratura*, 17 May 1834, p. 101.   15. Bull,
p. 89.   16. Ms. Library of Congress, Music Division, letter dated 10 February 1834.   17.
Ms. University of Chicago, Regenstein Library.   18. Merlin, *Madame Malibran*, vol. 2, p.
271.   19. Bellini, p. 290, letter dated 26 December 1831.   20. Ibid., p. 278, letter dated 1
September 1831.   21. Mackinley, *Garcia*, p. 108.   22. *Teatri Arti e Letteratura*, 24 May
1834, p. 116; Monaldi, p. 8.   23. Ibid., pp. 117, 109.   24. Ibid., p. 109, citing
L'Eco.   25. Ibid.   26. *Teatri Arti e Letteratura*, 24 May 1834, p. 117.   27. Ibid.   28.
La Gazette Musicale, cited by Bradi, p. 222.   29. Merlin, *Memoirs*, vol. 2, pp. 147–51; and
others.   30. Delacroix, cited by Giulini, p. 163.   31. Legouvé, p. 60.   32. *Teatri Arti e
Letteratura*, 31 May 1834, p. 120.   33. Ibid., p. 125.   34. *La Revue Musicale* 16 (1834):
176.   35. Malherbe, p. 225.   36. George Sand to Casimir Dudevant, 30 July
1834.   37. Malherbe, p. 226.   38. *La Revue Musicale* 16 (1834): 191.   39. Bunn, vol. 2,
pp. 121–22.   40. Anecdote paraphrased from Lanquine, pp. 107–8, citing Jules Bertrand,
La Malibran (Paris, 1864).   41. Ricci, p. 220.   42. Merlin, *Memoirs*, vol. 1, pp. 190–
91.   43. Malherbe, p. 212–15.   44. Pougin, p. 157.   45. *Teatri Arti e Letteratura*, 14
August 1834, p. 213.   46. *L'Eco*, 28 November 1834.   47. *Teatri Arti e Letteratura*, 30
October 1834, p. 75; 9 October 1834, p. 50.   48. Ibid., 30 October 1834, p. 75.   49. Ibid.,
6 November 1834, p. 83.   50. Giulini, p. 153. See also Merlin, *Madame Malibran*, vol. 1, p.
274.   51. Ibid., pp. 152–53.   52. *La Gazette Musicale*, 13 April 1834.   53. Bunn, vol. 1,
p. 247.   54. Heron-Allen, p. 6, letter postmarked 8 November 1834.   55. *Teatri Arti e
Letteratura*, 22 November 1834, pp. 110, 127.   56. Cottrau, p. 29, letter dated 20 November
1834.   57. Ibid., pp. 27–29, letters dated 2 August 1834, 18 September 1834.   58. Ibid.,
pp. 30–31.   59. Ms. Pierpont Morgan Library, Mary Flagler Cary Music Collection. Letter
from Maria Malibran to Parola in Naples dated February 1835.   60. Duprez, p.
117.   61. *Allgemeine Musikalische Zeitung* 37, no. 30 (July 1835): 501.   62. *Teatri Arti e
Letteratura*, 19 February 1835, p. 211.   63. Ibid., 14 February 1835, p. 198.   64. Heron-
Allen, pp. 8–10.   65. Ibid.   66. Legouvé, p. 108.   67. Cottrau, p. 29.   68. Bellini,
pp. 454–55, letter dated 13 October 1834 to Florimo.   69. Ibid., pp. 486–87, letter dated 30
November 1834 to Florimo.   70. Ibid., p. 493.   71. Ibid., p. 489.   72. Ibid., p.
493.   73. Ibid., p. 495, letter dated 5 January 1835 to Florimo.   74. Ibid., p. 497, letter
dated 5 January 1835 to Florimo.   75. Ibid., p. 517, letter dated 11 February 1835 to
Florimo.   76. Ibid., pp. 519, 521, letter dated 18 February 1835.   77. Ibid., pp. 526–27.
See facsimile between pages 520 and 521.   78. Cottrau, pp. 56–57.   79. Malherbe, p.
217.   80. Paraphrased from Merlin, *Memoirs*, vol. 1, p. 209.   81. Cottrau, pp. 32,
40.   82. *Teatri Arti e Letteratura*, 21 March 1835, p. 17.

Chapter 14   Venice: Il Teatro Malibran

1. Merlin, *Memoirs*, vol. 1, pp. 212–14.   2. Merlin, *Madame Malibran*, vol. 2, pp. 23–24.   3.
Legouvé, pp. 109–10.   4. Bielli, p. 34, citing Carlo Rusconi, *Rimembranze* (Rome,
1883).   5. *L'Apatista*, 20 January 1835.   6. Bernardi, p. 270.   7. Cottrau, p. 39.   8.
Merlin, *Madame Malibran*, vol. 2, pp. 15–18.   9. Ibid.   10. *Teatri Arti e Letteratura*, 9 April
1835, p. 42.   11. *L'Apatista*, 28 March 1835.   12. Cited by Bernardi, p. 272.   13. Cited
by Bernardi, p. 273.   14. Pougin, p. 183.   15. Bernardi, p. 274; and others.   16. *Teatri*

Arti e Letteratura, 16 April 1835, p. 52. 17. Liszt, p. 187. 18. *Teatri Arti e Letteratura*, 16 April 1835, p. 52. 19. Merlin, *Memoirs*, vol. 1, pp. 226-28. 20. A photograph of these medals appears in Soubies, p. 35. 21. Merlin, *Madame Malibran*, vol. 2, p. 34. 22. Bellini, p. 546, letter dated 29 April 1835. 23. Ibid., p. 575, letter dated 1 July 1835. 24. Ibid., p. 574, letter dated 1 July 1835. 25. Ibid., p. 575, letter dated 1 July 1835. 26. Bunn, vol. 1, pp. 239-40. 27. Ibid., pp. 240-43. 28. Ibid., p. 243. 29. Verdi, p. 205, letter dated 27 January 1877 to 0. Arrivabene. 30. *London Literary Gazette*, no. 958 (30 May 1835): 347. 31. Chorley, p. 39. 32. Ibid., p. 38. 33. Castil-Blaze, "La Revue," p. 143. 34. Von Raumer, pp. 309-10. 35. *Times*, 13 June 1835. 36. *Spectator*, 13 June 1835, pp. 561-62. 37. *Times*, 13 June 1835. 38. Chorley, p. 9. 39. Cottinet, p. 97. 40. Bunn, vol. 1, p. 246, my translation. 41. Ibid. 42. Merlin, *Madame Malibran*, vol. 2, pp. 35-37. 43. *Athenaeum*, no. 403 (18 July 1835): 552. 44. Bunn, vol. 1, p. 244. 45. Merlin, *Madame Malibran*, vol. 2, p. 38, letter dated 13 June 1835. 46. Bunn, vol. 1, p. 244. 47. Ibid., pp. 244-47. 48. Ibid., p. 247. 49. Merlin, *Madame Malibran*, vol. 2, p. 35. 50. Ibid., p. 42. 51. *Teatri Arti e Letteratura*, 22 October 1835, pp. 58-59; Merlin, *Memoirs*, vol. 1, pp. 238-42, vol. 2, pp. 157-58; and other sources.

Chapter 15 Madame de Bériot

1. *Teatri Arti e Letteratura*, 20 October 1835, p. 72. 2. Florimo, vol. 3, p. 213 fn. 3. *Teatri Arti e Letteratura*, 23 October 1834, pp. 65-66. 4. Zavadini, p. 362, letter dated 7 October 1834. 5. Ibid. 6. Cottrau, p. 30, letter dated 9 December 1834, with my corrections. 7. Zavadini, pp. 371-72. 8. Ashbrook, p. 175, unfootnoted. He assigns the date of 7 August 1835 to this letter, with a provenance of London, but this is impossible since Malibran was already in Lucca at the time. 9. *Le Catalogue Charavay*, no. 181, October 1895, p. 13, letter dated 9 December 1835 from Maria Malibran to Eugène LeBon. 10. Zavadini, p. 394, letter dated 3 January 1836. 11. *Teatri Arti e Letteratura*, 14 January 1835, p. 161. 12. Zavadini, p. 400, letter dated 8 or 9 March 1836. 13. *Teatri Arti e Letteratura*, 7 January 1835, p. 153. 14. Merlin, *Madame Malibran*, vol. 2, pp. 283-84. 15. Mackinley, *Garcia*, p. 117. 16. Merlin, *Madame Malibran*, vol. 2, pp. 277-79. 17. Ibid., vol. 1, p. 138. 18. Legouvé, pp. 91n94. 19. Bunn, vol. 2, p. 122. 20. *Times*, 10 May 1836. 21. *London Literary Gazette*, no. 958 (29 May 1835): 347. 22. Merlin, *Memoirs*, vol. 1, pp. 248-49. 23. Kenney, p. 108. 24. The plot appears in the *Times*, 28 May 1836. 25. Bunn, vol. 2, p. 58. 26. Macready, p. 337. 27. Ibid., pp. 30, 42. 28. Idid., p. 299. 29. Bunn, vol. 2, pp. 52-53. 30. Ibid., p. 53. 31. Ibid., p. 41. 32. Macready, p. 306. 33. Kenney, pp. 120-21. 34. Phillips, vol. 1, pp. 216-18. 35. Kenney, pp. 117-20. 36. *Times*, 27 May 1836; Bunn, vol. 2, p. 68. 37. Crowest, vol. 2, pp. 287-88. 38. Bedford, pp. 63-65. 39. Bunn, vol. 2, pp. 73-74. 40. Ibid., pp. 68-69. 41. Ibid., pp. 69-70. 42. Lennox, pp. 177-78. 43. Ibid., pp. 178-79. 44. Moscheles, pp. 225-27. 45. Merlin, *Madame Malibran*, vol. 2, p. 72. 46. Bunn, vol. 2, pp. 93-94.

Chapter 16 The End

1. Merlin, *Memoirs*, vol. 1, pp. 249-51. 2. Ibid., p. 251; and other sources. 3. Legouvé, p. 101. 4. Merlin, *Memoirs*, vol. 1, p. 262. 5. Moscheles, pp. 227-28. 6. Ibid., pp. 228-29. 7. Legouvé, pp. 101-2. 8. *Teatri Arti e Letteratura*, 15 September 1836, p. 16. 9. Merlin, *Madame Malibran*, vol. 2, p. 72. 10. Desternes, photo of letter following page 96. 11. Ibid., p. 161. 12. Merlin, *Memoirs*, vol. 1, pp. 271-72. 13. Legouvé, p. 100. 14. Cox, p. 238. 15. The information on the first days of the Manchester Festival has been compiled from several sources, including Merlin, *Memoirs*, vols. 1, 2; Bunn, vol. 2, pp. 103 ff.; Castil-Blaze, *L'Opéra-Italien*; Sir George Smart, various reports in journals of the time; and other contemporary accounts. 16. Bunn, vol. 3, pp. 216-17. See also *Gleason's Pictorial Drawing Room Companion* 3 (1852): 108; *Manchester City News*, no. 35 (31 August 1878): 228; *Musical Opinion* 60 (November 1936): 115-16. 17. The events of the last weeks of Maria Malibran's life have been culled from several sources, including Merlin, *Memoirs*, vols. 1, 2;

Bunn, vol. 2, pp. 103 ff.; and other biographical sketches. These facts were published in virtually every European newspaper and journal from England to Italy. Dr. Belluomini's journal was published in Malherbe, pp. 250 ff.   18. Bunn, vol. 2, pp. 101–2 fn.   19. Ibid., p. 102.   20. Ibid.   21. *London Literary Gazette*, no. 1030 (15 October 1836): 669; and others.   22. *Spectator*, 1 October 1836, p. 943.   23. *Athenaeum*, no. 466 (1 October 1836): 707.   24. Duprez, p. 118.   25. Phillips, vol. 1, pp. 218–19.   26. Merlin, *Memoirs*, vol. 2, p. 79.   27. Husk, p. 33.   28. Cited by Marix-Spire, p. 27.   29. Lamartine, p. 201.

Epilogue

1. *Le Moniteur Universel*, 16 November 1836, p. 2112.   2. *La Gazette Musicale*, 20 November 1836.   3. Mairet, p. 308.   4. Legouvé, p. 78.   5. *Athenaeum*, no. 602 (11 May 1839): 357–58.   6. De Musset, p. 721.

Additional Letters

1. Ms. Pierpont Morgan Library, Mary Flagler Cary Music Collection.   2. Cottinet, p. 96.   3. Ms. The Historical Society of Pennsylvania.   4. Trebbi, p. 51.   5. Bunn, vol. 2, pp. 120–21.

BIBLIOGRAPHY

Amateur. *The Star of La Scala.* London, 1837.
Ammirata, Giannina. *La Vita Amorosa di V. Bellini.* Milan, 1935.
Andersen, Hans Christian. *Dagbøger.* Vol. 1, 1825–1834. Copenhagen, 1971.
———. *The Improvisatore.* Translated from the Danish by Mary Howitt. Boston and New York, n.d.
———. *The True Story of My Life.* Translated from the Danish by Mary Howitt. New York, 1926.
Aniante, Antonio. *Vita di Bellini.* Turin, 1925.
Apthorp, Wm. F. *Hector Berlioz.* New York, 1879.
Archer-Shee, William. *My Contemporaries, 1830–1870.* London, 1893.
Armstrong, W. G. *A Record of the Opera in Philadelphia.* Philadelphia, 1884.
Arundell, Dennis. *A Critic at the Opera.* London, 1957.
Ashbrook, William. *Donizetti.* London, 1965.
Bailbé, Joseph Marc. *Le Roman et La Musique en France.* Paris, 1969.
Barbieri, G. *Notizie biografiche di M. F. Malibran.* Milan, 1836.
Baron-Wilson, Margaret. *Memoirs of the Duchess of St. Albans.* London, 1839.
Bauer, Karoline. *Memoirs of Karoline Bauer,* vol. 1. London, 1885.
Bedford, Paul. *Recollections and Wanderings.* London, 1867.
Bellini, Vincenzo. *Epistolario.* Edited by Luisa Cambi. Italy, 1943.
Benson, E. F. *Queen Victoria.* London, 1935.
Berlioz, Hector. "Revue Critique: Dernières Pensées Musicales de Marie Félicité Garcia de Bériot," *Revue et Gazette Musicale,* 2 July 1837.
Bernardi, G. G. "La Malibran a Venezia," *Musica d'Oggi,* August–September 1936, pp. 269–75.
Bielli, Domeniĉo. *Maria Malibran.* Lanciano, 1936.
Bordeaux, Henry. *Portraits De Femmes et D'Enfants.* Paris, 1909.
Bradi, Lorenzo de. *La Brève et Merveilleuse Vie de La Malibran.* Paris, 1936.
Bremont, Anna. *The World of Music: The Great Singers.* New York, 1902.
Bull, Sara C. *Ole Bull, A Memoir.* New York, n.d.
Bunn, Alfred. *The Stage,* vols. 1, 2, 3. London, 1840.
Cambiasi, Pompeo. *Rappresentazioni date nei Reali Teatri di Milano, 1778–1872.* Bologna, 1969.
Castil-Blaze [François Henri Joseph Blaze]. *L'Académie Impériale de Musique.* Paris, 1855.
———. *L'Opéra-Italien.* Paris, 1856.
———. "Revue du Monde Musical; Mme Malibran—Fin," *Revue de Paris* 34 (1836): 63–69, 139–45.
Chase, Gilbert. *The Music of Spain.* New York, 1941.
Chopin, Frederyk. *Selected Correspondence.* Edited by Bronislas Sydow. London, 1962.
Chorley, Henry. *Thirty Years Recollections.* New York, 1926.
Clayton, Ellen C. *Queens of Song.* New York, 1856.

Colombani, Alfredo. *L'Opera Italiana nel Secolo XIX*. Milan, 1900.

Cottinet, Edmond. "Maria Malibran & Alfred de Musset," *Les Lettres et les Arts* 4 (1889): 91–100.

Cottrau, Guillaume. *Lettres d'un Mélomane*. Naples, 1885.

Cox, H. Bertram and C. L. E. *Leaves from the Journals of Sir George Smart*. London, 1907.

Crowest, Frederick J. *A Book of Musical Anecdotes*. London, 1878.

Curtis, John. "A Century of Grand Opera in Philadelphia," *The Pennsylvania Magazine of History and Biography* 44 (1920): 122–57.

D'Agoult, Marie. *Mes Souvenirs*, by Daniel Stern. Paris, 1877.

DaPonte, Lorenzo. *Memoirs*. Translated from the Italian by Elisabeth Abbott. Philadelphia, 1929.

Day, Lillian. *Paganini of Genoa*. New York, 1929.

De Bassanville, Anaïs. *Les Salons D'Autrefois*, vol. 4. Paris, n.d.

De Filippis, F. and Arnese, R. *Cronache del Teatro di S. Carlo*, vol. 1. Naples, 1961.

Delacroix, Eugène. *Journal, 1822–1852*. vol. 1. Paris, 1932.

De Musset, Alfred. *Oeuvres*. Paris, 1883.

Derwent, Lord. *The Life of Rossini*. London, 1934.

Desternes, Suzanne and Chandet, Henriette. *La Malibran et Pauline Viardot*. Paris, 1969.

De Trémont, Baron. *See* Prod'homme, Jacques G.

Devrient, Eduard. *Letters from Mendelssohn*. London, 1869.

Doggett, John Jr. *Great Metropolis, or Guide to New York*. New York, 1846.

Duprez, Gilbert. *Souvenirs D'un Chanteur*. Paris, 1880.

Ebers, John. *Seven Years of the King's Theatre*. Philadelphia, 1828.

Edwards, Henry Sutherland. *Famous First Representations*. London, 1886.

———. *The Prima Donna*. vol. 1. London, 1888.

Ehrlich, A. *Celebrated Violinists, Past & Present*. Translated and edited by R. Legge. London, 1897.

Elson, L. *The History of American Music*. London, 1904.

Engel, Carl. "Again Lafayette and Maria-Felicia Malibran," *The Chesterian*, January–February 1925, pp. 105–10.

Escudier, Marie et Léon. *Vie et Adventures Des Cantatrices*. Paris, 1856.

Fétis, François. *Biographie Universelle des Musiciens*. Brussels, 1839.

Figarola, Domingo. *La Condesa De Merlin (Maria de la Merced Santa Cruz y Montalvo)*. Paris, 1928.

Finck, Henry T. *Success in Music*. New York, 1909.

Fitzlyon, April. *The Price of Genius*. London, 1964.

Florimo, Francesco. *La Scuola Musicale di Napoli*, vols. 3, 4. Naples, 1882.

Francis, John. *Old New York*. New York, 1865.

Gara, Eugenio. "Maria Felicita Malibran," *La Scala*, 15 December 1951, pp. 39–44; 15 January 1952, pp. 29–35.

Garcia, Manuel del Popolo Vicente. "Seis Cartas a la Duquesa De Osuna," *Anuario Musical*, vol. 2. Barcelona, 1947, pp. 98–105.

Garcia, Manuel, Jr. Letter to the Editors of *Le Figaro*, 15 April 1830.

Garcia, Maria Felicita. *See* Malibran, Maria.

Gatti, Carlo. *Il Teatro alla Scala*, vols. 1, 2. Milan, 1964.

Giulini, Maria Ferranti. *Giuditta Pasta e I Suoi Tempi*. Milan, 1937.

Gossip of the Century, vol. 2. London, 1892.

Groves, George. *A Dictionary of Music and Musicians*. Edited by J. Fuller Maitland. New York, 1908.

Guichard, Léon. *La Musique et Les Lettres au Temps Romantisme*. Paris, 1955.

Hensel, Sebastian. *The Mendelssohn Family*, vol. 1. New York, 1882.

Héritte de la Tour, Louis. *Une Famille de Grands Musiciens*. Paris, 1923.

Heron-Allen, Edward. "A Contribution toward an Accurate Biography of Charles Auguste De Bériot and Maria Felicia Malibran-Garcia," *De Fidiculis Opuscula*, vol. 6. London, 1894.

Hogarth, George. *Memories of the Musical Drama*, vol. 2. London, 1838.

Horowicz, Bronislaw. *Le Théâtre D'Opéra*. Paris, 1946.

Husk, William Henry. *Templeton and Malibran*. London, 1881.

Hutton, Laurence. *Portraits in Plaster*. New York, 1884. (Excerpts published in *Harper's Magazine*, vol. 85. 1892.)

Ireland, Joseph N. *Records of the New York Stage*. New York, 1866.

Jullien, Adolphe. "Maria Malibran," *L'Art*, vol. 2, series 3, pp. 305–16. Paris, 1902.

Kenney, Charles L. *A Memoir of Michael William Balfe*. London, 1875.

Krehbiel, Henry E. *Chapters of Opera*. New York, 1911.

———. *More Chapters of Opera*. New York, 1919.

Lafayette, General Marie. Correspondence with Maria Garcia Malibran and Charles de Bériot. Library of Congress, Music Division, Washington D.C.

———. Correspondence with Maria Garcia Malibran. Regenstein Library, Chicago University.

———. "Six Unpublished Letters from Lafayette to Maria Malibran," *The Chesterian*, March–April, 1926, pp. 147–50.

LaForêt, Claude. *La Vie Musicale au Temps Romantique*. Paris, 1929.

Lahee, Henry Charles. *Famous Violinists of Today and Yesterday*. Boston, 1899.

———. *Grand Opera in America*. Boston, 1902.

Lamartine, Alphonse de. *Portraits et Salons*. Paris, 1927.

Lanquine, Clément. *La Malibran*. Paris, 1911.

Larionoff, P. and Pestellini, F. *Maria Malibran y su Época*. Barcelona, 1953.

Lavignac, Albert. *Encylopédie De La Musique: Histoire De La Musique—Espagne-Portugal*. Paris, 1920.

Legouvé, Ernest. *Soixante Ans de Souvenirs*, vol. 2. Paris, 1888.

Lennox, William P. *My Recollections*, vol. 1. London, 1874.

Levien, John. *The Garcia Family*. London, 1932.

Liszt, Franz. *Pages Romantiques*. Paris, 1912.

Loewenberg, Alfred. *Annals of Opera*. Cambridge, 1943.

Mackenzie-Grieve, Averil. *Clara Novello*. London, 1955.

Mackinley, M. Sterling. *Antoinette Sterling and other Celebrities*. New York, 1907.

———. *Garcia the Centenarian and His Times*. London, 1908.

Macready, William C. *Diaries*. Edited by William Toynbee, vol. 1. New York, 1912.

Madeira, Louis C. *Music in Philadelphia and the Musical Fund Society*. Philadelphia, 1896.

Mairet, Jeanne. "Reminiscences of a Franco-American," *Putnam's Monthly*, June 1908, pp. 305–10.

Maitland, J. Fuller. *English Music in the XIX Century*. New York, 1902.

Malherbe, Henry. *La Passion de la Malibran*. Paris, 1937.

Malibran, Maria Garcia. Correspondence with General Marie Lafayette. Regenstein Library, Chicago University.

———. Correspondence with Giuditta Pasta and others. New York Public Library at Lincoln Center.

"Malibran and Mutlow." *The Musical Times*, 1 September 1901, p. 585.

Marix-Spire, Thérèse. *Les Romantiques et La Musique*, vol. 1. Paris, 1954.

Maynard, Walter. *The Enterprising Impresario*. London, 1867.

Merlin, Maria de las Mercedes. *Memoirs of Madame Malibran*. London, 1844.

———. *Madame Malibran*. Brussels, 1838.

Michaud. *Biographie Universelle*. Paris, 1843.

Monaldi, Gino. *Cantante Celebri*. Rome, 1929. *See also:* "Giuditta Pasta e Maria Malibran," *Nuova Antologia*, July–August 1903, pp. 100–106.

Moore, Lillian. "Malibran in America," *Musical Courier*, 11 May 1935, 18 May 1935.

Morgulis, G. "La Malibran en Italie," *Revue de Littérature Comparée*, April 1936, pp. 378–82.

Moscheles, Ignaz. *Recent Music and Musicians*, as described in the diaries and correspondence of Ignaz Moscheles, edited by his wife and adapted from the original German by A. D. Coleridge. New York, 1873.

Mount Edgcumbe, Lord Richard. *Musical Reminiscences*. London, 1834.

Nathan, Isaac. *Memoirs of Madame Malibran-De Bériot*. London, 1836.

Odell, George C. *Annals of the New York Stage*, vol. 3. New York, 1928.

Owen, Robert Dale. *Threading My Way*. London, 1874.

Pacini, Giovanni. *Le Mie Memorie Artistiche*. Florence, 1865.

Paganelli, Sergio. *Due Secoli di vita musicale: Storia del Teatro Comunale di Bologna*, vols. 1, 2. Bologna, 1966.

Parry, John Orlando. *Victorian Swansdown, Extracts from the early travel diaries of John Orlando Parry*. Edited by G. B. Andrews and J. A. Orr-Ewing. London, 1935.

Pearce, Charles E. *Madame Vestris and her Times*. New York, n.d.

Peña y Goñi, Antonio. *La Música Dramática en España*. Madrid, 1881.

Perugini, Mark E. *The Omnibus Box*. London, 1933.

Phillips, Henry. *Musical and Personal Recollections*, vols. 1, 2. London, 1864.

Phipson, Thomas L. *Celebrated Violinists*. London, 1877.

Planché, James. *Recollections and Reflections*, vol. 1. London, 1901.

Pleasants, Henry. *The Great Singers*. New York, 1966.

Pontmartin, Armand. *Souvenirs d'un vieux mélomane*. Paris, 1879. *See also*: "The Bath of Madame Malibran," *Overland Monthly*, Aug. 1892, pp. 214–18.

Porter, Andrew. "Bellini's Last Opera," *Opera Magazine*, May 1960, p. 315.

Pougin, Arthur. *Marie Malibran*. Paris, 1911.

Prod'homme, Jacques G. "The Baron de Trémont: Souvenirs of Beethoven and other Contemporaries," *The Musical Quarterly*, July 1920, pp. 366–91.

———. "Lafayette and Maria-Felicia Malibran," *The Chesterian*, September 1919, pp. 17–20. (Also published in *La Revue Politique et Littéraire (Revue Bleue)*, 3 May 1924, pp. 311–12.)

Quicherat, Louis M. *Adolphe Nourrit*, vol. 2. Paris, 1867.

Radiciotti, Giuseppe. *Gioacchino Rossini*, vol. 2. Tivoli, 1928.

Ricca, Vincenzo. *Vincenzo Bellini*. Catania, 1932.

Ricci, C. *Figure e figuri del Mondo Teatrali*. Milan, 1920.

Ritter, Frédéric L. *Music in America*. New York, 1883.

Rogers, Francis. *Some Famous Singers of the 19th Century*. New York, 1914.

Sainte-Beuve, Charles A. *Nouveaux lundis*, vol. 4. Paris, n.d.

Sales, Jules. *Theatre Royal de la Monnaie 1856–1970*. Nivelles, 1971.

Sand, George. *Correspondence*. Edited by Georges Lubin. Paris, 1964.

Schoen-René. *America's Musical Inheritance*. New York, 1941.

Seligman, Janet. *Figures of Fun (Jean-Pierre Dantan)*. London, 1957.

Soubies, Albert. *Le Théâtre-Italien De 1801 à 1913*. Paris, 1913.

Smart, Sir George. *See* Cox, H. Bertram.

Stendhal. *The Life of Rossini*. Translated from the French by R. Coe. London, 1970.

Stevenson, Robert. *Music in Mexico*. New York, 1952.

Stirling, Monica. *The Wild Swan: The Life and Times of Hans Christian Andersen*. New York, 1965.

Subirá, José. *Historia de la Música Española e HispanoAmericana*. Barcelona, 1953.

———. *Historico y Anecdotario del Teatro Real*. Madrid, n.d.

———. *La Tonadilla Escénica*. Madrid, 1928.

Teneo, Martial. "La Malibran d'après des documents inédits," *Sammelbände der Internationalen Musik –Gesellschaft [International Musical Society]* 7 (1905–6): 437–82. (Excerpted in *La Grande Revue*, 1904, pp. 25–29.)

Tiersot, Julien. *Lettres De Musiciens*, vol. 2. Paris, 1936.
——. "Bizet and Spanish Music," *The Musical Quarterly* 13 (1927): 566–81.
Tissot, Ernest. "Le Premier Mariage de Madame Marie Malibran," *La Revue Mondiale* 103 (1913): 506–24.
Towers, John. *Dictionary-Catalogue of Operas & Operettas*. New York, 1967.
Trebbi, Oreste. *Nella Vecchia Bologna*. Bologna, 1924.
Vaccaj, Giulio. *Vita di Nicola Vaccaj*. Bologna, 1882.
Verdi, Giuseppe. *Verdi Intimo—Carteggio di Giuseppe Verdi con il Conte Opprandino Arrivabene*. Edited by Annibale Alberti. Milan, 1931.
Viardot-Garcia, Pauline. "Letters to Julius Rietz," *The Musical Quarterly* 1 (1915): 350–80; 526–59; 2 (1916): 32–60.
Von Raumer, Frederick. *England in 1835*. Philadelphia, 1836.
Von Wolzogen, Alfred F. *Wilhelmine Schröder-Devrient*. Leipzig, 1863.
Weinstock, Herbert. *Bellini*. New York, 1971.
——. *Donizetti*. New York, 1963.
——. *Rossini*. New York, 1968.
White, Richard Grant. "Opera in N.Y.," *The Century* 23 (1882): 686.
Willis, Nathaniel. *Pencillings by the Way*. New York, 1852.
Wilson, James G. *The Life and Letters of Fitz-Green Halleck*. New York, 1869.
Zavadini, Guido. *Donizetti*. Bergamo, 1948.

Newspapers and Periodicals
Belgium: Courrier Belge
England: Athenaeum, Brighton Guardian, European Magazine, Examiner, Gloucester Journal, Harmonicon, London Literary Gazette, London Magazine, Morning Chronicle, Morning Post, New Monthly Magazine, Quarterly Musical Magazine and Review, Spectator, Times (London)
France: Annales du Commerce, Le Figaro, Galignani's Messenger, La Gazette Musicale, Le Globe, Le Ménéstrel, Le Moniteur Universel, Nouveau Journal de Paris, Paris Revue, La Revue des deux Mondes, La Revue Meridionale, La Revue Musicale, La Revue et Gazette Musicale.
Germany: Allgemeine Musikalische Zeitung.
Italy: L'Apatista, L'Eco, La Gazzetta Piemontese, La Gazzetta Privilegiata, Teatri Arti e Letteratura.
United States: Albion, New-York American, New-York Enquirer, New-York Evening Post, New-York Review and Atheneum Magazine, New-York Times, Philadelphia Gazette.

Other Sources
Les Archives Parlementaires; The Autographic Mirror (London, 18–, p. 45); Le Catalogue Charavay; M. Benjamin Fillon, *Inventaire des Autographs et Documents Historiques*, vol. 2 (Paris, 1879); Gleason's Pictorial Drawing Room Companion, vol. 3 (1852, p. 108); Longworth's American Almanac, New-York Register, and City Director; Revue des Autographs; Stefano Vittadini, *Catalogo del Museo Teatrale alla Scala*, Milan (Milan, 1958)

INDEX

ILLUSTRATION CREDITS

Page 45. Oval portrait of Malibran by Léon Viardot, 1831, published in *Les Lettres et les Arts,* 4 (1889): 91.

Page 46. *Upper left:* M. Sterling-MacKinley, *Garcia the Centenarian and His Times* (reprint Da Capo Press, New York, 1976).
Upper right: Blanch Marchese, *Singer's Pilgrimage* (reprint Arno Press, New York, 1977).
Bottom: M. Sterling-MacKinley, *Garcia the Centenarian and His Times* (reprint Da Capo Press, New York, 1976).

Page 47. *Top:* Henry E. Krehbiel, *Chapters of Opera* (New York, 1911).
Lower left: New-York Evening Post, 29 Novmeber 1825.
Lower right: Le Figaro, 14 January 1828.

Page 48. Firestone Library, Princeton University.

Page 49. *Top:* Firestone Library, Princeton University.
Bottom: Firestone Library, Princeton University.

Page 50. *Upper left:* British Museum MS ADD33965 106 M15398. Reproduced by permission of the British Library Board.
Upper right: Firestone Library, Princeton University.
Lower left: British Museum MS ADD33965 74 M15398. Reproduced by permission of the British Library Board.
Lower right: British Museum MS ADD33965 75 M15398. Reproduced by permission of the British Library Board.

Page 51. *Upper left:* Bologna, 1832. Firestone Library, Princeton University.
Upper right: Bologna, 1834. Firestone Library, Princeton University.
Bottom: Caricature by Chalon. Victoria and Albert Museum.

Page 52. *Top:* Giuseppe Radiciotti, *Gioacchino Rossini* (Tivoli, 1928), vol. 2.
Lower left: Maria de las Mercedes Merlin, *Memoirs of Madame Malibran* (London, 1844).
Lower right: Allgemeine Musikalische Zeitung, 37, no. 30 (July 1835): 500.

Page 53. Theatre Royal, Covent Garden, June 14, 1833.

Page 54. British Museum MS ADD35027 93 92. Reproduced by permission of the British Library Board.

Page 55. *Upper left:* François Gerard, *Portrait of Giuditta Pasta.* Reproduced by permission of the Metropolitan Opera Guild.
Upper right: British Museum MS ADD35027. Reproduced by permission of the British Library Board.
Bottom: Princeton University Library.

Page 56. *Upper left:* La Scala, May 13-17, 1834.
 Upper right: La Scala, May 24, 1834.
 Lower left: Gran Teatro della Comune, Bologna, March 1834.
 Lower right: Princeton University Library.

Page 57. *Autographic Mirror.*

Page 58. *Top:* Princeton University Library.
 Bottom: British Museum ADD 35027. Reproduced by permission of
 the British Library Board.

Page 59. Photograph by the Manchester Public Libraries. Reproduced by
 permission of the Manchester City Council Cultural Services Department.

Page 60. *Top:* Princeton University Library.
 Lower left: Princeton University Library Theatre Collection.
 Lower right: Teatri Arti e Letteratura, October 1836.